The Grandest Battle

Napoleon 1805

The Grandest Battle
The Campaign of Ulm and Austerlitz, 1805

ILLUSTRATED

George Armand Furse

Edited by John H. Lewis

The Grandest Battle
The Campaign of Ulm and Austerlitz, 1805
by George Armand Furse
Edited by John H. Lewis

ILLUSTRATED

FIRST EDITION

Leonaur is an imprint of Oakpast Ltd
Copyright in this form © 2019 Oakpast Ltd

ISBN: 978-1-78282-878-5 (hardcover)
ISBN: 978-1-78282-879-2 (softcover)

http://www.leonaur.com

Publisher's Notes

The views expressed in this book are not necessarily those of the publisher.

Contents

Introduction by the Editor	7
Military Education of the French Officers	11
Preparations in England	25
William Pitt	43
Villeneuve Sails for the West Indies	59
March of the "Grande Armée" to the Rhine	92
From the Rhine to the Danube	120
Ulm—Operations on the Right Bank of the Danube	148
Ulm—Operations on the Left Bank of the Danube	179
From Ulm to Vienna	199
Action of the Archdukes	232
The "Grande Armée" Enters Moravia	250
Dispositions for the Battle	275
Battle of Austerlitz	299
After the Battle	342
Appendix	367

Introduction by the Editor

There is no doubt that George Armand Furse (1834-1906) was a fine, thorough military historian and writer of his day. He was primarily a military man, an officer in the British Army and indeed, at one time Colonel of the Black Watch. Furse wrote a number of books concerning the business of war including works on marching, intelligence, logistics and provisioning among others. However, he also wrote two well regarded history books on the campaigns of the Napoleonic age, one of which was unambiguously titled, 'Marengo and Hohenlinden' and the other a book, which is the foundation of the edition you are now holding, which was originally published under the title, 'A Hundred Years Ago: Battles by Land and Sea: Ulm, Trafalgar, Austerlitz'.

Perhaps predictably for a book title containing twelve words this work was regularly catalogued as 'A Hundred Years Ago' and this choice of title, for those who were not aware of the book's existence and so were not pointedly seeking it, did not—even if had they accidentally stumbled across it—immediately reveal the nature of the book's contents.

Good writers cannot necessarily be relied upon to provide good titles for their books or give much thought (though it is a tactical consideration of a quite simple kind) to the adverse effect likely to ensue when a title references a point in time which applies only in the year that the book was originally published. That was in this case, as one may suppose, 1905.

In this lack of foresight Furse was by no means alone among authors either before or after his time. Authors have written about the, 'late war' and the 'great war' when they have been referring to recent events from their own perspectives which have included the Seven Years War, The Napoleonic Wars and—hopefully finally—The First

World War, 1914-18. The Second World War was actually 'greater', but writers had presumably learned their lesson by that point, even if those who actually start wars had not.

Similarly, 'the great rebellion' has been employed in titles when referring to The English Civil War, The Jacobite Rebellion, The American War of Independence and The American Civil War. At least one other publisher has appreciated the error of Colonel Furse's title by re-publishing it as, 'Campaigns of 1805'.

However, this is not the principal reason why this Leonaur edition has been given a new title, though it is certain that if this book was a straightforward reprint of the original it would not have been released under the title, 'A Hundred Years Ago' even with the addition of qualifications that might explain why such a title was inappropriate. All of that rather ignores the purpose of a title in the first place. Readers should also not assume that this view comes from innate wisdom, but from several hard-learned lessons. The excellent book, 'The War Drama of the Eagles' for example very rarely found a customer until the title was changed to, 'Napoleon's Eagle Standards'!

This publisher releases many books concerning naval history and the histories of armies at war since there exists an avid readership for both subjects. It is perfectly reasonable to propose that where those two events are essentially and inextricably intertwined, they should appear in the same book in detail, but it is the view of this editor (on this occasion) that this is not necessarily or essentially the case. There is no doubt that the majority of the original book concerned Napoleon's campaign of 1805 in which the battles of Ulm and Austerlitz were the principal engagements. That being the case and aware of the different preferences of readers of military history, it was decided the excise the quite expansive and detailed account of the actions at sea which culminated in the Battle of Trafalgar from this edition.

This decision was not taken in an arbitrary manner, however. A certain amount of background history of events leading to the Campaign of 1805 was included in the original edition and this has been removed since this publisher's readership—in the main—is interested in the specifics of military history and are not entirely new the entire subject of the wars of revolution which brought Napoleon to the position he held in 1805. The text concerning the state and position of the French Army in its camps around Boulogne has been retained, as has the position of the British Government and its forces during the same period. This is the legitimate opening scene of this drama, since one nation was awaiting the opportunity to launch an invasion across the English Channel and another was making its preparations to defend itself against that invasion.

It is at this point that the importance of the Royal Navy enters into the narrative if only briefly, since it was entirely because of the naval dominance of the British navy that a French invasion of Britain was impracticable. Quite simply, Britannia ruled the waves and both protagonists knew it to be so-one side with relief and the other with ill-concealed chagrin. So, Napoleon turned his back on Britain and marched towards the Rhine. His commitment to the campaign of 1805 began before the Battle of Trafalgar was fought and the outcome of that engagement came about because of the established superiority of the Royal Navy over that of the French despite being supported by the Spanish Navy. This was not the first occasion in which the Royal Navy under Nelson had given the French Navy a drubbing, but it underscored the power of the British in the general struggle against France by making it clear that despite the success of French armies under Napoleon's command, his broader machinations were in jeopardy by his inability to dominate the seaways which would always be vitally influential in a military and commercial sense.

A battle like Trafalgar, it may be argued, was inevitable, but it did not influence the prosecution of the campaign in Europe of that year which once again graphically demonstrated the prowess of the French commander and his soldiers. This book, therefore, confines itself to a detailed description of the battles fought in modern day Germany and the Czech Republic which brought about the dissolution of the Holy Roman Empire and effectively ended the War of the Third Coalition.

This editor hopes readers will agree that this gives the work considerably more focus. This surely is nothing less than it merits, for as Napoleon asserted, 'THE BATTLE OF AUSTERLITZ IS THE GRANDEST OF ALL I HAVE FOUGHT'.

This edition contains maps and illustrations which did not accompany the original edition.

John H Lewis
Leonaur, 2019

CHAPTER 1

Military Education of the French Officers

On the 5th of December 1804, three days after Napoleon's coronation, a grand festival was held in the *Champs-de-Mars*, when the emperor distributed the eagles (which the soldiers gave the name of *coucou*—cuckoo), to the regiments forming the garrison of Paris and to deputations of picked men belonging to all corps of the army and of the navy. This was one of the most splendid of the great pageants held during the Empire.

Napoleon addressed his troops thus:

Soldiers, behold your flags; these eagles will serve you always as rallying points; they will be wherever your emperor may judge it necessary for the defence of his throne and of his people. Swear to sacrifice your life to defend them, and to keep them always by your courage on the path of victory. Do you swear it?

Thousands of voices replied with enthusiasm, "We do swear it."

The army kept its oath, for in less than twelve months the same eagles, after a series of sanguinary combats, were waving on the walls of Vienna and floating in the breeze on the plateau of Pratzen. (The city of Paris presented a laurel crown in gold to the eagles of all the regiments which had fought at Austerlitz.)

Dumas (*Précis des Evénemens Militaires*) calls the camp of Boulogne:

The best and most complete war school that could have ever been conceived.

Alison writes:

The camps in which the soldiers were lodged during their long sojourn on the shores of the Channel were characterised by the same admirable system of organisation. They were laid out, according to the usual form, in squares intersected by streets, and composed of barracks, constructed on a uniform plan, according to the materials furnished by the country in which they were situated. At Ostend they were composed of light wood and straw; at Boulogne and at Vimereux of sharp stakes cut in the forest of Guenis, supported by mason work.

These field-barracks were extremely healthy; the beds of the soldiers, raised two feet above the ground, were composed of straw, on which their camp-blankets were laid; the utmost care was taken to preserve cleanliness in every part of the establishment. Constant employment was the true secret both of their good health and docile habits.

Neither officers nor soldiers were ever allowed to remain any time idle. When not employed in military evolutions they were continually engaged either in raising or strengthening field-works on the different points of the coast, or levelling down eminences, draining marshes, or filling up hollows, to form agreeable esplanades in front of their battalions, and where their exercises were performed. The different corps and divisions vied with each other in these works of utility or recreation; they even went so far as to engage in undertakings of pure ornament; gardens were created, flowers were cultivated, and, in the midst of an immense military population, the aspect of nature was sensibly improved.

What was said in praise of Soult at Boulogne and of Davout at Ostend could not be said of Ney at Montreuil.

It is astonishing to learn from an officer who was there, serving in the 59th Regiment belonging to Ney's army corps, how a very precious time was lost, inasmuch as the superior officers did not pay much attention to the drilling of the men. The Duke of Fézensac, afterwards general of division writes (*Souvenirs Militaires*):

> The regiment was rarely assembled for manoeuvring in a body (*en ligne*); some military promenades were made, which were nothing more than ordinary promenades like a short day of route marching; some target practice without any method, nothing in the way of skirmishing, no bayonet exercise, no fencing. It entered no one's head to throw up the simplest field

work. No officer was detailed to carry out the smallest reconnaissance.

General De Saint Chamans, who was at that time a young officer like Fézensac, writes in a different fashion of the Boulogne camp.

I do not believe, that there existed at any period, nor in any country, such an excellent military school as there was at the camp formed at Boulogne at that time; the general who had command of it, the generals under his orders, and the troops which it comprised were all drafted from the pick of the French Army, and the greatest general that had ever appeared, Napoleon Bonaparte, used to come himself frequently to inspect those old troops and the young fighting men who were being formed under those excellent models.

When in command at Boulogne, Soult was only thirty-five years old, but he sacrificed his pleasures and his rest to give himself up entirely to the most minute details connected with his army corps. He caused his troops to manoeuvre three times a week for twelve hours running; he was assiduous in his work, and formed a band of excellent officers which the best military school would with difficulty have turned out.

However poor and incomplete may have been, if we accept Fézensac's word, the instruction imparted, life in camp had the great benefit of accustoming the troops to live together and to become intimate with one another. Not only was camp life a good school for camping and marching, but the troops were trained together in the identical units and under the identical generals they were to serve under in war. The latter knew where to look for experienced officers to undertake any special service.

The generals, the staff officers, the senior officers of the various corps, by having been for a long time thrown together, had come to know and to appreciate each other. In this way, if the colonels of a brigade were indifferent, the general paid greater attention to the execution of his orders; if the general himself was not quite up to the mark, the colonels combined and showed him in a respectful manner what it was necessary to be done, and, when following their suggestions, the latter believed himself to be commanding. The hobbies, the defects of character, which on the part of a newcomer might have engendered mistrust, were appreciated at their full value. This union, this confidence, this appreciation of the worth, the talent, the qualities and even the defects of everyone were what so much contributed to the thorough success of the French armies, and all this was the result of the long stay the army had made in the camp.

There is a prevailing idea that the instruction the French officers had in the armies of the Republic and Empire was purely practical, nothing more or less than the result of what was acquired in the field, but it was not quite so, as can be seen by the testimony of Marshal Soult. This is what the marshal writes of the time when he was a simple sub-lieutenant in the battalion of the Haut-Rhin:—

> In all the staffs the work was incessant, embracing every branch of the service, and still it was barely considered enough; one aimed at taking part in everything that was done. I can truly say it was the period of my career in which I worked hardest, and in which my chiefs appeared most exacting; and though they did not all deserve to be taken as models, many of the general officers who at a later period came to the front, have come out of their school.

Soult spared no pains in supervising the instruction of officers and men, and could claim the merit of having formed in the camp of Boulogne a mass of excellent officers, who in later years were spread throughout the French Army.

Desaix was another studious officer. He had acquired a large store of knowledge, and was well acquainted with most battlefields, with all the most brilliant manoeuvres, and with all the most renowned acts of bravery.

Joubert was a good general, not only on account of his courage, but through his knowledge and military talents.

Ney, possibly because he had only an elementary education, was an officer who did not quite believe that brilliant fighting could be done without a certain knowledge of the principles of the art of war. He openly admitted the necessity for systematic military reflection.

> When the Marshal commanded the camp at Montreuil-sur-Mer, in 1804, having practically experienced the insufficiency of the regulations then in force, and seeing the necessity of instructing the officers under his command in the theory of war, he had a spacious room constructed in rear of each regiment, which he designated as the officers' council-room.
>
> Here the officers of the respective corps, from the colonel to the youngest subaltern, were obliged to meet and study their

profession together; the Marshal's idea being that solitary study often tends to engender error, which by public and general study and discussion may in most cases be avoided. Each officer was called upon to give an explanation of every manoeuvre in which he had taken a share in battle, discuss its utility, its advantages, etc. Ney would then briefly offer his own ideas, and argue each point familiarly with his comrades.

These rooms were, in fact, regimental schools for tactics. The Marshal regularly attended the council-rooms of every regiment in rotation, and generally gave out subjects for study. It was in this view, and for this object, that he wrote a great many papers on tactics, but, at the moment, without any other motive than the laudable desire of instructing his officers and making them conversant with his own evolutions; and he had the satisfaction to see that his labour was not in vain, for Ney's officers were confessedly the best instructed, the most ready and intelligent in the army. (Major A. James, *Military Studies by Marshal Ney*.

The discipline of some of the French regiments was not of a very high order when they first came into camp. Fézensac joined the 59th Regiment, and has something to say about it. Colonel Lacuée was one of Napoleon's *aides-de-camp*, but he held strong republican opinions, and had offended him by his strong advocacy of Moreau. To punish him, the emperor gave him the command of a bad regiment, the 59th, ordering him at the same time to bring it under subordination. (Colonel Lacuée was mortally wounded on the 9th of October at Gundelfingen, and died shortly after of his wound.) The 59th Regiment, better known at that time as the *Royal décousu*, lay encamped at Montreuil. It had a colonel who robbed the military chest of his regiment, and who was not ashamed to own that the centre companies of the regiment might be clothed in rags, provided that he had an imposing squad of pioneers, a good band, and a stalwart company of grenadiers!

Nothing is so absolutely necessary in war as timely and complete preparation, for once hostilities break out, events follow each other with startling rapidity. If matters have been foreseen judiciously, well and good; but if not, mishaps will follow one another, and the situation is certain to become worse every day.

Napoleon, who was endowed with superhuman strength and endurance, worked at his preparations with a frenzy of energy. He laboured continuously; he thought of everything, he provided every-

Garde Uniformen.
Russisches Militair.
Augsburg in Herzberg's Kunsthandlung.

Husar. Uhlane. Artillerist. Musquetier. Curassier. Dragoner.
Russisches Militair.
Augsburg in Herzberg's Kunsthandlung.

thing. His assiduous application was the best example, and it animated the others to exert themselves. He was not a man to do things by halves; with him no point which demanded attention was ever suffered to be overlooked. He certainly had the capacity for conceiving gigantic designs, mighty combinations; still he knew that conceiving was not all, so he went much further, he sketched out the operations down to the most minute and tiresome details. Nothing ever escaped his penetrating eye, nothing was ever too great or too small for his notice.

With all the unbounded confidence the emperor had in his ability, and though he appeared to trust greatly in his own good fortune, nevertheless he never neglected to take any precaution which it was possible to adopt. Being a deep thinker and a man of great circumspection, he never omitted to examine personally and in detail all the facts and circumstances of any enterprise he was seriously bent on. His grasp of practical details was very great, and came very opportune in this instance, for there was no lack of work to be executed.

An enormous number and a great variety of crafts had to be constructed; all their complicated gear to be procured, a great assortment of materials required for the expedition to be collected, the supervision of the large army assembled on the shores of the Channel to be attended to, a novel description of drill to be devised for men utterly unacquainted with the sea. Napoleon was untiring, he keenly scrutinised everything; and had it only depended on his forethought and on his fostering care, the expedition certainly held every prospect of turning out a success.

If there was a want, it was in horses for cavalry and transport. In preparing for the invasion, Napoleon had calculated on mounting a large number of his men after landing in England.

The morale of the army could not have been better; officers and soldiers were all animated by the prospect of humiliating the English in London.

Not only had this formidable army, with all its necessary equipment and materials, been concentrated on the coast of the Channel, but the construction of a large number of small vessels had been conducted nearly to completion. When the war was resumed, all the materials of the Republic were turned to account for constructing the 2000 vessels of the flotilla. Some hundred thousand trees were cut down in the forests and brought by land and by water to the shores of the Channel. The emperor had taken for model the crossing of the Channel as conducted by William the Conqueror, and caused an

Officer.   Gemeiner.
Kosaken vom schwarzen Meere.
Augsburg in Herzbergs Kunsthandlung.

Officer.   Gemeiner.
Kosaken vom schwarzen Meere.
Augsburg in Herzbergs Kunsthandlung.

enormous flotilla of vessels of various descriptions to he constructed and kept ready for ferrying his army across the Channel. The total number of transports and ships of all kinds amounted to 2293, and, with the object of infusing order and regularity in this large number of crafts, the flotilla was distributed into six divisions. Each division was under the command of a senior naval officer.

James, in his *Naval History*, gives the following account of the flotilla:

> The flotilla was separated into six grand divisions. The first, under the designation of the left wing, commanded by Rear-Admiral Jean François Courand, and stationed at the port of Etaples, was destined to carry the troops from the camp of Montreuil, commanded by Marshal Ney; the second and third, called the left and right wings of the centre of the flotilla, under the respective commands of Rear-Admiral Daniel Savary and Capitaine de Vaisseau Julien le Ray, occupied the port of Boulogne, and were destined to carry the troops from the two camps to the right and left of the town, commanded by Marshal Soult; the fourth, named the right wing of the flotilla, commanded by Capitaine de Vaisseau François Henri Eugène Daugier, occupied the port of Vimereux, and was to carry the corps of Marshal Lannes, composed of sundry divisions of light infantry, amongst which were those of the grenadiers of the advance and of the reserve.
>
> The Gallo-Batavian flotilla assembled at the port of Ambleteuse, under command of Vice-Admiral Ver-Huell, formed the fifth grand division of the expedition, and was to carry the troops commanded by Marshal Davout. (For the proposed invasion, Holland had to submit to heavy requisitions in men, ships, and money.) The sixth, or reserve division, lying in the port of Calais, under the command of Capitaine de Frégate Charles l'Evêque, was destined to transport the division of Italian infantry, and several divisions of dragoons, mounted and dismounted.
>
> The first four grand divisions only had a regular organisation; each was separated into two portions, called '*escadrilles*;' and each of the latter was to embark a division of the army, composed of four regiments of the line, and one of light infantry, with its cavalry, artillery, and baggage.

In view of the coming operations, the troops were exercised in such manoeuvres as they would be called upon to perform when landing in the presence of an enemy.

Napoleon, alluding to the preparations he was making for the invasion of England, said:

> The perfect order which reigned in this immense flotilla, the frequent exercises by which I habituated the troops to embark and disembark in less than an hour at an appointed signal, the care with which each man was instructed in his particular duty—in a word, everything had been provided that could secure success to this grand operation.

Anxious to have ocular proof of the degree of celerity with which the army could be embarked, Napoleon, who arrived at Boulogne on the 3rd of August, ordered the operation to be executed twice in his presence. The result surpassed his belief. Although the troops had to march from camps, the extremities of which were more than two miles from the point of embarkation, an hour and a half after the beating of the *générale* men and horses were all on board.

Various establishments on a very large scale were found indispensable at and near Boulogne. Great basins had to be excavated at Boulogne, Etaples, Ambleteuse, and Vimereux for the reception of vessels. Bonaparte procured the means for meeting the cost of all this by selling Louisiana to the United States of America for eighty millions of *francs*.

Five marches forward to the banks of the Thames would, in Foy's opinion, have carried the French further in the conquest of the world than thirty victories on the Continent. To obtain immense results it was not indispensable that the invasion should be complete and definitive. Retreat, it is true, presented almost insurmountable obstacles; but Napoleon's hopes of landing were so dazzling as to divert his thoughts from the difficulty of retreat. To retire unmolested might, after all, have been demanded and obtained from the vanquished. As he himself said:

> The nature of his plan, was so good that, in spite of all manner of obstacles, the most promising chances were in his favour.

Many incidents related about Napoleon belong to the realm of romance, and many of his sayings are nothing more than an expression. It is thus with his utterances with regard to the command of the Channel.

> Give me the command of the Channel for twenty-four hours, and England will have lived.

For all that, he knew much better what was required, for in another instance he writes:

Make us masters of the Straits of Dover, be it for five days.

But even that did not satisfy him, at another time he asks to be made complete master of the Straits for two or three weeks. The longer he needed to remain supreme in the Channel, the worse it would have been for him.

Nelson's opinion of the invasion was that the landing could not be effected, if it were only on account of the counter currents of the tide. As far as crossing by means of rowing-boats, humanly speaking, he held it to be impracticable. He wrote:

You are right to be on your guard against the folly of that man, but with the forces at my disposal I defy him to carry out his absurd plan.

James reviews, (*Naval History*), what might have occurred had the French become masters of the Straits of Dover, and carried their flotilla across to the English shore.

Even admitting that the Channel, Mediterranean, and North Sea fleets of England were away, were there no other ships to check the course of the flotilla? Let but a breeze have blown from any point of the compass, and innumerable frigates—heavy frigates too—sloops, bombs, gun- brigs, and cutters, would soon have been on the spot. No shoals or shore batteries would then have interposed to prevent the guns of the British from producing their full effect. The more numerous the French troops, the greater would have been the slaughter amongst them, the greater the difficulty for the sailors to manoeuvre the vessels. Confusion would have ensued; and the destruction or flight of a part of the flotilla would, in the end, have compromised the safety of the remainder. Every hour would have brought fresh British vessels to assist in the general overthrow.

James reviews the chances of the flotilla getting across in a calm. He pictures the difficulty of managing such a huge heterogeneous fleet, such a number of vessels possessing different powers of progression, with cross-tides and partial currents; and shows how the delays and confusion were likely to augment still more if a breeze had sprung up.

Thiers reviews at some length the problem whether Napoleon

would have been successful had he once placed his army on the shores of England. It will be as well to quote his exact words:—

> That is a question which will often be asked both in our days and by future generations, and which it is not easy to solve. However, supposing Napoleon to have once effected a landing at Dover, we do not affront the English nation in believing that it would have been vanquished by the army and by the Captain, who, in eighteen months, conquered and subjected Austria, Germany, Prussia, and Russia. Not a man was added to that ocean army, which at Austerlitz, at Jena, and at Friedland, beat 800,000 soldiers of the Continent. (Thiers, who wrote after the stubborn fights in the Peninsula, should have known what resistance the French would have had to overcome.) It must be added, too, that the territorial inviolability so long enjoyed by England has not familiarised her with the danger of invasion, or tested her means and courage to repel it; a circumstance which by no means diminishes the glory of her fleets and regular armies.
>
> It is therefore very improbable that she would have successfully withstood the soldiers of Napoleon, not yet exhausted by fatigue, and not yet decimated by war. An heroic resolution of her Government, taking refuge, for instance, in Scotland, and leaving England to be ravaged until Nelson, with the English squadrons, could come and cut off all retreat from Napoleon,—such a resolution, exposing Napoleon, the conqueror, to be made a prisoner in his own proper conquest, would, doubtless, have brought about some singular conjunctures; but it is beyond all probability to suppose that it would have been adopted. We are firmly persuaded that had Napoleon reached London, England would have treated.

★★★★★★

Note: Thiers speaks very confidently when he asserts that England would have been too ready to treat, had Napoleon readied London. He evidently forgot that England had such a minister as Pitt at the helm, and that suing for terms would have been the very last thing that great man would have ever consented to do.

★★★★★★

All the difficulty lay in the crossing of the Straits. Although the flotilla could pass in a summer calm, or in the fogs of winter, the passage wars full of danger. Accordingly, Napoleon had planned the co-operation of a fleet to cover the expedition. But then, it may be urged, the difficulty was, after all, coincident with the original one, that of being superior to the English on the sea. By no means. The point in question was, not to be superior, or even equal to them. All that he proposed was, by an able plan to bring a fleet into the Channel, by taking advantage of the chances of the sea, its immensity rendering encounters on it so uncertain.

The plan of Napoleon, so often modified, and reproduced with so much fecundity, had every chance of success in the hands of a firmer man than Villeneuve. Doubtless, Napoleon experienced here, under another form, the disadvantage of *his* naval inferiority. Villeneuve, keenly alive to that inferiority, became discouraged; but he was too much discouraged, and in a manner to affect his honour in the eyes of posterity.

After all, his fleet fought well at Ferrol; and if we suppose that he had fought before Brest the disastrous battle which he shortly afterwards lost at Trafalgar, Gantheaume would have run out; and as for losing that battle, would it not have been well lost, in order to secure the passage of the Channel? Nay, under such circumstances, could it be said to be lost? Villeneuve, then, acted wrongly, although he has been too much decried, as is usually the case with those who are unfortunate. A practical seaman, and unmindful that by dint of energy and resolute courage one can often supply what is deficient in *matériel*, he knew not how to elevate himself to the height of his mission, and attempt that which, in his situation, Latouche Tréville would assuredly have accomplished.

The enterprise of Napoleon, then, was no chimera: it was perfectly possible, as he had prepared it; and, perhaps, in the eyes of discerning judges, this unfinished enterprise will do him more honour than those which have been crowned with the most brilliant success. Neither was it a mere feint, as it has been supposed to be by some people, who discover depths where there are none. Some thousands of letters of the ministers and the emperor put an end to all doubt on that point. It was a serious enterprise, followed up and matured for several years with a real passion.

Napoleon urged Villeneuve to sail from Ferrol and throw himself on the squadron that was blockading Gantheaume in Brest. His orders were:

Give battle, risk all, lose all, provided you open the port of Brest.

His orders absolved Villeneuve of all responsibility. The dishonour of a lost battle could not be imputed to the commander who had faithfully complied with his orders.

It has been said—and this refuted the idea that the invasion of England was all a sham—that when Napoleon heard that Villeneuve had sailed out of Ferrol, and, as he imagined, to proceed to Brest, his excitement and anxiety knew no bounds.

What Napoleon needed to complete his military success was the humbling of England. In the eleven years in which he was at war with this country he was never able to score a single important success, while England, on the other hand, destroyed his fleets, conquered his colonies, and by arming Europe against him at length brought his domination to an end.

Chapter 2

Preparations in England

Since the resumption of the war the people of England had been kept in a state of constant suspense. The fear that the French might present themselves at the most unexpected moment was in every one's heart. The finances were not in a flourishing condition, and the ministers who had to make ready for a possible invasion found it a most difficult task to devise schemes for replenishing the war-chest.

It is barely possible for us now to conceive the virulence of feeling which existed against Napoleon in England in 1805. The high, the low, the rich, and the poor simply detested him. ("There had suddenly blazed up in the breasts of millions a fierce, uninquiring, unappeasable detestation of the individual."—Sir John Moore.) The lower classes regarded him as a ruffianly murderer. At the bottom of this feeling was a superstitious dread, for the impression which his fame and his extraordinary deeds had engendered had sunk deep in the mind of the people, who had come to look upon him as something more than human. Of the two arch-enemies of mankind Satan was less feared than Napoleon. He was not simply the great bogey of the nursery; his name was not only a bugbear for quieting obstreperous children, but conveyed alarm to full-grown and able-bodied men.

****

Chateaubriand said in the House of Peers, "Napoleon's greatcoat and hat placed on the end of a pole on the coast of Brest would make Europe run to arms from one end to another."

******

Narrow-minded men could or would not recognise any except the ordinary rules of inheritance as being the ones ordained to guide the destinies of nations. It was but natural that the monarchs, the men who had mounted the steps of the throne by strict succession, should uphold the divine right, that it should be extremely distasteful to them to see a man who by his rare qualities and good fortune had raised himself to a level with them. But there were others besides who remained obstinately blind to the fact that genius respected no laws, and this when they willingly shut their eyes to the eccentricities which their great naval hero permitted himself, which were often in opposition to the established rules of the service.

The *Times* was particularly virulent in its tone towards Napoleon; it called him the Corsican, the *soi-disant* emperor, the scourge of Europe, the Usurper.

★★★★★★

It strikes one as very strange that many years after the death of this great man persons who from their high position should have shown more delicacy, should have cast at him slurring reproaches. In a speech delivered at Erfurt in September 1891, William II. applies to Napoleon the epithet of *parvenu Corse!*

★★★★★★

That paper was not able to understand how much superior is the man who attains to greatness by sheer ability, by force of character, by a keen and grasping intellect, by strength of will, than one on whom eminence has been forced by the mere accident of birth.

Bonaparte had, in truth, to struggle hard against many difficulties. Born in Corsica in 1769, after that island had been annexed to France, which just made it possible for him to call himself a Frenchman, he was by origin an alien of a semi-obscure family, and not supported by any powerful party, but jeered at as the pauper child of a conquered race; a man who did not know where to turn to find money for a modest repast, and who starved himself rather than add to the family troubles, and if possible to mitigate them. So poor was he that we are popularly reminded that at one time he could not pay his washing bill.

All Europe had become familiar with the appearance of this little man in a cocked hat and long grey coat, with a pale and set face; with a thick neck, and a head fixed low in his peculiar square shoulders; with eyes that seemed to take in everything at a glance, and not that alone, but something beyond—eyes as the eyes of the man of action, not those of the man whose food is thought; eyes which at rest had a melancholy and meditative look, but when stirred to anger were fierce and menacing; endowed in his happy moods with a charming smile which altered his physiognomy entirely.

But with all his drawbacks of birth, so gigantic were his gifts that he did not experience any disadvantage from the want of either friends or means. He possessed a capacity and talent calculated to enslave mankind. He excelled most men in moral audacity and in vigilance; his activity was unremitting. Napoleon accounted for his superiority over other men by his power of being able to endure continuous brain work. He averred that he never knew any man that could equal him in this.

When about to undertake any military operations, he made a most minute estimate of the number of men, amount of money and munitions of every description which would be required, rating all at the highest figure, for in his preparations he was prodigal of everything which he deemed necessary to success.

******

It appears very singular that with all his foresight, Napoleon, when preparing for his campaign of 1812, should have omitted to foresee the rigour of a Russian winter, nor should have made any provisions for roughing the horses.

******

There was nothing above the reach of his mind; nothing seemed too low for him to bend over and touch. It was unerring foresight which raised him above all other men.

The first place was vacant; the most worthy was called to fill it: he had only dethroned anarchy.

So, it was said of Napoleon at the close of 1804. Some called him the usurper. The usurper indeed!

******

Was not Bernadotte a usurper, like Napoleon? Was not Victor Emanuel II., as King of Italy, a usurper? Still the people would have no other king. Why did no one question the popular right that led them to the throne?

******

Those who called him so had forgotten Voltaire's words: "*Le premier roi fut un soldat heureux.*" ("The first king was a happy soldier.) One of the Popes, (Zacharias), when asked whether it was the name or the fact which constituted the legitimate king, replied, "He is King who has the power." Queen Caroline of Naples, who had great reasons for hating Bonaparte, said of him: *S'il est arrivé à gouverner son pays, c'est qu'il en est le plus digne.* (If he has managed to govern his country, it is because he is the most worthy of it.)

******

Those who had remained faithful to all that was generous and patriotic in the Republican Utopias, objected to a sovereign of any kind, but with the majority of his opponents, Napoleon's greatest crime was to be a parvenu. *Il lui manquait d'être né sur le trône.* (He failed to be born on the throne.) It was the pride of his enemies which revolted at the bare idea of being ruled by one of their own class. With many, however, republicanism was not deep-seated. Murat and Bernadotte, who were at one time ardent republicans, full of ultra-revolutionary sentiments, altered their ideas so much as to accept a crown.

Murat was lieutenant-colonel commanding a cavalry regiment at Abbeville when Marat fell under the keen blade of Charlotte Corday in 1793, on which occasion he wrote to the Jacobin Club that, from sincere admiration of the illustrious deceased he intended to change the spelling of his name into Marat. His principles at that period were so extreme that after Robespierre's fall it was considered necessary to deprive him of his command. Bernadotte's attachment to democratic principles was well known. He was a violent democrat, and his republicanism was for a time proof against seduction. He was one of the first batch of marshals created in May 1804, and soon turned imperialist.

On assuming command of the Army of Hanover, he issued an order of the day in which occurred the following passage: . . . Cherish for ever the preserving hand which has saved your country; to your fathers it is a guarantee of their possessions, to you the reward of your services, and to all an undisturbed and happy old age. Shout with all your generals and with all good Frenchmen *Vive l'Empereur.*"

******

The most eminent statesmen, the most able and daring generals, often have not the talent to rule a state. They may shine in their own special line, but they shine not when they attain the supreme power. It was not so with Napoleon; he could command an army and rule a state equally well.

Nor had England any reason for being surprised at the event, for had not that able statesman Burke some years before prophesied that the French Republic would become the prey of the first ambitious chieftain, who might have sufficient boldness to avail himself of any fortunate train of circumstances for seizing the reins of government?

Napoleon himself said:

> I am a successful soldier. My dominion will not last beyond the day in which I have ceased to be strong, and consequently feared.

Most states in Europe had long acknowledged France as a Republic, and such an acknowledgment undoubtedly inferred that the pretensions of the Royal House of Bourbon were extinguished. Providence sided with genius; still, the crowned heads looked with jealousy on this intruder, and there was a desire abroad amongst the sovereigns of Europe to humble a person who from a private station had dared to aspire to sovereignty. He certainly lacked the *jus divinum*, but, after all, is there no other nobility but that which is inherited? Is no exception ever to be made in favour of the nobility of intellect, of the powers of ruling? It is a well-known fact that Louis XV, like his grandsire Louis XIV, firmly believed that kings were something different from and superior to other men. One day he told the Duke of Choiseul, his prime minister, that he would surely go to perdition; the minister reminded him that the same fate might someday attend him. The monarch replied:

> Not at all, I am the anointed of the Lord.

★★★★★★

Once the king had been consecrated, in the eyes of the people he was inviolable. The consecration of a sovereign was therefore not an empty ceremony. Of the European sovereigns at the commencement of the nineteenth century two were, if not actually insane, at least very eccentric, whimsical, and possessed with dangerous hallucinations. His divine right did not save one from being most brutally murdered by his nobles, nor prevent the other from being deposed by his subjects.

★★★★★★

Napoleon has often been accused of want of dignity in his deportment and in his manners. Though this may not be an unfounded charge, much of it evidently arose from the fact that his early friends were brusque and unpolished. Foljambe-Hall attributes this brusqueness to merely native "insularity."

Napoleon declared that his mission was not simply to govern France, but to bring under her dominion the entire world; for had he failed in this, the other powers would have to a certainty united to annihilate her. Bourbon rule was not such an unmitigated blessing that the removal of one of them should arrest the progress of the world; would they or any other monarch have done as much as Napoleon did for France at the commencement of his rule? Through his victories he had brought back peace by land and by sea. He had restored religion to the country by a concordat concluded with the Pope; a political arrangement, a manifesto against the Revolution, which as it drew to him a large section of the nobility and gave him influence on a certain number of the population, was of the highest importance.

On the 24th of March 1804 he issued a new code, a, model of sage legislation, an immortal digest of laws on which the happiness of many people is based. The most interesting effort in the direction of legal reform which has ever been made; a superb monument of jurisdiction which of itself alone would have sufficed to immortalise the name of the great emperor.

Pace data terris, animum ad civilia vertit.
Jure suum, leges que tulit justissimus autor.

He awarded merit in every class of society alike by creating the Legion of Honour. Such a well-chosen name and distinguished title! The cross, the coveted cross! what could not be expected from the soldier on the day of battle? What an incentive to gallant deeds, the thought of returning to his country decorated and of being saluted by every sentry as a noble soldier!

"When Bonaparte returned from Egypt without leave, after having sacrificed a fleet and abandoned an army which when it quitted the shores of France was the pride of the nation and the astonishment of the world, it might have been thought that he would have begun by explaining his reasons and excusing his conduct. An ordinary man would have done this, but not so Bonaparte. On the contrary, he at once took the Directory to task, and abused it severely for the state to which it had reduced France. In short, he acted as if he had already been the ruler and master of the country, and those who really were the rulers were struck dumb before him." (*An Analysis of the Talents and Character of Napoleon Bonaparte,* by a general officer.)

And why did he assume this imperative tone? why, in place of subordinating his person to the state, did he subordinate the state to himself, but because he had the occult right to dominate; a right which was inborn in him.

"Tyranny is a reed which bends before the wind and recovers itself." The truth of these words of Saint Just were confirmed eleven years after they were spoken. Bonaparte, who had been acclaimed First Consul for life, was set on the throne of France by the people on the 28th *Floral An. XII.* Public opinion was tending towards a return to a monarchical *régime*, but the French, who disdained and dreaded being dictated by one of the ancient Royal House of Bourbon, chose for their ruler the most fortunate and able of all the generals of the Republic. The old dynasty had been done away with, and, in the words of the Senate, "*Vons fondez une ère nouvelle.*" You create a new epoch. (On one occasion Bonaparte administered a sound kick to Volny for telling him too frankly that France wished the return of the Bourbons.)

The Revolution had swept away the Bourbons. They were numbered amongst the things which had seen their day. Twelve years had gone by since the death of the king, and in all the excesses and changes of those tumultuous days Bonaparte had had no hand. It was because the other nations chafed at their impotence that they railed at Napoleon. His genius could not be denied, and no better proof of this existed than the invectives levelled at his head.

The feeling in favour of a change of government was pretty general, 3,524,254 votes were in favour of the empire and of Napoleon being elected emperor.

★★★★★★

A parade was held in the various garrisons to proclaim the change of government. Mouton, a colonel of high stature and fine proportions, renowned for his daring, had the courage to call out in a defiant voice, "Silence in the ranks," as the troops lustily cheered the emperor. Napoleon showed his knowledge of men by not being offended by this republican manifestation. On the contrary, he promoted Mouton the next day to General's rank, and made him one of his *aides-de-camp*.

★★★★★★

Compared with other mortals, Napoleon seems to have been a man of quite a different breed. He laid down the law in council quite as imperiously as in his camp. He was a man of unconquerably restless disposition; action was a necessity for him. His inmost thoughts ran always on war; there was nothing he loved so passionately.

★★★★★★

At the surrender of Ulm, an Austrian general, seeing the emperor's uniform all soiled and splashed with mud, spoke to him of the hardships of such a campaign. To which observation he replied with a smile, "Your master wished to remind me that I was a soldier. I hope he will now admit that the imperial purple has not made me forget for a moment my original trade."

✶✶✶✶✶✶

He breathed combats; he loved the tumult of the fray, the intoxication of victory. Always bent on proving himself stronger that anyone else, he had a real longing for glory, for dominion; he had a passion for regulating everything, for ruling everybody, and, as Hanno said of Hannibal, "he was devoured by a burning thirst for reigning."

The more we examine the character of this most extraordinary man, the more we discover attributes for ruling which we rarely see united in one man. With all that, his conceptions were often impracticable, his dreams too vast. Fortune may have favoured his plans, but it was he who conceived them, and he could show equal ability whether fortune favoured him or not.

The fame of his name always preceded him, and such was his prestige that before a battle his troops never seemed to have any doubt but that victory would crown their efforts.

He only judged by results, and was only satisfied with success. When he desired to employ any person on some special service, he no doubt inquired, as Cardinal Richelieu did, "Is he fortunate? Is he enterprising?"

He inspired confidence by his brilliant talents and by his indomitable will. Thoroughly acquainted with the human heart, he attentively studied the character of those opposed to him, and knew with what ease he could turn their faulty dispositions and their personal failings to account. In men he saw only helps or obstacles to his designs. "*Ensorceler, captiver, épouvanter au besoin, en tout cela il était inimitable. Combien de gens, ses ennemis d'abord, devenaient sincèrement des amis à la première entrevue (Alexandre I.) c'était un hypnotiseur incomcient.* "To bewitch, to captivate, to frighten if need be, in all this he was inimitable. How many people, his enemies at first, were sincerely friends at the first meeting (Alexander I.) was an incompetent hypnotist."—*Boutades Militaires.*

Nerve, quickness of eye and readiness of resource he possessed to an immense degree. Never did his enemies make one false move without it being quickly detected by his eagle eye; never did he miss to give them bitter cause to rue their error. His anger, says Thiers, when honest, lasted not more than does a flash of lightning; when feigned, as long as the occasion required. But though endowed with an incredible daring to incur risks, he nevertheless displayed marvellous prudence in the midst of danger.

What his heart longed after, he wanted to possess principally to satisfy a kind of obstinate pride which he felt in succeeding in all his designs whatever might be the cost and the obstacles in the way. Patient and persistent, he unravelled all difficulties with a skilful hand. His savoir-faire enabled him to adapt himself to all with whom he came in contact. But under all his astuteness lay the domination of an iron will—a will, as it has been justly said, only second to the will of God himself—and a character decided and imperative. False and astute, gifted with matchless power of dissimulation, he deceived whilst he charmed.

It is greatly to the credit of such a man that he never abandoned a friend. It was a well-established fact that if a person had once served Napoleon well, he could always count on his protection for the future. In this he confirmed Paoli's saying, "What lasts longest in Corsica is the memory of benefits."

The great man loved praise, and it is just possible that fully one half of the faults he is reproached with in our days were due to his advisers and flatterers.

Napoleon had an intelligence of vast breadth and extraordinary penetration; he readily acquired a knowledge of anything worth treasuring. No labour could tire out his body or depress his spirits. His mind was always active; his repose was not, like that of the rest of us mortals, dictated by the night and the day, it was the time which was left to him after business that he consecrated to rest.

Knowing how often great events spring from trifles, he wanted to know everything, to hear everything. He often arrived unexpectedly to see for himself how matters stood, and to give no time to his ministers and generals to prepare for his coming.

There are men who appear to have been born to attract all the rays of the sun, and Napoleon was one of them. In the days of the Consulate, above all, everything seemed to smile on him. His fortune was great, his genius transcendent; decision flashed upon his councils, and with him to decide on the performance of an action and to carry it out was all one.

After all the outcry, after all the blood that was shed in the suppression of tyranny, after all the boast about equality, nothing reveals Napoleon's ability more than the way in which he cajoled the people, while the scenes of the Revolution were still quite fresh in their recollection, into offering him the crown.

Fascinated as one may be by the splendour of his intellectual gifts and by his brilliant successes, no one can nevertheless help grieving over his glaring errors, and the heavy price his country was made to pay for military glory. Whilst strongly opposed to his military despotism, all seem to agree that in him we behold a man never to be matched, that such a world conqueror will perhaps never be seen again. Some ninety years have passed (1905) since he was overthrown at Waterloo, and eighty-four since his mortal remains were laid under the shadow of the far-famed mimosa tree at St. Helena; still his fame is perhaps even greater now than when he was seated on the throne of France. People never seem tired of writing about him. The power of appealing to the imagination has survived Napoleon's death, for his mighty deeds have burnt his name too deep into the pages of the world's history.

If, as some writers allege, he strove to leave a memorable record to posterity, how gratified would he be could he know how thoroughly his ambition has been realised! His very death in a remote and ocean-girdled rock, dreaded by all the powerful rulers of the world, was a more befitting end for such a hero than the commonplace dissolution of the most renowned of sovereigns. Posterity has spoken, and continues to speak, but not to endorse the verdict of those who can see nothing but bad and vile in his character.

As Napoleon had no intimate friend, no one to whom he was in the habit of unburdening himself, of confiding his purposes, his ideas, his reasons, it will always be impossible to know what really regulated his actions. It would require nothing less than a genius to fathom the working of such a master mind, and evidently, we should abstain from judging his actions by the ordinary standard of men.

Such was the man, who, envious of our national prosperity, wealth, and liberty, had planted a hundred years ago a powerful army opposite to our Kentish shores and meditated an invasion of England. (Napoleon envied England the command of the sea and the immense power that command confers. His covetous spirit would brook no rival; he wanted to be great on land and also great at sea.)

Notwithstanding her close vicinity to France and the years she had been at war with that country, England had always relied on her navy, and did not possess an army at all in keeping with her power and with the extent of her territory and possessions. We find Lord St. Vincent writing to Lord Keith on the 12th October 1803:

Our greatest resource lies in the vigilance and activity of our cruisers; to reduce their number or to employ only a portion of them to guard our own coast, our harbours, our islands and our shores would in my opinion cause a disaster.

Had the British people not been so inexperienced in the terrible sufferings which are the necessary accompaniments of war, and less ignorant of what is required to defend a country from the devastation of a hostile army, they would not have been so averse to the maintenance of a sufficient force to defend their shores.

The spirit of the nation in 1805, however, ran high against Gallic invasion. The subject was of such vital importance that persons of all ranks were strongly agitated by the crisis. Unprecedented unanimity existed amongst the British people. Pitt, exerting all the powers of his exalted mind, of his forcible and brilliant eloquence, had roused the spirit of the country, and from one end to the other of the land the nation had burst into a blaze of enthusiasm, every person being actuated by the most determined resolution to perish rather than to submit. This was the nation which all Europe at one time looked to for salvation.

Still, as was natural, panics sometimes occurred. Many of the peaceful inhabitants of Dover and of the villages which lay along the neighbouring coast were so horrified at the idea of an invasion that they quitted their homes precipitately and retired to Canterbury and to London. The season and the long nights in the winter were held to be extremely favourable to the enemy for the purpose. When, Napoleon having gone to Boulogne, a general illumination ensued, many of the inhabitants of Folkestone and Sandgate became alarmed, and removed to the interior.

These panics were not confined to the coast of Kent and Sussex, they were also seen at Torbay, at Dublin, at Danbury. Such was the extent of coast to be guarded, that it was admitted as almost impossible to place the whole of it in an adequate state of defence.

In the latter part of July, the news of Calder's fruitless victory on the 22nd of that month, and that he had lost sight of the allied fleet gave rise to a state of great alarm throughout England. Everything gave way to a universal cry about invasion. Lord Minto speaks of Villeneuve's sailing from Ferrol as affecting the mercantile section of the population of London.

There has been the greatest alarm ever known in the City of London since the combined fleet sailed from Ferrol. If they captured our homeward bound convoys, it is said that the India Company and half of the City must have been bankrupt.

Our spirit of resistance was possibly greater than our strength, still at no previous period of her history had England made preparations on so large a scale. There were nearly 100,000 troops of the line, with 80,000 and upwards of first-rate militia, and these in point of efficiency were not far behind the regulars. Besides regulars and militia, a volunteer force, computed at 350,000 men, had come forward ready to defend their country. (Of the volunteers it must be remembered that a goodly number of individuals joined that body to avoid being forced into the militia.)

Amongst the regulars were the troops that had already fought the French in Egypt. With regard to the militia and volunteers, it is a fact that the longer such bodies are embodied the greater their efficiency becomes. Some years before, in 1798, armed associations were formed in all parts of England, and a great impetus was given to the volunteer movement. Now this shaped itself, for whatever real merit auxiliary services of this description possess as a defensive force, to be relied upon when called to oppose experienced troops, arises entirely from their approximation to the model of the regular army. At that period all patriotic men worked hard to attain efficiency.

The enclosed nature of our country was greatly in favour of auxiliary troops gifted with burning patriotism. It was also well adapted for troops that had to resist dense columns moving to the attack.

Talleyrand wrote, (*Mémoirs of Prince Talleyrand-Périgord*):

> The camp of Boulogne which he (Napoleon) formed at this period for the purpose of menacing the coasts of England, had for first result to make the war popular in that country, and to create there an as yet unheard-of thing, a numerous permanent army.

For a time, factions were done away with, and men of all shades of politics stood shoulder to shoulder in the ranks of the various volunteer corps. Sir Walter Scott says:

> On a sudden the land seemed converted into an immense camp, the whole nation into soldiers, and the good old king himself into a general-in-chief.

No one was ever so thoroughly in earnest as Pitt; he set a fine example by putting himself at the head of the Cinque Ports volunteers. Through his great energy and activity, he soon formed an excel-

PITT THE YOUNGER IN LATER LIFE

lent regiment 3000 strong, divided into three battalions. He was constantly on horseback, exercising and reviewing his men. The Prime Minister was continually riding from Downing Street to Wimbledon Common, and from Wimbledon Common to Cox's Heath, inspecting camps, attending manoeuvres and reviews, testing transport, and supervising many other military details.

At the beginning of the century the British Army was growing into strength as to numbers, and efficiency as to discipline. Had Bonaparte crossed the Channel in the winter of 1803-1804, our troops would have been found utterly unfit for battle. In 1804 they were better prepared; the line regiments were strong, and more fit for the field; the militia well disciplined, and the volunteer corps tolerably familiar with the use of arms.

Batteries were multiplied along the coast. A fortified camp had been formed at Dover, two others near Chatham and Chelmsford. Large bodies of troops were quartered in Essex, Kent, and Sussex; and a large camp of instruction was formed at Shorncliffe, near Hythe.

*****

The gross return of forces in Great Britain in September 1804 was—

Guards and regular infantry	75,000 men.
Regular cavalry	12,000 ,,
Militia	80,000 ,,
Volunteers and Yeomanry	343,000 ,,
Total	510,000 ,,

******

The earliest possible news of the invaders' approach was to spread right through the country. The hoisting of a red flag at any of the following stations was to ensure the lighting of all the beacons wherever established:—

Colchester.	Mum's Hedge.
Brightlingsea.	White Notley.
Earls Colne.	Ongar Park.
Gosfield.	Messing.
Sewers End.	Rettenden.
Littlebury.	Dunbury.
Thaxted.	Langdon Hill.
Hatfield Broad Oak.	Corne Green.

Beacons were in readiness for lighting in the most conspicuous points, in full view of and communication with each other. As it would naturally happen in such a high state of tension, false alarms sometimes occurred, but these served simply to show the spirit of readiness which animated the troops, who issued forth and stood to their arms at the first note of alarm, a promptness which demonstrated how dear to every man's heart stood the cause of his country. The efficiency of an army raised at the eleventh hour must always be a matter of doubt. However, the patriotic enthusiasm which pervaded the country in those days was a factor in the defence that was not to be despised. And there can be no question that had the French landed, whatever the final result might have been, they would have had a warmer reception than they expected.

In the former chapter we have shown the brilliant array of French marshals and generals who were ready to follow Napoleon across the Channel. England on her side had few able commanders to rely upon in repelling the invasion. Abercrombie, the most able and successful of her generals, rested in his grave at Malta, having succumbed to the wound he received at the Battle of Alexandria. Sir Arthur Wellesley—the *sepoy* general, as the emperor derisively called him—had displayed considerable ability as a general in India, had won the Battle of Assaye (23rd September 1803), and ended the Mahratta War; still he was little known in England, and did not begin to establish a reputation in Europe till some four or five years later. There was Sir John Moore and some few more generals—Stuart, Hill, Crawford, etc.— but no one who had yet held a large command in the field.

The country could not have relied on a more able soldier than Sir John Moore, in whom Pitt, a good judge of character, had found the one man fit to command. After having taken part in Sir Ralph Abercrombie's expedition to Egypt, Sir John received a home command, and at Shorncliffe he turned to account the experience he had acquired on active service by organising and training the light infantry brigade, which, a few years later, gained such renown in the Peninsular War. (The Light Infantry were modelled on the Backwoodsmen and American Indians.) Moore, who possessed real genius for war, knew the great superiority of an enterprising offensive over a purely defensive plan of operations, and was not pleased with the spiritless attitude which found favour with the Government. To Sir David Dundas he wrote:

> The measures hitherto adopted have been with a view to drive and retreat, which leads to confusion and despondency, and is inconsistent with a warfare in which the French excel and to which the English are the least adapted. The language and the

system should be to head and oppose, and no foot of ground ceded that was not marked with the blood of the enemy. Nothing would damp his spirits more than to see the country turned out against him.

A few years before (in 1801) Nelson had written in this spirit to Lord St. Vincent.

> I agree perfectly with you, that we must keep the enemy as far from our coasts as possible, and be able to attack them the moment they come out of their ports.

A few days later he wrote:

> Our first defence is close to the enemy's ports. When that is broke, others will come forth on our own coasts.

Sir John Moore had been the leader chosen to oppose the French landing in Kent; Pitt and Dundas constantly visited him and consulted him. (Some years later, in 1808, it was Sir John who baffled the Great Napoleon himself, and brought about the collapse of his plan for the subjugation of the Spanish Peninsula.) At the Shorncliffe camp he had the 4th, 43rd, 52nd, and 95th Regiments, with two more strong regiments of militia, the 14th Light Dragoons and a large body of artillery.

Caricatures and satire were very prolific. Stirring appeals to arms—handbills and the like—loyal and patriotic songs abounded, all mixed with a great amount of gasconading and braggadocio. However bad the taste may have been in all this, still it served to keep alive the enthusiasm, and prevented the people becoming careless and ignoring their danger, consequently it answered the purpose.

Generally speaking, these productions were a vilification of Napoleon, which only the irritable state of the population could excuse. Here is as an example, one by the brilliant Richard Brinsley Sheridan, who was said by Lord Byron to have made the best speech, written the best comedy and the best farce in our language:—

> Our King! Our Country! and our God!
> My brave associates—partners of my toil, my feelings, and my fame! Can words add vigour to the virtuous energies which inspire your hearts? No; you have judged, as I have, the *foulness* and the *crafty plea* by which these bold invaders would delude you. Your generous spirit has compared, as mine has, the *motives* which in a war like this can animate their minds and

ours. They, by a strange frenzy driven, fight for power, for plunder, and extended rule; we, for our country, our altars, and our homes. They follow an adventurer whom they fear, and obey a power which they hate; we serve a monarch whom we love, a God whom we adore. Whene'er they move in anger, desolation tracks their progress! Where'er they pause in amity, affliction mourns their friendship! They boast, they come but to improve our state, enlarge our thoughts, and free us from the yoke of error! Yes, they will give enlightened freedom to *our* minds, who are themselves the *slaves* of passion, avarice, and pride.

They offer us their protection; yes, such protection as *vultures* give to lambs—covering and devouring them! They call on us to barter all of good we have inherited and proved, for the desperate chance of something better which they *promise*. Be our plain answer this: 'The throne we honour is the people's choice; the laws we reverence are our brave fathers' legacy; the faith we follow teaches us to live in bonds of charity with all mankind, and die with hope of bliss beyond the grave.' Tell your *invaders* this; and tell them, too, we seek no change; and least of all, such change as they would bring us.

R. B. Sheridan.

The defensive measures not being considered sufficient, a debate took place in the House as to the expediency of calling to arms all able-bodied men within certain ages. The manhood of the country, however, had rushed so eagerly into the volunteer corps, that there was no necessity for a compulsory calling out of the male population.

The people had been invited to engage to act as associated volunteers bearing arms, as pioneers and labourers, as drivers of wagons. The volunteers drilled between services on Sunday, because the men could not be got so readily together on weekdays.

Fox said in a debate on obligatory service that the French could not bring over an armed peasantry, and that he looked on this as the greatest stumbling-block against the French invasion.

Pitt spoke in favour of strengthening the Metropolis and fortifying the principal headlands of the coast, in order to render landing by the enemy more difficult and laborious.

On the seas England had 570 ships of war of every description, and divisions of her fleet blockaded every French military port and all the ports in the Channel.

The coasts of Kent and Sussex were protected by batteries and Martello towers. The people were told to what places to conduct their families, cattle, and provisions, should the French land; the roads that were to be broken up. In case of necessity the horses, cattle, and all vehicles were to be removed far inland, or otherwise destroyed. The officers were recommended to avoid regular engagements, to take advantage of the hedges and enclosures to carry out a skirmishing war.

It had been arranged to have carriages and fish-carts in readiness, and these would have brought several thousand men to the threatened spot within a few hours.

Sir David Dundas, who held the chief command in Kent and Sussex, had intended, were he to be beaten at the landing between the cliffs of Dover and the border of Sussex, to throw back his right and retire on the intrenched camp at Dover. If the emperor disregarded him there, and marched straight on London, he would have sallied forth and pressed close upon the rear and right flank of the enemy's columns.

Transport is always the weakest spot in military organisation, and a committee sat both at the Mansion House and at the Thatched House Tavern to stimulate the patriotic ardour of owners of horses and carriages, in order that they might be induced to offer them for the use of the Government.

Whoever in this matter is guided by one idea only, economy, knows little about war. War is always costly; brilliant tactics, devotion, energy, must all fail if the means to conduct it are not provided. One of the principal needs is transport.

Several measures for the public defence were brought before the House of Commons, and the earnestness of the Government would have prevented Napoleon terminating the war by a Battle of Actium as he had foretold.

The Opposition scorned the timid measures of defence proposed by Addington. Pitt and Windham decried their efficiency, and strongly declared themselves against a war that should be purely defensive, for such a course they held would be ruinous and discreditable. Windham demanded an expedition of some sort, for which a large and regular army was absolutely necessary.

CHAPTER 3

William Pitt

Of all the statesmen who directed the policy of their country in the year 1805, the most prominent was William Pitt. Our countrymen are apt to forget what a deep debt of gratitude they owe to this distinguished son of Lord Chatham. In the years which have gone by they have lost sight of the fact that, if our country was saved from invasion in 1805, it was through William Pitt having devised the way for getting Napoleon to withdraw his formidable legions from the shores of the Channel.

The ordinary belief that the progeny of a pre-eminently able man is generally speaking disappointing was belied in the case of William Pitt. Without the least exaggeration it can be said that in this son of the Earl of Chatham, one of our greatest of War Ministers, was reproduced his genius in politics, and that entrancing eloquence which carried conviction to the minds of most of his countrymen.

William Pitt was born in the year 1759. He was the second son of William, first Earl of Chatham, and Lady Hester, only daughter of Richard Grenville and Countess Temple. From his early days the clearness of his intellect, combined with his assiduous application, his precociousness and eagerness, gave promise of a brilliant manhood. After a careful home training—for his health was so feeble in his early youth that he was unable to receive any very assiduous instruction—in 1773 he went to Pembroke Hall, Cambridge, at the very early age of fourteen. It might appear strange for a mere boy to be considered fit to follow the highest classes of education, but this was not unusual in those days; moreover, the young Pitt had received a careful teaching under the close supervision of his talented father, who had encouraged the lad to converse with him without reserve on every subject.

One might imagine that there was too considerable a disproportion between master and pupil; still this very constant intercommunication of these two exceptional intellects can have had no other but the most happy result. Nothing could have been better for modelling the youth and opening his mind. This was done in a more thorough manner than would possibly have been effected had he, removed from the society of his talented father, received the usual training of a public school. The first book put into his hands by the express desire of Lord Chatham, was the narrative of the great Greek tactician Thucydides.

It would not be quite true to say that Pitt forced himself to the front by sheer strength of character and ability, for the great reputation of his sire did much to give him a start. Nevertheless no one could have made better use of his opportunity than he did.

From the very earliest years, from his boyhood, Chatham had trained his son for the House of Commons, and had prepared him to excel as an orator. He had instilled into his mind very high principles, he had taught him how necessary it was for a man of his position to be laborious and self-denying, strongly patriotic, and prepared to accept without flinching that measure of responsibility which, he deemed necessary for the prosperity of his country.

The illustrious earl had fully gauged the ability and qualities of his son, and was in the habit of saying that "he would one day increase the glory of the name of Pitt."

William Pitt, as his noble father desired, belonged to his country; he did not disdain the prosaic cares of a political career; in 1781, at the age of twenty-two, he took his seat for the borough of Appleby. This occurred when Lord North's Administration was approaching its termination.

In his early parliamentary years, Pitt's efforts were directed towards peace, retrenchment, and reform. Notwithstanding his youth, gifted as he was with a fine penetrating intelligence, he was bound to make himself an early reputation in Parliament. This he did, so much so that at the end of the first session Fox, not a mean judge, declared him to be one of the leading men in the House of Commons, and soon was he to withstand in debate the resplendent talents of so great a man.

★★★★★★

Lord Chatham was a second son, and became Prime Minister of England. His rival and political opponent was Henry Fox, Lord Holland, likewise a second son. Lord Holland's second son, Charles Fox, and Lord Chatham's second son. William Pitt, were also rivals and antagonists. Charles Fox was born in 1718.

At the age of nineteen he was elected Member of the House of Commons, and appointed Lord of the Treasury. Having been removed from office in 1774, his powers as a speaker won for him the position of head of the Whig party. In 1782 he was appointed Chief Secretary of Foreign Affairs. He always displayed sympathy towards France and the Revolution.

★★★★★★

When Pitt commenced his political career, we should recollect that the House was adorned by brilliant talents. Fox, Burke, Dundas, George Canning, and a host of men of learning and splendid abilities held seats. Pitt was always equal to the occasion, so much so that Fox, at the end of his career of rivalry, declared that in all the years in which he had been opposed to Pitt the latter had never been caught tripping.

When only two-and-twenty, Lord-Advocate Dundas (Lord Melville) declared in Parliament that:

> He rejoiced in the good fortune of his country and his fellow-subjects, who were destined, at some future day, to derive the most important services from so happy a union of first-rate abilities, high integrity, bold and honest independence of conduct, and the most persuasive eloquence.

At the close of the session, on an observation being made that "Pitt promised to be one of the first speakers ever heard in the House of Commons," Fox, turning round to the speaker, instantly replied, "He is so already."

To England the moment Pitt begun public life was unfortunate, for it was the time when Cornwallis' inexplicable surrender completed the triumph of the American Republic. On the receipt of the news, Pitt exclaimed, "The sun of England's glory has set;" such was the despondency caused by the news. Had the great statesman lived to see our days he would have seen, notwithstanding the loss of the American Colonies, England's glory and power far, far greater than it was at the close of the eighteenth century.

England has never had a minister of whom such different opinions have been entertained; and, indeed, no previous one had ever been placed in such difficult circumstances. Besides governing his own country, Pitt was the mainspring which gave motion to many of the actions of most of the foreign Cabinets. And well has it been said of this resolute and solemn statesman, that on his head lay the weight of public care for all Europe.

After Rockingham's death, in the rearrangements of the Cabinet brought about by that event, Pitt became Chancellor of the Exchequer and leader of the House of Commons. This eminence he gained at an age scarcely beyond boyhood, for he was then only twenty-two.

He was excellent company, cheerful and witty. Reserve, calm sagacity, and ever-watchful caution—the qualities most necessary for a leader of the House of Commons—he possessed in a high degree. It was said of Pitt that "no speaker ever knew better how to tell all he chose to tell, and not a syllable more."

When the famous Coalition Ministry fell, Pitt crossed the Channel in company with Eliot and Wilberforce. This was the only occasion on which he travelled abroad, and some remarks he made when visiting France are still preserved. To the French: "You have no political liberty," said he; "but as for civil liberty, you have more of it than you suppose." It was five years after he had pronounced these words that the terrible Revolution commenced in France, to secure for the people that political liberty which they so eagerly coveted.

In December 1783 William Pitt, at the unusually early age of twenty-five, became Prime Minister. The prepossession, of the public in favour of the offspring of their much-lamented Chatham called him almost from the cradle to the helm of the State.

Though the fallen ministers ridiculed his appointment, and scoffingly declared that his Administration could not possibly last more than a very few days, still it continued for seventeen years. As Lord Macaulay observed, since parliamentary government was established in England, no English statesman had held, the supreme power so long.

Public life in England was in those days a very grand career. It was the steady patriotism of the great men which carried England through her troubles from 1789 to 1815. Now it is very different, for our people have become self-indulgent. Great men have certainly in all ages been lovers of pleasure, but pleasure was their relaxation, and not their only pursuit. Self-indulgence would never have made our country what it is now.

Pitt was a true leader, a politician of distinction and of immense influence; a man of great ability, an indomitably hard worker, clear-headed and practical. He possessed that rare faculty, the power of ruling men. He was gifted with every qualification for governing, and singularly able must have been the man who, young, unaided and alone could hold his own in the House of Commons in such a stormy period. Bold must have been the politician who, having as yet little personal experience, did not disdain to guide the destinies of a great country, to undertake weighty labours, to assume a most heavy burden of responsibility.

Alison, in his *History of Europe*, states that modern history has hardly so great a character to exhibit. Invincible in resolution, and yet cool in danger; possessed of a moral courage which nothing could overcome; fertile in resources, powerful in debate, eloquent in declamation, he exhibited a combination of great qualities which for political contests never was equalled.

Rigby declared in the House:

> His oratory was no less persuasive, his abilities no less powerful; nay, he would make no scruple to assert that he regarded him as a still greater orator than his noble and admired father.

Pitt's eloquence was like an impetuous torrent; his sarcasms blistered and burned.

The young statesman was faithful to his race and to his traditions; he was ever toiling for the country he loved so well. Evidently, as heir to an immortal name, his advent to power was welcomed by the country; still, that of itself alone would never have kept him in power for such a long period, and gained him the confidence of the people.

The new Prime Minister found it difficult to form an Administration. The majority of Parliament was against him, but he gradually diminished it till the Mutiny Bill passed without opposition.

He had acquired public favour because his sympathies were all with the middle classes, with those who at that period represented the views of the people. His well-deserved popularity was enhanced when he refused to secure to himself the Clerkship of the Pell, a sinecure office to which was attached a yearly income of £3000.

Men whose names are constantly before the world should keep them unstained and hold them high; it is only to men who govern with perfectly clean hands and with pure disinterestedness that the masses will generally accord their full confidence.

Besides having a strong sense of the integrity of his position, Pitt was not like some men who miss nearly everything in life which they very greatly covet. On the contrary, he was a man who at an unusually early age had already attained everything which position could give; he had reached the pinnacle of a political man's ambition, he had become Prime Minister, and as such, after the sovereign, he was above everyone in the land.

The popular sympathy evoked by his disinterested deed was, if anything, augmented by his escape from death when an ambuscade was laid for him by a gang of malefactors opposite to Brooks'.

Attention to commerce greatly distinguished Pitt's Administration. Perhaps there was no man in the kingdom better acquainted with the principles of trade than he was. The oldest and most experienced merchants were astonished at his readiness in conversing with them upon subjects of which they thought themselves exclusively masters. Many who waited upon him in full confidence that they should communicate some new and important information, to their great surprise found him minutely and intimately acquainted with all those points with which they conceived he was unfamiliar.

It must be evident how it was the close attention which that great statesman unremittingly paid to mercantile interests that enabled him, not only to face a most vigorous Opposition, but to carry into effect financial measures which until his time were deemed impracticable. Fortunately, England had at the head of affairs a statesman whose peculiar talent lay in the management of the public wealth, which was so essential in the national struggle with Napoleon.

> Under Pitt's administration, the revenue, trade, and manufactures of England were doubled, its colonies and political strength quadrupled; and he raised an island in the Atlantic, once only a remote province of the Roman Empire, to such a pitch of grandeur as to be enabled to bid defiance to the world in arms. (*History of Europe*).

The French Revolution convulsed the whole of Europe, and Pitt, after a few years of able administration, was called to encounter events the most singular and momentous. He then stuck to the principle of letting France settle her internal affairs as she chose, for at the time he was not alarmed at the possible spread of French doctrines in this country. The American War had so exhausted England that he considered that a period of rest had become absolutely necessary for her to recover.

On the outbreak of the French Revolution in 1789, English sympathy was strongly in favour of the movement. Burke's attacks upon the Revolutionists and his defence of the Monarchy brought about a great change in public opinion; and when Britain was led to declare war against France, it was with the object of aiding the French royal family basely molested by the revolutionary party. The British Government did not take up a publicly hostile position towards France until Louis XVI was beheaded.

In 1791, two years after the Revolution had upset the established Government in France, Pitt just escaped a war on the question of the cession of Ocksakoff—a miserable fort in a swamp—which Prince Potemkin had captured from the Turks. Pitt, nevertheless, was eager for peace, and no statesman shunned war more. Peace, reform, retrenchment, free trade, these were his objects; but the events on the Continent of Europe stood in his way, and he was never destined to attain the noble aims he had set before him.

He was formed to steer the barque of state through a convulsion altogether new, fierce, and beyond the calculations of the old public wisdom of Europe.

But wars often break out when they are least expected. In 1792 Pitt declared in Parliament:

> Unquestionably there never was a time in the history of our country when, from the situation of Europe, we might more reasonably expect fifteen years of peace than at the present moment. (The Earl of Rosebery, *William Pitt*.)

He clung to peace, as Lord Rosebery tells us, with the tenacity of despair, and when France, on the 1st of February 1793 declared war against England, and compelled him to draw the sword, he did so with the full belief that it would be returned to the scabbard in a few months.

Sir John Jervis (afterwards Lord St. Vincent) fell into the same mistake. Writing to Parker's father, he says that:

> From the aspect of foreign affairs there is small probability of a war arising.

Only five years after writing this he won the Battle of Cape St. Vincent.

How frequently does history repeat itself! In 1870, before the outbreak of the Franco-German War, as Leopold de Hohenzollern withdrew his nomination to the throne of Spain, Émile Olivier gaily announced in the lobby "*C'est la paix!*" ("It is now peace.") Public opinion, however, was too strong, the excitable nation craved for war, and in a very few days it was declared.

Pitt had no notion of the immense recuperative power which constitutes one of the marked characteristics of the French nation. He failed to gauge accurately the patriotism of the people, and, as he did at a later period, before the campaign of Marengo, built up his hopes on their bankruptcy. In place of fifteen years of peace and tranquillity, England was to be distracted by a ruinous war, which, but for a brief interval, lasted twenty-three years. A sorrowing nation laid Pitt in his grave at Westminster Abbey by the side of the ashes of his most renowned sire ten years before peace was ultimately restored to Europe.

The characteristics of the French Revolution were a universal spirit of aggression, hatred of all settled authority and its universal appeal to the power of the population. The greatest votary of peace could hardly have expected that the English Government would have refrained from taking any steps to safeguard the interests of England and of her allies when seriously threatened by the Republican uprising. Nevertheless, it was said of Pitt by those who knew him best that "he was dragged into the contest with as much reluctance as a man of conscientious principles into a duel." (Alison, *Wilberforce's Life*.)

In the long period of years that Pitt governed England he had the support of his sovereign, George III., who in the beginning of his reign was unjustly unpopular, though he was true, patriotic, and intrepid in public life, anxious only for the common good, and willing to sacrifice all private predilections to the national advantage.

After the Austrian defeat on the Tagliamento, 16th of March 1797, and the capture of Tarvis, Bonaparte, whose position from various causes was very precarious, wrote a letter to the Archduke Charles to ask whether he could not exert himself to bring about an end to the miseries of a fruitless war. In that letter, with considerable effrontery, the general, whose capacity for chicanery and machination his warmest admirers have never denied, accused England of having embroiled France and Austria, two powers which had no grievance against each other.

For all that, no one knew better that it was the Emperor Francis' designs on Venice and the march of the Archduke Charles through the Tyrol that had brought on the war. (It had come to the knowledge of the Venetian Senate, through its agent in Paris, that at the conclusion of peace Austria would indemnify itself with Venetian territory for the loss of the Milanese.) It was on this letter, which the archduke passed on to the Cabinet of Vienna, that Thugut agreed to open negotiations.

The conditions of peace between Austria and France were settled at the Castle of Göss at Leoben on the 18th of April 1797. The Treaty of Leoben seemed to Pitt to offer a favourable opportunity for reopening negotiations with the French Republic. He was more than ever desirous to do this, as his party had reaped little success in the military operations, and the opposition in Parliament was daily ac-

Archduke Charles

quiring strength. Always eager for peace, he could not let the occasion escape, and entrusted Malmesbury with the mission. Malmesbury, however, held very opposite views to those of the French Revolution, and believed that no peace was possible until France was rendered powerless. He was received with distrust, many believing that he had mainly come over to France to reorganise the Royalist party.

England declared itself ready to give up the French colonial possessions seized during the war would France in return give up Belgium. France would not listen to the terms offered, England insisted, and Malmesbury was allowed forty-eight hours to leave the country. In July Pitt tried again to come to terms, and negotiations were reopened at Lille, when Malmesbury proposed terms which were more favourable than any which England had hitherto offered. Nevertheless, Pitt's efforts were doomed to serious disappointment, for from the very beginning of the congress the French commissioners showed no conciliatory dispositions whatsoever.

Matters became even worse, for the Directory, emboldened by the victory scored on the 18th *Fructidor*, recalled Maret, the principal delegate, replacing him by a fresh plenipotentiary, and added to their demands.

******

Maret was captured by the Austrians whilst on his way to take up his post as ambassador at the Court of Naples. He was confined in the fortress of Brünn, and with Sémonville exchanged for Maria Teresa, daughter of Louis XVI. During the Empire he was created Duc de Bassano, and succeeded Talleyrand as Secretary of State for Foreign Affairs.

******

By asking too much the Directory lost the best chance of peace they ever had; the conditions Bonaparte obtained by the Peace of Amiens were nothing as favourable.

Malmesbury, admitting the utter impossibility of coming to a settlement, returned to England.

Pitt was not the only statesman who desired peace. In a speech delivered at the commencement of the Devolution, Mirabeau posed the following principle: "*L'homme n'est fort que par l'union; il n'est heureux que par la paix.* ("Unity alone renders man strong; he is only made happy through peace.") After the 18th *Fructidor*, Barras wrote to Bonaparte for "Peace, peace, but an honourable peace. None of Carnot's worthless suggestions." After the Italian campaigns came the

Treaty of Campo Formio; but this treaty did not deceive Thugut. "Peace! peace! Where is it?" he exclaimed. "I cannot discover it in the treaty."

In 1801, having met with very serious opposition in Parliament, and finding he could not do justice to the Catholics as he would have liked, Pitt resigned the Premiership.

In the early part of 1802, the concord between the two countries was re-established by the Treaty of Amiens. For a very brief period of fourteen months England breathed again; in this short time internal affairs, and principally the Act of Union, absorbed the attention of the Cabinet.

Pitt, who at heart cordially disliked war, approved of Addington's negotiations for peace. He believed that now that Bonaparte had obtained the supreme power he might probably be satisfied. With the support of Pitt and the general feeling of the country, the Ministry found in Parliament large majorities in favour of peace. However, many of Pitt's late colleagues, among others Grenville, Windham, and Spencer, were fully of opinion that Bonaparte's policy would continue to be one of aggression, and that for the honour of England and the safety of Europe the war should continue.

As the First Consul's conduct was rendering a renewal of hostilities inevitable, a feeling gained ground that when the war came it should find England in the hands of its ablest statesman, and not in those of a weak man like Addington. Addington could not be made to acknowledge his incapacity and to advise the restoration of Pitt. He was obdurate, he would not listen to Canning nor to Lord Malmesbury, who urged him to resign; and Pitt, rather than force him out of office, withdrew for a short time from Parliament.

When, later, dark clouds of invasion hung low over the land, the popular voice designing Pitt as the only statesman capable of steeling the country through the approaching storm could not be stifled. Well has it been said that a great man is the property of his country. On the 20th of April 1801, the Addington Ministry resigned, as the enormous expenditure with inadequate results had caused great dissatisfaction and a widespread feeling of uneasiness. It was on the 10th of May, eight days before the First Consul was proclaimed Emperor of the French, that Pitt resumed office as Prime Minister.

In most glowing and animated language, he had expressed his indignation at the menaces of the insolent and vainglorious enemy who threatened to invade England, the seat of public liberty. His return to power simply signified the resistance of a united England to Napoleon and all his works. Whether this was to be on British soil or by a coalition of the great powers on the Continent, it did not greatly matter.

The Opposition, which in former years had extenuated all the excesses of the Revolution, opposed his policy, censured his system of finance and the subsidiary arrangements which had so long kept the calamities of war remote from our shores. Had not Pitt been able to cover our shores with our most efficient squadrons, squadrons of the best navy in the world, the history of Europe might have taken a very different turn from what it eventually did. (In 1798, Pitt fought a duel with Mr. George Tierney, stung to the quick by the latter's remarks over the Bill for manning the navy.)

It was in the following year, the last of his life, that Pitt rendered his greatest service to his country. Napoleon was then bent, either really or not, as some writers argue, on the invasion of England. For that purpose, he had concentrated on the shores of the Channel his best troops. To command them he had gathered the best generals in France, distinguished soldiers who had made their reputation in the battles of the Republic. With feverish activity and hitherto unseen energy, he was pushing forward gigantic preparations for ferrying his army across. Pitt admitted that England should not engage in war on land. The war on the Continent should be carried on by the continental powers by means of combinations, and he strained every nerve to array them against France. Alive to the imminent danger his country was exposed to, he set himself to bring about the Third Coalition.

He laboured incessantly to frame amongst the discordant and selfish Cabinets of Europe a cordial league for their common defence. The negotiations were often difficult, requiring much tact and forbearance. With indomitable perseverance he braced himself to overcome every obstacle. He never despaired; what he knew he could not accomplish with the small army of England—an army officered by wealthy and well-connected men who then, as at present, displayed little real talent for war—he did by paying liberal subsidies to the larger armies of the great European powers. The burden was heavy, but there can be little fault to find in his administration of the finances, when we look at the miserable state Europe had fallen into, and at the great difficulties Pitt had to contend against.

If he failed, it was not in the original conception or arrangements, it was owing to the fatal errors of those who had to carry out the details. The management of the armies was the province of the generals of the allied armies, not his.

He was foredoomed to failure because he pitted himself against a colossus, against the greatest genius for governing and for war which the world has ever beheld; to contend against whom were men bound by old traditions, of whom only very few had any real aptitude for war. Even the few who had were shackled by the orders of their respective Governments, whilst Napoleon as general and emperor was absolute, being served by a host of young leaders, who, though not always quite able to act by themselves, were constantly victorious when giving effect to the conceptions and orders which emanated from such a master mind.

Pitt conducted the negotiations with consummate skill, though his patience was often severely taxed by the feebleness and the irresolution of the powers he had to deal with. The past French victories had inspired such terror in the foreign Cabinets that they were not at all eager to draw the sword again; only the injuries they had sustained, and the serious loss of prestige caused by their many defeats, had driven the roots so deep into the soil, that as long as there remained a chance of getting revenged, it was possible to stir them into action. By promising large subsidies, as he had done before, Pitt eventually succeeded in organising a powerful coalition. This was a costly way of getting rid of the French on the shores of the Channel, but he reflected that, as the country was wealthy, it was sound policy to purchase immunity from attack, and restore confidence to the mercantile enterprise of the country, which had suffered considerably under the dread of invasion.

The success with which he trampled over the jealousies of the European courts showed the extent of his diplomatic ability.

The year 1805 was fertile in great events. Whilst Napoleon's gaze seemed fixed westward on the bold cliffs of *Perfide Albion*, striving to find a way for putting his troops ashore in the fair county of Kent, our artful statesman was arranging and providing means for Austria and Russia to assemble a mighty army with which to attack the French in the east. If the compact could be concluded, Pitt had every reason to believe that the threatening attitude of those two powers would make Napoleon uneasy about the safety of France, and would induce him to shift his troops to the neighbourhood of the Rhine.

As it will be shown in the course of this narrative, his object was attained in the last days of August, and as the mighty host, the *Armée d'Angleterre*, set its face eastwards to gain fresh laurels on the Danube and on the plains of Moravia, England could breathe freely once more.

Pitt's triumph was of short duration, for of the two brilliant victories—one by sea and the other by land—which made the year 1805 memorable, the last shattered Pitt's great coalition and dealt a death-blow to the eminent statesman who had brought it about.

What had considerable effect in shortening his life was the charges brought against his old friend Melville, the First Lord of the Admiralty. Then came the news of the capitulation of Ulm, which depressed him greatly.

One last happy moment did this one of the greatest of English statesmen enjoy, when the news of the victory of Trafalgar and the destruction of Villeneuve's fleet raised the enthusiasm of the entire nation to a pitch hitherto unknown. Well might Pitt have been proud of that event; still, he took what share was due to him with singular modesty. At the Lord Mayor's banquet, in responding to the toast of his health, he said:

> I return you many thanks for the honour you have done me. But Europe is not to be saved by any single man. England has saved herself by her exertions, and will, as I trust, save Europe by her example.

As victory sided with the great British admiral at sea, so it sided with the great French general on land. Austerlitz quickly followed Trafalgar. Pitt was distracted by the disaster which had overcome the coalition. As he returned dejected and heartbroken to his villa at Putney, it has been written that as his eyes rested on a map of Europe, he exclaimed, "Roll up that map; it will not be wanted these ten years." Never was prophecy more true, for the mighty conqueror of Austerlitz was to be for ten more years the arbiter of Europe.

At the meeting of Parliament, at the end of December 1805, Pitt displayed his troubled mind, his wasted form, and his rapidly declining constitution. His last illness originated in extreme debility, brought on by excessive anxiety and unwearied attention to business.

Wilberforce, it is often said, was wont to describe Pitt's careworn and unhappy mien as the "Austerlitz look." Earl Stanhope, however, states, (*Life of the Right Honourable William Pitt*), that Wilberforce never once saw Pitt after the Battle of Austerlitz.

Pitt's career was destined to be short, for he had never spared himself, and his physical strength, at no time overgreat, was spent. The patriotic statesman had for some time looked fatigued and unwell. Times in England were troubled, and political life was stormy and thankless.

Every year that the struggle went on the more useless it appeared, and with the Battle of Austerlitz all hope seemed definitely lost. The first accounts spoke of a success for the allies, and the news of their defeat which quickly followed was a most grievous blow to the English minister. The disappointment was more than Pitt's delicate constitution could bear, and Napoleon's stupendous success hastened his end.

He died on the 23rd of January 1806, at the early age of forty-seven. His spirit passed away, but not before his work was accomplished, when the aggression of Austria had diverted the storm which menaced Great Britain. Pitt's last words were:

> Oh, my country! How I leave my country!

The expiring statesman, with many others, fully believed that after his splendid victory on the field of Austerlitz, Napoleon would resume his measures for invading England, and that with added prestige and power he might probably succeed.

The aspect of affairs was gloomy; all dreaded the power and the genius of the conqueror. How frequently, however, do we see the unexpected occurring! Who, in that dire moment, when the spirit of England's saviour was flitting away, would have ever imagined it possible that in less than ten years Napoleon's splendid legions would have found their match on the field of Waterloo? Who would have dreamt of seeing the tents of a British Army pitched in the Bois de Boulogne, within sight of the Arc de Triomphe?

William Pitt was buried in Westminster Abbey, by the side of his immortal father. It was this circumstance that made Lord Wellesley exclaim:

> What grave contains such a father and such a son? What sepulchre embosoms the remains of so much human excellence and glory? (*Life of Pitt.*)

Chateaubriand said:

> While all other contemporary reputations, even that of Napoleon, are on the decline, the fame of Pitt alone is continually increasing, and seems to derive fresh lustre from every vicissitude of fortune.

In these few past years there has been a revival of Napoleonism, the Naval League have done much to keep fresh the memory of the immortal Nelson; but Pitt, the wise and all-enduring statesman, who saved England from invasion, has been well-nigh forgotten. *Sic transit gloria mundi!* What does the majority of the nation know now of the memorable effort which forms the brightest page of his life?

There are many graves of great men in Westminster Abbey, but for the most part the men who lie in them have come to be little more than names to the general sight-seer. It is only the student of history who learns from the most interesting records what really made them great during life.

Men of genius, the Pitts and Carnots, who organise victory, are very rare. Bitter experience, harsh lessons, and repeated defeats bring them to the front.

Providence had chosen England to be the great agent to bring back to the Continent of Europe that peace of which she had been robbed by the events of the great Revolution in France. It was to Pitt that was given to lay the foundations of that peace.

CHAPTER 4

Villeneuve Sails for the West Indies

In Napoleon's campaigns there was something extraordinarily out of the common which captivated the mind. There was no one like him for original inspiration. The prosaic formalities of war so cherished by the martinets of the seventeenth and eighteenth centuries were thrust aside by the youthful general, and were replaced by striking innovations. Thus, in his first campaign in Italy we behold a youthful commander reviving the forgotten principles of Julius Caesar, and, descending from the Maritime Alps with an army whose soldiers were half starved and wanting in most necessaries, defeating the enemy in battle after battle with the same regularity as the waves beat on the shore. In his next, the troops are led against the Mameluke intrenchments at Embabeh under the shadow of the great pyramids of Cheops.

The victory in itself was not a great one, but the great age of the world-renowned monuments added to it a signal brightness. In the third, the ice-covered Alps are not sufficient to stop the progress of his army, and infantry, cavalry, and artillery are to overtop those stupendous heights, and go crushing down like an avalanche on the unsuspecting foe in the fertile plains beyond. The campaign of 1805 was not to be an exception to the rest; the events embraced both naval and military manoeuvres ending in terrible conflicts by sea and by land, in battles which even now, after the lapse of a hundred years, are related "with bated breath."

Napoleon's opinion had considerably changed from the time when he looked upon an invasion of England as a dream, a hazardous undertaking which could never be carried into effect. The French people had resigned into his hands the destinies of the country, and he was not loath to show the world how far his genius and his power combined would carry the French name. To a brave heart nothing is impossible; and if the undertaking was still encompassed with risks, a way would be found to overcome them, and great would be the glory in carrying to a successful issue an operation which to many minds seemed impracticable.

The French Army lay encamped on the shores of the Channel, and the preparations for ferrying it across to the British shore were steadily progressing. The enemy was, however, known to be on his guard, and to have a large number of warships protecting the coast. (In 1802 the British, navy numbered 700 sail, of which 148 were of the Line.) These ships were commanded by dashing captains seconded by hardy crews, and in all the encounters which had taken place since the commencement of the war the British seamen had shown splendid courage and fighting qualities of the very highest order.

Napoleon made no secret of the difficulties which encompassed the undertaking. He had long ago realised the fact that it was absolutely necessary for France to have a strong navy; this necessity pressed more than ever at that period, considering how the British navy was daily acquiring greater power. The impotence of the French fleets had always a very irritating effect on Napoleon, and we can well imagine how deeply he deplored the heedlessness of the Convention which had been so detrimental to the maritime branch of the service.

As far back as 1798, before he set out for Egypt, he had recommended that it would be prudent to spend the summer months in fitting out the fleet at Brest for an invasion of Ireland. The difficulty of an attack on England had struck him in all its force. A proof of this will be found in his letter to the Directory of the 23rd of February 1798, in which he wrote:

> To make a descent upon England without being masters of the sea, is the boldest and most difficult operation that can be attempted.

******

> Note: Sir Geoffrey Hornby, in defining the command of the sea said: "I consider that I have the command of the sea when I can inform my Government that a military expedition may be safely transported across it."

******

Thoroughly convinced that supremacy at sea was what was principally needed for the success of his measures for the subjugation of England, he seriously set about to devise some way to obtain it. To a perfect master of strategy this was not difficult and the plan he conceived has received, as it justly deserved, the approval of all historians and soldiers.

Napoleon kept himself acquainted with every movement of the navies of France, Spain, and Holland. In 1804 there were in France several fleets more or less ready for sea. At Toulon was Latouche Tréville with—

12 ships of the Line.
6 frigates.
5 corvettes and brigs,

Missiessy was at Rochefort with a smaller squadron. Gantheaume, at Brest, had a fleet of twenty-one war-ships. In addition to these, a Spanish fleet commanded by Admiral Don Frederico Gravina was at Cadiz, another at Carthagena.

The purpose of Napoleon's scheme was no other than to combine these various fleets into a powerful Armada, which by a simultaneous movement would eventually acquire the control of the British Channel. But he clearly saw no hope of effecting this unless by some artifice he could entice away from Europe a considerable portion of the British naval forces.

The essence of his plan lay in inducing the British fleets, and above all the one commanded by Nelson, to follow in pursuit of the French. The latter at a given moment were to change their *modus operandi*, alter their course, and make for the Channel in one imposing body, sweep away all opposition, and leave the way clear for the crossing of the flotilla.

★★★★★★

When Gantheaume got out of Brest in January 1801 with reinforcements for the army in Egypt, Bonaparte tried to lead the enemy into error by giving out that the destination of the Rear-Admiral was St. Domingo.

★★★★★★

Had not destiny hitherto given everything to Napoleon which he could possibly have desired? In this instance he no doubt counted somewhat, as he generally did, on his luck, and no one probably ever had as good a reason for doing so. From the earliest days of his career, fortune, it was clear, had constantly sided with him. In 1790 Rampon's determined resistance at Monte Legino, and Augereau's daring bravery at. Lonato had saved his enterprise from dismal failure. Twice, at

Lodi and at Arcole, he had escaped death; in the latter battle through the devotion of his *aide-de-camp* Muiron, who shielded him and met death in his stead. At Valeggio and at Lonato he just escaped being made prisoner. Never did fortune in one single campaign show such regard for any commander. But what more than anything else demonstrated that luck was on his side was the escape of his fleet between Malta and Alexandria from the ever-vigilant eye of Nelson. Had that daring seaman when off Cape Passaro not recalled the *Leander* and got in sight of the French fleet, history would have recorded a disaster not much unlike the attempted passage of the Red Sea by Pharaoh's host.

★★★★★★

At daybreak on the 22nd of June 1798, two frigates, supposed to be French, were seen by Nelson, and, according to the Vanguard's log, the *Leander* was sent in pursuit of them. The ship was recalled on the information obtained from a Genoese brig.

★★★★★★

In Egypt he almost fell into the hands of the Bedouins. A fold of ground hid him from a mass of horsemen who harassed the flank of the French Army. In recognising the danger, he had escaped, Bonaparte exclaimed irreverently:

"It is not written above that I am to be captured by the Arabs."

For crossing the Channel, Napoleon had taken for his model the arrangements made by William the Conqueror, and had ordered a multitude of small vessels of various descriptions to be built. But it was one thing for William the Conqueror to command success when Harold's fleet had dispersed with the object of refitting and his army had gone north to do battle with Harald Hardrada, and quite another for the emperor to reach the British coast when the approaches were guarded by British warships, and the shores teemed with determined men armed and prepared to contest the landing.

Once having set foot on shore, Napoleon felt thoroughly confident of being able to overcome the English. But a landing in face of an enemy is a risky undertaking, and there could be little prospect in this case of taking the English unawares. He rightly judged that only the presence of his fleet would secure him a careful preparation by artillery fire.

Napoleon, an adept in making false demonstrations, tried to win by skill what he saw he could not obtain by force. To devise a safe way of landing, he called his fertility of resource to his aid. Never did a commander resort to a more brilliant stratagem. His conception in this instance was a real stroke of genius, a parallel to which we may seek for in vain in the history of naval warfare.

******

Keralio had prognosticated, "This boy would make an excellent sailor," and Napoleon was originally destined for the navy. The applicants for that favourite branch of the service were too numerous, and want of influential friends and family arrangements made it necessary for the youth to adopt a military career.

******

If this artifice in the end did not meet with success, it was because the man who had been selected to carry it into effect failed to do his duty, and had neither the ability nor the audacity required.

It was from Mayence that Napoleon directed the sailing of the two squadrons designed to be the first movement towards the contemplated invasion of England. One commanded by Villeneuve was to sail from Toulon, the other under Messiessy was to go from Rochefort.

As the British fleets blockaded the principal French ports, the French fleets were driven to inaction, and had no opportunity of putting out to sea. All possibility of manoeuvring was lost, the consequence being that their tactics deteriorated. The navy possessed no daring officer, there was no Ney, no Lannes, no Murat in that service. No admiral showed any boldness in issuing forth to attack the enemy, and a notion soon obtained amongst French naval officers that they were not competent to contend against ships which for years had kept the sea, and which, possibly, had not cast anchor in a harbour except when absolutely compelled to do so for repairs.

One of the main requisites in fighting is confidence; so much so that it is an old saying that an unwilling commander is half beaten before the battle commences. Brueys, the unfortunate admiral who commanded the French fleet at the battle of the Nile, reflected the little confidence the French naval officers had in the following passage contained in a letter he wrote on the 9th of July 1798 to the Minister of Marine:

> Our crews are too weak in number and quality of men. Our ships, generally speaking, are very badly armed, and I consider that it needs a good deal of courage to burden one's self with the leading of fleets so badly furnished.

Thanks to Augereau's troops, the Directory on the morning of the

18th *Fructidor* found in their hands the entire control of the city of Paris. The Government no longer resorted to the terrible guillotine for debarrassing itself of its political opponents; it simply sent them to languish and die in the pestilential swamps of Cayenne. After the 18th *Fructidor*, Carnot, warned in time, took refuge in flight; Barthelemy, less fortunate, was cast into prison; Pichegru, with forty-two deputies from the Five Hundred, and 148 other persons, most of them journalists, were proscribed.

After Bonaparte's return from Egypt and the 18th Brumaire, a further number of men, too openly opposed to his measures, were removed from the country in a similar manner; still the police found, or pretended to have found, men who were plotting against the life of the First Consul, and after the explosion in the Rue Nicaise, 24th of December 1800, some of these guilty, others innocent, were tried and executed. This attempt did much for Bonaparte, for his miraculous escape was by many of the more religious of the population accepted as an omen that Providence kept a careful guard over his own elect.

The police remained very active, and many months after reported having discovered a plot to assassinate the First Consul, in which Pichegru, Georges Cadoudal, and others, were said to be implicated. Though some of the leaders were executed or put away like Pichegru, Bonaparte, weary of the endless plotting which aimed at his life, longed to make such an example as would inspire terror in the Royalist party. With this object, he violated the territory of the Grand Duchy of Baden by despatching a body of soldiers to arrest the heir of the Condé family, the Duke d'Enghien, at the time residing at Ettenhein, a manor-house in Baden, situated some sixteen miles from Strasburg. This step was decided at a council of state presided over by Bonaparte on the 10th of March 1804, though very strongly opposed by Cambacérès, the Second Consul, to whose remonstrances Bonaparte replied:

> I will not submit to be killed without defending myself. I am determined to make these people tremble; I shall teach them to remain quiet.

Sloane states that Bonaparte was determined to stun the already prostrate Bourbons and to render them harmless for years to come. Another writer, Schoell, holds that this crime was committed when the First Consul was greatly irritated by the refusal of Louis XVIII and the Bourbon family to give up to him their rights to the throne of

France. It was more likely done when seriously irritated by the long series of attempts made to murder him.

******

No greater or more barefaced falsehoods have been uttered regarding the conspiracy of Georges Cadoudal, the tragic end of Pichegru and the Duke of Enghien, and Moreau's complicity in the plot. This originated in the suggestions of the police, and most of the conspiracy was fictitious. Fouché, the most able and unscrupulous intriguer, proposed Moreau's exile. The general was hurried away out of the country, for the attitude of his well-wishers was beginning to inspire alarm.

******

D'Enghien was both clever and fearless. When England was threatened with invasion, he sought permission to enter the British service and to fight in the defence of our country, but the Government would not permit a Bourbon prince to draw sword on British soil.

He had been repeatedly warned of his danger, and advised to take refuge in England, but he was not to be intimidated.

General Ordaner was sent from New Breisach with three hundred *gendarmes*, and arrested the unfortunate prince at night on the 15th of March, brought him to Vincennes, where he was tried for having borne arms against France, and shot in the early hours of the 24th of March 1804.

******

With the duke were arrested the Marquis Turnery, whom the *gendarmes*, through the bad pronunciation of German, had erroneously represented to be Dumouriez, Saint-Jacques, his secretary, and others. Dumouriez had never been at Ettenheim, and would not have been received by the duke had he gone there. It was Thiard, one of the First Consul's staff officers who pointed out this error to Napoleon.

It was at Vincennes that the great Condé had been imprisoned for having taken up arms against France.

******

Of this lamentable episode which evoked horror and indignation in France and throughout Europe, the First Consul said:

It will clearly be seen, from the fate of the Duke d'Enghien, that I shall spare no man.

Talleyrand's sarcasm was far too true:

That the death of the Duke d'Enghien was worse than a crime, that it was a blunder. (*Quela mort du Duc d'Enghien était plus qu'un crime, que c etait une faute.*)

With regard to Talleyrand's verdict, Napoleon in his *Mémorial de St. Helene*, wrote:

He (D'Enghien) died, victim of politics and of an unheard-of combination of circumstances.

In reality the tragic death of the prince had not produced less sensation abroad than it had caused at home. Personally, the *Czar* emphasised the indignation of the Court of Russia. This glaring violation of neutrality and iniquitous execution irritated more than ever the foreign powers, and was one of the principal causes of a fresh war.

★★★★★★

In the way of a protest, Louis XVIII sent back to the King of Spain the order of the Golden Fleece which had also been conferred on Bonaparte, saying that there could be nothing in common between him and the murderer of the Duke. Gustavus Adolphus likewise returned the order of the Black Eagle to the King of Prussia, declaring that according to the rules of chivalry he could not be a brother in arms with d'Enghien's assassin.

★★★★★★

Another cause was the jealousy and hostility the European sovereigns felt for the simple fact of Bonaparte having placed himself on their level by getting himself crowned Emperor of the French. It does, however, seem strange that at the very time when foreign powers and the foreign press were levelling accusations against Bonaparte for d'Enghien's execution, the senate should offer him the crown.

The execution of the Duc d'Enghien was the most wicked deed that Napoleon committed in his career. He felt this, hence all he wrote and said to excuse it. He vainly endeavoured to justify the deed under the plea of political expediency, regarding the execution as a state necessity, but neither his words nor the arguments of his most devoted adherents will ever succeed in effacing the remembrance of the bloody tragedy enacted in the moat of Vincennes. (Napoleon did not pay much heed when his detractors accused him of cowardice or questioned his generalship. When, on the other hand, he came to be charged with poisoning and assassination he became furious.)

The population of Paris, accustomed as it had been to all the horrors which accompanied the Revolution, was struck speechless, and

Napoleon's staunchest partisans were filled with consternation.

✶✶✶✶✶✶

It is a fact that more than two-thirds of the population had no knowledge who the prisoner shot at Vincennes was. The emperor accuses Fouché of having organised the intrigue which caused the taking of d'Enghien's life; that it was Fouché who put him on his guard against the secret meetings of the Royalists on the right bank of the Rhine, for he had spies everywhere; that he persuaded him to sacrifice the Duke to show the Jacobins that he was in no way favouring the Bourbons.

✶✶✶✶✶✶

Far from being sanguinary and cruel by nature, Napoleon was full of pity and indulgence for human weakness, of which no one could be a fairer judge. Nevertheless, when the political situation demanded, he could harden his heart, and was able to master without the slightest scruple every benevolent feeling. He often repeated that the heart of a statesman should have its seat in the head, and not in the breast.

There is some truth in what he said regarding d'Enghien's execution; that he had sent the terror as far as London, and it had succeeded. From the day of the execution conspiracies ceased.

✶✶✶✶✶✶

"Monsieur de Talleyrand," writes Alison, *History of Europe,* "aware of the imminent danger which the Duke ran if he continued in his residence at Ettenheim, had secretly sent him warning to remove through the lady to whom he was attached at that place, and similar intelligence was at the same time transmitted by the King of Sweden, by means of his minister at Carlsruhe. It augments our regret at the issue of this melancholy tale, that he was only prevented from availing himself of the intelligence and escaping the danger by the tardiness of the Austrian authorities in procuring him the necessary passports. Upon receiving the warning he resolved to join his grandfather, but to do so it was necessary that he should pass through part of the Austrian territories. The English ambassador at Vienna wrote for this purpose to the Austrian Government to demand a passport for the Duke, and it was their tardiness in answering that occasioned the delay, which permitted his arrest by Napoleon, and cost him his life."

Much was based on the statement that a person evidently of high standing, to whom the principal conspirators showed marked attention, had interviews with Georges. This mysterious person was supposed to be the Duke d'Enghien, who had for a time been lost sight of. It was only a faint supposition. An officer of *gendarmes* sent to inquire was told that the Duke sometimes went to Strassburg to the play. The truth of this report was denied by his secretary, though he admitted that the Duke took walks on the banks of the Rhine. It was thus that on very insufficient data he was made the soul of the conspiracy.

******

The cruel fate of the Duke d'Enghien and other charges brought against Napoleon have to be commented on, not merely to show that he could act wrongly at times, like any other mortal, but because the execution at Vincennes had much to do in bringing about the third coalition.

******

Thiard, who when in Condé's corps had served as intermediary between the Austrians and the Duc d'Enghien, had several conversations with Napoleon about the unfortunate prince after his death. It was from what he had elicited from Thiard that he exclaimed, "But he was really a man then, this prince!" ("*Mais c'était donc réellement un homme que ce Prince là!*")

******

In a former chapter we have remarked on the extraordinary ability with which Napoleon had devised a plan for enticing the British naval forces to a distance from the English Channel. It was left to Pitt, a statesman who excelled in diplomacy and finance, to devise some way for causing the withdrawal of the French force from their threatening position around Boulogne.

The impending danger had aroused alarm in England, and the people had demanded Pitt to undertake the saving of their country. He might have waited patiently to meet the French after they landed on the shores of Sussex and Kent. It was not likely that the British, the descendants of the brave men who conquered at Crécy,—where by Napoleon's own estimate 26,000 English utterly defeated 100,000 Frenchmen—Agincourt, and Blenheim, that those soldiers who had fought so gallantly in Egypt, and who shortly after showed such stubbornness and spirit in the Spanish Peninsula and other fields, would have been easily subjected by the French.

******

"The success of the English in Egypt," wrote General Andréossi, "seems to have made them fancy themselves able to act a part as land troops." Napoleon and some of his marshals could well testify, to their sorrow, that they were fully able to play such a role.

✶✶✶✶✶✶

There were, indeed, men so confident that they openly expressed a wish that the French might land.

Until Napoleon went to Spain, he had never gauged the real strength of an armed population. It seemed to him impossible that the people, stirred to resistance by patriotism and despair, could for a long time hold out against troops which had routed the best armies in the world.

In England all ranks of the population alike were imbued with a strong spirit of patriotism, and the able-bodied men who had enrolled themselves into volunteer corps were likely to become every day better adapted to confront the enemy. French soldiers when led by Napoleon and his marshals might certainly do much; nevertheless, in Egypt lately, when opposed to British valour and stubbornness, they had signally failed. It was this very obstinacy which caused the British troops to be accused of gross ignorance by more than one French historian, inasmuch as they could not perceive when they were beaten. These words, uttered in scorn, were, however, the most honourable testimony which could ever be paid to the prowess of any army. (Even Waterloo had not shaken Napoleon's confidence in the excellence of his army. "Look at the English," he said; "they conquered us, and yet they are very far from our equals.")

England's gifted minister, Pitt, very naturally alarmed by seeing his country so closely threatened, tried to avert the blow by setting alight a Continental war. He endeavoured to find some formidable combination which would put an end at once and for all to the possibility of an invasion. He well realised the fact that the best way of dealing with any danger is to remove the cause rather than to guard against the effect.

Schoell, on the question of who was the originator of this European league, writes, *Histoire Abrégée des Traité de Paix*:

> This confederation owed its origin to the British Ministry, which, however, were strangers to the faults committed in the redaction and execution of the military plan of operations. The feeble Ministry which had ruled Great Britain since the month of March 1801 had employed intrigues to divert the French

forces from a project of invasion, by occupying the attention of that Government through troubles fomented in the interior of the country, and some of the British ministers accredited abroad have even been accused of having abused the character they held to foment troubles in France. Pitt, who returned to the Cabinet in the month of May 1804, disdained using such ignoble methods for injuring the enemies of his country.

He conceived the idea of a grand European league; and, justly attributing to the feebleness of the means employed the unfavourable issue of former coalitions, gave to his scheme the colossal proportions which were needed for a successful issue. His plan failed once more, and this mighty minister carried to his grave the fear of the misfortunes which threatened England. She, however, escaped them all, and it was really Pitt's genius that saved Europe eight years later, for it was the league, as he had originally conceived it, that vanquished Bonaparte in 1814.

Schoell, in his *Recueil de Pièces Officielles destinées a detromper les François, Tome Septième*, quotes a communication made to the Russian ambassador in London on the 19th of January 1805, which very clearly shows that the proposal for a coalition originated with the British Cabinet, and not, as was often supposed, with the Czar Alexander.

The interests were so conflicting that a league of states at one time seemed almost impossible; some of the sovereigns were very loath to arm. England made her first attempt at St. Petersburg, as, owing to her geographical position, Russia had less to lose from failure than any of the other states. To give the *Czar* the opportunity of playing the leading role on the Continent did not alarm England half as much as the threatening armaments at Boulogne.

Austria temporised, desiring to gain time and prepare for those redoutable blows which the Cabinet of Vienna knew too well from recent experience, would, in the event of hostilities at the first go off, be directed against her. She hesitated a long time in taking part in the new war, and there was much truth in Mack's statement after the fall of Ulm, that the Emperor of Austria had not been desirous of war, but had been driven to it by Russia.

Should Prussia and Bavaria refuse to join the coalition, there was no other ally left to Austria but Russia, a country situated too far from her eastern frontier. Austria temporized, whilst England's interest was for the league to declare itself at once and give rise, without further loss of time, to a powerful diversion.

Prussia coveted Hanover, and did not relish alienating France in the event of the fortune of war siding with Napoleon. Sweden and Prussia were at variance regarding Hanover, and in fact the fickle character of the Swedish monarch militated against any serious operations being undertaken.

Pitt had also no small difficulty in bringing the views of the Cabinet of St. Petersburg to a reasonable bearing, for the young *Czar* held philanthropic views which were not very practical. Alexander dreamt of a happy, lasting, and universal peace which was to be brought about by a close union of all the European sovereigns. He wanted the Christian nations to form one family under the protection of the Almighty. Possessing a noble heart, he cherished illusions; he advocated many measures which the statesmen of Europe were not slow to recognise as being surrounded by insuperable difficulties.

Austria and Russia had already signed a defensive treaty on the 6th of November 1804, though nothing at all was done in virtue of that agreement. When, in January 1805, Napoleon's encroachments in Italy roused the indignation of Austria, Cobentzel, the head of the peace party, resigned, and was succeeded by Count Baillot Latour. The war party then became predominant at Vienna.

The first to show a feeling of enmity towards France was the ardent and chivalrous King of Sweden. Hatred of Napoleon was the guiding motive of his life; this joined to a question of legitimacy, an ardent desire to see the restoration of the Bourbon dynasty, made him eager to join the coalition against France. His wife was one of the three princesses of Baden who showed such decided animosity against Napoleon. On the 7th of September 1804, the king abruptly announced the termination of all friendly communication between the Governments of Sweden and France. (In bad style, the communication to this effect was addressed to Monsieur Napoleon Bonaparte.) His action was, however, contrary to the wishes of his people.

On the 14th of January 1805, a convention was signed between Russia and Sweden, by virtue of which these two powers bound themselves to resist the ambition of France, to maintain the equilibrium of power in Europe and the independence of Germany.

Pitt had taken speedy advantage of this unfriendly disposition of the King of Sweden; he had entered into a secret compact with the Swedish Government on the 3rd of December 1804, one clause of which was the enrolment of an Hanoverian legion in Stralsund in the island of Rugen, and the issue of a subsidy of £80,000 for the defence of Stralsund. The French, who got wind of this treaty through Monsieur Laforest, persuaded the Court of Prussia to remonstrate with the King of Sweden, who indignantly objected to have his system of alliances discussed.

✶✶✶✶✶✶

The King of Sweden's project of uniting the troops of England and Russia to his own, which eventually resulted in the siege of the small fortress of Hamlen, contributed not a little to alienate the affections of his subjects, who feared lest they might be the victims of the revenge roused by the extravagant plans of their king They dreaded the insults he had permitted himself to heap on Napoleon, particularly since the execution of the Duke d'Enghien,

✶✶✶✶✶✶

Next to show hostility to the ruler of France was the Sultan. He refused to acknowledge Napoleon as Emperor of the French, and after a long delay Marshal Brune, the French ambassador, found himself compelled to quit Constantinople.

Russia and Sweden, the first two powers which joined the coalition, had no very powerful reasons for declaring against Napoleon. Though the Court of Russia had gone into mourning for d'Enghien's death, that sad event did not affect her particularly. The *Czar* had strongly protested against the violation of the neutral territory of Baden, but his reclamation received scanty attention. In any case, as his own territory was far away to the east, he had not any very powerful grounds for dreading Napoleon's ambition.

No other state in Europe had so little interest as Sweden in restoring the family of the Bourbons to the throne of France. Sweden was independent of all foreign influence, and, like Russia, she was far removed from the emperor's blows, therefore she had possibly even less reason than that power for going to war with France. Gustavus Adolphus IV. seems to have been actuated by a silly desire to interfere in the affairs of Germany. It was this that made him foster the coalition against France. The execution of the Duke d'Enghien, a crime which appeared to go unpunished, made him a bitter enemy of the French Government.

Having combined with Russia, the King of Sweden concluded two conventions with England, bearing date the 31st of August and the 3rd of October 1805. The first of these, signed at Helsinborg, was only intended to strengthen the previously mentioned secret convention of the 3rd of December 1804, and related to the sum of £1,800 to be paid by England monthly for each 1,000 men added to the garrison of Stralsund.

The second treaty, signed at Beckaskog, referred to a corps of 12,000 men to be landed in Pomerania to combine with a Russian corps, paid for by Great Britain, and provided that the subsidy agreed upon should continue to be paid for three months after the conclusion of peace.

On the 31st of October 1805, Gustavus Adolphus IV declared war against France. A sovereign, who found difficulty in furnishing 12,000 men, and whose ruined finances did not enable him to keep even this small force in the field, boasted that he would act with energy for the re-establishment of the general tranquillity of Europe. He was not a very redoubtable enemy, certainly not one the French should fear.

England had proposed to the Emperor of Russia a plan for a powerful coalition to wrest from France the countries she had subjugated since the commencement of the Revolution. To restore peace and happiness to their countries, and get them to form a barrier against further projects for the aggrandizement of France, the allies were to place in the field an army of 500,000 men.

Baron Winzingerode, Prince Schwarzenberg, and General Mack, held a conference at Vienna, and on the 10th of July adopted a plan of operations proposed by the Austrian generals, to which Russia offered a few observations. The Austrian Cabinet, nevertheless, believed it to be desirable to delay the commencement of the operations, and to keep the peace, waiting for events which might hold promise of better success. It considered it difficult to attack the French on the Rhine and wiser to remain quietly on the defensive on the Danube.

Had the great powers understood their real interests, had they forgotten their rivalries, how much bloodshed and suffering would have been spared. Towards the end of the previous year, Nelson had written words full of wisdom to the Queen of Naples:

> Never, perhaps, was Europe more critically situated than at this moment, and never was the probability of universal monarchy more nearly being realised than in the person of the Corsican. I can see but little difference between the name of emperor, king, or prefect, if they perfectly obey his despotic orders. Prussia is trying to be destroyed last; Spain is little better than a province of France; Russia does nothing on a grand scale. Would to God

these great powers reflected, that the boldest measures are the safest! They allow small states to fall, and to swell the enormous power of France, without appearing to reflect that every kingdom which is annexed to France makes their own existence, as independent states, more precarious.

Prussia and Austria, in their desire to avoid going to war with France, had lost sight of the latter point. Austria, besides, needed peace to re-establish her finances, ruined by the past wars. In 1804, came the d'Enghien execution; the very name of Napoleon at that time inspired such terror that no power, except Russia, dared to manifest thoroughly its indignation. It was then that the ambassadors were recalled, and all friendly relations between the Cabinets of Russia and France ceased.

The *Czar*, in an autograph letter to the Emperor of Austria, wrote:

> The French Government, made strong by the fear which it has been able to inspire more than by its own might, desires to turn to profit the isolation in which the great powers continue to remain; and the Ettenheim event proves sufficiently, had one failed to be persuaded of it long ago, that Bonaparte has no other rule of conduct than an unquenchable thirst of power, coupled with a desire for universal dominion.

The Emperor Francis replied:

> In the present state of affairs, I consider our union, our thorough understanding, as the only hope which remains for the safety of Europe.

His Majesty proposed to conclude a defensive treaty, which was signed on the 10th of October 1804. Russia bound herself to send 115,000 men to aid Austria in the event of her being attacked.

Russia and Prussia also signed a treaty, in virtue of which they engaged to guarantee the independence of Northern Germany; and to prevent Napoleon extending his dominion over it. The Kings of Sweden and of Naples declared themselves prepared to make common cause with the *Czar* of Russia.

The conditions for combined action were at that moment especially favourable, for after the murder of the Czar Paul, his successor, Alexander I., had lost no time in reopening an amicable intercourse with the Emperor of Austria. The new *Czar* had protested against Bonaparte's acts of aggression in Switzerland, in Italy, in Holland, and in a special manner against the occupation of Hanover, as the integrity of that country had been guaranteed by a special treaty concluded between France and Prussia. To all of these representations the *Czar* only received evasive answers.

The precarious state in which Bonaparte had found himself previous to the Treaty of Campo Formio, and which had compelled him to moderate his demands, did not escape the attention of the foreign powers. Austria had with great persistence raised one army after another to oppose Bonaparte, and, though she had officially complimented him on his new dignity, it was believed, might be induced to fight him again.

******

Previous to Napoleon's coronation, the Emperor Francis addressed a letter to him acknowledging his imperial dignity, and relinquishing for himself all claim to the title of Emperor of Germany.—*Tomass*, vol. i.

******

Pitt deemed that the Cabinet of Vienna might be found willing to entertain any proposals which would promise ample sinews of war. Before that painful episode, the murder of d'Enghien, was permitted to be forgotten, he proposed to himself to cement the concord of Austria and Russia with English gold, and in this manner to form a powerful coalition in the centre of Europe, which, by alarming Napoleon, owing to the danger which menaced his eastern provinces, should compel him to withdraw his troops from the shores of the Channel.

The enticing of Nelson's fleet to the West Indies in search of fleets which were to evade him, return, and unite in the British Channel, was the most masterly feature of the emperor's combination for the conquest of England. His scheme for obtaining the command of the Channel by the withdrawal of the British fleet, has always been regarded as a real stroke of genius, and the same, in all truth, can be said of Pitt's plan for drawing the French troops eastwards from the camp of Boulogne. The plan the British minister prepared for the allies was nothing less than a masterpiece.

Pitt strove to thwart Napoleon's boundless views and his insatiable ambition by bringing all the nations of Europe together to attack him. He would have broken his power, had not the military inability of the allies enabled the French to score an easy victory at Ulm and at Austerlitz.

Russia, Sweden, and Naples at first joined the coalition. With the exception of the first, the other powers were little to be dreaded, for they could not contend with France on any footing of equality. Napoleon knew the movements of the Russian forces, and that Russia was making preparations on a large scale. He knew that her troops were in motion in every quarter; that Buxhowden, Lascy, and Kutuzoff had received important commands.

On the 5th of August 1805, Austria, who felt aggrieved by France's encroachments in Italy, sided with the other three powers. Prussia still held aloof.

Fully aware of Austria's animosity, Napoleon continued to carry on negotiations, Austria all the time complaining of the non-execution of the Treaty of Lunéville.

At that period all sorts of diplomatic deceptions and subterfuges—*on ignore toujours le mot de mensonge dans la haute politique* (we still do not know the word lie in high politics)—were employed both in Vienna and in Paris to prolong the explanations. Both sides wished to secure the advantage of a formidable aggression. Napoleon desired to carry to termination his naval expedition, and was not deterred by menace and futile demonstrations, as long as he had any prospect of displaying the superiority of his naval forces in the Channel.

The Austrian ambassador in Paris had a difficult task to discharge; he had to maintain the resemblance of amicable relations with the French Government, well knowing all the time that his Cabinet was openly elaborating measures for commencing hostilities.

The Emperor Francis was deeply irritated by the news of the coronation at Milan; and the recent annexation of Genoa to France furnished Austria with one more subject of complaint. Napoleon's main reasons for uniting Genoa to the empire had escaped him; it was to form of Liguria a recruiting ground for his navy. To Lebrun, who had been charged with the government of Liguria, recently annexed, Napoleon wrote:

Je n'ai réuni Génes que pour avoir des marins... (Sailors, old sailors, are the contribution I require.)

When Napoleon went to Italy to be crowned, and collected a body of troops to give a representation of the battles he had fought in that country, the Austrians concentrated troops in the Tyrol. To Napoleon's remonstrances the Austrian Government replied that the large concentration of French troops appeared to be in excess of what was needed to give a certain amount of brilliancy to public rejoicings.

Austria argued that the Treaty of Lunéville guaranteed the independence of the Italian, Helvetic, and Batavian republics, and promised them the liberty of choosing their form of government. On this point she insisted that the treaty had been infringed, and consequently that she had just cause of complaint.

★★★★★★

Napoleon's original design was to have erected the Cisalpine Republic into a separate kingdom with his brother Joseph as King. Joseph Bonaparte, however, would only accept the crown under certain distinct conditions; this made Napoleon change his mind, and he resolved to place the crown of Lombardy on his own head. He cunningly made his views known to Count Melzi, and a deputation of the Italian Republic, which had come to Paris to be present at the emperor's coronation, made the proposal appear as if coming from them. Things were done speedily, and on the 19th of March the Act of settlement of the Italian crown was read, when Napoleon declared that he was ready to accept and defend the iron crown. He appointed his stepson, Eugène Beauharnais, to be Viceroy, and on the 31st of March received the homage of the principal authorities.

On the 2nd of April Napoleon set out from Turin, and a series of splendid entertainments and magnificent pageants marked his progress through Northern Italy. At Marengo he proceeded to the historical battlefield and had a mimic representation of the battle. A force of thirty-four battalions and seven squadrons manoeuvred under Lannes, who had borne so large a share of the brunt on the memorable 14th June 1800.

In all this splendour Napoleon never forgot his designs for the humiliation of his foes. Never for a moment did he permit the festivities to interfere with the performance of his work; his orders were issued with singular ability, and with an indefatigable activity of mind which has been seldom equalled.

★★★★★★

Napoleon despised Austria, and did not believe her to be powerful enough to act against him. In 1805, that power still needed some years of rest to recover her strength and recruit her finances. Nevertheless, all the statesmen of Europe were fully convinced that in any coalition which might come to be formed, and which offered a fair prospect of success, Austria should take a prominent part.

Four days after the opening of the Parliamentary session of 1805,

Pitt lay before the Russian ambassador in London the headings for a combination, and on the 11th of April 1805 Russia entered into a treaty with England, which was the base of the third coalition. The treaty was signed by Lord Granville Leveson-Gower on the part of England, and by Adam Czartorinski and Nicolas de Nowosilzoff for Russia. Its object was to restore peace, independence, and happiness to Europe, of which she had been deprived by the endless ambition of the French Government, and by the supreme influence it strove to arrogate. This coalition did not remain such a secret as the allies flattered themselves to be.

The contracting parties to the treaty bound themselves to oblige the French executive to withdraw its troops from Hanover and North Germany, to recognise the independence of Switzerland and of Holland, and to reinstate the King of Piedmont. To promise the future safety of the kingdom of Naples, and the total removal of French troops from Italy, including the island of Elba.

An important clause was that all the Governments who subscribed to this league bound themselves not to conclude peace with France unless with the full consent of the other contracting powers.

The army of 500,000 men which Pitt had calculated putting in the field, not being so easily procurable, it was agreed to commence operations as soon as 400,000 men were forthcoming. Of these Austria was to furnish 250,000, Russia 115,000, and the rest was to embrace the contingents furnished by Naples, Hanover, Piedmont, etc. England promised to provide 35,000 men; mercenaries whom she proposed to enlist or to pay.

England engaged to undertake minor armed descents on the Continent, to contribute to the common effort with all her forces military and naval, and with ships for the transport of troops. To pay £1,250,000 for each 100,000 regulars the powers would furnish.

Pitt demanded from Parliament £5,000,000 with which to subsidize the foreign powers, a sum which afterwards, when Prussia refused to join the coalition, was reduced to £3,500,000.

Russia made this treaty known to the Cabinet of Vienna, but the Austrian Government exaggerated the difficulties in which it was placed. Before coming to a final decision, it wished to weigh well all the chances of war. It believed, besides, that without the concurrence of Prussia it would have been impossible to triumph over Bonaparte.

Strange enough that though Austria was still holding aloof, this treaty fully specified the role she would have to play, the contingent she would be bound to provide, the subsidies she would receive. Russia was willing to place 180,000 men in the field, and expected 250,000 more from Austria.

Still, believing she would be the first to bear Napoleon's attack, and already half ruined by the disasters of the past campaigns, Austria joined the coalition with the greatest unwillingness, and for a long time felt reluctant to enter into any engagement. In any case, the Cabinet of Vienna held back, and would not be a party to any agreement until fully convinced that the Austrian Army would be supported in sufficient time by Russia.

The powers were not of accord in their aims. England needed a powerful and early diversion on the continent; Austria selfishly hoped to mature her preparations whilst the French Army was occupied and enfeebled by the expedition to England. The British Cabinet wanted Austria to advance boldly and force the smaller German states to declare for the coalition and give up all hopes of maintaining an equivocal neutrality.

Napoleon recognised how Austria's hostile attitude effected a real diversion in favour of England. In the impossibility of keeping a maritime war going, he marched to overthrow Austria and to compel her to sue for peace.

Prussia remained obstinate in her indecision. She had been tempted by the offer of Hanover, which the great Lord Chatham invariably pronounced to be a mill-stone about England's neck. Even this offer did not quite satisfy her; she demanded, besides, the independence of Holland and Switzerland, but this Napoleon would not concede. Consequently, instead of co-operating with the French, she decided to remain neutral.

The feeble but upright Frederick William III had ascended the throne on the 16th of November 1797. Firmly believing that it was impossible to beat Napoleon, he desired to remain at peace with him at any cost. He refused to take the field, reminding Russia that his engagement with her only related to Northern Germany.

His policy was very short-sighted, and his vacillation was not long in bringing about his own destruction. It turned out disastrous in the end for the two powers who had been the first to unite against the French Republic in 1792, to oppose Napoleon separately, and not to have made their defence a common object. When Napoleon resolved to attack the Emperor of Austria in 1805, Prussia might have stepped boldly into the field and cut off all communication with France. The

French Army, when it penetrated into Moravia, later on, was at such a distance from home that, with a powerful enemy in rear as well as in front, it must have been in the greatest peril, and might probably have been forced to capitulate.

✶✶✶✶✶✶

Some few years later, in 1808, Napoleon saw the whole of his plan of campaign for the subjugation of Spain upset, because Sir John Moore, by advancing, with his little army on Sahagun, threatened his communications. The emperor's vast army of 300,000 men depended entirely for their supplies on the line of communications with France, and even a menace directed towards that tender point sufficed to cause him the greatest alarm.

✶✶✶✶✶✶

The Prussian Government, owing to its rivalry with the Emperor of Germany, had for some years past kept aloof from any dispute with France. Its object was that Prussia might derive some adequate benefit in the strife between Austria and France, such as some enlargement of territory. The king had acknowledged the title of Emperor which Napoleon had assumed, and had hastened to decorate the new monarch with the Order of the Black Eagle.

A reaction was, however, preparing in the mind of the nation, and especially of the Prussian Army, which aimed at making a stand against the progressive enlargement of the power of France, now that it had become an empire. A crisis was at hand, brought about by the prospect of a war between Austria and France. The men of action in the army were clamorous for war, and loudly declared for the interference of Prussia.

The English made strenuous efforts to gain the co-operation of the King of Prussia, and were profuse in their offers of subsidy, so much so that Napoleon had good reasons to fear that the king would eventually join the coalition. England eagerly desired to gain this end, for 109,000 good soldiers put in the field by Prussia and added to the rest of the allied forces would have made the execution of Napoleon's campaign absolutely impossible.

The British agents kept reminding the king of the past glory of Frederick II. You have, they said, numerous troops trained in the same evolutions; some of the generals of the memorable Seven Years' War are still to the fore, who wish for nothing better than to add to their glory and renown.

In the presence of several distinguished diplomatists, the king pronounced himself in favour of neutrality. All the endeavours of Stackelberg, of Prince Metternich, of several Russian generals, did not succeed in making him change his determination.

Frederick William issued a proclamation in which he informed all his states that he was resolved to maintain a strict neutrality. No passage of troops or of escorted transport would be permitted to take place without the consent of the king. All billeting, letting of horses, deliveries of supplies, and the like was strictly prohibited. All exportation of provisions, of horses, etc., was forbidden.

The pacific feeling of the king towards France at this time is hard to understand. One would think he might have surely have expected that France had not quite forgotten Prussia's hostility in the early days of the Revolution. But he remained blind to what was in store for him, and when he could have, made Avar with a great probability of success, having both Austria and Russia to assist him, he held aloof, only to feel the full weight of the French Army in the following year.

Napoleon had neither magnanimity nor pity for the Prussians. The timid policy of the king robbed him of respect, without diminishing the dangers which threatened him. His own brother, the nobility, and most of the officers of his army, were only too eager for war; they blamed his conduct, and with very good reason too, considering that it endangered their country.

The king and Haugwitz—who exercised a great influence in politics—both seemed to be troubled by a presentiment that ruin was soon to overtake their country. They persisted in opposing the views of those whom they stupidly accused of working for the ruin of Prussia.

The Prussian ruler adopted a system of vacillation and tried to protract arrangements with the two emperors at a time when the calamitous circumstances of the war on the Danube were growing daily more and more critical.

Herr von Alopaeus, who had been for many years, Russian ambassador at Berlin, was instructed to ask permission for a Russian Army to march through Silesia, hinting at the same time that there could not be the least doubt that Prussia would join in the work of delivering Europe from French dictation.

According to the plan of operations agreed between Austria and Russia, it was arranged that Michelson should in the beginning of September enter the Prussian states at the head of Benningsen's, Buxhowden's and Essen's corps; that he should march with Benningsen's corps in the direction of Southern Germany, sending Buxhowden and Essen to rejoin Kutuzoff. Alopaeus received an order to obtain from the king permission for the Russians to cross his states. In case of refusal, Michelson was to enter by force; in the event of armed resistance, he was to treat Prussia in the light of an enemy.

The intention was clearly intimated to the Court of Berlin of compelling Prussia to join and take part in the war by fair means, or, if necessary, by force. The Russians were not loath to fight the Prussians. When Czartorinski saw that Prussia hesitated, he advised the *Czar* to attack her, feeling positive that after her first defeat she would be too ready to treat.

The King of Prussia refused to let the Russian troops march through his states. He stated his determination to resist to the very last, and hinted that he might be forced to make common cause with Napoleon.

Russia pushed forward her negotiations, and from persuasion passed on to threats. Had the *Czar* put greater pressure on the King of Prussia than he did, there is little doubt that it would have ended in driving him into the arms of France.

When, as a matter of precaution, Prussia made preparations for war, Russia, at first, imagined that these might probably be intended for an attack on her.

As it came to be recognised that Prussia would not join the coalition of her own free will, the *Czar* conceived the idea of forcing the king into it by putting on moral pressure. With this object he concentrated an army of 40,000 men on the Russo-Polish frontier. This measure so irritated King Frederick William that he placed his army on a war footing. For though the king was feeble and irresolute, when pushed too far he became irritable and obstinate. Being in this mood, he mobilised 80,000 men. The *Czar* then proposed an interview—this could hardly be refused; but even then, as the king had no taste for such meetings, the interview was held back till the first days of October.

Prince Dolgorouki, one of the *Czar's aides-de-camp*, a nobleman full of ardour and spirit, but without the qualities needed for undertaking a delicate mission—in Prussia, above all, where strict etiquette kept the diplomatic corps at the greatest possible distance from the Court—was to predispose Frederick William to this friendly meeting of the two sovereigns.

Duroc and Laforest were labouring to counteract these Russian influences, striving to secure Prussia's aid by the offer of Hanover. This offer seemed to have some effect on the young king, while Hardenberg had to rack his wits to find some plausible pretext which would save his monarch's honour in this transaction.

Duroc, who arrived at Berlin on the 1st of September, had lost no time in explaining his mission to the king. On the 3rd he wrote to Talleyrand to say how the proposition on the part of the Emperor of the French had much surprised the King of Prussia. Later on, on the 8th of the same month, Duroc wrote a letter to Napoleon to announce the probable failure of his mission. He did more, for he hinted very strongly to the emperor that any passage of French troops through Prussian territory would be a dangerous step, which, if possible, should certainly be avoided.

It was soon after the receipt of this letter, which counselled him to treat Prussia with forbearance, that orders were sent to Bernadotte to march through the territory of Anspach. A man who had not scrupled to violate the territory of Baden to seize a harmless prince, was not the person to hold back when the violation offered his army a chance of success. Napoleon was not the man to be restrained by any prudent advice or by diplomatic considerations when anything stood in the way of his strategy.

Bernadotte was ordered to advance by the shortest route; he received the following instructions:

> Cross these territories, but avoid making any stay there; be profuse in protestations in favour of Prussia; show much attachment towards her, the greatest possible regard for her interests, still pursue your march swiftly, alleging as an excuse the impossibility of acting otherwise, for, after all, this impossibility is really a fact.

Napoleon could very well have avoided irritating the Prussian nation by drawing the 1st and 2nd corps towards him, thus avoiding their treading on Prussian ground at all, but his great strategical movement contemplated the Danube being crossed as far in rear of Mack's army as possible, in case that general should have retreated from the Iller to the Lech. There was a very important strategical reason, therefore, for the line of advance marked out for the two marshals, inasmuch as the emperor intended them to strike the Danube at Ingolstadt. To reach that city Bernadotte had to take the shortest road, and that led through the Prussian possessions in Franconia. Nothing but his march through there would have got him up in time to co-operate with the other corps.

Besides the 18,000 men which Bernadotte had brought from Hanover, he had 23,000 men of Marmont and Hesse Darmstadt and 22,000 Bavarians, making a total of 63,000 men. The centre column, composed of two divisions from Hanover, marched by Anspach, the Gallo-Batavians by Gunzenheim, all making for Ingolstadt. The march was as rapid as the circumstances demanded. The troops were concentrated round Eichstädt on the 8th of October; Marmont, forming the advanced guard, was on that day at Nassenfeld, four leagues only from the Danube, between Neuburg and Ingolstadt.

The French march through Anspach was a master stroke, for it placed them in a most skilful manner in rear of the Austrians, whilst Mack remained tranquilly in his position on the Iller.

The indignation of the entire Prussian nation when it came to learn the news of the violation of the territory of Anspach knew no bounds. Its pride was wounded to the quick in beholding the utter contempt with which Napoleon treated their country. Prussia remonstrated indignantly, and as the irritation gradually augmented, the king, though loath as ever to declare war, seemed to be inclined to resort to hostile measures. Haugwitz, the great advocate for a temporizing policy, lost the confidence of the nation, and was replaced by Baron Hardenberg.

The King of Prussia affected, it was believed, to be more irritated than he was in reality. The Russians wished to march through Silesia to Bavaria, to which the king was strongly opposed, but the fact that the French had marched through Anspach forced his hand and militated against this objection. He now could hardly refuse to Russia what had, in a way, been accorded to France. The desired permission was granted.

With regard to this incident Prince Metternich writes:

> The attitude of the King of Prussia was founded on strict neutrality, and in this he acted in good faith. The violent measures of Napoleon and Alexander, similar in character and coincident in time, left the king only the choice which of the two insults he should resent; he chose without hesitation to pass by that which in form was the most injurious. Alexander had made known to the king, in a manner as peremptory as unusual, his determination to violate the neutrality of Prussia. Napoleon, on the contrary, admitted the neutrality of this power, and yet violated it. The king felt Napoleon's proceeding to be the more bitter insult. (*Autobiography of Prince Metternich.*)

Napoleon directed his representatives at Berlin and at Würzburg to declare that nothing had occurred to change the terms of the convention which existed in the former war relating to the neutrality of Anspach, which therefore could by right be crossed by French troops; that the emperor had fully believed that things would stand on the same footing as in the last war.

Thiers tries to excuse the violation of the Prussian territory by the excellent behaviour of the troops. He states that the French troops were misrepresented as having crossed the territory of Anspach in an overbearing manner. That all that was taken was paid for in ready money, and the most rigid discipline was observed. The people, well paid for the bread and meat they had given to the French soldiers, seemed to be in no way irritated by the violation of their territory.

He endeavours to show how Napoleon crossed the neutral territory of Anspach in all good faith; that the irritation of Prussia was a mere pretext.

★★★★★★

When alluding to Bernadotte's march across the territory of Anspach, Count Pelet de la Lozère, *Napoleon in Council, or the Opinions delivered by Bonaparte,* gives a different version from the ordinary one,

By the advice of Monsieur Otto, the French Minister at the Court of Bavaria, the Elector had quitted Munich and repaired to Würzburg. But no sooner had he got there than the Ministers of Austria and England set to trying to persuade him into joining their side, by offers of augmentation of territory and of royal dignity.

Austria could back her offers with troops, as her troops had already occupied part of Bavaria. It was at this moment, when the Elector appeared to be on the point of giving up treating with France, that Otto rendered a good service to the emperor. Otto put an end to the Elector's indecision by sending an extraordinary courier to Marmont and Bernadotte to represent to them the state of affairs, urging them to move at once by forced marches for Würzburg without waiting for Napoleon's orders. It was the arrival of these two divisions which re-established the preponderance of France in the councils of Bavaria.

★★★★★★

To Prussia the emperor said that the former conventions covered the case of the violation of the territory of Anspach; that had these been considered as abrogated, he should have been warned of the fact. But to this explanation he added in the shape of a warning that France had not for the first time had the whole of Europe on her hands, and that such an event did in no way terrify her.

When the Prussian Government protested, Bernadotte was well forward towards the Danube. The indignation of the court and of the people Alison declares to have blazed forth on the 14th; but, as on the 8th Bernadotte's advanced guard was already on the banks of the Danube—between Neuburg and Ingolstadt—it is not quite clear how a declaration of war could have had any effect in staying his march for the Danube.

Whatever measures Prussia might have taken to arrest Napoleon's progress, neither Prussia, Austria, nor Russia had capable enough commanders to contend against the French emperor or his marshals. Nor were their troops animated by the same spirit of confidence in the ultimate success of the campaign. Had Prussia joined the coalition in October 1805, more battles would have been fought, and the French would have gained more victories. Napoleon had not then marched so very far from the Rhine as to endanger his communications to any appreciable extent.

Well aware of the little cordiality existing among the great powers, and of Frederick William's earnest desire of avoiding going to war, it is reasonable to suppose that Napoleon did not anticipate anything beyond strong protests for the violation of Prussian territory.

The march across the territory of Anspach had helped the French invasion considerably, and the king considered that this unfriendly action absolved him from his engagements. The *Czar*, who was then at Pulavy, in Poland, learning the great ferment caused all through Prussia by the above violation, imagined that he could improve the situation by going to Berlin.

On the 25th of October, the very day the French troops stationed round Munich opened their march for the Inn, the Czar Alexander arrived in Berlin. There he employed all his charms, all his captivating manners, (Czernichef gave the *Czar* the title of "the bewitching"), and used every possible argument and wile to induce the king to assume a bolder attitude. Russia and Austria promised him Hanover; England engaged to find her compensation in Holland.

Prussia had no need to seek for a pretext for casting her lot with the coalition, for the violation of her territory was enough reason already. Her Government, however, only agreed to take up arms on the side of the allies on condition that Prussia should be rewarded with Hanover. The treaty signed at Potsdam was once on the point of not coming into effect on the discussion of this point. French influence now rapidly declined, and on the 2nd of November Duroc quitted Berlin and made for the French headquarters, which he joined at Linz. By working on the king's indecision, he and Laforest had succeeded in gaining time, which was invaluable to Napoleon, for when the king's determination was taken, his co-operation had lost much of its value; the situation of Austria was more than critical, nearly one-half of her army had been destroyed or captured.

Frederick William became alarmed at the favourable reception of the *Czar* and the influence he seemed to exercise on the Court of Prussia. He recalled Haugwitz, his old counsellor, and demanded his advice for getting out of the embarrassment he had been thrown in by Hardenberg espousing too readily the cause of the allies. The king and Haugwitz resisted for a long time the pressure put on by the *Czar*, and held that possibly the whole of Europe united was incapable of resisting the power of Napoleon.

The result of the *Czar's* visit, the solicitations of the queen, the arguments of Prince Louis, and the outcry of the Prussian staff, conquered the king's reluctance. A secret convention was signed at Potsdam on the 3rd of November by the rulers of Prussia and Russia; a treaty offensive and defensive for the re-establishment of peace in Europe much on the basis of the Treaty of Lunéville.

The existence of this treaty was denied by Baron Hardenberg, until placed beyond a doubt by a proclamation issued to the Austrian Army announcing the conclusion of a triple alliance between Austria, Prussia, and Russia.

This treaty had left open an avenue of escape, the king having insisted that he would let the Emperor of the French know on what conditions he was prepared to continue his neutrality. Hostilities were not to commence for a month, the Duke of Brunswick having declared that the Prussian Army would not be quite ready to take the field before the beginning of December. In the meantime, the Prussian Army marched towards the Upper Danube in the direction of Regensburg.

Haugwitz was to carry the notification of this convention to Napoleon, and to offer a continuance of former friendship and an alliance with the Prussian nation, if he was willing to accept its terms, or a declaration of war should he reject them. He was instructed to intimate in the latter case that hostilities would commence on the 15th of December.

Louise, wife of Frederick William III., already exceedingly popular through her great beauty, dignity, and grace of manners, added much to her popularity by the patriotic spirit she displayed at this period. (Napoleon, after having seen the Queen of Prussia at Tilsit, declared her to be the handsomest woman in the world.) She endeavoured to cement still further the alliance between the two sovereigns by a solemn oath taken at night over the tomb of the great Frederick. There the two sovereigns took an oath of eternal friendship; they were never to separate their cause nor their destinies.

★★★★★★

The moment the *Czar* had got well clear of his redoubtable enemy after Austerlitz, he sent the Grand Duke Constantine and Prince Dolgorouki to Berlin, and having in mind the oath he had taken on the tomb of Frederick the Great, but forgetting the severe lesson he had just received, placed all his forces at the disposal of the Berlin Cabinet if the king would only prosecute the war.

★★★★★★

The effects, however, of this somewhat theatrical scene were not long-lasting. A few hours after the occurrence, Alexander started for Galicia, and with his departure the King of Prussia relapsed into his usual habit of temporising. Haugwitz, who had to deliver the ultimatum, did not set out from Potsdam for Napoleon's headquarters before the 14th of November. Undoubtedly what perplexed the king was the news of Napoleon's victories round Ulm, which had been brought to Berlin by the Archduke Anthony. The events were no doubt of a kind to make the Prussian Cabinet thoughtful, but only by energetic action could Prussia restore the chances of war in favour of the allies.

The indignation of the Prussian Court was seriously modified by the startling reports which were continually coming of the success of the French Army. It was not likely that the king should be eager to take part in the contest when from the very commencement things had turned out so unfavourably for the Austrians.

Pitt had warned Prussia in a most absolute manner of her danger. No one could have made it clearer than he did that, should Napoleon succeed in overcoming his present enemies, he would next turn his forces against Prussia. England, true enough, set the king a bad example. Eager that he should decide in favour of the coalition, she held back her own troops. There can be no question that a vigorous demonstration in Flanders would have most probably determined Frederick William to join the other European powers then under arms.

A few days after Haugwitz had left for the French headquarters, Lord Harrowby and Mr. Hammond reached Berlin with offers from Pitt of ample subsidies which would have enabled the Prussian Army to take the field. The *Czar* also wrote to the king from Weimar:

> The state of affairs becomes worse every day; since my departure from Berlin every moment becomes more precious; the fate of Europe lies in your hands. I begin to feel uneasy with regard to Kutuzoff's position; his troops fight bravely, but, contending alone against superior forces, they will be obliged to give way before numbers. I place all my hope in your Majesty, in your friendship, in your firmness.

However, all this insistence to accelerate the commencement of hostilities proved of no avail. The dilatoriness of the king in making up his mind apparently sprung from a desire to see what turn affairs were likely to take.

Prussia was principally answerable for the disasters of the campaign. Here was a golden opportunity thrown away for putting an end to the enemy's advance by threatening Napoleon's communications with the Rhine.

Pitt's conceptions were on a large scale. He had evolved military projects thoroughly in keeping with the immense political matters at issue. He aimed at obtaining what had not been possible since the commencement of the hostilities with France, *viz.* Austria, Prussia, and Prussia closely bound together. He contemplated nothing less than 500,000 veterans arrayed for the fight and led by their sovereigns in person.

There were to be four attacks. One in the north of Germany, by a united force of Russians, Swedes, and English; the second in the valley of the Danube, by the armies of Russia and Austria; a third in Upper Italy, entrusted to the Austrians alone; the fourth in Southern Italy, by a united force of Russians, English, and Neapolitans.

Relying on the powerful influence of Russia which had already overcome the hesitations of the Cabinet of Vienna, Pitt hoped that power would in a like manner be able to persuade the Prussian monarch in casting his lot with the coalition. Counting on this, he had framed the above programme and dreamt of a simultaneous and immediate course of action on the part of all the armies of Europe, supported by the navy of Great Britain.

Whilst the Austro-Russian forces were to advance towards the Upper Rhine, the Prussian Army was to cross the Lower Rhine, and later on an Austrian Army, reinforced by Neapolitan troops, was to push into Lombardy.

An English corps was to make its way along the mouths of the Scheldt, and a combined English, Swedish, and Russian force was to invade Hanover, the latter forming two powerful diversions which would much facilitate the success of the principal operations. In this way Napoleon would have been anticipated in every direction and compelled to maintain an absolutely defensive attitude. Nowhere in the North, in Germany, nor in Italy, could he concentrate forces approaching in number to the armies of the allies, and the French would at last be made to taste the calamities of war and to bear its cost.

Though his inclinations were principally for peace, Pitt was not devoid of that barbaric instinct which lies sleeping in the blood of all men of high courage and strong feeling. He had devised a scheme which would cause the French Army to turn its back on the Channel and make the mighty host encamped around Boulogne go and seek for fresh renown somewhere in the centre of Europe. He well knew that with the object of concentrating his forces on the sands of the Channel Napoleon had left the eastern frontier of France unprotected and totally ungarnished of troops. All that he needed to carry out his plan was soldiers, and as England had them not, all that was left to him was to cultivate the friendship of the Continental governments which had already many causes of quarrel with France, but who needed the means to enter into a state of war and keep the field.

Pitt had the gold, the sinews of war, and used it unsparingly. The object was good—the freedom of his beloved country. He had the courage to incur heavy responsibilities. The moment the continental powers had accepted her subsidies they had become dependent on England, and as Pitt supported their armies, he came to have a powerful voice in the planning of the operations.

But all England's millions were not able to produce an officer of the same calibre as Napoleon. The generals who were opposed to him in 1813 and 1814, after Pitt's death, notwithstanding all the experience they had gained in their wars against the French, agreed to attack the French only when Napoleon was absent. The Archduke Charles might have anticipated Waterloo by half a dozen years, had he known at Essling that the French were running short of ammunition, and that a rise of the Danube had carried away the bridges in their rear. But at that time Napoleon's star was still in the ascendant.

If the army of England was incapable of great things, the armies of the continent were not much better. When looking at the earliest years of the contest against France, at Yalmy, at Marengo, at Austerlitz, at Jena, at Auerstädt and at the Prussian retreat after the last two battles, we see how, through adhering to obsolete methods, the armies of Europe had rendered themselves unfitted to contend on even terms with the more mobile and pliable armies of the French Republic and Empire, led by generals young in age but old in experience, and free from all the pedantry and rigidity of movement which Europe had copied from the great Frederick.

Bülow, in his book on the campaigns of the French in Germany and Italy in 1800, writes contemptuously of the British Army of those days. Had he written a few years later, after the battles of Jena and Auerstädt, when in less than a month the Prussian Army had been swept into space, he might have been, more charitable in his remarks. In true German dictatorial style, he declared the British soldier to be devoid of discipline and the officers to be totally ignorant of their profession. (Bülow, the writer of *Spirit of Modern Warfare*, was brother to the brilliant general, later on Count von Dennewitz. He died in prison because his contemporaries scorned him and disliked the unpleasant truths he uttered. They strove to make people believe he was insane.)

Who could ever have believed it possible that a military power like Prussia would in the space of six weeks have been entirely disarmed and occupied.

We do not wish for a moment to deny the little pains our officers have always taken in mastering the principles of their profession, or their general distaste for learning. No doubt the Prussian officers were very far in advance of them on that point; nevertheless, all their learning stood them in no good stead in the campaign of 1806, because, as Gneisenau himself confesses, in the years of peace the officers had got accustomed to accord enormous importance to insignificant minutiae, and to elementary tactics invented to please the public. Proud of having the reputation of being the best army in Europe, the army imagined itself invincible; whereas in 1806 it was not up to the new order of things. Because it had conquered under a given style of fighting, it considered all changes unnecessary. What progress Prussia made after her humiliating defeat! How little did her army of 1813, the army of Blücher, Gneisenau, Bülow, York, resemble that of Brunswick, of Hohenlohe, and other chiefs! There lies the lesson.

CHAPTER 5

March of the "Grande Armée" to the Rhine

Whilst busy organising and exercising his army at Boulogne, Napoleon's mind kept soaring across the Atlantic and following in imagination the onward course of his great scheme. The time for his gaining the control of the Channel was fast approaching. True enough, things had not quite turned out according to his wishes; Missiessy had brought back his fleet from the West Indies, and Gantheaume had not found a day in which to lead his fleet out of Brest. These were sinister indications; nevertheless, the emperor continued steadfast in trusting in his star.

He could not believe that fortune, which had already so often befriended him, would desert him in this instance. No, he would be able to ferry his victorious legions across, attack, and humble the proud nation which always stood in his way, and whose wealth made it the soul of every coalition on the Continent. (Napoleon's idea was to make England disgorge a very considerable war indemnity, to be used in preparations for the reduction of the continental powers.)

Many of Napoleon's ardent admirers have striven to prove that he was never really serious in his avowed intention of invading England, and that all his preparations around Boulogne were simply undertaken with the object of lulling Austria into a sense of security.

Miot de Melito writes:

> We were soon aware that the emperor, in the execution of a plan already abandoned, had made such demonstrations only to increase the security of the continental powers and lull them to some decisive step which would permit him to speak out and act.

Bourrienne is of the same opinion. He states that Napoleon never seriously entertained the idea of an invasion of England; that he made use of it as a pretext to assemble together a large army. This is the impression that Napoleon was anxious to give.

> To raise such forces in time of peace, there was need of a pretext in order to levy and bring them together without raising the suspicion of continental powers. The pretext was afforded by the project of landing in England.

In his memoirs, Prince Metternich relates a long conversation he had with Napoleon in 1810, in the course of which the emperor admitted that his preparations at Boulogne were principally made to hide his hostile intentions against Austria; that to England he simply intended to cause uneasiness. As it appears that the question had been put by Metternich, it is not unnatural that, by simply giving an affirmative reply, the emperor would have taken to himself merit for the events. In any case, so greatly did Napoleon fail in the matter of veracity as to make his acknowledgement to Prince Metternich a point of little value. It may have pleased him to disown all intention of invading England, and to have assigned a different reason than the true one for the collapse of the undertaking.

Metternich may have imagined himself astute enough to have detected Napoleon's subtle scheme for deluding the Austrians into a sense of perfect security, or, like a fawning and scheming diplomat, may have put to Napoleon a question which he fancied would have flattered his *amour propre*. He could not, however, but have known from the familiar intercourse he had with the French imperial court, how bent Napoleon had been in 1805 to invade England, and how he desired nothing so much. His preparations were in a very forward state, and Austria was still undecided whether to take up arms or not.

As to Napoleon, one can hardly place much reliance in the words he used at a council of state held in January 1805.

Moreover, at that time the powers had not yet been worked up to such a pitch as to indicate an approaching war. It was only some months later that the arrangements for the coalition were sufficiently matured.

Bourrienne's words are:

> England was never so much deceived by Bonaparte as during the period of the encampment at Boulogne.

The lack of common sense, he states, led to a panic in England.

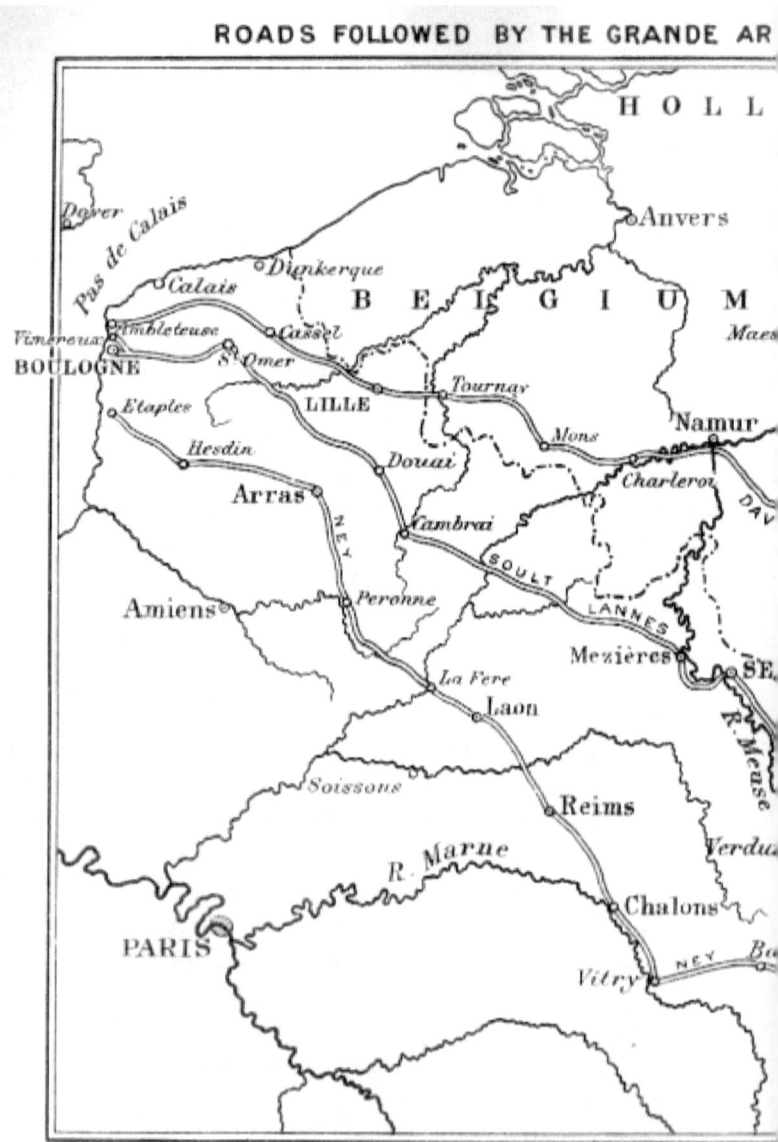

Napoleon, in his manuscript from St. Helena, writes:

> But as menaces cost me nothing, and I had not then any employment for my troops, I thought I might as well garrison them on the coast as anywhere else. It obliged England to raise armaments and provide other means of defence, and as all this pressed hard on her finances, I gained some advantage thereby.

Not only English historians, however, but several eminent French writers, are convinced that Napoleon was fully bent on the invasion, and that war with Austria was an afterthought. Earlier we quoted Thiers' words, and to these we can add those of General Foy:

> We have no doubt that it was his intention to attempt a landing. (*History of the War in the Peninsula under Napoleon.*)

As late as the 22nd of August the emperor wrote to Decrès: "*Pour mois je n'ai qu un besoin, c'est celui de réussir.*" ("As for myself, I need only one thing, and that is to succeed.") He wrote in these terms, for he had foreseen Villeneuve's failure. His foreign minister, nine days before, on the 13th of August, stated that Napoleon had already suspended the execution of his hostile projects, having recognised that he could not go to England with 150,000 men when his southern frontiers (*frontières du midi*) were threatened. To the Austrian officers, whilst Mack's army was laying down its arms, he said:

> I do not know for what reason we are at war; it was not of my seeking. I only wanted to go to war with the English, when your sovereign provoked me.

The following story is given as authentic. On the 29th of October 1804, the emperor was entertaining himself familiarly with his relatives before retiring, and the question under discussion was the invasion of England. Napoleon explained to those present all the measures that had been taken. He concluded by saying that all was arranged, and that he would either perish or plant the French flag on the Tower of London. All his people pressed round him, beseeching him to abandon the enterprise, as his life was too precious for France and for Europe. How cruel of him, they declared, to jeopardise his family and his dearest ones. All the dangers of the enterprise were then painted to him in the most vivid colours; Napoleon was touched by these expressions of attachment, and retired deeply agitated. His family were enchanted at having won him over, as he had been moved even to tears.

There are too many facts to show that Napoleon desired to do something more than frightening England; it would appear from his very words as if he had fully made up his mind to conquer it. He had put all his energy, all his talents into the preparations; he had done everything that it was possible for mortal man to achieve in order to lead the undertaking to a successful termination. His daily increasing animosity towards England, his hopelessness to do anything as long as England possessed the means for subsidizing his enemies on the continent, all spurred him on to remove from his path this great obstacle to universal dominion. I)o not all his words stand as witnesses against him? Can anyone who reflects on all this still believe that the intended invasion was only a make-believe?

What makes it difficult to determine with certitude, whether Napoleon had decided to invade England might be imagined to have been the necessity of imparting his ideas to as few persons as possible. Secrecy was necessary for the success of the undertaking. Thiers believes that the fact has been placed beyond question by the forthcoming correspondence, he writes:

> It has sometimes been doubted, but can be doubted no longer by anyone who sees, as I have seen, several thousands of letters which all combine to the same point.

★★★★★★

Note: Napoleon had determined to carry his enterprise shortly into effect. He desired to cross the Straits about the month of July or August 1804; and if the unbelievers who have cast doubts on his designs could read his confidential correspondence with the Minister of Marine, the endless number of his orders, the secret confiding of his hopes to Cambacérès the High Chancellor, they would entertain no longer any uncertainty regarding the reality of this extraordinary resolve.—Thiers, *Con. et Emp.*

★★★★★★

As one of the proofs, and not the least, Lanfry adduces the commemorative medal prepared for issue. The medal bore the image of Hercules stifling in his arms the giant Anthaeus, with *Descente en Angleterre*; underneath, in small letters, was—*frappée à Londres en 1804.*

★★★★★★

The story is told of Monsieur Denon, director of the emperor's numismatic collection, how he one day presented his master with a medal having Napoleon's head on one side and on the reverse the figure of an eagle strangling a leopard. "And what may this mean, sir?" said the emperor. "Sire," replied Denon, "it is a French eagle choking with its claws the British leopard, principal element in the coat-of-arms of that nation." "Vile flatterer," cried Napoleon, "how dare you say that the French eagle chokes the English leopard! I cannot put to sea a single fisherman's boat that the English don't capture it. Have this medal melted at once, and never show me the like."

******

Count Mathieu Dumas, the very able author of *Précis des Événements Militaires*, reviews the naval forces Villeneuve could bring up Channel. After having combined the squadron at Carthagena with the allied fleet, he could put to sea with forty-three ships of the Line, and, should he come across Lallemand's fleet, he could appear before Brest with a mass of fifty ships, clear the way for Gantheaume, enter the Channel with sixty-eight ships, and cover the getting under sail and crossing of the flotilla. Admiral Collingwood, who was cruising in the neighbourhood of Cadiz with eleven ships, would have taken refuge under the guns of Gibraltar; Lord Cornwallis, rallying for a second time Cochrane's fleet, could not prevent the blockade of Brest being raised, nor oppose more than forty ships to this immense agglomeration of forces. What a combination was this, which, notwithstanding so many contrary chances and such grave faults, still left the possibility of such an enterprise!

Was it possible, after all, that the emperor, who cannot but have known the great inferiority of his navy, would have risked his fleets to be beaten by making them go to the West Indies and back for no reasonable purpose? Baron de Meneval—and he, if anybody, had opportunities of knowing the truth—asserts that no project was more seriously entertained by the emperor than the descent on England, and that Villeneuve's retirement into Cadiz and Austria's declaration of war were the causes of its adjournment. He uses the word adjournment to indicate that Napoleon contemplated at the time returning someday to Boulogne and resuming his preparations for the invasion.

When he quitted Boulogne for Paris on the 4th of September, most minute instructions were given for the protection of the flotilla. He left Marshal Brune with thirty-six battalions for its protection and ordered extensive earthworks to be thrown up round Boulogne to cover the immense magazines he had caused to be formed. The Minister of Marine was ordered to remain at Boulogne to inspect the crews, to arm them, and to form them into battalions. He was also directed to give minute instructions to Rear-Admiral Lacrosse, urging the importance of defending the flotilla and territory.

Notwithstanding the departure of the *Grande Armée*, the English were still disquieted by the presence of the flotilla at Boulogne, by the camps being still garrisoned by troops, and the batteries being kept in a proper state of defence. The British Admiralty believed that the boats of the flotilla could be easily destroyed by fireships. An attempt was made on the 30th of September 1805; it utterly failed, and was not renewed.

******

At the end of September Sir John Moore was sent on board H.M. ship *Antelope* to report as to the possibility of a landing on the French coast near Boulogne with a view to the destruction of the flotilla. His report was that any attempt at landing would be attended with too much risk.

******

In the early part of August, Napoleon apparently did not attach any very great importance to the armaments of the coalition. If fortune would only let him ferry his army across the Channel, he believed that he could have brought the invasion to a conclusion before the Austro-Russians had time to reach the banks of the Rhine.

The emperor was then still over confident in the ultimate result of his plan; he was sanguine of success. On the 2nd of August, as he left for Boulogne, Gantheaume was ordered to keep the Brest fleet in the Bertheaume roadstead ready to sail. This hopeful feeling, however, was not shared by others. His naval experts persisted in taking a gloomy view of the attempt, and did not anticipate a favourable result. His own Minister of Marine, Decrès, much to his vexation, had declared the emperor's plan to be horribly dangerous.

By degrees, it dawned on Napoleon's mind that his great scheme for the invasion of our islands ran a good chance of collapsing. But for this uncertainty he could find no remedy, for all the prospects of glory, all his inducements and words of encouragement, were to all appearance inadequate to raise the courage of his admirals to the necessary pitch.

We can well understand how his proud spirit must have chafed against the discomfiture of his cherished plans. It was a grievous disappointment indeed, and most humiliating to be baffled when everything seemed to promise so well. However, Napoleon was not a man who would stake his success upon one plan alone; like a prudent soldier he had accustomed himself to make his plans in two ways, so as never to be taken unawares, and, thanks to this sensible precaution, he could now conceal the irritation he felt and hide from every one the mortification he had to experience in having to change the destination of his army.

In a conversation he had with Roederer in 1809, the emperor told him:

> I am always at work; I meditate a good deal. If I seem always ready to reply to everything, to face every eventuality, it is because before undertaking anything I have for a long time meditated, I have foreseen what might occur.

At the time when he was devoured by the uncertainty whether Villeneuve was steering for Brest or for Cadiz, the reports from Austria were becoming more alarming. Austria now scarcely aimed at concealment; her troops were assembling in considerable numbers upon the banks of the Adige and the Inn, and were threatening Italy and Bavaria. Everything indicated deep hostility, and a fixed resolution to recommence the war. Napoleon desired a rupture, and was preparing for it.

Fortunately for his plans, Austria had already furnished sufficient provocation, and the news of the formation of a fresh coalition offered him a fine prospect of employment for the army he had gathered round him at Boulogne. By the preparations she was making, Napoleon had been able to foresee that a war with Austria was imminent. Very slowly he had come to recognise that the opinion of his naval advisers was a just one, that nothing was to be hoped for from Villeneuve; that he had reckoned badly when he had placed faith in him, for he was not the man to whom such a task should have ever been assigned.

In his early career Napoleon had always been fortunate, and in this instance, fortune still befriended him in giving him an opportunity for hiding his disappointment, and a promising field where his magnificent army could gather fresh laurels. This was not the only instance in which he hid his discomfiture by finding a field of action elsewhere. Lanfrey has laboured to demonstrate how the emperor worked up a war with Austria in 1809 to hide his failure in Spain.

Whilst Napoleon was in this dilemma, with singular imprudence the Austrian Government offered him an escape from his awkward situation, and a battlefield which, up to that moment, he had been looking for in vain.

Since the division of the Germanic indemnities, Bavaria had become hostile to Austria, and the Cabinet of Vienna was determined that she and; the smaller principalities of Germany should join her standards and make common cause with her against France. It was then that the emperor made up his mind, that he decided to adjourn the invasion of England and to despatch his troops without a moment's loss to the eastern frontier.

Napoleon had a fertile imagination, and no one need ever hope to turn out a great captain without it. Never in the history of wars has a more beautiful conception of a campaign been recorded, or a more masterly handling of an army so strong and so pliant.

One may try to speculate as to what might have happened had Napoleon succeeded in the perilous operation of disembarking in England in spite of the innumerable number of vessels of every size which were ready to dispute the crossing. We know too well that his fleets and flotilla could not maintain a permanent control of the sea. This command would have soon passed away, as all our war vessels then afloat would have combined to attack the French covering fleet. His army of 160,000 men would have found itself in a hostile country without a base of supplies or line of communications. Its position would have been precarious and dispiriting.

England had raised a large number of volunteer corps, numbering, some say, no less than 400,000 men. The regulars, aided by these, and backed up by an intensely patriotic, proud, bold, and combative people, would have paralyzed all his efforts and worn out any force he could have kept together. General Foy (*History of the War in the Peninsula under Napoleon*), states:

> Our soldiers who had returned from Egypt talked to their comrades of the indomitable valour of the English.
>
> ★★★★★★
>
> Note: Sir John Moore writes in his diary: the French prisoners declare that they have never been fought till now; that the actions in Italy were not to be compared to those they had engaged in since we landed.
>
> ★★★★★★

The stubborn resistance the British troops were renowned for would have prevailed; in any case the French forces would have been detained long enough to allow the troops of the coalition to invade

France, which would have been left undefended. No, the expedition to England was not likely to turn out an easy success, nor would Napoleon have been able to borrow for his bulletin the well-known words once uttered by a successful invader of ancient Rome—*Veni Vidi Vici*.

However, whilst no one can but agree that a descent on the coast of Great Britain was a difficult enterprise indeed, we cannot subscribe to the opinion that it was impracticable. Napoleon himself told Lord Whitworth that there were a hundred chances to one against him; still, as circumstances had favoured him in other undertakings, why should they not have come to his aid in this one?

A man of the time wrote:

> Twenty defeats in England after having effected a landing would not give Bonaparte half the uneasiness as finding that he could not effect a landing at all. The chief bent of his mind evidently turned on being able to show his country that he could land, that nothing was impossible to him.

No one has been able to state positively the exact day on which the decision to abandon the operations for the invasion of England was taken. There can, however, be little doubt that it was only when the news of Sir Robert Calder's attack off Finisterre made him acquainted with the fact that the English were on the look-out, and that little of real consequence could be hoped for from Villeneuve. The emperor was well aware how threatening affairs were in his rear, how Russia was advancing, how Austria was arming. He was fully instructed of the Austrian movements both in the Tyrol and on the Danube, and no peaceful protestations on the part of the Austrian Government had been able to put him off his guard. Still it was desirable to surprise the enemy, and the best way for lulling the Austrian cabinet into a dangerous security was, in his opinion, to push forward with more ostensible energy his preparations for his great project, the invasion of England.

We should not possibly be far wrong in assuming that the emperor's mind was made up on the day he dispatched Duroc on a mission to Berlin to secure the co-operation, or at least the neutrality, of the Prussian monarch.

✶✶✶✶✶✶

Michel Duroc, son of Chevalier du Roc, joined the Artillery in March, 1792. During the first Italian campaign Marmont introduced him to Bonaparte, who took him on his staff. With him he went to Egypt and Syria, and was badly wounded at

Saint Jean d'Acre by a shell. Up to the day of his death, no one was more faithful and devoted to the emperor. Many and many were the occasions on which he prevailed on Napoleon, arrested his outbursts of temper or momentary irritation, and turned him from a purpose on which he had set his heart. Duroc knew how to bring him back to a more amiable mood. As he was dying, he said, "I have lived as an honest man; I have nothing to reproach myself with." What an epitaph for any man! Duroc was a safe adviser, a faithful friend, and one of the bravest officers Napoleon ever had.

He was the only person who possessed Napoleon's intimacy. With his death at Reichenbach the world lost much, for had it pleased Providence to spare his life, how many doubtful points in the career of his master would have been cleared, and how many errors would have received authentic correction.

★★★★★★

Duroc quitted the Imperial headquarters on the 24th of August. On the previous day Berthier had written a letter to Marmont to inform him that, should the allied squadrons be prevented by contrary winds from coming up Channel, the emperor would adjourn the expedition to England to the following year. But, added Berthier, before that he would find himself compelled to dissolve the concentration of Austrian troops in the Tyrol.

Napoleon's correspondence with Talleyrand and Cambacérès contains the clearest possible evidence of how frequently he had pondered over the possibility of counter-marching his army. In the long waiting for Villeneuve's arrival he had had plenty of leisure to work out the details of the march to the Rhine. There may have been the simulated agitation which Thiers describes when Napoleon, irritated beyond bounds by Villeneuve's retreat into Cadiz, dictated at one breath his orders for the march of the several army corps with the utmost completeness, but the march had been long thought of and studiously prepared in all its details.

A man of such power of mind cannot but have entertained a suspicion of the uncertainty attending the success of his plans for the humiliation of England, and where it was possible to conceal the fact, he was the last man to show that he had been foiled. If he were able to substitute another purpose for the invasion and hide the discomfiture of his plans with regard to England, it would be a considerable gain; afterwards he might even pretend that the invasion of that country had never been intended, and that the camp was formed at Boulogne solely with the intention of throwing Austria off her guard. Metternich did ask him if such was not the case, and Napoleon did not deny it; the ruse being greatly to his credit, it would have been strange had he disavowed it.

Napoleon may probably have dictated something to Daru, but not the complete programme uttered without pause, when overpowered by anger, and which was punctually followed day by day, league by league, until after the capitulation of Ulm. How could this have been possible, when on the 23rd of August Mack's army was still on the Traun in the camp of Weis, thirteen or fourteen marches from Ulm, and that it did not reach that city before the 20th of September?

The formation of a plan of campaign is a matter that pertains, strictly to the general, and the general who desires to succeed must keep it concealed as long as possible from his adversary. Hardly anyone should share the secret with him, lest it should be divulged. Only a very few discreet officers, very trusted coadjutors, should be taken into confidence, very prudent men on whose discretion the general can safely count.

The utmost possible secrecy was required in this instance, and nothing was omitted to keep the march of the *Grande Armée* from being known. All communication along the left bank of the Rhine was suspended, and the post-offices were occupied. To the Minister of Police, the emperor wrote:

> Forbid the Rhine newspapers to speak of the army: let it be as if it did not exist.

The *Moniteur* abstained from publishing a word of politics, restricting itself simply to commonplace subjects. It only informed the public on the 22nd of September that the Austrians had crossed the Inn on the 7th of that month.

Thinking it was almost impossible to keep his immense movements entirely concealed, the emperor authorised his ministers to acknowledge how, as a precautionary measure, he was despatching 30,000 men to the eastern frontier. He thus repeated what he did in 1800, when he gave out that the Army of Reserve was nothing else but reinforcements intended for Moreau's army in Germany. In Italy the viceroy received the following instructions, "to talk of peace, but to work for war." Bernadotte had orders to tell everyone that he was merely taking the route he was following to conduct his corps back to France.

As the troops marched across the north of France, Paris was likely to remain in ignorance of the movements of the army for some time to come, and with the slow rate of travelling which obtained at that period, the news would have leaked out very slowly. The French Army, in short, marched so quickly that it outran the rumour of its coming. Its appearance on the banks of the Rhine was totally unexpected, for up to the moment when the news startled the Austrian authorities, they still believed it to be placidly resting on the shores of the ocean. The secrecy of the march had been well kept throughout.

As the troops were marching by different roads, it was not likely that the people would have taken in the full extent of the movement, or the greatness of the army that was marching. The Austrians had not reckoned on the possibility of such swift marching, consequently they were not on the look-out for the French; they did not suspect their being so close at hand.

This march can be taken as an excellent example of such an operation, and it is worthy of being closely studied. Rapidity in marching is one of the principal elements of a surprise, and the rapid marching of the French in the Austerlitz campaign frequently helped Napoleon to conceal his purpose. The soldiers avowed that the emperor made more use of their legs than of their bayonets. (In the present war between Japan and Russia the rapid tactical movements of the Japanese have had a considerable influence on their successes. These swift movements enabled them to outflank the strongest Russian positions.)

The happy result of this march must be principally attributed to the following favourable circumstances. First, the *Grande Armée* was marching to the Rhine by three distinct roads, each corps being fractioned into several echelons; the troops, being divided into small units, could consequently undertake longer daily marches. Secondly, there was not the slightest possibility of the enemy obstructing the march. Thirdly, the resources of the country were fully utilized, the local authorities assisting the *Intendance*, the troops being fed and sheltered by their countrymen. Fourthly, the weather was all that could be wished, for it was only when the French Army reached the Danube that it changed and became detestable. To all these favourable circumstances should be added the enthusiasm of the troops, who had in prospect a spell of fighting under the guidance of their beloved emperor.

Officers furnished with funds were sent in advance along these three routes, to look after the collection of provisions and forage for the troops that were coming, and to arrange for quarters. (On the right road Chef d'Escadron Mergez, on the centre one Adjutant-Commandant Dalton, and on the left Chef de Bataillon Lejeune, were the staff officers sent forward to look after the billeting and feeding.) The *prefects* and other officials had also been written to and enjoined to have all that was likely to be required by the soldiers collected in their respective departments or localities. As the troops came up by ten or fifteen thousand at the time, they were provisioned and made comfortable without any serious difficulty or loss of time.

Napoleon, who wished Austria to commit herself so far as to offer him a reasonable pretext for attacking her, had intimated that he would consider an attack by Austria on Bavaria as equal to a formal declaration of war. The Austrians seem to have crossed the Inn at Braunau and at Schoerding on the 8th of September. Murat, travelling incognito in Germany, reported that the Austrians occupied Ulm on the 18th of September. Either date would show that the French were well forward on their march to the Rhine before Austria had taken any decided step. If we accept the first date as correct, the French would have been over two weeks on the march before receiving any actual provocation from Austria.

The emperor, at all times famed for the great pains he took to be well informed, was not likely to neglect that highly important point in the present instance. He knew his men well, for he was remarkably clear-sighted; to gather information, he selected officers of tact and determination who were certain to comply with his directions. Duroc, the Grand Master of the Palace, an officer renowned for his tact and taking manners, was sent, as we have said, on a political mission to Berlin on the 24th of August. He was to seek the co-operation, or, in default of that, the neutrality, of Prussia in the approaching contest with Austria. At the Court of Prussia, he was likely to gather many important details which would prove invaluable to his master.

******

General Rapp states: "Duroc was a man whose services were almost indispensable to the emperor; he always enjoyed the highest favour and the greatest confidence, which he in every respect deserved. Few men were so distinguished by tact, spirit of business, and skill, as Duroc; and at the same time, few men were so remarkable for modesty. His devotion to the emperor was without bounds."

******

Murat had been sent to Bavaria under the assumed name of Colonel Beaumont, with injunctions to examine and reconnoitre the country and procure maps. Lagrange was sent to the Elector to make him decide to co-operate with France. Savary and Bertrand were dispatched to Franconia, Suabia, and Bavaria to explore, to ascertain the nature of the routes which led from the Rhine to the Danube. General Thiard was sent to Carlsruhe to negotiate an alliance with the Grand Duke of Baden.

Mouton was sent to gain over the Elector of Würtemberg, as the French had to march across his states. Mouton had a difficult nut to crack, but he was firm, and succeeded. "*Que vient faire ici votre Bonaparte? Un prince de hier, un souverain parvenu me faire violence! a moi, prince ancien et de race de princes.*" ("What is your Bonaparte doing here? A prince of yesterday, a sovereign who has managed to do violence to me! to me, old prince and race of princes.") Very fine words; but he soon began to bargain, and, as the price of his friendship, asked for some possessions which encroached on his, and that the electorate should be turned into a kingdom. When the A.D.C. reported the result of the interview to Napoleon, he burst into a loud laugh and replied, "Very well, I do not wish anything better. Let him be a king, if that is his desire."

It was at Boulogne, in the summer of 1805, after the troops had commenced to march for the Rhine, that Napoleon constituted the *Grande Armée*. Its organisation was the subject of an order of the day issued on the 30th of August. This army, of which he was so justly proud, and in speaking of which he said, "I had the best army in the world," had been gathering for the last two years on the shores of the Channel. It was originally intended for the invasion of England.

How often have we to repeat Rüstow's saying, "*Une bonne préparation à la guerre a été de tout temps un moyen essentiel de victoire, de succès.*" (A sound preparation for war has been at all times an essential factor of victory and success.) For his purposed invasion of England, the emperor had collected his troops round Boulogne, Ambleteuse, Vimereux, and Ostend. Always careful in looking after the superiority of his forces over those of the enemy, he had drawn to these camps the very best soldiers of the empire. In these camps, the French soldiers had been steadily drilled in all kinds of evolutions and manoeuvres, being in that way accustomed to every description of work, and at the same time hardened to bear serious and continuous fatigue. Exposed to unbroken labour and subject to a rigorous discipline, the French were formed in these camps into perfect soldiers, so that at the outbreak of the war Napoleon had at his command a body of drilled men the like of which it had never been his good fortune to command in his former campaigns.

The other armies still adhered to the Prussian school, which demanded extra accuracy in the manoeuvres, measured and well-timed evolutions; but the first battle of the Revolution had suppressed that system. The Revolution had likewise swept away from the French Army the immense importance hitherto attached to minutiae. The soldier had ceased to be regarded as a machine. The army was full of enthusiasm, a quality so necessary, above all in an offensive war, a war which is so well adapted to the fiery character of the French. Astonishing was the enthusiasm shown by all ranks of the army on learning that they were to march into Germany.

Besides the troops encamped on the shores of the Channel, Bernadotte held Hanover with his army corps, and Marmont had another in Holland. These two corps, being the 1st and 2nd, were destined to form the left wing of the *Grande Armée*. Massena was intended to replace Jourdan in the command of the army of Italy, and his corps, the 8th, was to constitute the right wing of the same. The centre was to be formed of the troops coming from Boulogne, the 3rd, 4th, 5th, and 6th Army Corps and the reserves, amongst which was comprised the 7th Corps.

When at its full, the *Grande Armée* stood as follows:—

	Commander.	Strength.	Generals of Division.
1st Corps,	Bernadotte,	17,000 men	La Raffinière, d'Erlon.
2nd ,,	Marmont,	20,000 ,,	Boudet, Grouchy, Dumonceau.
3rd ,,	Davout,	26,000 ,,	Friant, Goudin, Boursier.
4th ,,	Soult,	40,000 ,,	Vandamme, Legrand, Saint-Hilaire.
5th ,,	Lannes,	18,000 ,,	Oudinot (Grenadiers), Suchet.
6th ,,	Ney,	24,000 ,,	Dupont, Loison, Malher.
7th ,,	Augereau,	14,000 ,,	Baraguay d'Hilliers (Foot Dragoons), Mathieu, Dejardins.
Imperial Guard (Infantry and Cavalry),		7,000 ,,	Mortier, Bessières.
Cavalry Reserve and Horse Artillery,		22,000 ,,	
	Total	188,000	

The Artillery numbered some 340 pieces.

The cavalry reserve was composed of six divisions, two of heavy cavalry, *carabineers*, *cuirassiers*—nicknamed *gros-talons* on account of their heavy boots—and four of dragoons. The first division of heavy cavalry was commanded by General Nansouty, and the second by General d'Hautpoul. General Bleim commanded the first reserve of

CUIRASSIERS 1805

dragoons, General Walter the second, General Beaumont the third, and General Bourcier the fourth.

Each corps was complete in infantry, had the necessary guns, and some regiments of light cavalry, hussars and *chasseurs*, just what was needed for outpost and reconnoitring. Murat was to command the cavalry reserve, but the emperor retained under his own immediate direction a large reserve of cavalry and artillery. From this reserve he intended reinforcing with guns and cavalry any of his corps which he might detach to carry out some special operation.

Napoleon looked on the Imperial Guard as the reserve of the whole army, and as such he held it more immediately under his personal control. The soldiers of the guard were the *crème* of the whole army, the strongest and the bravest men. At a later period, of infantry there was the old guard, the middle guard, and the young guard. Admission to the first required twelve years' service in the army, to the second eight, to the third four. Soldiers who had served in two campaigns were selected for transfer to the guard. The guard marched on the high-road and fought in full dress.

As the veteran soldier reserves his cartridges for the most important moments, so did the emperor keep his guard to be employed in the crisis of the battle. The Imperial Guard was reserved to join in the fray on urgent occasions only, consequently it was sparingly brought forward to fight. The soldiers of the Line who envied their privileges, called, on this account, their comrades of the guard the immortals.

Almost equal to the guard in appearance was a *corps d'élite*, all picked men, formed by Junot at Arras, generally known as Oudinot's Grenadiers. *C'est le coeur qui fait le grenadier,* (It's the heart that makes the grenadier.) This famous corps consisted of ten battalions each of 800 men, drafted from the grenadier companies of regiments not intended to take part in the campaign. The grenadiers formed part of Lannes' corps, the 5th.

At Arras, in mid-winter, these grenadiers, formed into battalions, were exercised morning and evening in a new description of manoeuvres which had been assigned to them for trial by the First Consul, and which he intended to have performed before him.

Besides the seven corps as given above, there was the 8th, Massena's, which was to operate in Italy, and 25,000 Bavarians. The smaller German states furnished a contingent of 12,000 men, who, if not the best of soldiers, were still useful for guarding the communications.

At the end of August, the 1st and 2nd Army Corps were in Hanover and Holland. Bernadotte, who commanded the 1st, received his orders on the 1st of September to set out on the following day. He was to concentrate his corps at Goettingen by the 6th, and to time his march so as to reach Würzburg by the 20th of September. The difficulty in his case was to conceal the real object of his march; and, to put people off their guard, he spread a report that the movement of his troops was being effected in compliance with orders he had received for withdrawing beyond the frontier.

Napoleon had ordered him to dissemble as long as it was possible; by his speech and that of his generals, he was to add strength to the already prevalent report that he was conducting his troops back to France, and that the march of the corps coming from Holland had no other object but to replace the troops which had evacuated Hanover.

Bernadotte deposited all the artillery captured from the Hanoverians in the fortified city of Hameln, stocked the place with provisions and ammunition for three months, and left there as a garrison all the soldiers who were not considered robust enough to endure the severe strain of a campaign. This done, he marched out of Goettingen on the 12th of September at the head of 17,000 able-bodied men.

The marshal was called to display considerable tact, and had to humour the Elector, the nobility, and the army of Hesse, as all combined to look upon the crossing of their territory by a foreign army in the light of a stain on their honour. As the Elector had considerable means of resistance at his disposal, it was necessary to maintain all the order and discipline that was to be expected from friendly soldiers, and to observe the utmost punctuality in all payments.

Bernadotte marched due south; the French troops were concentrated at Münden on the Weser on the 15th of September, and on the following day bivouacked on the border of the forest of Münden, two leagues from Cassel. The corps was at Cassel on the 17th, at Giessen on the 20th, and on the 27th the marshal had his headquarters at Würzburg, the whole of his troops being assembled round that city.

The emperor expressly wished Bernadotte to bring his troops fresh into Würzburg, but the marshal gave them unnecessary marches, so that they were quite fatigued on reaching that city.

The two divisions of infantry commanded by Generals Rivaud and Drouet, the cavalry under the orders of General Kellermann, and the artillery under those of Eblé, crossed Cassel, marching past the guard and a portion of the electoral troops which were drawn up under arms. (The lesser German states on the Rhine, influenced by Prus-

INFANTRY OF THE LINE

INFANTRY RECEIVING CAVALRY

sia, did not keep to their engagements. The Elector of Hesse-Cassel had given. Bernadotte a free passage through his States for thirty-five days. But he soon revoked this permission and declared his neutrality.)

At Würzburg, Bernadotte received Napoleon's intimation that the Bavarian troops were placed under his orders, and were to form part of his corps. To effect a junction with the French, the Bavarians had been ordered to ascend the Rednitz by Forcheim and Nuremberg and proceed to Weissenburg. Bernadotte's divisions were to reach the latter place, marching by Offenheim, Anspach, and Gunzenhausen. As Mack was holding his forces concentrated at Ulm, Memmingen, and Stockach, it was almost a necessity for Bernadotte to cross the territory of Anspach, form a junction with the Bavarians at Weissenburg, and march to the Danube. On the 6th of October, Bernadotte was at Weissenburg, Davout being then at Monheim, Soult at the gates of Douauwört, Ney at Giengen, Lannes to the west of Nördlingen, and Murat close to the banks of the Danube.

A courier left Boulogne on the 28th of August bearing orders for Marmont from the chief of the staff. The general was directed to break up his camp at Zeist on the 2nd of September, and to march at the head of 20,000 men, 5000 of whom were to be Dutch. He was to take with him forty pieces of artillery, well horsed, two French cavalry regiments, and as much Batavian cavalry as he could; with this force he was to march by the left bank of the Rhine to Mayence. Marmont's corps was to march by three roads, so arranged as to concentrate at Mayence by the 27th. The march was to be resumed on the 27th, the corps to proceed by way of Frankfurt to Würzburg.

Marmont's corps comprised two divisions of French infantry, the divisions of Boudet and Grouchy, and one division of Batavians under Dumonceau. The infantry numbered thirteen French and eleven Batavian battalions; the cavalry seven French and four Batavian squadrons. All computed, the corps numbered 21,000 infantry and 3000 cavalry. With this was a fine body of artillery.

The march of the 2nd Corps was very creditable. The general, who made use of the Rhine for the transport of his war materials, was at Nimèguen on the 12th, and by the 18th had reached Cologne. On the 22nd and 23rd he was at Mayence, on the 25th and 26th he quitted Mayence, and on the 30th of September and the 1st of October he approached Würzburg. His troops marched for twenty consecutive days without a halt, nevertheless on their arrival at Würzburg there were only nine men who had not been able to keep up with the rest. This was very remarkable, for it is at the commencement of a campaign when the marches always tell most on tender constitutions; it is then that nature compels many willing soldiers to remain in the rear.

The troops of the Elector of Bavaria were to join the French. Deroy's troops were concentrated at Bamberg by the 1st of October. Wrède remained at Ulm till the 16th of September, almost up to the very day the Austrians appeared under its walls. On the 27th he took post on the right of the Mein between Altheim and Klein Ochsenfurt.

General Deroy had collected at Bamberg all the troops quartered at Munich and Ratisbonne, 16,500 in all, Wrède brought 6000 from Ulm, and 4500 were in Franconia.

The Bavarian troops were divided into six brigades, under the orders of a commander-in-chief, General Deroy, aided by a second in command, General Wrède.

In the last days of September, the left wing of the *Grande Armée* had completed its concentration, and Napoleon had in Franconia, six days' march from the Danube—

Bernadotte with	17,000 men
Marmont ,,	20,000 ,,
The Bavarians	27,000 ,,
Total	64,000

The orders for the march of the centre were issued on the evening of the 27th of August. The army was to march forthwith by three routes and by divisions in three successive days—that is, the first division of each corps was to set out on the first day, the second division was to follow on the second day, and the third division on the third day.

The march of the *Grande Armée* for the Rhine actually commenced on the 26th of August with the departure of Nansouty's division.

The troops from Ambleteuse, under the orders of Marshal Davout (3rd Corps), were to march off between the 2nd and 5th of September by way of Cassel, Lille, Namur, Luxembourg, Sarre-louis, and Deux Ponts on to Mannheim, and to arrive at the last place by the 25th.

The troops from Boulogne, under Marshal Soult (4th Corps), were to begin to get under way on the 29th of August, marching by Saint-Omer, Douai, Cambrai, Mézières, Sedan, Verdun, Metz, and Landau, making for Spires, which they were likewise to reach on the 25th of September.

The 5th Corps, under Marshal Lannes, was to set out from Vimereux on the 30th of August, and to reach Strasburg on the 23rd of September, preceding the 4th Corps as far as Metz by one day's march.

The troops from Etaples (6th Corps), commanded by Marshal Ney, were to start on the 28th of August, moving by way of Hesden, Arras, Péronne, La Fére, Reims, Toul, Nancy, Lunéville, and Zabern, being timed to reach Hagenau on the 25th of September.

The Imperial Guard was timed to arrive at Strasburg on the 22nd of September, and the headquarters of the army were to be established in that city.

The two reserves of cavalry were to precede the army, and to be in the departments of the Upper Rhine at Pirmasens, Schlettstadt, Molsheim, and Obernheim between the 16th and 21st of September; Murat's headquarters were to be at Schlettstadt.

It was calculated that the entire force could thus arrive on the banks of the Rhine between the 21st and 25th of September. It was intended that the army should occupy a position with the extreme right at Strasburg, the centre at Spiers, and the left at Mayence.

The 7th Corps from Brest, under Marshal Augereau, 14,000 men, principally from troops destined to embark at Brest in Gantheaume's fleet, was not supposed to reach the Rhine until fifteen days after the others; being fifteen days behind the rest, it was to be considered in the light of a reserve. Augereau was instructed to form his two divisions in Brittany, to march by Alençon, Lens, Langres, and Belfort. His corps was to cover the right flank of the *Grande Armée*, and extend from the Black Forest to the Tyrolese Alps.

Napoleon, who witnessed the departure of most of the divisions of his army, was much gratified in beholding how full of ardour the soldiers were, and how the promise held out to them of a great and eventful war had rendered them happy. The men were mostly tried soldiers—men who had fought in Italy, in Egypt, and in Germany. They stepped out lustily, with a martial appearance, which inspired confidence. Old associations and recollections were acting upon their mind; their buoyant spirits spoke well for the coming operations. All were animated by a too eager desire to come to blows with the foe. Most of the soldiers had already drunk deeply enough of the intoxicating draught of applause; a far-off expedition, toilsome marches, heavy fatigues, and bloody combats seemed welcomed as holding for them so many further chances of satisfying their ambition and desire for glory.

Though there were a goodly number of conscripts in the ranks,

Cuirassier

they bore the march admirably. There were few sick, no laggards, and what told most in favour of the soldiers was that the men who were given leave, or who took it without asking, to spend a few hours with their families, had almost all rejoined before the army crossed the Rhine. Soult's army corps, the most numerous, went from Boulogne-sur-mer to Spires in twenty-nine days without losing a single man by desertion or sickness.

Looking at the large number of men marching, what seems almost incredible is that an army which had marched 400 miles at the end of the summer and at the commencement of the autumn, with very few days of rest, should have been so free of sick and laggards.

Not a single complaint was uttered against the troops; their discipline on the march was all that could be desired. The army crossed France without causing any trouble or doing the slightest damage. Everything was done with surprising order. A stay of a couple of years in the camps by the Channel had greatly improved the discipline of the French troops.

The weather was fine, the soldiers well cared for, and the people glad to see them, consequently every condition was favourable. The people stood at their doors or windows watching their gallant troops as they went by, and many a tender-hearted woman offered a fervent prayer for a blessing on their arms.

Napoleon had already laid solid foundations in Germany. Bavaria had promised her armed co-operation; Würtemberg, Baden, and Hesse Darmstadt were willing to remain neutral.

The march to the Rhine was the first act of this prodigious campaign: The frontier was to he attained by rapid marches; few or no convoys were allowed, the troops had to subsist as well as they could on the resources of the country. The essential point was to get over the ground quickly, to surprise the enemy by the rapidity of the march, and in such a manner that it might become quite impossible for him to alter his dispositions and to concentrate his forces at the right time in the most necessary points. The legs of the soldier, as a French writer puts it, behold in them the instrument of surprise!

People who are accustomed to give a willing ear to the croakings of our special correspondents, of inexpert critics, would derive a good deal of instruction by learning how an army which had been preparing for two years, which was commanded by an autocrat, by the greatest genius for war the world has ever seen, by a leader renowned for the attention he paid to the details of his military machine, left for the frontier incomplete in many respects.

Looking at the suddenness of the movement, all the steps taken for collecting provisions, forage, and fuel were not pursued in all places with the same energy. The warning sent to collect a certain amount of supplies in some localities arrived too late, the notice received was far too short. To get billets ready was not as difficult a matter as to collect provisions. From the official correspondence still extant, it appears that the population did not everywhere show the same alacrity in preparing what was needed by the troops.

According to Captain Romagny, it was intended that each division should canton every evening with a depth equal to its echelon of march, and, as far as it was possible, along the road itself—an arrangement which would have relieved the troops from much unnecessary tramping. However, with regard to billeting, complaints were prevalent that the civil authorities had often billeted the soldiers out in the country, several miles away from their headquarters, which led to unnecessary fatigue, both at the conclusion and at the commencement of the day's march, whereas all should have been lodged as near as possible to the road they were marching on.

In his preparations for the invasion of England the emperor had experienced considerable difficulty in getting remounts for the artillery and cavalry, so much so that it had been his intention, had he landed in England, to mount 8000 dragoons on English horses. When he turned his back on England and marched his army to the Rhine, he had to resort to all kinds of measures to obtain horses; he got them from farmers, he got them from Italy, he got them from Hanover, still many horsemen left for the Rhine on foot, to be mounted later as opportunities occurred. Commandant Gérome (*Essai Historique sur la tactique de la cavalerie*) states that in 1805, for want of horses, the emperor formed each dragoon regiment of two battalions; the first mounted, the second on foot, waiting until it could receive horses either captured or requisitioned.

Later on, bad weather, the bad state of the roads, and the inexperience of the riders over-fatigued the horses. Many, thin, galled, and out of condition, soon became inefficient. What much led to their wasted condition was that they did not receive the oats their exertions demanded.

But the principal deficiency, and the one most felt, was money. There was not enough to pay the troops with, to purchase necessary articles of equipment—boots and overcoats—to pay the drivers of requisitioned transport, etc.

The difficulty of land transport was considerable; the carriages obtained had no covering, and the goods were destroyed. The drivers taken across to Germany, much against their will, deserted with their horses. In one corps alone (Soult's) 300 requisitioned horses disappeared after the crossing of the Rhine.

In short, the condition of the *Grande Armée*, when it crossed over into Germany, was not quite satisfactory. The supplies were scanty, and the marshals had procured the transport present with the troops at the last moment, and by resorting to all manner of expedients.

Napoleon's genius did not allow his initiative to abate for a moment through these deficiencies.

Besides the troops left at Boulogne under Marshal Brune for the protection of the flotilla, as we have already said, the emperor, always foreseeing, decreed the reorganisation of the National Guard. He also called to the colours the levy of that year, and the remaining part of the contingent of the preceding years; besides, by an anticipatory levy he drafted into the army all those who would have attained the required age in the first three months of 1806. These levies gave him a reserve of 150,000 men, who were to be concentrated on the Rhine, and there trained and exercised under the supervision of Marshals Kellermann and Lefebvre.

Early in September Pitt had attained his object. The legions which had threatened to invade England were well forward in their march to the Rhine. The Franco-Spanish fleet lay intact in Cadiz, and when on the following month issued from port, it headed for the Mediterranean, and not for the Channel.

Chapter 6

From the Rhine to the Danube

Until war was declared the allies believed that they had all the time required for collecting their forces. Napoleon had, however, calculated the march of his army with great accuracy, and the secrecy of the movement had been well kept. Whilst the Austrians believed the French troops peacefully encamped on the shores of the ocean, behold, here they were on the Rhine, ready to overrun Southern Germany.

The astonishment of the allies, indeed, was great. They had not reckoned on such rapid marching; when they had persuaded themselves that it would take the French at least sixty-five days to get from Boulogne to the Lech, there they were on the Rhine already in twenty-seven days.

Well has it been said that the good marcher is the best of soldiers. With very good reason the emperor could boast that in this campaign he had destroyed the enemy more by his rapid marching than by anything else, that victory depended on the soldiers' legs.

With regard to marches, the following is what occurred to Baron Lejeune when orderly officer to Marshal Berthier at Boulogne, as narrated in his memoirs.

After he had made all his preparations to follow the Imperial Staff to Alsace, he received orders from Berthier not to leave Boulogne till he had sent off by the quickest route to Germany 300,000 pairs of shoes, which were to be delivered to him from the military stores. This order upset him entirely. He was only able to rejoin the emperor after the Battle of Elchingen. Lejeune, *Mémoires*, says:

> In giving the emperor an account of my mission, and saying to him, 'The shoes are there,' I could not help grumbling at having been reduced to the position of a mere army contractor,

and deprived of the honour of being present at the opening scenes of the campaign; to which he replied with a smile, 'What a child you are! You do not seem to understand the importance of the service you have just rendered; shoes help on marches, and marches win battles; you will get your turn as everyone else.'

What immense alterations these past hundred years have brought about in the art of war! One might at first sight feel disposed to think that it is well-nigh impossible to gather useful principles from the wars of the past; but it is not so.

The campaign of Austerlitz, for example, was principally remarkable for its strategy, and strategy has not undergone anything like the alterations tactics have experienced. Nor have all the improvements in range and accuracy of fire-arms affected greatly the military administration and the maintenance of an army in the field. The alterations principally regard the battlefield, the conduct of the action itself; what relates to the measures taken to mystify the enemy, to conceal from him our intentions, and to baffle his plans, are as much the outcome of forethought, calculation, and knowledge of human nature as heretofore.

Strategy, the clever hoodwinking of the adversary, in which our troops suddenly appear where they are least expected and defeat by the effect of the surprise more than by anything else, has been more or less the same in all ages.

Strategy is, first of all, an affair of the intellect; none but a very able commander can plan out a brilliant campaign. In this, time has wrought no change. But, to carry into effect the plan once formed, it must be kept secret, and it is on this point that strategy has been undermined by the inventions which have been introduced and perfected during the last century. The electric telegraph, the speedy travelling by rail, the extension of the public press, the great postal development, have all combined to lift the veil of secrecy, so much needed to hide the movements of armies. The march of Napoleon's *Grande Armée* to the banks of the Rhine would in our days soon have been wired or communicated to all foreign powers. It might have certainly been hidden by resorting to all manner of pretexts and false reports, but the greatest artifice and the most cunning measures taken to keep it from getting abroad might possibly have turned out insufficient.

Wireless telegraphy, which has only begun to be employed in war, is certain to render immense assistance to an army. There are no wires to cut and interrupt communication, whilst this can be established in

MARCH OF THE GRANDE

ARMÉE TO THE DANUBE.

far less time than would be required to run up an ordinary telegraph line. The whereabouts of corps and divisions of an army settling late after sundown in their bivouacs can be soon ascertained, all such being placed in communication with headquarters and each other. The difficulties experienced under the present system in issuing orders and instructions to them and to the depots in rear, particularly by night, may be reduced to a minimum when wireless telegraphy can be employed.

Strategy therefore has, though to a much lesser extent than tactics, been modified by modern inventions. Much talent can nevertheless still be displayed in concealing the concentration and movements of an army. Of this we have a fine example in the massing of the German armies in 1870 in front of Weissenburg and Forbach. Besides, have we not seen former and forgotten methods often revived, altered, necessarily, in such a way as to suit the circumstances? The student will recall as one of the most remarkable the large employment the German staff made of cavalry to screen the advance of the German armies in the 1870 campaign. Moltke had made a thorough study of war, and with the most happy results.

What was most admirable in the campaign of 1805 was Napoleon's strategy; it was simply a masterpiece.

Alison relates how the French soldiers said to each other:

> The little corporal has discovered a new method of carrying on war; he makes more use of our legs than of our bayonets.

The fact was that counting on the mobility of his army over the tardiness of the allies, he had foreseen all the advantages this would have on the carrying out of his plan.

Whatever alterations may have taken place since those years, the endurance of man has not decreased; he can march now as well as ever, and the general who can urge his army to get quickest over the ground will always have an immense superiority over his adversary. In war there is absolutely nothing so precious as time. It is possible to make up for other shortcomings, but never for loss of time. By a rapid march to the Rhine and timely preparations, Napoleon gained immensely over the allies who had greater distances to march, and made a much later start. In every period of the campaign, Napoleon was prompt to act; he was resolute, and lost no time.

All was ready for the crossing of the Rhine. General Songis had constructed two bridges, one in front of Spires, the other near Knielingen, on a level with Durlach. A portion of the *Grande Armée* was already on the rght bank of the river when Napoleon arrived at Strasburg on the evening of the 26th of September.

In point of administration, the lessons taught by this campaign are very useful. It must at any time, without proper and timely preparation, be a most arduous enterprise to move an army of 180,000 combatants through any country, however friendly and well-disposed its inhabitants may be. In the campaign of 1805, even the march of the French Army across French territory was not quite free from hardships. The population of every halting station alike was not well-pleased to part with a large portion of their provisions and forage. It was this excessive demand that gave rise to many complaints. There being no magazines, no sooner had the troops set foot on the enemy's territory than the subsistence of the troops became very precarious. It was all very well to assign to each army corps a given zone of country from which it was to draw the supplies it needed; but as the troops were always moving, there was not the time necessary for serving the requisitions and collecting the supplies.

The allies were not in a very much better plight; they had not long gathered round Olmütz at the camp of Olschan when it was found that supplies were already becoming scarce; so much so that Kutuzoff recommended retiring a few marches in order to abandon a country which had become exhausted.

By means of prodigious marches, Napoleon carried his army from Boulogne to the Rhine. Then, whilst by false demonstrations he kept Mack's regard steadily turned towards the Black Forest, he hastened to occupy the line of the Lech in rear of the Austrians, in this way closing their natural line of retreat on Vienna, and by detachments on the northern affluents of the Danube, their indirect line of retreat on Bohemia. This done, he turned against the Austrians echeloned round Ulm.

The crossing of the Rhine was turned into a veritable festival by the French troops. The soldiers, who had bedecked their head-gear and adorned their uniforms with sprigs of oak and green leaves, marched past their generals uttering loud shouts of *Vive l'Empereur!* The presence of Napoleon was hailed by his soldiers as a certain pledge of victory.

The recruits emulated the ardour of the veterans. The latter pointed out to them far beyond the river the mountains they had crossed several times before, and the direction of the battlefields on which they had already fought and won. This stimulated the earnestness of the young soldiers, who were most eager to come across the enemy.

On the 25th of September, Murat, with the main part of the cavalry, three divisions of dragoons commanded by Klein, Beaumont, and Walther, about 7,000 men, with Lannes at the head of Oudinot's fine division of grenadiers, from 7,000 to 8,000 strong, supported by 2,000 heavy cavalry under d'Hautpoul, crossed the Rhine at Strasburg by the Kehl bridge, as if making for the defiles of the Black Forest.

Napoleon, who left Paris on the 24th of September, in two days was at Strasburg. That day, the 26th, the 6th Corps crossed the Rhine by a bridge thrown across it, in front of Durlach, and marched for Stuttgard by way of Winsheim. The 4th Corps crossed the river by a bridge of boats at Spires, and moved on Heilbronn on the 27th; the 5th crossed at Mannheim, its advanced guard moving on the heights of Ingelfingen. The human tide continued to flow hour after hour; there was no pause.

Much of the art of war lies in deceiving. By demonstrations and false reports, Napoleon induced the Austrians to believe that it was his intention to advance through the passes of the Black Forest by Gengenbach and the Hornberg; nevertheless, he was working by his left. In this manner he succeeded in getting between the Russians and the Austrians, and after several conflicts and most brilliant strategical manoeuvres, he cut Mack's army from its line of communications and shut it up in Ulm.

This was a line piece of deception, and, as such, the evolution should interest us greatly, for we, of all nations, understand so little the value of circumventing our opponent in war.

Napoleon employed his cavalry to deceive Mack with regard to the line of advance which his army would follow. For this purpose, no other arm can secure the same effect. Cavalry can push boldly forward for a considerable distance, can perplex the enemy by appearing in many quarters almost at simultaneous moments; it can convey the idea that it is covering the advance of a very large army. This is all due to rapidity of motion, which enables cavalry to be very enterprising, whilst, if adroitly handled, it can withdraw from any impending danger. Infantry might find itself drawn into a fight and lose good men in a manoeuvre which is nothing beyond a feint. Cavalry, on the other hand, can clear the ground quickly, leaving the enemy puzzled and unable to grasp the real object the mystifying horsemen had in view. Murat appeared in succession at the end of each of the mountain passes, but he simply showed himself, and this done, speedily withdrew. Some provisions had been demanded in that direction with the object of inducing the enemy further into error.

The operations for the capture of Ulm after the 6th of October were carried out in detestable weather. It had been moderately fine up to the crossing of the Danube, then of a sudden the weather broke, and became dreadful; it rained first, then snow fell heavily; this melted, turned into thick mud, and rendered the roads nearly impracticable.

The march of the French to the Rhine was a masterpiece, and the same may be well said of the march from the Rhine to the Main and to the Danube. If there ever was a commander who mystified his adversary in any campaign, it was Napoleon in 1805. With the corps of Guards, he quitted Strasburg on the 1st of October, and arrived at Ludwigsburg on the 3rd; there he concluded an alliance with the Elector of Würtemberg on the 4th. He then directed the march of his army so as to be in a position to concentrate at any moment 86,000 men belonging to the Imperial Guard, reserve cavalry, the 5th and 6th Corps, and one division of the 4th.

Whilst Soult and Davout were advancing in the valley of the Neckar, and Ney on Stuttgart, Lannes and Murat were making constant demonstrations at the entrance of the Black Forest, with the object of imposing on Mack, and of confirming him in the belief of a coming frontal attack. Soon Murat was recalled, but be left in front of the Black Forest Bourchier's dragoon division, which had lately arrived. Murat, with his other divisions, marched on Stuttgart and Ludwigsburg.

Nothing took place but slight cavalry skirmishes with the Austrians. There was no indication whatsoever that Mack intended to molest the flank march which was to lead the French on his rear. Napoleon expected to have to fight in the plains of Nördlingen, and had taken dispositions to meet such an eventuality.

One thing especially needful before drawing the sword is to select able leaders and officers to fill the most important posts, and to let the choice fall on men of reputed ability, who enjoy the confidence of the Government and are popular with the troops.

No officer in the Austrian Army enjoyed such a well-earned reputation as the Archduke Charles. He was the only military competitor Napoleon had reason to respect. The archduke, however, tried his very utmost, as he had already done in 1800, to dissuade the Emperor of Austria from going to war with France. He pointed out that Prussia was not at all likely to be persuaded to give up her neutrality, that the contingents of the minor German states were of little worth, and that the combined forces of Austria and Russia would not be sufficient of themselves to battle with success against Napoleon. The most forcible argument he adduced was that Austria would be made to feel the weight of Napoleon's first blows before the Russians could put in an appearance on the field.

✶✶✶✶✶✶

Another officer who had never offered any but wise counsel to his sovereign, and who afterwards played a distinguished part in this campaign, the Prince of Lichtenstein, was also strongly opposed to the war.

✶✶✶✶✶✶

Russia nourished a double resentment against the Archduke Charles. One of old date, which arose from the defeat of the Russian forces at the battle of Zurich; the other, a more recent one, was the well-known opposition of the prince to the war. Russia intrigued to have the archduke sent to command the Austrian forces in Italy, so that there should be no able competitor to claim the supreme command of the allied armies in Germany, or any Austrian commander to reap the lion's share of the glory accruing from any brilliant success that might follow.

In an evil hour for Austria its Cabinet assigned to the archduke the command of the army in Italy, for in Italy were the provinces which it had the greatest desire to recover. The nominal command of the army of the Danube was conferred on the Archduke Ferdinand, though its real commander was Field-Marshal Lieutenant Mack.

The Archduke Ferdinand of Este, a youth of twenty-five years, had behaved very creditably in the campaigns of 1799 and 1800. In 1805 he showed that if he had less experience than Mack, he far surpassed him in spirit and enterprise.

✶✶✶✶✶✶

Mack was conspicuous for the bravery he had displayed in the Seven Years' War and against the Turks. He had been chief of the staff of the Austrian Army in 1793 at the Battle of Neerwinden. On the 27th of March he and Dumouriez held a conference, in which the treason of the French general was settled. He was already celebrated for his ill-luck when commanding the Neapolitan army in 1798- 1799. On that occasion he occupied Rome, from which city he was chased by General Championnet. After this he evacuated, almost without firing a shot, the position taken to cover Naples. On the 21st of December 1798, King Ferdinand fled to Sicily, and on the 10th of January Mack signed a capitulation, by virtue of which he surrendered all the fortified places and all the magazines to the French and agreed to pay a contribution of ten millions.

To save himself from being torn to pieces by the Neapolitans, Mark had to take refuge in Championnet's camp. He was sent to Paris, a prisoner on parole, and exchanged for General Alexander Dumas, the celebrated novelist's father, who had been captured coming from Egypt, when the ship *Belle Maltaise,* from stress of weather, and being in a very leaky condition, had been compelled to put in at Taranto.

******

Metternich, (*Memoirs of Prince Metternich*), writes:

> Taught by the defeats of the earlier campaigns, and convinced by experience that the. means applied in these campaigns were insufficient, and that Napoleon must be met by other generals than those who held the command in previous wars, the emperor had singled out General Mack, who stood high in the estimation of the army. Events afterwards proved how unhappy this choice was. Mack possessed many estimable qualities, but he should never have been raised to the post of supreme command. His intelligence, industry, and perseverance fitted him for the place of Quartermaster-General: the task of commanding an army was beyond his powers.

Sloane states that Mack enjoyed a swollen reputation, and that Nelson, amongst others, had expressed his contempt for him.

******

> By this ship (the *Agamemnon*) his lordship received some newspapers from England, one of which contained a paragraph stating that General Mack was about to be appointed to the command of the Austrian armies in Germany. On reading this, his lordship made the following observation: 'I know General Mack too well, the sold the King of Naples; and if he is now entrusted with an important command, He will certainly betray the Austrian monarchy.'—Beatty, *Authentic Narrative of the Death of Lord Nelson.*

******

The great master of war himself, who came across Mack in Paris whilst he was a prisoner of war there, had formed a very poor idea of him. Without for a moment foreseeing that he might someday find himself opposed to him, he prognosticated that, should Mack find himself contending with a first-rate French general, he would most likely receive a severe lesson.

Cobenzel and Pitt allowed Mack's plausibility to impose on them, and they fell into error when they recommended the Cabinet of Vienna to appoint him to the command of the German Army of the Danube. A general can elaborate a promising plan of campaign, but it does not follow that he has the talent required to carry it through with success. In every army there are officers who are as excellent at their desk as they are inefficient as executive officers in the field.

The two statesmen, however, were not the only persons who had formed an over-estimate of Mack's ability; the Emperor Francis himself was swayed greatly by his advice, even to the point of allowing it to override that of the Archduke Charles, by far the most able of his generals. For Mack at that time enjoyed a great reputation, and all his blunders in Naples were laid down to the cowardice of the Neapolitan troops. He was not popular, as Metternich says, nor was he beloved by his soldiers; and in political circles his knowledge and ability were not admitted.

Nominally the army of the Danube was under the orders of the Archduke Ferdinand. This was plainly demonstrated at a council of war held on the night of the 14–15th of October, when Mack silenced the achduke by producing the emperor's orders, appointing him the *de-facto* commander-in-chief of that army. The rank of the archduke could not be called in question, but it led to a dual command. This, as it invariably does, caused friction and disunion, which certainly did not forward the Austrian operations round Ulm.

In the south, Field-Marshal Zach was appointed as chief of the staff to the Archduke Charles. Zach was an able general, but he was the officer whom the Austrians saddled with all their misfortunes at Marengo.

The Archduke Charles had made a very fair estimate of the troops in Germany. He urged that he should be allowed to assume the offensive in Italy, so as to take full advantage of the numbers and excellence of his army, combine operations with the Archduke John in the Tyrol, and penetrate into the heart of Lombardy. He wisely recommended that the Archduke Ferdinand should be enjoined to remain on the right bank of the Inn, in the Weis camp, there to await the arrival of the Russians, so that the allied armies might open the campaign together.

The third Austrian Army, the Army of the Tyrol, was to be led by the Archduke John, the same commander who in 1800 was beaten at

Hohenlinden. Though five years older than he was when he suffered defeat at the hands of Moreau, the archduke had since then found no opportunity of acquiring experience in the field.

Amongst other Austrian officers who held conspicuous positions in 1805, we should not omit to mention Weyrother, the officer who drew up the plan for the allied armies at Austerlitz. Weyrother had been Alvinzi's chief of the staff at Rivoli and counsellor to the Archduke John at Hohenlinden. He was Quartermaster-General of the Austrian Army in 1805. General Schmidt, an officer of superior merit and talents, had been selected for the post by the Court of Vienna. This officer was killed at Dürrenstein, and Weyrother was appointed. Weyrother was a more presumptuous than capable officer; he lacked the calmness, the prudence, the firmness of Schmidt.

The French Army in 1805 had received a preparation for war which no other army of Napoleon ever had. Besides greater readiness, the French had an enormous advantage in having their operations directed by one man, and that man an experienced soldier, a genius for war. The Austrians had to comply with the dictates of the Aulic Council, of the same body that, by discrediting the existence of the French Army of Reserve in 1800, had been the cause of their disasters in Italy.

The Russians did not quite suffer from the same disadvantages as the Austrians with regard to their commanders, but they were dilatory, and in the end their tardiness proved fatal. Their action was a thorough contrast to Napoleon's, and not only had their columns to march greater distances and over badly kept roads, but their lumbering convoys were suffered to march with their columns, and this militated, as it invariably does, against rapid marching.

Alexander Paulovitch, the *Czar*, ascended the throne on the murder of Paul I. (Napoleon tells us that he had abundant proofs of the conspiracy on foot to dethrone Paul I., and that he regretted not having warned him. He adds that he did not believe the thing possible.) Though entirely innocent of that barbarous crime, Alexander was nevertheless well aware that a powerful conspiracy was on foot for the dethronement of his father. (Rostopehine, who had always remained faithful to Paul, though devoted to Russia, did not love Alexander. He dared to insinuate unjustly that Paul's successor had reasons for reproaching himself for the assassination of his father.) Though the late *Czar*, fearing him as a possible rival, hated and detested him, the bloody sceptre which the conspirators laid at his feet and the crown which they placed on his brow never effaced the memory of Paul's tragic end.

★★★★★★

In a voyage which Alexander made in the Crimea, news reached him of a vast complot prepared by some secret societies, the principal act of which was to be his assassination. "It is a just retribution he exclaimed," the horrible tragedy which ushered in his reign coming back to his mind. He returned to Taganrog, where he had been compelled to go for the health of the Czarina Elizabeth, who needed a mild climate for the winter, and there he died of fever at the age of 43.

★★★★★★

During the whole of his life most remarkable was the goodness of his heart; never did he willingly tolerate anyone to suffer. He was a kindly and romantic dreamer; to be a general benefactor, the liberator of the oppressed, the promoter of concord and peace, such were his aspirations. He aimed at making his people happy and promoting their civilization and prosperity. (Alexander was always ready to plead in favour of some unfortunate who had fallen under his father's displeasure. At times, after some exceptional act of violence, Paul was heard saying, "I should have consulted the Grand Duke Alexander.")

The Czar Alexander was enthusiastically beloved by his subjects. From the very commencement of his reign he grew attached to England, for he conceived himself under an obligation to that country, as she, by her influence, had in a certain way secured him his elevation. He entered warmly into the French project of elevating Prussia at the expense of Austria in the division of the German indemnities.

At first, he was an admirer of Napoleon, as he fondly imagined that in every one of his victories, he detected a step towards universal peace. When, however, Napoleon's unbounded ambition and succeeding acts of annexation had removed the bandage from his eyes, he did not delay a moment in openly declaring himself his most deadly foe.

The young sovereign eagerly desired to fight and to render his first military exploits illustrious by measuring his strength with so formidable a competitor.

Though full of energy, Alexander, who was slightly deaf, was also impulsive and vehement, always in danger of acting rashly, and viewing things from the standpoint of his favourite ideas. On coming to the throne, he surrounded himself with a set of persons of his own age, whom he honoured with the name of friends. Dolgorouki was one of those general officers from whom His Majesty constantly took counsel.

In point of men, the *Czar* engaged himself to provide more men than he could accomplish, and never complied to the full with the 5th article of his treaty with England. For though urged the previous year to recruit largely, he could not be made to see the necessity for it. There was, besides, much indecision when the time came for concentrating the Russian forces.

By an act dated the 16th of July 1805, Russia bound herself to send forward by the 16th of the following month a preliminary force to consist of 51,916 men, 7920 horses, and 200 guns. This army was to time its march so as to arrive on the Inn by the 20th of October. A second army was to set out on the 20th of August, make a demonstration on the Prussian frontier, and follow the first in the direction of Switzerland.

Kutuzoff had concentrated 46,000 men at Radziwiloff; he crossed the frontier at Brody on the 25th of August and commenced his march. He divided his troops into six columns, from 7000 to 8000 men strong, commanded by Prince Bagration, Generals Essen 2nd, Dochtouroff, Chépeleff, Maltitz, and Rosen. These columns were to march with one day's interval from each other. The route followed was the only one which from Poland leads to the capital of Moravia, crossing Austrian Galicia by way of Lemberg, Tarnow, and Teschen. Of these columns the last was sent back to Podolia, when the *Sultan*, at Napoleon's instigation, began arming; later on, it followed the others, but only rejoined Kutuzoff as he was recrossing the Danube.

When on the 22nd of September the Austrian Government learnt for certain that the French Army was in full march for the Rhine, it urged Kutuzoff to hasten his progress. To aid in this, it placed a number of vehicles at his disposal. This enabled the infantry to march from twelve to fifteen leagues a day, the first half being performed on foot, the other in carts, which were found awaiting them at the various stages. Relays of horses were also furnished to assist the artillery, and vehicles to carry the valises and equipment of the cavalry.

But the weather had changed for the worse; the continuous rains had softened the roads and made marching very fatiguing. With the utmost activity the first Russian column did not reach Braunau before the 11th of October, the fifth on the 19th, the very day on which Mack's troops laid down their arms.

The second Russian Army assembled in rear of the Bug under Michelson, and Buxhowden was not timed to reach the Danube before the end of November. As we shall see hereafter, it never reached it at all, for events compelled it to halt in Moravia, far from that river.

The Russians, who were then in the Ionian islands, and the English at Malta, were to land at Naples and move northwards to join the Austrian Army.

The Austrians fixed the strength of their forces at 315,000 men and 39,860 horses. Of these 142,840 men with 13,440 horses were to constitute the army of Italy; 53,440 men and 2440 horses were to be employed in the Tyrol; 89,280 men and 22,682 horses were for the army of Germany. There still remained 29,440 men with 1254 horses; these were to be held in reserve, available for any detached expeditions.

The *Czar*, unfortunately, had not a single general able to inspire complete confidence to his army. Kutuzoff, its commander, was far advanced in age, blind of an eye, the sight of which he had lost through a wound in the head, very portly, idle, greedy, and fond of pleasure. For all that, he was intelligent and as crafty in mind as he was heavy in body, expert in the habits of the court, and capable of commanding in situations which demanded good luck and prudence.

Destiny had singled him out to command armies where success was doubtful and the enemy had the best of the situation. In this campaign he was obliged to arrest Napoleon's victorious army with 50,000 men. In 1811, he fought the Turks in a war which his predecessors had imperilled; in 1812, he was placed at the head of the Russian Army at the eleventh hour, when the French were already beyond Smolensko, marching on Moscow. Still, however unfavourable the circumstances might be, the honour and glory of the Russian Army was always safe in Kutuzoff's hands, and he always justified the confidence the Emperor Alexander placed in him.

The second column was commanded at first by Michelson, afterwards by Buxhowden; in numbers it should have been equal to the first. With the object of deciding Prussia to join the coalition it tarried on the Vistula, and on the day of Austerlitz it numbered only 30,000 men, indifferently organised.

The *Czar* wished to do everything himself, to prove to all that he was not guided by any one, and that he possessed the necessary abilities to direct his troops. Czartorinski raised objections to his being with the army, on the ground that his presence would destroy all the responsibility of his generals. He argued that they would cease to occupy themselves with all the measures necessary for making matters go well; that there had been no opportunity yet for showing that the *Czar* had ability for commanding, and whether it was in his nature to take prompt and important decisions. He recommended that it would be better if the *Czar* only joined the army after the operations had taken a favourable turn. Alexander had admitted to his confidence a certain number of persons to form a vast plan, but ceased to listen to them the moment its execution was about to commence.

Others, besides the highest officials, had been regularly admitted to his confidence, and had been consulted on political affairs, which for many reasons was very hurtful. This introduced a certain disaccord between the views of the Cabinet of St. Petersburg and the *Czar*, which was readily observed when he visited the King of Prussia at Berlin.

The Archduke Charles dreaded Mack's incapacity, to which he was no stranger, and this mistrust it was that kept him inactive on the Adige. That experienced soldier had foreseen that, Mack, not being able to hold his own in Suabia, nor to effect anything of importance on account of the inferiority of his forces, would in the near future ask for reinforcements. As these could only be drawn from the Tyrol or from the army of Italy, he felt sure that he would be called to repair any disasters which might befall the Austrians in the Danube valley, that he would soon be crippled and placed in a state in which it would be impossible for him to undertake any offensive operations.

This eventually occurred. No sooner had Mack crossed the Lech (15th and 17th of September) than the Aulic Council, alarmed by the news which had reached Vienna of the operations of the French left wing and the defection of the Bavarians, took thirty-two battalions from the army of the achduke and transferred them to the army of Suabia.

No doubt the archduke, of whose military ability there was not the least question, would have been by far the most capable general to pit against Napoleon. When the Austrian Cabinet saw that the French Army was heading for the valley of the Danube, they should have called up their best and most experienced commander. The Government of Austria and the leaders in the administration were, however, jealous of the Archduke Charles, of this man who had saved the country more than once already. The Government, having always at heart the recovery of Italy, had assigned to him the command of the army in that country, and he was intended to crush Massena and reconquer Lombardy.

It was only on the 20th of September that Mack reached Ulm; the intrenched camp had been demolished some time before. Murat, writing to Napoleon, set down Mack's army at 72,000 men; the Archduke Ferdinand, writing to Kutuzoff on the 8th of October, gives the same number of men.

The Austrian troops crossed Bavaria by forced marches. A considerable column entered Augsburg, took post on the Iller, and occupied

Ulm. Ulm belonged to the Elector of Bavaria, and had quite lately been evacuated by General Wrède. Mack took steps to place it in a state of defence.

The Austrian Government had formulated the following plan of campaign. Mack was to march swiftly into Bavaria, so as to compel the Elector to make common cause with the coalition. In Italy it had located 100,000 men, its strongest army under its best general, bent on reconquering the much-regretted Lombardo-Venetian provinces. The Archduke Charles was to assume the offensive, attack Massena, overpower him and drive him out of Lombardy. The army of the Tyrol was to connect the other two, and act according as circumstances might demand.

As soon as the Russians succeeded in forming a junction with Mack, it was arranged that the combined Austro-Russian armies were to march to the Rhine, enter Switzerland, and invade France by the Jura and the Franche Comté. After all the outcry that was made when Bernadotte crossed the neutral territory of Anspach, it is worthy of notice that the plan of the allied commanders contemplated the violation of the neutrality of Switzerland.

Other smaller corps in concert with Sweden and with the English were to effect diversions. A landing of English, Russian, and Swedish troops was to operate against the French in Hanover. An attack by an Anglo-Russian corps in the Gulf of Taranto was to recover the kingdom of Naples and draw it into the coalition, threatening at the same time Massena's rear.

Looking at the very little good these diversions effected, it seems that it would have been better if Russia had used the troops she sent to the north of Germany and Naples for strengthening her main forces in Moravia.

The Austrian staff never imagined that the troops at Boulogne would follow the shortest road to Austrian territory and make it the theatre of war. Their eyes were steadily fixed on Italy.

Their plans erred conspicuously on three points. They, first of all, prepared to face an offensive war in Germany with the weaker of their two principal armies. Secondly, they remained on the defensive in Italy, where the largest army of the monarchy was opposed to an inferior force. Thirdly, they kept idle in the Tyrol an army which might have given considerable assistance and gained the victory had it been judiciously combined with either of the other two.

While Mack, with 80,000 men, was to withstand Napoleon, the

Archduke Charles, at the head of above 90,000 men—the only Austrian Army that was really ready—was detailed to confront Massena, who could hardly muster 50,000 men.

The campaigns of Jourdan and Moreau, in the valley of the Danube, apparently had not been able to indicate to the members of the Aulic Council in what direction the storm was most likely to burst. They could not see that the direct line Paris-Vienna was the one best adapted as a line of operations for the French Army, and that it presented few obstacles to their advance.

Napoleon, fortunate in commanding the finest, the best-drilled, and the most compact army France had yet possessed, desired to assume a brisk offensive in Germany. In Italy, on the other hand, he thought it was desirable, for the time being, to remain on the defensive.

His plan was to disregard all secondary attacks, and to confine himself in Italy to a purely defensive attitude, until his victories in Germany would force the Archduke Charles to retire. He himself would anticipate the Russians, and crush Mack before the latter's forces and the Russians could come together. The idea of surrounding the Austrian forces in Ulm was not conceived, however, until after Napoleon arrived with his army on the Danube.

The emperor took measures for facing the armies in the valley of the Danube and in Lombardy. He counted on the distance the Russians had to march, and consequently calculated that they were not likely to come to the assistance of the Austrians for some time. He foresaw that the Austrians, eager to enter Bavaria and occupy the position of Ulm, would add to the distance the Russians had already to overcome. He decided to inflict a severe defeat on the Austrians before they were joined by the Russians, then to attack the Russians when they could no longer rely on the main Austrian Army.

By the middle of September, the original conception formed at Boulogne underwent considerable modification; it ceased to satisfy him; it was necessary to turn the Austrian Army, and not simply to content himself with beating it, but strive to surround it, capture it, and send the soldiers prisoners to France.

By the end of September, the French had possession of all the passages over the Rhine, and through the arrangements entered into with their allies much of the resources of the country on the right bank were at their disposal.

It was desirable to avoid any violation of the neutrality of Switzerland; also, it was necessary to abstain from making a frontal attack across the defiles of the Black Forest—a mountainous country, very dangerous, because it would lead the French to expose a flank to the Austrian Army of the Tyrol. Besides, a direct attack on this line would not have led to any decisive results, for were the Austrians beaten, they would simply have had to fall back leisurely on their reinforcements and their resources.

These and other considerations made the emperor decide on turning the Black Forest by the north. It was the adoption of this plan that led him in the first instance to direct the march of his columns towards the Middle Rhine, where he counted on joining his left, composed of Bernadotte, Marmont, and the Bavarians, about the Main. He would then skirt the Black Forest and descend on the Danube, narrowing his front gradually as he closed with the enemy and as the chances of battle augmented.

Mack imagined that Napoleon would respect the territories of Anspach and of Hesse. Was it likely that he would do so when it was a question of consolidating the left wing of his army in Franconia? Napoleon's strategy always aimed at an overwhelming surprise; in this campaign, when the Austrians expected to be attacked in front, he carried his army rapidly round and attacked them from the rear. On the Austrian side, a dangerous element was the indifference of the troops.

Alison, *History of Europe*, writes:

> The soldiers went into the field resolute and devoted, but rather with the resignation of martyrs than the step of conquerors. Their repeated defeats had rendered them nearly hopeless of success.

The Austrians had calculated upon being joined by the whole forces of Bavaria; they never conceived that the Elector might deem it his best policy to throw the whole weight of the electorate into the opposite scale.

The Elector Maximilian was personally well disposed towards France. Before assuming the electoral dignity, he had served in the French Army. His eldest son was in Paris, and with the recent fate of the unfortunate Duke d'Enghien before his eyes, the Elector was alarmed by the perils which the young prince would be exposed to should Bavaria declare against the French. Montgelas, the Bavarian prime minister, was also attached to the Liberal party; both were disposed to think better of the French principles and of the French alliance than of those of Austria. Maximilian felt a sincere admiration for Napoleon, and France; he had already, by the late treaties, obtained for

Bavaria an important augmentation of territory.

The Electress Caroline, daughter of the hereditary Prince of Baden, and sister to the Empress of Russia and the Queen of Sweden, belonged to the anti-Gallican party. It was through her that the Austrian minister demanded the dismissal of Monsieur de Montgelas and a close alliance with Austria.

Bavaria had become hostile to Austria since the division of the German indemnities. Maximilian mistrusted Austria's ultimate views; he feared that, should the coalition turn out victorious in the end, Bavaria might experience the same fate as Venice and be used as an indemnity. On the other hand, in the event of victory siding with France, Napoleon might be inclined to enlarge the Bavarian territory so as to make of it a buffer against her former rival. What applied to Bavaria applied with equal force to Würtemberg and Baden; and, indeed, more strongly still, seeing how those principalities were situated much closer to France.

The Elector had good reason for his indecision, for all engrossed as Napoleon was with his preparations for the invasion of England, the French Army was to all appearances too distant to come to his aid. Thiers relates how Napoleon wrote to the Elector in his own hand and announced to him, as a state secret confided to his honour, that he was about to adjourn his projects against England, and was at once marching with 200,000 men to the centre of Germany, adding, "You will be helped in plenty of time."

Austria attempted to act towards Bavaria as Russia was acting towards Prussia. The Cabinet of Vienna decided to surprise her and drag her into the war. The Elector, who was not a very strong-minded person, was being persuaded by Otto that his country only existed through Napoleon having afforded him his protection, and that only by leaning towards him could Bavaria save herself from the covetousness of Austria. He reminded him how in 1803 she had received a fair share of the German indemnities, principally through the intervention of France. Persuaded by these arguments, the Elector agreed to execute a treaty of alliance with France. This treaty was drawn up on the 24th of August, but was to remain a profound secret.

The Elector had agreed that in the event of his territory being violated he would put his forces at Napoleon's disposal. Donauwörth had been fixed as the point where the Bavarian troops were to join the French.

A few days later, on the 7th of September, Prince Schwarzenberg arrived in Munich. He was commissioned by the Emperor Francis to urge the Elector to declare himself in favour of the coalition, to join his troops to the Austrian, to consent to their being incorporated in the Imperial Army—one regiment being drafted into each Austrian division. The allies had a strong suspicion with regard to the real feelings of the Bavarians, and doubted their being disposed to give up their territory and their magazines to them. The prince was authorised to offer, should it be necessary, as a bribe, a compensation in the territory of Salzburg, or even in the Tyrol, in the event of the allied armies reconquering Italy, and reinstating in that country the collateral branches of the Imperial House which had been driven away.

The Elector of Bavaria had written to the Emperor of Austria:

On my knees I beg you that I may be permitted to remain neutral.

This humble appeal was disregarded, and the Austrian troops in Bavaria conducted themselves, it is said, as in an enemy's country.

Schwarzenberg, greatly aided by the Elector's wife, a fascinating woman, distinguished for her animosity towards France, and who worked on the vacillation of her husband, shook his determination for a moment, and prevailed on him to side with Austria.

★★★★★★

There were three princesses of Baden, all handsome women, who married the *Czar*, the King of Sweden, and the Elector of Bavaria; all remarkable for their hatred to France. The wife of the Elector was the most implacable of the three.

★★★★★★

Schwarzenberg had the Austrian Army at his heels, which probably proved a very strong argument. The Elector having sent to warn Otto of his sudden change of mind, the latter hurried to his side and showed him the danger he was running by his defection, and the certainty that Napoleon would soon enter victorious into Munich and conclude peace with Austria by sacrificing Bavaria.

The proposal of breaking up the army and of drafting the various regiments amongst the Austrian divisions had deeply offended the Bavarian officers, and when it became known that without waiting for the Elector's consent the Austrian Army had crossed the Inn, public opinion was much incensed by this violation of territory. Otto and the very able Bavarian minister, De Montgelas, under these irritating circumstances, had no great difficulty in persuading the prince to cast his lot with France.

He was recommended to take refuge in Würzburg, and to order his army to follow him there. To gain some time, Schwarzenberg was told that a Bavarian officer, General Nogarola, a well-known partisan of Austria, would be sent to Vienna to treat. Then, on the night between the 8th and 9th of September, the Elector and his court left for Ratisbonne; from Ratisbonne they went on to Würzburg, which was reached on the 12th of September. The Bavarian troops concentrated at Amberg, and at Ulm received orders to march on Würzburg, but to avoid any collision with the Austrians. Though the latter advanced by forced marches, the Bavarians had the start of them; the invaders were unable to overtake the Bavarians, who, having crossed the Danube, were already beyond reach.

In the early days of August, the Austrian Army of Germany was concentrated in the camp of Weis on the Traun, distant not more than three or four marches from the Inn. It had been arranged that this army should await the Russians before commencing operations on the Upper Danube. Mack, however, alarmed by the reports which came from France, began to believe that the enemy might forestall him at the issues of the Black Forest. As supplies were running short at Weis, it had become necessary to spread out to find sufficient nourishment for the army. Impressed by these circumstances, he urged that the Inn might be crossed without delay, reasoning that by hastening matters there was a better chance of gaining over the Elector of Bavaria, Maximilian Joseph. If this could be secured, not only would there be an addition of 25,000 men to the army, but the theatre of war would be removed from the hereditary states almost to the borders of the Rhine.

The Austrian advanced guard under Klenau, thirty battalions and thirty squadrons strong, quitted Weis on the 4th of September, and marched in two columns towards the Inn. That river, which constituted the frontier of Bavaria, was crossed on the 8th at Braunau and Schoerding. From Braunau, the first column went by way of Alt-Œtting and Hohenlinden to Munich, which was entered on the 11th. The second from Schoerding marched by Eggenfelden, Vilsbiburg, and Landshut on Freising, with the object of cutting off the retreat of the Bavarian garrisons.

The Austrians assumed the initiative, hoping thereby to secure the co-operation of the Bavarian forces. When this hope was frustrated, it is inconceivable why they should have pushed as far as Ulm, and so retarded their junction with the Russians, more so that the co-operation of the latter was the essential condition of the plan of operations in Germany.

But there was still another reason for these over hasty movements of the Austrians: their eagerness to show that alone they were able to enter successfully into the struggle and carry the day. A more far-seeing leader than Mack would have kept his forces on the line of the Inn, which extends from the Tyrol to the Danube by Passau, a strong defensive line on which he might have waited in comparative safety the arrival of the Russian forces.

The Inn is the most important of the rivers which rush down from the Alps to swell the stream of the Danube. It has a large volume of water, and flows with considerable velocity. From Kufstein as far as Mühldorf, it runs in a deep bed, which the vehemence of its current has cut through the solid rock. Both banks are quite precipitous, and the few places favourable for the passage of an army are strongly fortified. This powerful line has on its lower reach the fortress of Braunau, on the upper that of Kufstein.

The Cabinet of Vienna had evidently been assured by their agents in Paris—misled, no doubt, by the activity at Boulogne—that in a few days Napoleon would be at sea, so that Austria might safely act without waiting for the Russians. The principal cause of the Austrians' defeat was their precipitate action in crossing the frontier without waiting for their allies. Their forcing on the hostilities before the arrival of the Russians was the ruin of this campaign.

At a council of war held at Hetzendorf on the 29th of August, the Archduke Ferdinand observed that Napoleon would be at Munich with 150,000 men before the Russians could reach the Inn. He therefore demanded that 30,000 or 40,000 men might remain in Bavaria, thus obviating a possible general retreat, which he declared could not but have a most deplorable effect. In this he was supported by the Archduke Charles, by Zach, and the Emperor Francis. Mack, however, succeeded in overriding their objections, and the emperor yielded.

★★★★★★

Mack had acquired an immense ascendency over the emperor. The emperor was to be commander-in-chief, with himself as quartermaster-general. As such he apportioned the commands, he introduced reforms, which, pressed at a moment when the army was taking the field, proved often injurious.

★★★★★★

The Archduke Ferdinand did not at all approve of Mack's move on Ulm, which could not be occupied without crossing the Bavarian frontier. He would have preferred taking post on the Isar and on the Lech. The two commanders, the nominal and the real, were already beginning to quarrel, so much so that the Emperor Francis thought proper to proceed himself to Landsberg, to put an end to the new-born misunderstanding. At a council of war which was held on the 25th of September, Mack defended his own plan. He demonstrated the advantages the line of the Iller possessed, and the importance of the city of Ulm, with a double bridge head, which allowed manoeuvring on both banks of the Danube. He showed how by extending his left as far as Kempten to the foot of the mountains he could connect with the Tyrol, and indirectly with the army of Italy; how the right solidly rested on Ulm, and the line of operations was sufficiently protected by the Danube, whilst its affluents formed so many barriers favourable for defence, and offering good positions in the event of his being compelled to retire.

Fools dream, wise men act. Mack was obstinately rooted in the opinion that it would be impossible for Napoleon to cross the Rhine with more than 70,000 men. He expected a front attack, and imagined that the French would advance by no other roads than those which led direct on the position he occupied, and the issues of which were guarded by his troops. He did not take in the gist of the emperor's manoeuvres; he never so much as dreamt having his right flank menaced, and even less finding the enemy ready to fall on his rear.

Napoleon skilfully led the *Grande Armée* round the flank of the Austrian Army and on its rear, thus threatening Mack's line of communications. In full confidence of his security, Mack all of a sudden beheld the advanced guard of the *Grande Armée* appearing in the most unexpected localities; he was seriously disturbed, and hesitated as to the best course to pursue.

Whilst Bernadotte and Marmont were marching from north to south, Napoleon's troops from Boulogne were marching eastwards. An advance of the latter by way of the Black Forest was simulated, but in reality the army was to leave that country well on its right, inclining to the left, passing through Württemberg with the intention of forming a junction with Bernadotte and Marmont and of crossing the Danube below Ulm, somewhere in the neighbourhood of Donauwörth. Having crossed the Danube, the French were then to manoeuvre so as to cut off Mack's retreat, close every point of issue, surround him, and capture him. Once free of the Austrian Army, Napoleon intended to march in the direction of Vienna to confront the Russians.

To Talleyrand and Augereau Napoleon wrote:

> The Austrians are in the issues of the Black Forest. Please Goodness they may remain there. My only dread is that we cause them great awe. . . . If they will only allow me to gain a few marches on them, I hope to turn them and to find myself with my entire army between the Lech and the Isar.

His plan was to defeat the Austrian forces before the arrival of the Russian troops, which were coming to reinforce them; to prevent the junction of Mack with Kutuzoff. Before reaching the valley of the Danube, he had not quite decided what course he would follow; it was only when he heard that Mack was in the neighbourhood of Ulm that he foresaw how by seizing that general's communications he could best prevent the Austrian commander joining forces with the Russians.

Mack either failed to grasp the scope of the grand movement made by the French Army or refused to give credence to it; but there were Austrian generals who understood it too well. Murat's demonstrations in the valleys of the Murg, Rench, and Kinzig had been thoroughly successful in their object, inasmuch as they had fully convinced the commander-in-chief of the Austrian Army that it was only on his front that he could expect to be attacked. The Austrian advanced posts reported again and again that the issues of the Black Forest were on the point of being forced by numerous columns. When it was seen as plain as it could well be that the French were marching on the Wernitz and were approaching the Danube, not above, but below the confluence of the Iller, Mack believed that by simply closing up his cantonments to the south of Ulm he Mould be able to face every eventuality.

At this period Werneck approached Ulm and took post between the Iller and the Günz. Auffenberg, who had been recalled from Kempten, joined him there. Jellachich was ordered to collect his troops, at that moment scattered on the northern shore of the Lake of Constance, and to close on Biberach. Wolfskehl was to hold Stockach with two battalions and eight squadrons, and Lindau with one battalion.

The greater part of Kolowrat's and Schwarzenberg's corps were brought up to the Iller and located between Ulm and Illeraichheim. The latter place was occupied by a new corps under Loudon, formed of fifteen battalions drafted from the Austrian Army of Italy, and others taken from Auffenberg's command.

Mack did not ignore the presence of the two corps of Bernadotte and Marmont in the direction of Würzburg, but, as he adduced in his defence, he relied that the neutrality of Anspach would be respected. On his right rear he had, moreover, Kienmayer with 20,000 men, located between Ingolstadt and Neuburg.

It would seem natural that, having a force of seventy-six squadrons of cavalry, Mack should have been well informed of Napoleon's movements. It was only on the 5th of October, when the whole of the French Army was deployed between Heidenheim and Weissenburg, and ready to engage in a general action, that the Austrian commander-in-chief for the first time appeared to have felt any apprehension of his danger. It was then that he made a few tardy dispositions with the object of concentrating the main portion of his army between Ulm and Günzburg, facing northwards.

In the first week of October, 180,000 French were advancing on a front twenty-six leagues in extent, their right skirting the mountains, their left converging towards the plains of the Higher Palatinate, able in a few hours to find themselves concentrated in number from 90,000 to 100,000 on either wing. Extraordinary as it might appear at first sight, they could effect this concentration without the Austrians having the least notion of this vast operation.

Napoleon could not bring himself to believe that the Austrians would remain stationary on the Iller. He fully conceived that their general, warned of the peril which menaced him, would hasten to carry his forces over to the left bank of the Danube and contest the crossing of that river. Accordingly, having given Donauwörth as the objective of the several columns, he expected to have to fight a battle on the plains of Nördlingen. With that view he had traced the march of his columns in such a way as to be in a position to concentrate his army at any given moment to fight.

For Bernadotte and Marmont to join the *Grande Armée* in the direction of Nördlingen as speedily as practicable there was no other course but to cross the territory of Anspach.

Napoleon, considering it extremely probable that he would have to fight a battle in the neighbourhood of Nördlingen on the 6th or 7th of October, halted his army on the 5th in the following positions: Murat was at Heidenheim, having beyond it detachments as far as the Danube. Ney, a little to his rear, was between Weissenstein and Heidenheim. Lannes was at Aalen, Soult in front of Ellwangen, Davout between Dinkelsbühl and Œttingen. Marmont had taken post to the west of Gunzenhausen, Bernadotte between Gunzenhausen and Spalt, the Bavarians to the north of Weissenburg. The emperor's headquarters and the Imperial Guard were at Gemünd, in rear of Aalen.

On the 6th the French moved forward towards the Danube. Nostitz and Kienmayer, the former with a feeble advanced guard of three battalions and a regiment of hussars, the latter with sixteen battalions and thirty-two squadrons, could not attempt to defend the passage of the Danube against a large army.

The expected battle between Gôppingen and Nördlingen had not come off, as Mack remained on the Iller, facing in the direction of France. Napoleon had succeeded in his manoeuvre far beyond his anticipations. Complete success only depended on the future dispositions of his forces. Mack was at Ulm on the Iller, with Kienmayer, who was to connect him with the Russians, on his rear. The march of the French had already driven the latter general well on the other side of the Danube. The emperor's first care was to take up a position between the Austrians and Russians so as to be able to prevent their junction. Had Mack understood his business, he would have quitted the banks of the Iller and fallen back on the Lech, passing through Augsburg to join General Kienmayer, who was at that time on the Munich road.

Nostitz retired to Eichstädt. Kienmayer had skirmished with the French advanced guards about Eichstädt and Nördlingen. Surprised at the size of the columns which were approaching the Wernitz, he withdrew in all haste to Neuburg, having left three battalions and one and a half squadrons at Donauwörth, Rain, and Ingolstadt. The bridges were not destroyed. Napoleon ordered his marshals to cross the Danube at once. Murat, Soult, and Lannes were to go in the direction of Donauwörth, Davout and Marmont to cross at Neuburg, Bernadotte and the Bavarians at Ingolstadt.

Ney was to remain on the left bank of the Danube and take post on the Brenz, fronting Günzburg and Ulm. He was posted there with the object of closing the road from Ulm to Donauwörth and of defeating any attempts Mack might make on the rear of the French Army. His corps was made up to 30,000 men by placing under his orders as a temporary measure one of Lannes' divisions (Gazan's), Baraguay d'Hilliers' foot dragoons, and Bourcier's division of dragoons.

The French Army, with this exception of Ney's corps, crossed the Danube on the existing bridges without experiencing any opposition or the least delay. Without any effusion of blood, but only by combinations and precision of marches, it had intersected the enemy's line of operations and all communication with the hereditary states. A retreat through Bavaria was out of the question, for Napoleon, with the intention of enveloping Mack's army, had sent several of his corps and the Bavarians in the direction of Munich.

It was one of Napoleon's maxims that rapidity of movement is the stamp of the operations of all great captains, and immobility that of passable generals. The latter remain rooted to one spot simply because they know not bow to move; incapable of manoeuvring, they seek safety by holding too long to a position. A truth which was demonstrated too often in this campaign.

CHAPTER 7

Ulm—Operations on the Right Bank of the Danube

Napoleon, with the Imperial Guard, entered Donauwörth on the evening of the 7th of October. From that day up to the 12th he remained in a state of great uncertainty. Nevertheless, after his arrival in that city he lost no time in making his dispositions for investing the Austrian forces in Ulm, and for holding in check the Russian Army under General Kutuzoff, which was already reported to be approaching the Inn.

Bernadotte, Marmont, Davout, and Soult's corps arrived at the same time on the left bank of the Danube. From the 6th to the 7th of October, in twenty-four hours, these four army corps, in round numbers 100,000 men, crossed the river at Donauwörth, Neuburg, and Ingolstadt.

Murat and Lannes were to march up the Danube, hold the road leading from Ulm to Augsburg, and pursue the troops which had been worsted at Donauwörth. Murat, who was then at Rain with 7,000 horsemen, received orders to recross the Lech at once and to march on Zusmarshausen and Burgau. He was enjoined to take with him three divisions of dragoons and two of heavy cavalry with their guns. Lannes' cavalry division was directed to march for the same destination, Murat being authorised to take two of its regiments to scout for his heavy cavalry. With the rest of his corps Lannes was to cross the Danube at Münster, and make for Wertingen. He was to push forward an advanced guard on the road from Burgau to Ulm.

Soult was ordered to quit the mouth of the Lech and to march up that affluent of the Danube as far as Augsburg with his three divisions, St. Hilaire's, Vandamme's, and Legrand's. By these dispositions the emperor intended to close the road leading to Munich.

With regard to what concerned the Russian advance, Davout was directed to hasten the crossing of the Danube at Neuburg and clear the passage of that river at Ingolstadt. After that he was to proceed to Aichach on the Munich road, driving Kienmayer's troops before him. Davout's corps was destined to constitute the rear-guard of the French forces which were about to gather round Ulm.

Marmont and Bernadotte were to hasten their movements, cross the Danube at Ingolstadt, and march on Munich, where Bernadotte and the Bavarians were to reinstate the Elector. By these dispositions Napoleon could confront the Russians with Bernadotte and the Bavarians, and, if necessary, also with Marmont and Davout. The two latter, according to circumstances, were to be prepared to march either in the direction of Munich, or of Ulm to complete the investment of Mack's army.

On the same day, at four o'clock in the evening, Mack arrived at Günzburg, and there the news of the occupation of Donauwörth by Marshal Soult reached him, also that Bernadotte had crossed the neutral territory of Anspach. As the reports did not mention aught else than a surprise of the bridge at Donauwörth, and only spoke of one French division as having passed over to the right bank of the Danube, he determined to attack it with superior forces. Baron Auffenberg, with seven battalions of grenadiers, two of fusiliers, and four squadrons of cavalry, about 8,000 men in all, received orders to proceed at once in the direction of Donauwörth by way of Wertingen. The other corps called up from the Iller were to support Auffenberg, and as the heads of the French columns would cross the river, one after the other, they were to be attacked and crushed in succession.

It is more difficult than it is generally believed to be informed in a reliable manner of the enemy's movements in sufficient time to regulate one's own. The most able commander is he who decides on the most reasonable conjectures.

But to be informed to some purpose one must have made his arrangements well beforehand, must have enlisted the services of the best men, have assigned to them a certain zone of country, and initiated them in the description of information which will be profitable to acquire and which will be of most value to him. In this case, as Mack did not dream of an enemy advancing on his rear, he had made no previous dispositions for acquiring information from the neighbourhood of Donauwörth.

Before issuing his orders, Mack should have waited for more complete information, then he would not have exposed his lieutenant to a serious defeat. On the following day, the 8th of March, Mack was apprized that it was not only the bridge of Donauwörth that had fallen into the hands of the French, but likewise those of Neuburg and Ingolstadt, and that it was not simply with Soult's advanced guard that Auffenberg would have to contend, but that he would possibly have to encounter the whole of the 4th Corps, if not three more, besides the whole cavalry reserve, all of which were ready to support Vandamme's division. On the receipt of this report Mack could no longer persist in disbelieving the presence of the French Army on the Danube below Ulm. He became perplexed, and strove to find some way of escape. Pressed by the Archduke Ferdinand, he made a change of dispositions; orders were issued for the Austrian forces to march in an easterly direction, and to open for themselves a passage by way of Augsburg towards the Isar, and from that to the Inn.

Auffenberg was already in the neighbourhood of Wertingen when Mack came to this decision. He had barely reached that village, at seven in the morning, when fresh orders reached him from Mack. He was no longer to advance in the direction of the Lech, but to fall back on Zusmarshausen, to cover the Augsburg road. He was to consider himself the advanced guard of the Austrian Army. As to the French troops advancing in his direction, he heard that they had passed the village of Norndorf.

On the 8th of October, the day in which Mack adopted this second plan of operations, the various corps of his army were disposed as follow :—

At Wertingen was Auffenberg, with 9 battalions and 4 squadrons of cavalry.

Covering the bridges of Günzburg and Leipheim and watching Marshal Ney was Werneck at Günzburg. He had with him Kerpin's and Hohenzollern's divisions—16 battalions and 9½ squadrons. A contingent consisting of 3½ battalions and 6 squadrons, under d'Aspre, was at Riedhausen, on the left bank of the Danube.

Of Riesch's corps, Loudon's division, 15 battalions, were at Günzburg. The divisions of Hesse Homburg, and Giulay, making together a total of 17 battalions and 28 squadrons, were on the march from Ulm to Günzburg.

Schwarzenberg's divisions, Klenan's and Jottesheim's, 21 battalions and 26 squadrons, were marching from the Iller to the Günz.

Jellachich, with 16 battalions, was on his way to Ulm, coming from the direction of Biberach.

Spangen, who was bringing 11 battalions and half a squadron from the Tyrol, was at Mindelheim.

There remained Kienmayer's 10 battalions and 22 squadrons, which had become separated from Mack's army by the speedy advance of the French.

Mack had at his disposal, not counting the latter and a few detachments on the Lake of Constance, 109 battalions and 761 squadrons, which made a total of 66,000 men and 9000 horses.

Notwithstanding his orders and the intimation, he received of the enemy's advance, Auffenberg halted at Wertingen. With three battalions he occupied the gates; the grenadiers were posted in the streets and the cavalry outside the walls. At about noon his scouts fell back and reported the advance of the enemy. Already his advanced guard at Pfaffenhofen—a battalion of infantry and two squadrons of cavalry—charged impetuously by the French, had been compelled to withdraw in disorder.

General Dinersberg had divided his detachment into two and advanced along both sides of the Zusam on Thurheim and Frauenstetten. Both these parties were overpowered and soon driven back in the direction of Wertingen.

Auffenberg disposed his troops as follows: four battalions of grenadiers on the heights to the left of the Günzburg road, with two squadrons of *cuirassiers* on the right, one battalion in front of the Augsburg gate, another and two companies of Stuart's corps were posted in front of the Pfaffenhofen gate; the three battalions of Reuss-Greitz occupied the town.

A brisk fusillade from Hohenreichen disturbed a regiment of French dragoons which led the advance. Exelmans, at that time one of Murat's *aides-de-camp*, had been attracted to the spot by the sound of the fusillade. He at once got about 200 dragoons to dismount, take to their carbines, and dislodge the enemy. This was done in very gallant style.

After this Murat approached with his cavalry, formed up in line on the heights of Gottmanshofen, and manoeuvred so as to outflank the Austrians on both sides. The latter were not long in evacuating Gottmanshofen and retiring to Wertingen.

Lannes, who had crossed the Danube that very afternoon at Minis-

ENVIRONS D'ULM.

ALBECK
Horfelingen
Witthau
Haslingen
Unt. Elchingen
Morixen
Kesselbrunn
CL. ELCHINGEN
Iungingen
Thalfingen
Haslach
Leibeh
Boffingen
Strass
Burlefingen
Pfuhl
Rᵗᵉ d'Augsbourg
Roth R.
Offenhausen
Steinheim
ULM
Holzheim
Finingen
Marbach
Reute
Idelhausen
Holzschwang
Kirchberg
Hausen
Aufheim
Senden
Route de Memmingen
Iller

ter, was at Thurheim at 3 p.m., just after Murat had commenced his attack. He made his troops step out, and was soon in view of Wertingen.

After a serious resistance, some dismounted dragoons and skirmishers of the 5th Corps got possession of the bridge over the Zusam at Wertingen. Klein then directed his division on Roggten, with the object of turning the Austrians from the south; at the same time Lannes, with Fauconnet's brigade of *Chasseurs à Cheval* and Oudinot's grenadiers, endeavoured to steal round the enemy under cover of a wood, and thus cut him off completely.

Having crossed the Zusam by a rickety bridge in single file, and got beyond the village of Roggten, Klein came face to face with a body of the enemy formed up close in front of the Binswangen wood. The 1st Dragoons, led by Colonel Arrighi, charged the Austrian *cuirassiers*, who were supported by infantry and four guns. The dragoons pursued the enemy up to the wood and captured some prisoners.

Auffenberg found himself compelled to fall back on Zusmarshausen. The retreat was seriously molested by Murat's and Lannes' horsemen. To keep them at a distance, the Austrian general adopted a square formation; however, instead of forming several squares in echelon, which would have flanked each other with their fire, and could have moved with greater ease, he formed his infantry into one large square, on the flanks of which, to the right and left, he posted two squadrons of cavalry. A bulky square of that dimension is anything but manageable; this one, though it had commenced retiring in good order, charged in front and menaced in the rear, soon began to waver and was broken; the soldiers got scattered, and only by taking shelter in the woods close by were they able to escape and reach Burgau.

It is astonishing that Auffenberg's force, being almost entirely composed of infantry, should not have made a better stand against cavalry, particularly when defending villages. In point of numbers the two sides were nearly equal. Had it not been for Oudinot's grenadiers and their guns, possibly the Austrians might have made their retreat good, for the repeated charges of Nansouty's heavy dragoons did not make very much impression on the Austrian square. Auffenberg, however, did not display the same skill as Dupont did three days later at Haslach; had he done so, the first action of the campaign would not have gone to inspirit the French by its successful termination.

Whilst Murat lost no time in attacking Auffenberg with his 7,000 horsemen, there was one of Soult's divisions not far from Wertingen. De Ségur had been sent to overtake General Saint-Hilaire, and to order him to occupy Augsburg with his division. As Napoleon's object was to turn the Austrian Army, it was consequently important for him to gain possession without delay of the city of Augsburg. De Ségur came up with Saint-Hilaire in the neighbourhood of Mark, where the general, startled by a heavy cannonade on his right, had halted.

Just at that moment one of Murat's staff officers rode up from Wertingen, and in the name of his general asked for assistance. Saint-Hilaire hesitated, uncertain if he should obey the special orders sent by the emperor or follow the rule of marching in the direction of the cannonade. He changed his mind with every fresh argument adduced by the two staff officers, and, when he finally decided to go to Murat's aid, it was so late that he arrived on the scene of the conflict at midnight to find there neither friends nor foes.

Auffenberg, who was himself captured during the retreat, lost in the engagement 334 men killed and wounded, 1,469 prisoners, 3 flags, and 6 guns. Murat occupied Zusmarshausen early the next day, and there in the evening he was joined by Lannes' troops.

The fugitives from Wertingen brought to Burgau, where Mack had gone to, the unwelcome news of Auffenberg's defeat. This news went far to demonstrate that Napoleon was in sufficient strength on the Lech to arrest the progress of the Austrian forces.

Mack at first imagined that he could prevent the passage of the Danube by pushing his right towards Rain under Kienmayer, and posting his centre at Günzburg and his left at Ulm. The bulk of the enemy's forces had, however, overlapped his right. He then made a change of front right back, with his right at Memmingen, his centre between the Iller and Günzburg, and his left at Ulm.

Napoleon felt almost certain that the Austrians were bent on retiring in a south-easterly direction. That Mack would ever dream of a north-easterly move he considered as a very unlikely eventuality; nevertheless, that such an effort on his part was feasible, he had clearly shown by preparing for such a case. He had left Ney on the Brenz with over 30,000 men to repel an attack in that direction.

In most of the engagements and battles fought in the Austerlitz campaign the Austrians behaved with great courage; nevertheless, they always suffered themselves to be overcome by the French. Can the severity of the weather, the numbing cold, the fatiguing marches over bad and almost impassable roads, the cheerless bivouacs in rain and snow, have brought about this inferiority? Hardly, for what applied to the Austrians on these points applied equally to the French; the latter,

Obermedlingen
Bergenweiler
Faimingen
Echenbrunn
BRENZ
GUNDELFINGE
Bachingen
Riedhausen
NIEDERSTOZINGEN
Offingen
Rettenbach
GÜNZBURG
LEIPHEIM
Tettingen
Limbach
Gros Koz
Klein Koz
Gros Kussendorf
Riedheim
Ochsenbronn
Waldstetten
Wettenhausen

OF ULM.

besides, had to face all these sinister conditions in a semi-starving state. Nor could the Austrians plead want of experience in war, for their army had fought in several campaigns since 1792. Their recent campaigns, for all that, had not taught the Austrian staff the secrets of the art of war. The cause of this inferiority, when closely examined, was to be found in the obsolete tactics, rigid formations and slow movements borrowed from the Prussian system, and even more than that in the spirit of confidence which the French had in their prowess, in the ability of their generals, and in the genius of their emperor.

The day after the engagement at Wertingen, Napoleon proceeded to Zusmarshausen, where he reviewed the troops which had been engaged. He distributed crosses and eulogised the officers who had principally distinguished themselves. (To Exelmans, who by his promptitude has achieved the first success, he said, "I know that no one can be braver than you, and I name you officer of the legion of honour.") He never let a brilliant action go unrecompensed, and, when possible, he rewarded on the spot in sight of the recipient's comrades. All ranks alike were eager to distinguish themselves, and strove to attract the attention of Napoleon.

No one knew better how to turn fanaticism to proper account. (It appears strange that Napoleon had it in him to inspire in others sentiments which he could not feel himself.) Indeed, the world has seldom seen a ruler who understood so completely the art of calling forth the enthusiasm of his followers and stirring their emulation by distinctions promptly conferred on merit. All ranks alike could aspire to some reward, and the success of the *Grande Armée* and other armies which Napoleon commanded was due in great part to the morale of his troops, roused by rewards conferred, or even the slightest notice taken by the emperor of individuals.

In 1800, before setting out for the Alps, the First Consul had instituted arms of honour—sabres and muskets—to which double pay was attached, to be conferred on soldiers as a reward for bravery and highly distinguished service in the field. After the Marengo campaign in May 1801, he had gone still further and had submitted to the Council of State the question of establishing a legion of honour not to be confined to military men.

★★★★★★

Routier writes of this order: "*Création si belle selon le coeur français et qui devait faire enfanter tant de nouveaux prodiges.*" ("Creation so beautiful according to the French heart and which was to bring forth so many new wonders.")

"Of all the orders ever created, ancient or modern," said the emperor, "there never was one which has paid so well those who instituted it as the Legion of Honour. It was my doing, it is my masterpiece; no one either at present or in the future can dispute the glory of it with me; I owe to it a considerable portion of my triumphs."

★★★★★★

In this he was seriously opposed, and only carried the measure by fourteen out of twenty-four votes. It was evident at the time that the majority of the French were still opposed to the issue of any personal distinction, to the creation of a privileged class which might become the origin of a patrician order. However, the taste for such distinction rapidly gained ground, and on the 29th of *Floréal*, year X. (19th of May 1802), the order of the Legion of Honour was founded.

In the summer of 1804, Napoleon proceeded to Boulogne to review the army of England, and on that occasion, he distributed crosses of the new order to deserving officers and soldiers.

To give special importance to the consideration he desired to be attached to this reward, to excite by *éclat* still more the enthusiasm of the army, the emperor proceeded to the headquarters of the army at Boulogne on the 26th of *Thermidor*, year XII. (14th of August 1804), to invest with his own hands the most worthy of the army with the insignia. He was determined that the ceremony should be of a most imposing description, calculated to impress itself strongly on the mind of all who witnessed it. To this effect, Marshal Soult was ordered to assemble near Caesar's tower on the 15th of August, the anniversary of the emperor's birthday, 80,000 men from the camps at St. Omer and Montreuil. The plain in this spot has the form of an amphitheatre, and the troops in dense columns were disposed in a large semi-circle facing the sea. On the flanks were posted the cavalry and artillery. In front of the columns were the regimental flags, and beyond these the officers and men who had been named to receive the cross.

In the centre of the semi-circle, on a high mound of turf, was a platform, and on this was placed an iron throne of gothic design, which tradition said to have belonged once to Dagobert. A flight of steps had been cut out leading to this throne, behind which was a huge trophy of arms and colours captured in various battles, all surmounted by a massive crown of laurels. On either side of this mound, as well as in rear, were posted the Imperial Guard, the regimental bands and drums, and the staff.

Punctually at noon, Napoleon took up his position in front of the throne, saluted by flourishes of trumpets, the rattle of drums, and discharges of artillery. He was surrounded by a brilliant retinue of civil and military officers. The emperor's *aides-de-camp* stood on the steps; in front of them other officers held Duguesclin's and Bayard's helmets and shields filled with crosses. The spectacle was superb, and Napoleon had a right to feel proud of his army. The officers and men to be decorated advanced with their banners to the steps of the throne; the emperor standing addressed his soldiers in a loud voice:

> And you soldiers! swear to defend, at all hazard of your life, the honour of the French name, your country, and your emperor.

This was the most stirring moment of the performance; with one voice the army replied:

"We swear it." Carried away by their enthusiasm, the soldiers raised their caps and head-dresses on their bayonets, and loud shouts of *Vive l'Emperor*! ran through the serried ranks of that imposing host.

Then followed the distribution of the crosses, the proceedings ending with a march past of the vast army. The troops went by in perfect order, and well could Napoleon boast that he had the finest army that could anywhere be found.

Glory is a seductive mistress, and almost every page of this volume will show how gallantly the French soldiers fought and died to keep the oath they had taken at Boulogne to lay down their life for the honour of France and their emperor.

Bourrienne does much credit to Napoleon's knowledge of human nature in trying to expose a singular piece of charlatanism he often had recourse to. The private secretary writes:

> He would say to one of his *aides-de-camp*, 'Ascertain from the colonel of such a regiment whether he has in his corps a man who has served in the campaign of Italy or of Egypt. Ascertain his name, where he was born, the particulars of his family, and what he has done. Learn his number in the ranks, and to what company he belongs, and furnish me with this information.'
> On the day of the review Bonaparte, at a single glance, could perceive the man who had been described to him. He would go up to him as if he recognised him, address him by name, and say, 'Oh, so you are here! You are a brave fellow—I saw you at Aboukir—how is your old father? What, you have not got the

cross? Stay, I will give it to you.' Then the delighted soldiers would say to each other, 'You see, the emperor knows us all; he knows our families; he knows where we have served.' (*Memoirs of Napoleon Bonaparte* republished in 3 volumes by Leonaur.)

One of his sayings was, "*La question tactique est peu de chose, la question morale tout!*" ("The tactical question is little, the moral question all!") We should not run away with the idea that it was always praise that the great leader bestowed on his soldiers; he could reprove his troops, and to a purpose. In 1798, the French troops had become disgusted with the Egyptian expedition by reason of the hardships they were compelled to endure.

A grenadier, bolder than the rest, on one occasion dared to address him. "Well, general," he said, "are you going to take us to India?"

"It is not with such soldiers as you that I would undertake the voyage," replied Bonaparte. This scornful remark humiliated the troops, they braced themselves up and marched with great swiftness. It is astonishing what power a few words of praise or of disdain have. No one was ever able to resist Napoleon's.

With just a few words, he had an unfailing way of infusing spirit in his men. As the troops were marching briskly into action at Austerlitz, he met the 28th of the Line, a regiment composed mostly of conscripts from Calvados. I trust," he said, "that the Normans will distinguish themselves today." Soon after, coming across the 57th, he called out, "Remember that I have named you the *terrible.*"

But not only could the great chief reproach in words, but also in deeds. At Elchingen the *chasseurs* of the guard had arrogated to themselves the best available quarters, ignoring the requirements of the headquarter staff. The emperor, deeply irritated, sent them off at once to Murat, to be employed without privileges like any other cavalry regiment—a punishment which they turned to good account by behaving in a most gallant manner, and in this way returning speedily into favour.

To the very last hour Napoleon was the darling of the army; and what right had he not to their gratitude? His generals and marshals owed to him alone their titles and their wealth; it was through him that the veteran revelled in his gains, and the capital, gorgeous with the spoils of art, became the metropolis of the universe.

A man who had such followers as Napoleon was indeed fortunate. The soldiers simply believed him invincible. There was a kind of intoxication in this universal faith, in this general belief, that marching under his orders was to march to sure victory. Returning from Moscow, notwithstanding all their sufferings, all the horrors of the retreat before their eyes, the soldiers believed the disaster to be only a passing one. Soon, they held, would their emperor revive in all his pristine glory and disperse his enemies.

He closed his eyes to the depredations of his greedy lieutenants, as long as they served him well and forwarded his designs. He rewarded his marshals and generals with great generosity, and gained the affection of his soldiers by rewarding their merits and offering a willing ear to their complaints. It must, however, be said that rarely those he rewarded or honoured did not deserve it.

Thiers, after having remarked on the danger arising from a dissemination of forces in war, and showing how Napoleon by his wise dispositions averted the danger in the Austerlitz campaign, adds:

> But, after having admired this profound and incomparable art, so surprising by its very simplicity, one is still bound to admire in this manner of operating another condition, without which any combination, even the most able, may become a danger, that is, such perception in the soldiers and lieutenants, that on coming face to face with an unforeseen circumstance, they know by their energy—as General Dupont's soldiers at Haslach, Marshal Mortier's at Dürrenstein, and Marshal Ney's at Elchingen—how to give to the supreme conception which directed them the leisure to come to their assistance and repair such errors as are inevitable even in the best-conducted operations. Let us repeat what we have said before, that it is necessary to have a great captain for valiant soldiers, and also valiant soldiers for a great captain. The glory, as well as the merit for the great deeds which they achieve, should be common to both.

The French soldiers did not take the number of their adversaries into account. As brave soldiers they had faith in their own valour. All ranks alike showed the same zeal, the same eagerness to go beyond their simple duty. If one distinguished himself, the others strove to surpass him by their courage, their talents, and their initiative. This was the only road to advancement, mediocrity had not the least chance.

Napoleon, wishing to tighten his grasp on Ulm, ordered Ney to march up the left bank of the Danube and seize all the bridges on the river, so that his army might be free to operate on either bank.

The marshal was also to give him warning of any attempt which the enemy might make to regain Bohemia by passing across the rear and communications of the *Grande Armée*.

Murat and Lannes were at the same time to march up the right bank of the Danube and co-operate with Ney.

During the night of the 8th and 9th of October, Ney heard from Berthier. The chief of the staff wrote:

> ... In one word, you are enjoined to watch the corps in Ulm. Should it march on Donauwörth, you must follow it; if it marches on Augsburg, you will have equally to go after it, keeping always on its left, that is to say between it and Donauwörth, and you should keep always a division half a day's march in rear (Berthier's meaning was not very clear) to form your advanced guard, and to find yourself always athwart the enemy and Donauwörth, should he at any time move in the direction of that city.

Ney, in short, was intended to frustrate any movements which the Austrians from Ulm might attempt to make on Augsburg or Donauwörth.

From having taken part in Moreau's campaign in 1880, the marshal was pretty familiar with the locality.

On the morning of the 9th, Ney directed Dupont's division on Albeck, Loison's on Langenau, and Malher's on Günzburg. He had other divisions besides his own which had been attached to him temporarily, but he left Gazan's at Gundelfingen and Baraguey d'Hilliers' at Herbrechtingen. These two divisions were by a later order to march for Augsburg, the emperor being under the impression that Mack had quitted Ulm and intended to give battle somewhere near Augsburg. In fact, we find Berthier writing to Ney the same day that, as at the most Ulm was occupied by 3,000 or 4,000 men, he was to send one of his divisions to turn the Austrians out of it. However, should the enemy be found holding the city with considerable forces, he was to march against the place with the whole of his army corps, carry the city, and capture many prisoners, after which, according to the enemy's movements, Ney was to follow him to Augsburg, Landsberg, or Memmingen.

On the 9th, Ney's divisions marched from their camps on the Brenz. On the right, at the break of day, Crabbé, an *aide-de-camp*, moved off with a detachment of Dupont's division on Albeck.

★★★★★★

Crabbé was Marshal Ney's *aide-de-camp*. He was a most en-

The Battle of Ulm

terprising officer whom the marshal entrusted with every description of service. He has been described as being himself the advanced guard of the 6th Corps from Lauterburg up to Ulm.

★★★★★★

After a slight skirmish near Hausen, Crabbé was attacked by superior numbers, and retired on to the woods in rear of Albeck. There he was joined at 6 p.m. by Dupont's division. Dupont showed a bold front, and the Austrian posts withdrew; the French ended by bivouacking in front of Albeck.

In the centre Loison's division marched from Burberg to Langenau by a narrow, sunken road, and took post in rear of the Langenau stream. During the night (9th-10th) Villate's brigade marched on Ober Elchingen with a squadron of hussars and two 8-pdrs. The hussars rushed the Austrian picket on the left bank. The 6th Light Infantry then crossed the bridge as well as they could over the trestles, for the Austrians had removed part of the planking. The battalion left by the enemy for the defence of the bridge retired, leaving in the hands of the French 57 prisoners and a gun.

Malher's division was told off to carry the bridges of Günzburg. These bridges were three in number; the principal was in front of the small town of Günzburg, the second above it in front of Leipheim, the third below, in front of the small hamlet of Reissenburg. The division was split up into three columns. One column, under Lefol, composed of 6 companies of grenadiers, 3 of carabineers, 3 of *voltigeurs*, and 20 *Chasseurs à Cheval*, went direct to Leipheim across the marshes, lost itself, and only turned up at Reidhausen in the middle of the night. Malher marched with the central column at the head of Marcognet's brigade. This column consisted of 3 battalions of the 25th Light Infantry, 1 battalion of the 27th of the Line, and 2 of the 50th, with 4 guns, and marched by Brenz, Sontheim, and Reidhausen. On reaching the woods which line the Danube, Marcognet fell in with the enemy.

The river in this section of its course flows in a very irregular narrow bed, and is cut up by many islands and small arms covered with willows and poplars. The French advanced guard forded all the small rivulets on their way and captured Baron d'Aspre, who was commanding at that point, with some few hundred Tyrolese. When they came upon the principal branch of the river, they found the bridge damaged, as the Austrians on retiring had destroyed one of the trusses. Malher tried to have it repaired, but the Austrians had posted several regiments with a number of guns on the right bank of the Danube, and the Archduke Ferdinand had hastened to the spot with considerable reinforcements. A heavy musketry and artillery fire was opened on the French, and many of the men who were trying to repair the bridge were killed and wounded.

The troops, who were in the open on the gravel banks of the river, were fully exposed to the enemy's fire, and Malher, not to incur a useless loss, made them fall back and seek shelter in the wooded islands. The attack had cost the French a few hundred men.

The third column was more successful. General Labassée had taken with him the 59th Regiment, having at its head Colonel Lacuée, and struck the Danube on the shore of the great branch. Here also the Austrians had rendered the bridge impassable by removing one of the trusses. The destruction, however, had been done carelessly, and the French were able to repair the bridge. The 59th, headed by the gallant Lacuée, who fell in the attack, rushed the bridge and carried Reissenburg and the surrounding heights in the face of forces three times as numerous. The Austrian cavalry hastened to the assistance of the infantry, and seeing that only one infantry regiment had crossed the Danube, rushed impetuously at the 59th. That regiment formed in square, received three charges without flinching, and the Austrians were compelled to leave the French masters of the field.

Malher had succeeded in getting possession of one of the three bridges, and towards the end of the day brought the 50th to Reissenburg alongside of the gallant 59th. The Austrians after this ceased to dispute the bridge of Günzburg, and at night withdrew from that town and retired on Ulm, leaving in the hands of the French 1,000 prisoners and 300 wounded.

On the 10th of October Malher crossed the Danube at Günzburg and occupied the ground between that town and Leipheim; Loison concentrated his division at Langenau, and Dupont continued at Albeck. Gazan's division still remained at Gundelfingen, and the foot dragoons at Herbrechtingen. Seeing how the Austrians had drawn reinforcements from Ulm the previous day, Ney wrote in his report:

> The enemy in Ulm is stronger than it was supposed.

A statement which does not appear to have carried conviction to the mind of the emperor.

Everywhere the bridges were found more or less damaged, but generally speaking, the enemy had withdrawn without offering a really serious resistance. The bridges which Ney's divisions attacked on the 9th appear to have been just sufficiently damaged as to render them impassable, otherwise their repair under fire would never have been attempted. This fact may be taken to indicate either that their destruction was taken in hand at too late a period, or that the Austrian staff considered it likely that they would have to use them sometime soon for their own army.

In the fight on the 9th, as it had occurred at Wertingen, the Austrian troops showed a lack of tenacity; they did not disdain to admit themselves beaten; they gave up the contest too soon, even when in superior numbers. Looking at the importance of the bridges, theirs should have been a *combat à outrance*.

The reason why Napoleon was disposed to accord less importance to an Austrian retreat into Bohemia than to one in the direction of the Tyrol was that he judged that the Austrians and Russians could sooner come together in the latter direction. He consequently looked forward to a battle on the Iller, where he conceived the bulk of the Austrian Army to be. All the measures he took naturally tended to close the Tyrol route. Nevertheless, the emperor still held in mind the other alternative open to Mack—a retreat by the left bank of the Danube. This can be clearly seen by his having made Ney's corps so strong before the rest of the army crossed the Danube, and by having in a special manner detailed him for service on the left bank of that river.

He was not likely to have overlooked Moreau's success on the Danube in 1800, and how, after his defeat at Höchstet, Kray, leaving a large garrison in Ulm, quitted that city and retired by Neresheim and Nördlingen to come down on Neuburg, recross the Danube and occupy the line of the Lech. It was possible for Mack, on finding the enemy in his rear, to adopt a similar course. In this instance the matter required closer attention, as the magazines and depots of the *Grande Armée* were on the left bank of the Danube, and in dangerous exposure.

On the 10th of October, Ney had brought Loison's and Malher's divisions across to the right bank of the river, with a view of connecting with Murat and Lannes, who were coming from Burgau. On the arrival of the two marshals, Ney intended that his two divisions should cross to the left bank of the river, in order to bar the enemy's retreat into Bohemia.

Murat had quite misunderstood the emperor's instructions, which enjoined concentrating towards the Iller as many troops as possible. This order did not apply to the 6th Corps, for which special dispositions had been made. Murat ordered Ney to gather all his forces,

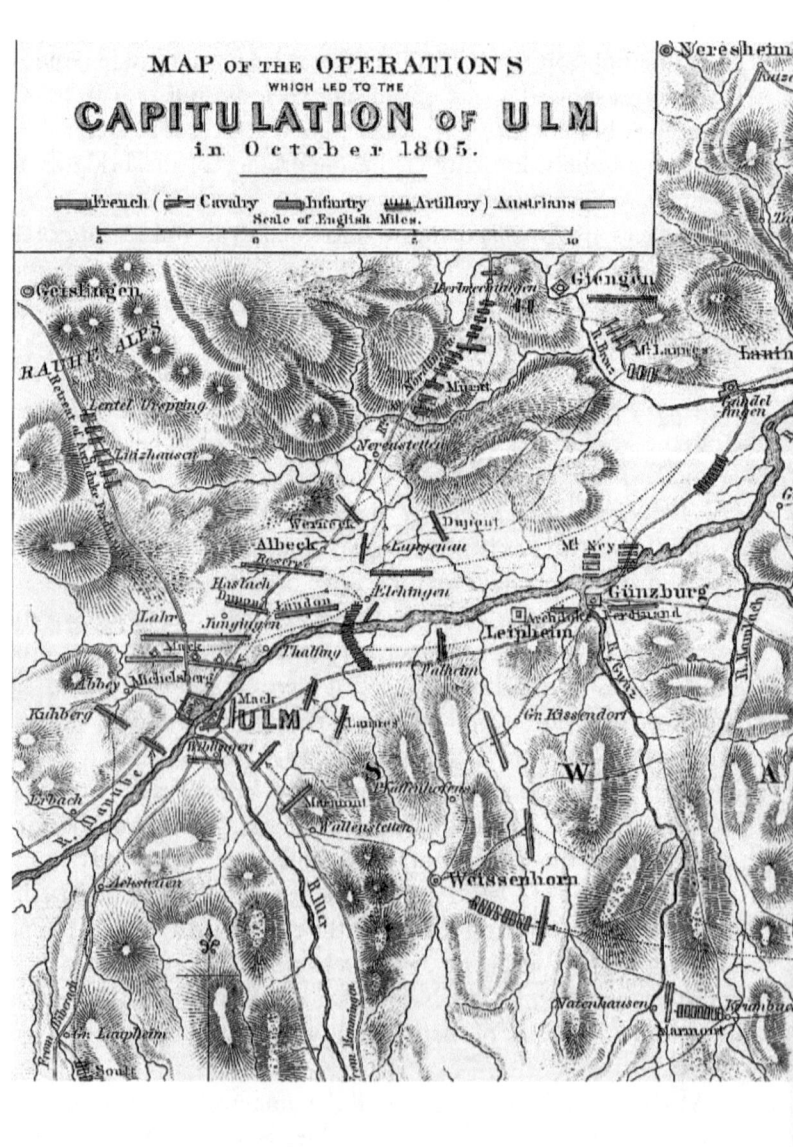

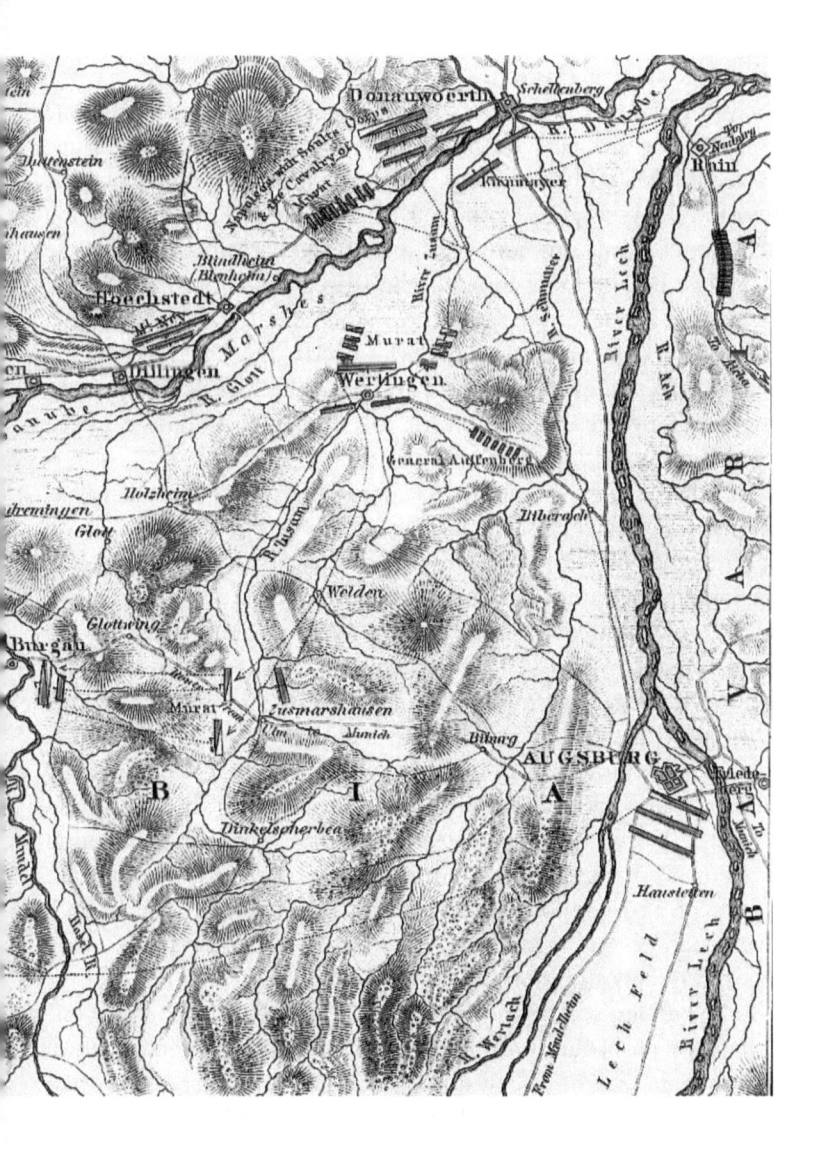

including Dupont's division, and to move from Günzburg and Elchingen on Wiblingen and the Both, which would have left the French communications uncovered. Tardy orders were dispatched to Dupont, and fortunately Napoleon's conception was not spoilt, for the Austrian advance compelled Dupont to remain on the left bank, where, complying with the original order he had received, he fought a stubborn engagement at Haslach.

Ney was fully alive to the strangeness of his position, with one division on the left bank of the Danube and two on the right bank. He asked himself why should not the Austrians seize such a favourable opportunity for escaping by the left bank of the river, and capturing all the French parks and convoys, he discussed the situation with the chief of his staff, Colonel Jomini, who shared the same opinion. On this point he had a serious altercation with Murat, who insisted that there was not the least danger, and who declared that he held identical views with the emperor; that a battle on the Iller was imminent; consequently by keeping Dupont on the left bank his division would be out of reach the day of the great battle.

From the very beginning of the campaign it was evident that little harmony reigned amongst the marshals. If they were not cordial with each other, the whole of them were unfriendly to the chief of the staff. To maintain peace amongst his senior officers Napoleon had to allow them a considerable amount of latitude. Ney resented Murat having been placed above him in this instance, as not being in any way his superior with regard to military ability. Certainly, it must be owned on this point that Murat in this campaign gave repeated proofs of a heedless and rash disposition, obdurate and not likely to be influenced by other people's arguments once he had formed his own opinion on any subject. He was not reliable, and had more courage than sound ability. For headlong courage he had possibly no equal, if we except Ney himself. Though nothing delighted Napoleon more than Murat's brilliant courage, yet he could not overlook his thoughtlessness, ostentation, and restless ambition.

Murat, besides, was wrong, for the emperor admitted the possibility, if not the probability, of the Austrians retiring by the left bank of the Danube; in fact, he believed the whole of Ney's corps to be then on that bank of the river. Its withdrawal from the left bank of the river, as Murat had ordered, was a serious blunder, for it amounted to nothing else than a gratuitous uncovering of the Austrian line of retreat into Bohemia.

Berthier was of the same way of thinking as the emperor; he imagined that, being bent on moving for the Tyrol, Mack would take with him most of his troops, leaving only a very limited number to garrison the city of Ulm.

On the 11th of October, whilst Ney was directing the bulk of his troops on the right of the Danube towards the Roth, and at Murat's headquarters the discussion ran high regarding Dupont's division, whether it should remain on the left bank of the Danube or not, that general, approaching Ulm, came into contact with 25,000 Austrians, which had issued from Ulm to open the way for the march of the archduke. A council of war had determined that at the head of that number of troops the Archduke Ferdinand should quit Ulm and fray himself a passage towards Bohemia by the Heidensheim and Nördlingen road.

Uncertain on account of the conflicting orders he had received, Ney had obeyed Murat only in part, and complied with Berthier's orders of the 9th. Dupont's and Baraguey d'Hilliers' divisions remained on the left bank of the Danube; Dupont being ordered to carry Ulm, and Baraguey d'Hilliers to support him.

The conveyance of these orders, and the manner in which they were obeyed, gave rise to several mischances, and only good fortune averted a disaster in the end. The orders, being for two generals, of whom one was at Albeck, the other at Stötzingen, places about ten miles apart, should have been conveyed by two staff officers; in this case they were entrusted to one, who was ordered to proceed first to Stötzingen, and afterwards to Albeck. Chef d'escadron Rippert, the officer in question, left Günzburg at 3 in the morning of the 11th, and lost his way in crossing the Donau Moos.

Having wandered about the swamps in the dark, as day broke, he found himself close to Langenau and Albeck. Rippert then considered that being so close to Albeck he should invert his order of going by delivering to Dupont his orders first, and then proceed to Stötzingen. Dupont received his at 8, and Baraguey d'Hilliers his at 11 (a disputed point, Baraguey d'Hilliers insisting that he only got them at about noon). So dilatory, however, was the latter in his arrangements for the march, that his division did not leave Stötzingen before 3 in the afternoon.

Dupont, who, as we have seen, had received his orders at 8 a.m., proceeded to carry them out at 11 a.m. He had with him—

The 9th Light Infantry	... ...	1,763	of all ranks.
,, 32nd of the Line	... ...	1,662	,, ,,
,, 96th ,, ,,	... ...	1,721	,, ,,
,, 15th Dragoons } ,, 17th ,, }	... ...	673	,, ,,
,, 1st Hussars ...	... ...	375	,, ,,
Gunners ...	... ...	250	,, ,,
Total		6,444	

Guns—two 4-pdrs., two 12-pdrs., six 8-pdrs., one howitzer, and three cavalry howitzers; in all 14 pieces.

His division was not strong, but he relied on being supported by the 4,500 men of Baraguey's division, as he knew through Rippert that they had received orders from Ney to support him.

Dupont marched from his camp at Albeck in the direction of Ulm. On reaching the village of Haslach, he was surprised to see the heights of Michelsberg occupied by the right wing of the enemy under arms. That day the Austrians were commencing their march northwards, and came unexpectedly across Dupont's division. The Austrians numbered 25,000 men, the French were only 6,444 strong.

Ney had enjoined Dupont not to hazard an engagement with overwhelming forces, but Dupont justly reflected that, were he to retire, he would thereby expose the weakness of his forces, encourage the enemy to assume a vigorous offensive, and show to him that the Nördlingen road was open. On the other hand, if he were to brave it out, be believed he might succeed in deceiving him. If he commenced the combat, the Austrians would naturally be led to believe that his division formed the advanced guard of the entire French Army. Dupont thereupon made his dispositions for battle; he deployed his division in a single line, the flanks resting on Haslach and Jungingen.

The Archduke Ferdinand, as Dupont had foreseen, took this division for the advanced guard of Ney's corps. Seeing that it halted at Haslach, the Austrians deployed several regiments, and soon tried to overlap both flanks of the French. Dupont had on his left the village of Haslach, surrounded by a small wood. He ordered General Rouger to deploy the 9th Light Infantry in front of the village; the 17th Dragoons were keeping the *Uhlans* in countenance. General Marchand had deployed the 32nd to the left of the 9th, the 96th were held in reserve at Haslach, and the 1st Hussars covered the French left.

Perceiving that he was being turned on the right, Dupont took the 96th in that direction, not far from the 9th, and supported by a goodly portion of his artillery. Feeling that his division would be destroyed by musketry alone, were he to allow the enemy leisure to deploy, he ordered the 9th to charge the Austrian column. That regiment advanced into the plain without firing, and rushed at once on the nearest corps. The 96th charged alongside of the 9th, and the two regiments overthrew the enemy's first line, and captured between them some 1,500 prisoners.

A battalion of the 32nd, judiciously posted between the wood which lies in rear of Jungingen and that village, held the Austrian cavalry in check. Some companies, by occupying the small woods along the French front, hid from the enemy the weakness of their centre.

The 15th and 17th Dragoons, deployed in two lines, charged the enemy's cavalry, which was overlapping the French right flank. The 15th, overcome by superior numbers, were borne back and compelled to retire; but they quickly reformed in rear of the 17th, which charged in its turn. The cavalry, however, had to contend against superior numbers, and was forced to retire into the wood. There a general *mêlée* occurred, for the French and the Austrians entered the wood together. In this action, out of a total of 673 officers and men, Dupont's cavalry brigade lost in killed, wounded, and prisoners 152 officers, non-commissioned officers, and men.

The Archduke Ferdinand, who evidently imagined that he had to contend with a very considerable body of the enemy, lost much time in manoeuvring, thus enabling Dupont to prolong the contest till night.

The 9th and 96th had to contest the ground between Haslach and Jungingen for fully three hours. The last village was captured and recaptured five times. Every time the Austrians were driven out of it, they lost many prisoners. These prisoners were sent to Haslach, where the 32nd, in spite of continuous attacks, managed to hold its position.

Under cover of darkness, and having picked up his wounded, Dupont fell back on Albeck; he then moved eastwards on Langenau and Brenz, so as to get within easy reach of Ney on the morrow.

This determined resistance had cost Dupont one-third of his force, which had been placed *hors de combat*. The Austrian cavalry, two regiments of *cuirassiers* (Mack and Archduke Albert), and La Tours light horse, had during the contest driven the French cavalry back to Albeck; they then swept along the French rear and captured Dupont's park and baggage. In consequence of the orders which were badly carried and leisurely executed, Baraguey d'Hilliers, though close at hand, at Langenau, had not moved to Dupont's assistance.

Notwithstanding the heavy loss of the French on the 11th, the combat had marked consequences; it showed Mack what little prospect there was that his army would be able to withdraw into Bohemia by way of Albeck.

At Haslach things did not occur quite in the manner in which Dupont reported them. Writing to General Sanson, he says:

> The success was complete; night had come on, and we remained masters of the battlefield.

The Austrians retired, true enough, but the French had lost two eagles and ten guns. The Austrians claimed the victory. Nevertheless, Dupont remained on the ground till he had collected all his wounded, and retired with his prisoners, over 4,000 in number.

The Austrians do not seem to have displayed much skill in the attack; in any case, their efforts were not simultaneous. They did not derive full advantage from their superior numbers from a want of unanimity between Mack and the Archduke Ferdinand. One directed the operations on the left, the other on the right, in accordance with their special views, and there was no supreme control over the two.

While the Austrian cavalry raided in rear of Dupont's division, it foiled to ascertain, what was most precious at that moment for the commander-in-chief, whether the French force was an isolated division or the advanced guard of the French Army.

With regard to the infantry, their battalions advanced only to be broken in succession, and the French, having in every turn of the action to contend against inferior forces, were able to have the best of it in several partial affairs. They fought valiantly against an adversary strong enough to annihilate them.

An officer, a captain in the Austrian staff, writes in the *Rélation de la prise d'Ulm*:

> Some battalions (Ludwig, Reiner, and Kaunitz) conducted themselves in a miserable way, and were mostly taken prisoners by a handful of skirmishers.

Haslach may be regarded as the most important of the minor actions of the campaign, for had Dupont not shown the bold front he did for several hours, and had he retired when he suddenly beheld the enemy's great strength, the entire course of the campaign would have been altered. The Austrian commander did not know how to turn to account an important capture made by his cavalry in rear of Dupont, for in this raid were found Dupont's papers, with the orders for

Capitulation of the Austrian Army at Ulm

the 6th Corps to capture Ulm by an advance by the left bank of the Danube, whilst the rest of the army was manoeuvring along the right bank of the river. These papers put the Austrian staff in possession of the exact situation of the French Army, and nothing would have been easier with a little energy than to steal two or three marches on the route to Bohemia. As the spirit of his troops had been restored by the supposed victory of Haslach, Mack made a plan to effect a junction with the Russians at Ratisbonne by marching- down the left bank of the Danube, thus threatening the enemy's communications and rear.

There was indeed on this occasion an uncertainty in the emperor's mind, similar to that which worried him in the Marengo campaign, *viz.* to discover the course which Mack would most likely pursue. The Austrian commander had two ways open to him for getting out of the dangerous strait he was in; a retreat into Bohemia, or one towards the Vorarlberg. As usual with him, Napoleon conceived that the Austrian commander would follow the latter, which was by far the easiest plan. He believed that in the difficulties Mack was in, the best course for him to follow would have been to work southwards in the direction of the Tyrol, which he could reach in three marches by Memmingen and Kempten. This would have enabled him to effect a junction with the Archduke John, and place himself in communication with the Archduke Charles.

We may pause a moment and examine what was Napoleon's conception of the state of affairs about the 11th of October. The emperor was principally disposed to believe that the Austrian Army was posted on the Iller; however, an erroneous report that the Archduke Ferdinand was at Munich made him believe it possible that the Austrians might have escaped by the way of Füssen. Murat wished to attack them on the Iller on the 12th, but Napoleon enjoined him to delay the attack till the 14th, as he contemplated making a general attack, in which Soult would take part. The latter was to come up with 30,000 men, overlap the Austrian right and turn it, which would lead to a sure and decided success. Napoleon assured Murat that the affair would be serious and conduce to important results. Berthier, writing to Davout, stated that the emperor estimated the Austrians to be 80,000 or 90,000 strong.

Napoleon, however, was not certain, as can be seen by Berthier's dispatch to Bernadotte:

Prince Ferdinand's presence at Munich makes His Majesty fear

The Capitulation at Ulm

that the enemy who was on the Iller may have escaped and retired towards the Tyrol.

Berthier writes to Soult:

> The enemy is on the Iller, the left resting on Ulm, the right on Memmingen. Prince Murat, with whom are Marshals Lannes and Ney, is confronting him, his left being at Weissenhorn, his right at Albeck.

With this prospect of a probable battle on the Iller, Napoleon had ordered up two of Marmont's divisions to take post at Krumbach between Murat and Soult.

Napoleon foresaw all the possible alternatives—Mack's movement towards Nördlingen, as well as his retreat into the Tyrol. He did not neglect the probable operations on the northern bank of the Danube. To that effect, he ordered Murat to repair, or to throw a bridge opposite to Albeck. Murat repaired the one at Leipheim, and informed the emperor that on the morrow be would recapture those of Elchingen and Thalfingen.

On the faith of incomplete and inexact intelligence, the emperor had formed quite a false idea of the situation. The orders sent by Berthier to Davout show to the full his conceptions and projects on the 12th of October—

> On the 22nd *Vendémiaire* (12th of October) there will be a great battle on the Iller, near Ulm. Marshal Soult, with his army corps, is on the march from Memmingen. General Marmont, with the two French divisions of his army corps, is on the march so as to place himself on the heights of Illertissen, on the Iller. Marshal Lannes is at Weissenhorn, Marshal Ney athwart the Danube near Ulm. Lastly, the Imperial Guard is marching on Weissenhorn.
>
> On the 21st all the dispositions will have been taken; the 22nd, the day of the battle, the enemy shall be destroyed, as he is encompassed all round.
>
> This affair once settled, His Majesty will return so as to cross the Inn at once. Marshal Bernadotte and you, sir, will be two large operating corps, the remainder being your auxiliaries.

CHAPTER 8

Ulm—Operations on the Left Bank of the Danube

Whilst Napoleon was imagining this coming Battle of Weissenhorn, or of Illertissen, Lannes was writing an important letter to Murat, in which he declared that the emperor had made a very inexact estimate of the situation, and demanding to be permitted without delay to cross over to the left bank of the Danube. He wrote:

> The enemy's army is on the left bank of the Danube. At this moment in Ulm there are no more than 4,000 or 5,000 men, and what he has on the right bank is very trifling. Everything seems to show that the enemy purposes retiring by way of Franconia, and I have not the least doubt that he will commence his movement this very night.

Lannes pointed out the urgency of the case, and requested that a very considerable portion of the prince's forces might be sent at once across the Danube. Also, that Murat might consider it fit to acquaint the emperor with this state of things.

Murat, who several times in the course of this campaign showed little judgment, did not share Lannes' opinions, his most plausible reason being a desire not to derange the emperor's plan, and leaving it to him to order the movement across the Danube. A more forcible reason was the weather, which was indeed most dreadful, and the heavy rain to which the troops had been exposed had retarded their march, so much so that they had only settled in their positions by ten that night; it did not consequently appear desirable to him that they should recommence marching at daybreak.

Lannes' letter and the news of Dupont's fight at Haslach drew Napoleon's attention to the left bank of the Danube. He began to doubt if the battle on the Iller would ever come off, and to look on a retreat of the Austrians into Bohemia by way of Nördlingen as not an unreasonable step.

He hastened from Augsburg to the Danube, being followed by Marmont's corps and the guard. He arrived at Günzburg on the 13th; there and at Pfaffenhofen he tried, but in vain, to acquire an exact account of the positions held by the 6th Corps. He imagined that Loison's and Malher's divisions were cantoned in the villages of Leipheim, Falheim, and Nersingen, that they occupied Elchingen, and that Dupont was holding Albeck.

Soon, however, he was undeceived, for news came in that Dupont, with the enemy all round him, was at Brenz; that of the 6th Corps only Marcognet, with a battalion of the 25th Light and forty hussars, had gone to Ober-Elchingen. Marcognet, his task done, came suddenly face to face on the plateau with three Austrian battalions and four squadrons, but as he considered he had complied with his orders, he retraced his steps.

In front of the bridge of Elchingen there were only three companies of grenadiers forming part of Loison's division.

Evidently during the emperor's absence at Augsburg his lieutenants had shown very little enterprise; they had failed to acquire a full knowledge of the enemy's movements. It was high time for him to be present, for him to take the management of the operations under his personal direction.

Napoleon was anxious and impatient, and not without reason, for he had learnt from Murat that the Austrians were not in front of him, that they had crossed to the left bank of the Danube. During the night 10th-11th of October his attention was more and more directed to what was passing on the left bank of the Danube. He then began to realise that the principal stroke might be expected to be delivered by the enemy in that direction. He consequently instructed Lannes to come as speedily as possible in support of Ney. Marmont would replace Oudinot in the positions occupied by that general.

Mack, driven back on the right bank of the Danube, had formed a plan for withdrawing into Bohemia by taking the Albeck-Heidenkeim-Nördlingen road, a plan somewhat similar to Kray's evacuation of Ulm in 1800.

To mask this manoeuvre, he had ordered Jellachich, with six battalions and two squadrons, about 5,000 men in all, to remain on the

Iller. In point of fact, Jellachich's orders were to move in the direction of Memmingen, following the left bank of the Iller, destroying all the bridges over that river as he went.

He was ordered to leave five battalions to garrison Memmingen, keeping the rest of his troops and those of General Spangen in the neighbourhood of that city. To put the French on a wrong scent, Jellachich crossed the Danube at Gaegglingen below Ulm, and marched to Ochsenhausen by way of Laupheim.

Ulm could not be invested entirely, nor the road to the Tyrol cut off unless by capturing Memmingen, crossing the Iller, and occupying Biberach. Two days after Dupont's fight had taken place at Haslach, Soult, who was advancing from Augsburg, made his appearance in front of Memmingen. The fortifications round that city had been repaired, and the city had been placed in a state to offer a certain amount of resistance. General Spangen commanded a force of eleven battalions, half a squadron of cavalry, and ten field guns, but he had no ammunition, and few supplies. The population was hostile to the Austrians, and, when Soult appeared before the place on the 13th, became very troublesome.

Spangen, seeing no chance of being supported, capitulated on the 14th of October with 5,000 men. His capitulation was hasty; in any case he might have tried to join Jellachich, who was near Ochsenhausen, only one day's march from Memmingen. In point of fact, he had received orders to do so.

Jellachich, being confronted by an army corps 30,000 strong, found himself in a dire predicament; nevertheless, he did not relish attempting to make his way back to Ulm. He adopted a bold plan, threw himself into the mountains, and escaped southwards to the Vorarlberg.

The action of some of the Austrian commanders strongly indicated their distrust of Mack, and the want of unanimity reigning at his headquarters.

Kienmayer, cut off from Ulm by Soult's arrival at Donauwörth, moved by Rain and Aücha without making any effort to rejoin Mack, and only halted after he had crossed the Inn. Jellachich, with his division, as we have said, looked for safety in the Vorarlberg.

Neither Murat nor Ney showed much talent in this instance. It must be pleaded in their extenuation that, having demanded blind obedience from his marshals and generals, Napoleon had deprived them of most of their initiative and power of reflection. What were they when away from him, and when consequently they had to take immediate decisions?

They hesitated, they groped about in the dark, and often ended by failing in their operations. Napoleon's system is revealed in a letter be wrote to Berthier, his chief of the staff, on the 14th of February 1806:

> *Tenez vous-en strictement aux ordres que je vous donne. Exécutez ponctuellement vos instructions: que tout le monde se tienne sur ses gardes juste à son paste. Moi seul je sais ce que je dois faire.* (Keep strictly to the orders I give you. Execute your instructions punctually: let everyone stand on guard just at his desk. I alone know what I have to do.)

It needed Napoleon himself to take up the threads of the operations which Murat had messed. It was at this period that, writing to Murat, the emperor enunciated the following principle:

> March against the enemy wherever he may be, but with caution and unity. . . . Nothing should be risked, and the first of all rules is to possess a numerical superiority.

On the 12th, the day after the fight at Haslach, the disappearance of Dupont's division had raised Mack's spirits. He came to the hasty conclusion that the French had entirely abandoned the left bank of the Danube, and that he was free to march with his army into Bohemia.

To turn out a success, this movement along the left bank of the Danube needed boldness and energy, elements which were wanting in the Austrian Army. It required the marching powers of the French, which it lacked.

True enough it was carried out in inclement weather, with roads muddy and sodden by heavy rains. Still, under the same conditions, we shall see a little further on how briskly Oudinot's grenadiers could march.

Mack probably hesitated to press on the operations, having learnt through a false spy, and from rumours which had reached him from Von Steinherr, that a report was current that the English had landed an army at Boulogne, and that the French were retreating hurriedly on Stuttgart.

On the 13th his army, formed into two powerful columns, advanced; one column, the left one, with the reserve artillery and baggage, marching by the Albeck road, the other, the right, by the heights of Elchingen and Langenau. The advance guard of Werneck's column got as far as the Brenz at Herbrechtingen, nineteen miles from Ulm, the same night.

The right column, under Riesch, was directed at the last moment on Gündelfingen, to protect the right flank of the retiring army.

Loudon, who marched with this column, went by way of Thalfingen, and reached Ober-Elchingen a little after noon, having a skirmish with a battalion Ney had pushed forward. This battalion was dislodged from the village and driven beyond the bridge over the Danube. Loudon then waited for Hesse-Homburg's division, which was so retarded by the bad state of the roads that it prevented the column from getting beyond Unter-Elchingen that night. On the following day, as the Austrians were about to resume their march for Bohemia, they were attacked by the French.

Napoleon felt alarmed by the news of the combat at Haslach, and, fearing that the left bank of the Danube would be found denuded of troops, proceeded, as we have seen, in all haste to Küssendorf, to make Ney recross the Danube and reoccupy as soon as possible the positions on the left bank of the river, which had been imprudently abandoned.

The jealousy and dissensions which existed amongst Napoleon's marshals, and which often proved detrimental to French arms, is notorious. This showed itself at a very early date. The emperor had left Ney, Lannes, and Murat in the neighbourhood of Ulm to contain Mack. The chief command was given to the latter, possibly in virtue of his title of Prince, or of his being the emperor's brother-in-law. This arrangement, however, did not please the other two marshals.

Ney was nettled by bitter reproaches he had received from the emperor, but even more hurt by stinging remarks Murat had indulged in a few days previously. When rejecting some explanations, Murat had told him that he never made any plans except in the presence of the enemy. On the morning when he was about to attack Elchingen, Ney, being in full uniform, conspicuous by his orders, his face expressing all the firm and haughty resolution of his soul, took the prince by the arm in presence of the emperor and the whole of the headquarter staff, and told him, "Prince, come with me to make your plans in the presence of the enemy."

Having spoken which words, he rushed in the midst of a most tremendous fire to take the personal direction of the operations.

The other divisions of the 6th Corps, Malher's and Dupont's, had fought at Günsburg and Haslach; the second, Loison's, had not yet had a chance of doing anything in the campaign, and was eager to get an opportunity of distinguishing itself; on the 14th it was its turn. Ney had about 8,800 troops:

Villatte's brigade	6th Light Infantry	... ...	1,740 men
	39th of the Line	... ...	1,640 „
Roguet's brigade	69th „ „	... ...	1,720 „
	76th „ „	... ...	1,800 „
			6,900

Cavalry—3rd Hussars	... ...	340 men	
„ 10th *Chasseurs*	... ...	350 „	
„ 18th Dragoons	... ...	335 „	
„ 19th Dragoons	... ...	440 „	
„ 25th Dragoons	... ...	490 „	
			1,955 „
	Total	...	8,855 „

Elchingen lies about five miles from Ulm. The village in the form of an amphitheatre rises from the banks of the Danube up to a spacious abbey, which crowns the summit of the ascent. When Marcognet withdrew from Elchingen the previous night, he had rendered the bridge impassable. The Austrians guarded it on the right bank with two battalions and a couple of guns.

Riesch, who had passed the night at Elchingen, was about to continue his march towards Brenz. At daybreak Mecsery, with the advanced guard, four battalions and five squadrons, had set out for Langenau, and was followed by ten battalions commanded by Loudon. As Riesch was about to follow, he received word that the French were advancing to the attack, that they had occupied the island of the Danube opposite Elchingen, and that Unter-Elchingen was threatened. Loudon and Mecsery were at once recalled, but the latter was already contending with Dupont's division near Langenau.

Riesch posted a battalion in the village of Ober-Elchingen, another in the buildings of the Benedictine abbey (a Gothic edifice of immense extent), the remainder of the troops he kept in hand in rear of these two posts. All the exposed points on the heights were commanded by artillery, and the windows of the abbey were filled with musketeers. Loudon, posted between the abbey and Unter-Elchingen, commanded the left wing; the right wing, which extended in the direction of Thalfingen and the Danube, was under Hesse-Homburg.

Riesch reinforced the troops guarding the bridge by two more battalions and four guns, with orders to hold the position to the very last. General Schönhals states that these reinforcing infantry did not, however, arrive in time to co-operate in the defence of the bridge. As Riesch saw the French crossing, he judged that it was no longer in his power to stave off a serious engagement.

The attack presented some difficulty, for the chesses of the bridge, a wooden one from eighty to a hundred yards long, had been removed, and the damage had to be made good under a murderous fire. Ney, with eleven guns, silenced those of the Austrians; but he was eager to close with them. Captain Coisel, aided by a pioneer of the 6th, commenced to replace the chesses, but fell severely wounded. The flank companies of the 6th and 39th then rushed forward to undertake the repairs. The boldest crossed by the girders, reached the left bank of the river, and spread out as skirmishers.

The French, having driven away the Austrians from the Custom House buildings, repaired the bridge as well as they could. Loison lost no time in crossing with Villatte's brigade, and pursued the enemy up to the foot of the slope on which the abbey stood. No one equals the French at an attack, but the village and convent were stoutly defended; they consequently suffered severely. Loison had already failed in two attacks, when Malher's division reached Unter-Elchingen.

Inspirited by the arrival of this reinforcement, the 6th Light Infantry made a furious attack on the abbey and succeeded in driving the enemy out. The abbey was the key of the position, and its capture broke the Austrian line of battle; the right wing, nevertheless, continued the contest for some time under cover of a wood situated to the west of Elchingen. The left, which rested on the chapel Sanct-Wolffgang, succumbed at last to several charges of light cavalry and of Bourcier's dragoons. Riesch, being unable to reform his troops in rear of the Kesselbrünn ravine, decided to retire on Ulm by way of Haslach.

The French pursued with great vigour, captured 2,000 prisoners and almost the whole of the Austrian artillery. The village of Elchingen was completely sacked, the abbey left full of dead and wounded. Ney directed the whole of the operations, and effected all this with great dash and brilliancy. (Such was Ney's reputation, that it is related how Jourdan and Kleber actually quarrelled as to who was to have the advantage of his services.)

In no other field, except in the retreat from Moscow, did he display more conspicuous bravery. He was always in the thick of the fight, present always with the foremost, and for his share in that day's fighting was afterwards awarded the title of Duc d'Elchingen—a title he bore up to the Battle of Borodino, when he was created Duc de la Moskowa.

★★★★★★

Fortunate for Ney, who had jested with death many a time in

many battles, had he fallen, like Desaix, at the head of his troops in the hour of victory. It pleased Providence to spare him, but cruel was his fate in the end. Who can but regret that so much heroism should have been laid low by a discharge of musketry in an obscure corner of the Luxemburg? The convention of the 3rd July 1815 between the allies and the military government, which should have been a sacred guarantee, did not protect him against the reactionary hatreds. Really the Bourbon revenge has made people almost forget the marshal's treason.

★★★★★★

Beaten on every side, the Austrians were pushed back from one position to another up to the main road of Albeck.

In this fight the Austrians did not contest the passage of the Danube with anything like spirit.

Napoleon would not rest satisfied with simply defeating the Austrians at Elchingen, he wanted over and above this to seize the heights which commanded the bridge-head of Ulm, so as to prevent all further attempt to a retreat. His intention was communicated to the troops in a proclamation issued at Pfaffenhofen on the 13th of October:

> Soldiers, tomorrow will be a more renowned day than the one of Marengo. I have placed the enemy in the same position. . . . but to conquer him is to do nothing worthy of your emperor; it is imperative that not a single man shall escape!

The 15th was to be the decisive day. The emperor, whose headquarters were established in the abbey of Elchingen, had during the night of the 14th-15th issued his orders to thrust Mack back within the walls of Ulm and to achieve his ruin. These orders were punctually executed.

Ney undertook a long flank march, which led him to the north of Ulm in front of Michelsberg, with his right at Blau. He had to endeavour, by the aid of Bourcier's dragoon division, to close the circle. Lannes was to cross by the bridges of Elchingen and replace Ney on the Albeck road, with his left resting on the Danube and Thalfingen. He commenced his march at one o'clock in the morning under torrents of rain. Suchet and Oudinot crossed the Danube by the bridge of Elchingen and took up the positions quitted by the 6th Corps between Thalfingen and Haslach. Gazan, a little later, crossed at Thalfingen, followed by Klein's dragoons. Nausouty and the Imperial Guard followed Oudinot. Marmont brought forward one of his divisions towards Kapellenberg, and caused the other one to close on the bridge-head. Beaumont's dragoons occupied the interval. Soult was on the left bank of the Iller, ready to move up to Ulm.

Towards noon on the 15th, the French troops, formed in columns of attack, advanced on the city. Ney, with three battalions of Malher's divisions, assaulted and carried the principal redoubt on the Michelsberg. Another portion of his troops attacked the intrenchments on the west and drove in the Austrians lodged in the suburbs. Suchet attacked on the east of the Michelsberg and drove the enemy step by step back to the foot of the ramparts. It was after this first success that, expecting to be adequately supported, he ordered Claparède to carry the Goensethor gate with one battalion of the 17th Light Infantry, whilst Vedel, with the second battalion, stormed the Frauenthor gate. Suchet was not supported, the enemy already driven into the town took heart and resumed the offensive, with the result that Colonel Vedel and a large portion of his troops were made prisoners.

To make the best use of victory requires more talent than to win it. There could be no possible doubt as to the result in this instance. Had an assault of the city of Ulm been ordered, it would, however, have led to what was rightly considered in the actual circumstances of the case an unnecessary loss of life. So thought Napoleon. He therefore made his troops draw back from the suburbs, and satisfied himself by throwing a few shells into the city, after which he sent De Ségur to intimate to Mack that nothing was left to him but to surrender.

The weather continued very inclement; it rained incessantly. On the 16th a terrible hurricane swept over the country round Ulm; the Danube swelled very considerably, and carried away nearly all the bridges, so that the French Army, which occupied both banks of the river, in order to blockade Ulm, was separated into two portions, quite unable to communicate with each other. This state of things lasted three days, and had Mack only known how to profit by this circumstance, he might have got out of his fix. He could by using the permanent bridge over the Danube at Ulm have attacked with the whole of his forces the most feeble half of the French Army thus separated.

The emperor himself was not free from discomfort. Writing to Josephine from Pfaffenhofen on the 10th of October, he says that all promises that the campaign will be short and brilliant, but always in the wet, in most frightful weather which forced him to change his clothes twice a day. Neither did he fare sumptuously. The emperor spent the night after Ney's sanguinary combat at Elchingen, under the roof of a poor country curate at Ober-Falheim. Everything had been looted; he had not a drop of his favourite Chambertin wine, and an *aide-de-camp* had to cook him an omelette.

Prince Maurice of Liechtenstein was sent to the French Army headquarters to negotiate. He was conducted before Napoleon on horseback, with his eyes bandaged. The bandage was not removed until the prince was in the emperor's presence. Rapp relates that the prince was covered with confusion on finding himself suddenly face to face with Napoleon; that he did not even know that the emperor had joined the army; how he uttered an exclamation of surprise and candidly confessed that General Mack was not aware of his presence under the walls of Ulm. It seems strange, inasmuch as having captured the 17th Light Infantry with Colonel Vedel at their head, the Austrian staff should apparently have been better informed.

After the repeated defeats the Austrian Army had suffered, Mack's headquarters were in a great state of confusion. Notwithstanding mutual recriminations, all combined to lay on the shoulders of the *de facto* commander-in-chief the main cause of these disasters. At a stormy meeting held on the night of Elchingen, the Archduke Ferdinand, Schwarzenberg, and other generals were strongly of opinion that the army should fray itself a passage, if not to Bohemia, at least to the Tyrol.

The archduke took matters in his own hands, and on the night of the 14th-15th of October quitted Ulm at the head of his cavalry, twelve squadrons, commanded by Prince Schwarzenberg. He followed the Blaubeuren road, making a long detour to the northwest so as to avoid falling in with Dupont's outposts, then moving on Geisslingen and Aalen to endeavour to discover the exact position of Werneck's corps.

Werneck, who had been cut off from Ulm by Dupont, was ordered by the archduke on the 16th to join him on the Nördlingen road. The two together threatened the French communications, and captured some of the French parks and convoys. Werneck, however, had imprudently drawn attention to his corps by retracing his steps with the intention of attacking the French rear during the engagement at Michelsberg. Napoleon, warned that at Albeck, in his rear, Dupont's division was engaged with the Austrians, became alarmed, and there and then dispatched Murat with Klein's dragoons, a portion of the *Chasseurs à Cheval* of the guard, and Ney's light cavalry, on the Nördlingen road, to be followed by Dupont's infantry.

Murat set out at daybreak on the 16th, overtook Werneck's rear-guard at Nerenstetten, and defeated it, capturing 2,000 men. On the 17th be drove him out of Neresheim, then marched to Heidenheim, and on the 18th surrounded him at Trochtelfingen near Nördlingen, and made him surrender with all the infantry he still had, 8,000 men. (Of the Austrians taken prisoners in the positions of Langenau and Nerenstetten, Clarke writes, "*L'ennemi est en déroute et se rend facilement.*" "The enemy is routed and easily surrenders.") Werneck's cavalry, though bound to capitulate like the rest of his force, made off and joined the archduke at Œttingen. Somewhat to the left, at Bopfingen, Fauconnet's dragoon brigade captured the great park of 500 carriages which had escaped from Ulm, and all the materials and treasure which had been taken from the French in the few preceding days.

The Austrian troops which had escaped from Elchingen and Langenau had retired in a north-easterly direction; this made Napoleon anxious for the safety of his communications. On the 15th, he had sent to General Rivaud, who had been left at Ingolstadt by Bernadotte, an order to go with a portion of his division to Rain and Donauwörth to watch the enemy's movements.

Being much disturbed by the scarcity of news, he dispatched on the 18th Oudinot's grenadiers and Nansouty's *cuirassiers* to reinforce Murat. Oudinot's grenadiers distinguished themselves on this occasion by their marches, making several of fourteen and fifteen leagues in one day. The Austrian cavalry could barely keep in advance of them, and was several times overtaken by these indefatigable marchers.

The archduke, having already managed to reach Œttingen with his cavalry, continued his march towards Bohemia. Murat overtook him at the passage of the Altmühl by Gunzenhausen, and captured all his baggage and his last few guns. Gunzenhausen was on the Prussian frontier of Anspach, and a Prussian officer came to reclaim its neutrality. As the Austrians had received permission to cross the country in their flight, Murat paid no attention to such reclamation, and followed the archduke. Again, on the 20th, beyond Nuremberg, he overtook the Austrians, and at Eschenau captured their rear-guard. Murat did not pursue them any further. The archduke had not more than 1,500 horsemen left him; he was without a single gun or carriage.

From the very first this act of indiscipline—for, though bold, it could be called by no other name—promised, little success. No doubt the condition of the Austrian Army in Ulm was deplorable, and it must have been provoking for a high-spirited soldier not to be able to shake Mack's resolution to concentrate his forces in Ulm and there to await the arrival of the Russians. As Kutuzoff's advanced guard had appeared on the Inn by the 11th of October, it was within the range of possibility that he would make an effort to approach Ulm. But as the archduke and Mack, even on the eve of the capitulation, had concealed their defeats and only announced successes, there was no special reason why Kutuzoff should have pressed forward. The weather, besides, was so inclement that he had already been compelled to leave behind many sick and footsore men.

The archduke showed a bad example. To surrender as a prisoner of war to Napoleon may most certainly have been most distasteful to him; still for a soldier to evade sharing the bad fortune of his brother officers was a very reprehensible action. His was the third large detachment lost to Mack. Besides the heavy losses incurred in battle, that unfortunate general had been deprived of some 33,000 combatants. Kienmayer had gone with some 12,000 men, Jellachich with 5,000 or 6,000, the Archduke Ferdinand and Werneck had tried to escape with 15,000 more.

The only chance of saving this last detachment for future action lay in speedy marching; but the troops were hampered by a convoy of 500 vehicles, a most serious drag to rapid movement. To save the men, the convoy should have been sacrificed, or, better still, used as a decoy to put the pursuers on a false scent, gaining thereby one or two marches on them.

In pursuit of the Archduke Ferdinand, Murat captured 12,000 men in four days, during which he had kept up the pursuit incessantly, marching about 30 miles a day. In addition to the prisoners, he had captured 120 pieces of cannon, 500 laden wagons, 11 flags, 200 officers, and 17 generals.

On the 17th of October, Mack had declared himself ready to surrender the city of Ulm in ten days, unless an Austrian or Russian force should approach to raise the blockade. But when Napoleon heard of the capture of Werneck's corps, it struck him that he could hasten Mack's surrender, and so be able to continue his operations. On the 19th, he invited the Austrian commander-in-chief to his headquarters, then at Elchingen, and exposed to him the severe privations both armies were exposed to. Mack was told how on the 16th Murat had overtaken the Austrian forces only one day's distance from Ulm and inflicted on them a loss of 2,000 men; how, on the 17th, he had chased Werneck from Neresheim, and coming up again with him on the 18th, had surrounded him near Nördlingen and compelled him to surrender with all the infantry that remained with him, over 8,000 men.

Thus, all the troops who had quitted Ulm, with guns and 500 carriages, but eight days before had been captured. The Archduke Ferdinand had also been overtaken, compelled to abandon his army corps and fly to Bohemia with a few squadrons. That in the opposite direction Bernadotte, Davout, and the Bavarians, making a total of 60,000 combatants, occupied Bavaria and confronted the Russians, who had not yet appeared on the Inn. On being assured that there was not a single Austrian soldier between Ulm and the Inn, that Werneck had surrendered, and that Soult was blockading the issues of the Tyrol, Mack, overwhelmed by his misfortunes, consented to evacuate Ulm the following day.

So, Ulm surrendered after fourteen days of manoeuvring and fighting. Some people endeavoured to spread a report that Mack had been bribed, but that report was utterly devoid of truth. With very good reason he has been very much blamed for letting himself be persuaded by Napoleon's arguments into hastening the surrender of the city. It has been demonstrated that to keep a victorious army inactive for five more days could not have been a matter of pure indifference. Mack, however, had stipulated that Ney's corps—12 regiments of infantry and 4 of cavalry— should not quit Ulm and a radius of ten leagues round it until midnight of the 25th of October. If he considered it necessary to so paralyze a single corps, why should he not *a fortiori* have endeavoured to paralyze, the whole French Army?

A sufficient body of troops would have had in any case to be left in Ulm to guard the city and the Austrian prisoners till their departure for France. (Many of the prisoners escaped, as the French soldiers, finding escort duty distasteful, kept insufficient watch over them.)

On the 20th all the troops the Austrians could muster, 30,000 men, of whom 2,000 were cavalry, quitted the city and defiled before the emperor at the foot of the heights of Michelsberg and Frauenberg. The French divisions crowned the heights, formed up in line of columns facing the city of Ulm and the Danube, and beheld the Austrian troops, with Mack at their head, march past and ground their arms. The Austrians were in full dress, smart and clean, for they had barely been campaigning a couple of weeks.

Sixty guns with their teams and 40 flags fell to the victors; 18 generals surrendered as prisoners of war. The officers were permitted to return to their homes on parole, the soldiers were sent to France as prisoners of war. Invaluable to the French were the 3,500 to 4,000 horses captured at Ulm; an entire division of dragoons was mounted on these captured animals.

In summing up the results of the fall of Ulm in his proclamation of the 21st of October, Napoleon tells his soldiers:

> What will England care for our success? What she wanted she has obtained; we are no longer at Boulogne.

The emperor, in these few words, testified to the success of Pitt's scheme.

Whilst he was addressing to the captured generals these words:

> *Je ne veux rien sur le continent; ce sont des vaisseaux des colonies, du commerce que je veux, et cela vous est avantageux comme à nous.* (I do not want anything on the continent; they are ships of the colonies, of the trade I want, and that is advantageous to you as to us.)

The first triumph of his campaign was on the point of being tarnished by the terrible battle off Cape Trafalgar, a battle which at one blow deprived him of the means necessary for obtaining what he so ambitioned.

In the operations round Ulm, at Wertingen, Günsburg, Elchingen, Memmingen, Albeck, Langenau, and Neresheim, the French captured almost all the Austrian generals; 40,000 men; more than 40 stand of colours—in his proclamation Napoleon said 90—a great number of cannon, baggage wagons, etc., while a very small number of men on their side were killed or wounded. The army, nevertheless, was dissatisfied, for, after all the severe marching, the exposure and dire privations, it had not fought the battle the emperor had promised with such confidence. Fully five-sixths of the army had not fired a single shot. The soldiers longed to distinguish themselves, but circumstances had put it out of their power.

Most of the Austrian generals had been struck by the inevitable consequences of the capitulation of Ulm and by the great loss of prestige the Austrian Army had suffered. They deemed it desirable to turn to profit the pacific words Napoleon had addressed to them at the time of the capitulation. His friendly dispositions, after all, appeared simply paraded to induce the Emperor of Austria to withdraw from the coalition. General Giulay easily obtained leave to proceed in person to lay before the Emperor Francis an exact picture of the affairs of the empire, and to repeat Napoleon's utterances for peace.

That Napoleon was keen to enter Ulm can be easily understood if one only reflects how he had massed the greater portion of his army round that city, and how precarious the situation of his army with regard to supplies had become, particularly now that the overflowing of the Danube prevented the French drawing any supplies from the country on the right bank of that river. But there were also other reasons which spurred his haste, such as the desire to add to the vividness of his triumph by its rapidity, the need for leading his forces on Vienna before that city could have time to recover from its amazement, and to give no time to the Russians to place it in a proper state of defence.

Writers are generally silent on certain important matters which have great effect on the result of military operations. The student consequently sees nothing beyond the bright side of the picture, and knows nothing of the sufferings and privations which have accompanied the triumphs of the victors. In this instance, excessive fatigue, want of provisions, cold, wet and boisterous weather, and the disorder which accompanies marauding, were all there to add to the ordinary hardships of the campaign.

The subsistence of the troops during war is often a more difficult task than that of commanding them. Napoleon in 1805 acted on the principle of *bellum alit bellum*, (the war feeds the war).

Marshal Berthier, Chief of the Staff, wrote:

> In this war of invasion which the emperor makes, there are no magazines; it lies with the generals to procure the means of subsistence obtainable in the country they pass through.

As, however, the generals had not the time nor the means for procuring in a systematic manner all that was needed, they had forcibly to close their eyes to pillage. The troops suffered from hunger during the entire campaign.

They were to live on requisitions, each corps making its demands in the zone which intervened between it and the corps on its left. It was only the cavalry which was authorised to requisition on its right.

There was little found in Ulm in the way of provisions, as can be seen by Mack asking permission before the capitulation was actually signed for supplies to be allowed to come into the city. After the capture of that city, matters became worse, as nearly 60,000 prisoners had to be fed in addition to the invading army.

Murat's cavalry, as cavalry must generally do, subsisted on the resources of the country. Ney, who laid down a set of instructions for the troops, directed that they should be fed by the inhabitants in every case in which no other system of provisioning was possible. This cannot but have been the ordinary rule in the campaign of 1805. Davout and Soult intended that the troops should be fed by regular distributions. These two marshals strove to make their commissariat officers requisition bread, meat, forage, and firewood locally, to be afterwards distributed to their divisions. It having come to Davout's knowledge that Nansouty, who had been placed under his orders, intended to make his cavalry live on the resources of the country, he rigorously prohibited it. Soult issued strict rules on requisitioning. The chief commissary alone was empowered to do so, the commissaries attached to divisions were to requisition in exceptional cases, and only when they were ordered to do so. Soult established magazines at Heilbronn during the time the 4th Corps remained there.

Saint-Chamans was detained at Elchingen, waiting until the Danube subsided to carry dispatches to Marshal Soult. He, and others like him, had nothing to eat! They were billeted on a poor curate, who spoke no French, whilst the officers knew not a word of German. The conversation had to be carried out in Latin, what Saint-Chamans calls *vrai latin de cuisine*, as it related in every instance to a demand for food.

Fézensac, who fought gallantly by the side of Ney at Dorogobouge in the retreat from Moscow, relates an instance which well deserves being repeated. At a time when the troops were suffering grievously from hunger, a body of prisoners crossed the French ranks; one of these prisoners carried a loaf of ammunition bread. A man of the regiment Fézensac belonged to took this loaf away by force, for which act he was reproached by one of his comrades. A discussion ensued whether it was lawful to take away provisions from a prisoner. The first man alleged the rights of war, their own pitiable state, the need for securing their sustenance; the other argued principally in favour of the dictates of humanity.

The discussion was long and animated, and in the end the possessor of the loaf told his comrade, "The result of all this is, that I shall not give you a morsel of it."

"I don't ask for it," replied his comrade. "I would not eat a mouthful of that bread."

We should recollect, adds the duke, that this resolution was formed by a man who was worn out with fatigue, and who was almost perishing with hunger. Contrary to the English system, which is to prepare the provisions and necessaries long beforehand, and to pay for everything obtained in the theatre of war, the French had to live the best way they could on *enforced requisitions,* for a soldier never steals.

Fézensac relates how one day a man belonging to his company, and who was under some sort of an obligation to him, crept up to him by stealth and brought him a piece of ammunition bread and half a fowl, the whole wrapped up in a dirty shirt. Notwithstanding the dirty shirt, the duke assures us that in his life he had never made a heartier meal.

Bugeaud (afterwards marshal), writes to his sister about the Guard:

Just fancy, can 10,000 men, arriving in a village, easily find all that one needs in the way of eating? What troubles me besides the distress are the thefts the poor peasantry have to endure; their poultry, their firewood, their larder, all carried away by goodwill (*de gré*) or by force. I do not do such things, but when I am really hungry, I tolerate them and partake of my portion of the plunder. (D'Ideville, *Le Maréchal Bugeaud.*)

In order to draw out the resources of a country, these must be sought for, and often guessed at; the good-will of the possessors must be gained over, and they must be impressed with a sense of their personal interests. All this is very difficult in brisk operations, in which the troops are constantly in motion. There is quite an art in this, and we quite believe what General Foy says, (*History of the War in the Peninsula under Napoleon*), that 20,000 French would live for nothing when 10,000 English would die of hunger with money in their hands.

Whether in peace or in war, provisions require transport. An army cannot be fed unless a sufficient quantity of it is forthcoming. In the other continental armies heavy convoys militated against rapidity of movement; in the *Grande Armée* their absence caused sufferings to the soldier.

A contract signed in May 1805 with the Compagnie Breidt was originally to provide 30 brigades of wagons; however only 6 with 163 carriages were ready in time. Of the carriages eventually furnished by the Breidt company, 546 in number, few reached the Rhine, and none went beyond the Inn. Amongst the reasons adduced for this failure was that the company furnished only one driver for each four horses, and once this man fell sick, there being no one to replace him, the carriage remained stationary. Complaints were rife that the company took extra care of its horses, and, by putting an excessive limit to the daily marches, made the movements of the transport very slow. The vehicles taken from the peasants in the Duchies of Baden and Würtemberg were badly horsed, badly driven, and progressed very slowly. Before the army reached Donauwörth a great portion had lost their horses, and a large number of the drivers had deserted.

In the ten days, counting from the 7th of October (the day the French commenced crossing the Danube) to the 17th, when Mack declared himself disposed to surrender, the weather, contrary to the general custom at that season of the year, was bad. It rained steadily, often melted snow and rain combined. The cold and heavy falls of snow in open bivouacs caused intense sufferings to the soldiers. The rain stopped the lighting of fires, and the soldiers plunged up to their knees in cold slush. The march consequently became more laborious. Every day the roads became a deeper quagmire from the unceasing rain and the constant passage of troops, guns, and transport wagons, and added enormously to the ordinary fatigue. As few of the roads were metalled, the troops had to follow secondary roads, and even march across fields, which kept them on their feet the whole day. Sometimes they were on the tramp for fifteen hours.

The troops were worn out with incessant toil, exposure, and want of food. The correspondence and reports of the generals are full of complaints on this point. Their reclamations received scanty attention. Berthier reminds Marmont that no one should be better acquainted than he as to the manner in which the emperor carried on war.

One day, the 16th of October, was memorable for its tempestuousness. It was the worst the troops had to face. On that day not a soul remained at his post. There were no guards, no vedettes, no sentries; the guns even were left unguarded. Every individual was striving his best to get under some sort of shelter. It was during that dreadful storm that Count de Ségur had to find his way into Ulm to summon Mack to surrender. (Fézensac, *Souvenirs Militaires*.)

Bad weather and the want of food soon developed insubordination, slack discipline, and marauding. When the soldiers were detailed to proceed to a village to procure provisions, they were tempted to remain there, and in that manner the number of absentees from their corps soon rose to a considerable figure. At no other time, except during the Russian campaign of 1812, writes de Fézensac, have I suffered so much or beheld the army in a similar disorder. (The staff of the French Army was ignorant of administrative details. It could not be otherwise in an army in which the soldier generally appropriated the resources of the country.)

Napoleon was fully aware of the fatigue and heavy sufferings of the troops, of the difficulties, of the impossibility of feeding them. The complaints of his marshals, the repeated remonstrances of the directors of the administrative services, even those of the soldiers, could not move him. The result he well knew would repay these very painful efforts. This can be gathered from a letter he wrote to Soult on the 12th of October:

> Had I only desired to beat the enemy, I should not have needed so many marches and fatigues . . . but my desire is to capture him, audit is necessary that of this army not a single man remain to convey the news to Vienna.

Napoleon had the iron resolution, the great will to conquer, however much his troops might be demoralised by hardships and want. As long as they were ready to support manfully all the sacrifices, he imposed on them, he was ready to accept any risks; he felt full confidence in his being able to lead them to victory.

To be strong, in a fit condition to undergo long and distressing marches, to remain for hours under arms, to fight bravely, the soldier must be adequately fed. The Church of Rome, so rigorous in all that relates to fasting, makes an exception with regard to soldiers; that they may be at all times in a robust condition, they are dispensed from fasting. Mohum-dari-bah, chief of the Mandingoes, told the writer that during the Ramadan fast his warriors never fought, being debilitated through abstaining from food from sunrise to sunset.

The only soldiers who have fought great battles and have achieved remarkable things under trying circumstances since the Napoleonic wars were the troops of the Southern States of America under Lee and Stonewall Jackson. The men were badly clothed, and worse shod, badly fed, often starving, exhausted by heavy marches; what exposure they experienced, what hardships they underwent, will never be known. However, greatly to their praise, all this was not sufficient to shake their confidence in their heroic leaders, to break their spirit or undermine their discipline.

Nogaischer. Krimscher.
Tataren.
Augsburg in Herzbergs Kunsthandlung.

Chapter 9

From Ulm to Vienna

Having destroyed the Austrian Army of Suabia by turning to account its isolation and the distance which separated it from its Russian allies, Napoleon set to to carry out the second part of his programme. Prussia, nevertheless, could easily have upset these plans of the emperor by employing her army in Franconia or Bohemia. Thiers explains how:

> An ordinary general, on receiving the news of what was occurring at Berlin, would at once have stayed his advance, would have fallen back and taken up a position closer to the Rhine in order to prevent his being turned, and there at the head of his concentrated forces would have waited the development of the Potsdam Treaty. Acting in this manner, he would have given certainty to dangers which were then only presumable; he would have given to the armies of Kutuzoff and Alexander time to gather together, to the Archduke Charles time to come from Lombardy to Bavaria and join the Russians, to the Prussians time and boldness to offer inacceptable proposals and to enter the lists. In less than a month the emperor would have had on his hands 120,000 Austrians, 100,000 Russians, and 150,000 Prussians, concentrated in the Upper Palatinate or in Bavaria, and would have been crushed by a mass of troops double his own in number.
>
> To adhere more than ever to his conceptions, that is, to march forward, drive the principal armies of the coalition to a remote corner of Germany, listen to Prussia's complaints at Vienna, and fling at her his triumphs in reply, was the wisest course he could adopt, though in appearance the most adventurous. Let us add

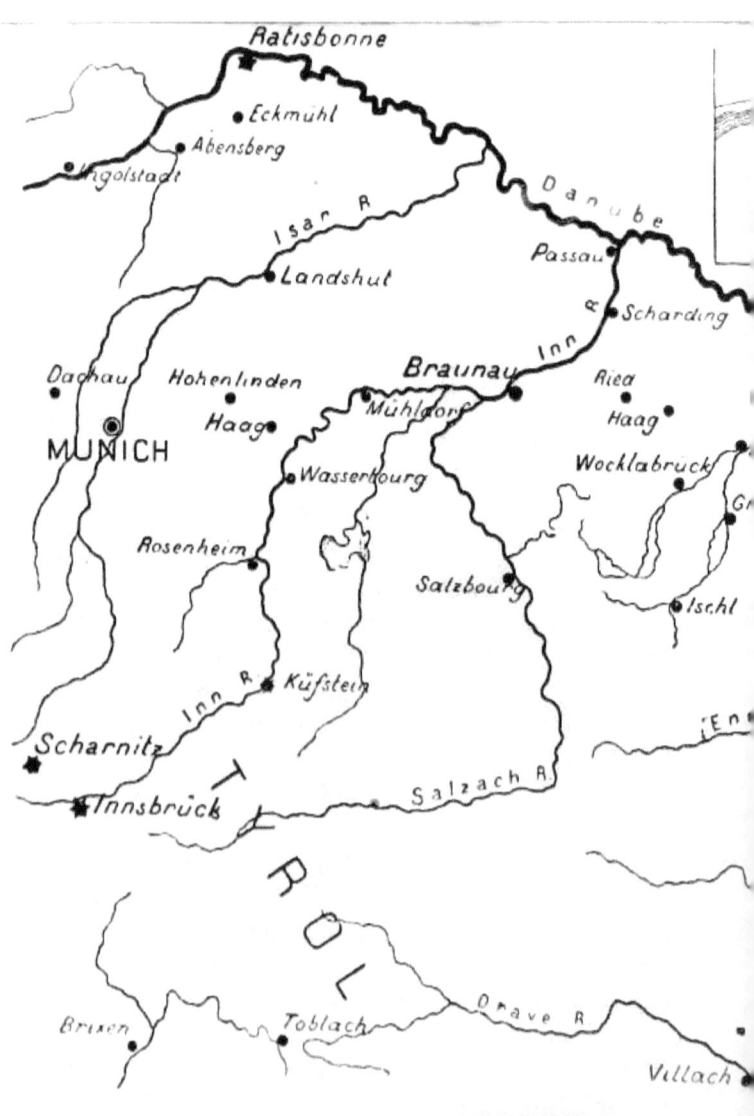

FROM ULM

TO VIENNA.

that bold resolutions of this nature are made by great men, where ordinary men would succumb; moreover, that they not only require a superior genius, but the possession of absolute authority. To be free to advance or retire advisedly, it is necessary to be the centre of all the movements, of all the information, of all the minds; it requires to be general and head of the empire; it requires to be Napoleon and emperor.

Napoleon had succeeded in destroying Mack's army before the arrival of the Russians, for it was not before the 20th of October that Kutuzoff had the bulk of his forces on the Inn. He now hoped to defeat the Russian commander before the arrival of Buxhowden and of the Archdukes Charles and John. There was consequently no time to lose, and immediately after the surrender of Ulm he set his forces in motion, advancing on the Isar and the Inn.

When the French were seen streaming rapidly down the Danube valley, the Austrian Government, with the object of arresting their progress, endeavoured to concentrate their armies. The Archduke Charles was bidden to hasten with his troops to the scene of danger. The Archduke John was directed to evacuate the Tyrol, to unite his forces with those of his brother, and to cover Vienna.

Since the 28th of September, on which day the Archduke Ferdinand had written to him that the Austrian Army was intact and full of spirit, Kutuzoff, then at Braunau, could acquire no news whatsoever of Mack's army. His cavalry patrols sent to reconnoitre in Bavaria could not take a single prisoner, but were themselves all captured by the enemy. The emissaries' reports were conflicting and full of exaggeration, and all communication coming from the west was intercepted by the French.

The last Russian columns, composed principally of cavalry and artillery, had reached Braunau in a deplorable state of exhaustion, after forced marches performed in most inclement weather; their shoes worn out so that many of the soldiers marched barefooted. The Russians had dropped as many as 6000 sick on the march, and there now remained to Kutuzoff little more than 32,000 combatants.

At this time, an unexpected reinforcement joined him. Kienmayer, cut off from Mack's army at Donauwörth, arrived at Braunau with 24 battalions and 60 squadrons, a total of 18,000 men. Nostitz followed him with 3 battalions of Croats and Prince Hesse-Homburg's hussars. Both of these officers could give no authentic information of what was passing round Ulm, and it was only on the 23rd of October that Mack, on his way to Vienna, revealed the extent of the disaster. He then told Kutuzoff how of an army of 70,000 men he had only been able to save 10 battalions, which had marched towards the Tyrol, and 14 squadrons, which had escaped into Bohemia with the Archduke Ferdinand. Mack begged him not to think of attacking Napoleon, who was then concentrating his army at Munich with the intention of moving on Vienna.

Kutuzoff's instructions from Vienna were to avoid the risk of defeat, to keep his troops intact, not to be led into any fighting with Napoleon, but to delay him at every favourable place so as to gain time for the Archdukes Charles and John and for the troops on the march from Russia to reach the theatre of war. On the receipt of these instructions, Kutuzoff felt bound to observe to the Emperor Francis that were he to dispute every inch of territory to the enemy, he would be exposed to be attacked, that his troops, once engaged, might have to be largely supported, and this might bring on a general action, the results of which might be unprosperous.

The Russian general had barely 50,000 men all told, and he did not consider it prudent to attack a more numerous army, and one which was already inspirited by victory.

There remained two alternatives, either to assume a purely defensive attitude before the *Grande Armée*, or to fall back steadily on the second Russian Army, which was marching with the Czar. Without the slightest doubt the latter alternative was the best, for it would have given time for the Archduke Charles to come up from Italy, whilst it would have secured the co-operation of Prussia, which was at that moment apparently inclined to join the coalition. Kutuzoff also believed that the more the *Grande Armée* pushed onwards in pursuit of the Russians, the more it would become compromised.

All this had not escaped Napoleon's attention. He thoroughly understood how expedient it was for him to hasten his movements so as to prevent the Russian general joining forces with the *Czar*. Still, before pushing on, he deemed it necessary to form large magazines at Ulm, at Augsburg, and on the Lech. These magazines were to be protected by fortifications and garrisoned by sufficient troops, to guard against a *coup de main*.

Ney, who had remained at Ulm till the 25th of October in accordance with the engagements entered into with Mack, received orders to march his whole corps into the Tyrol. Augereau, who had recently crossed the Rhine at Hüningen, was directed to occupy Augsburg and the line of the Lech, which was destined to be the new base of operations of the French Army.

The main army sped on in three formidable columns, which kept moving close to each other. It left the banks of the Isar on the 26th of October, and marching through the forest of Hohenlinden—the scene of Moreau's victory in 1800—reached the rocky banks of the Inn on the 28th and 29th. On the left Lannes marched on Braunau; in the centre Murat, Soult, Davout, and the Guard advanced on Mühldorf; on the right came Bernadotte, Marmont, and the Bavarians, making for Wasserburg, Rosenheim, and Salzburg. The right had instructions to outflank steadily the Austro-Russian left, by crossing the upper reaches of such rivers as the enemy might feel disposed to turn to account as lines of defence.

Kutuzoff still held Braunau, waiting to see the development of Napoleon's plans. Of the Austrians, he had posted Kienmayer at Salzburg and Nostitz at Passau. Both were placed under the orders of Count Merveldt, who had been appointed by the Emperor Francis commander-in-chief of all the Austrian forces attached to the Russians. All the sick in the Braunau hospitals were sent to the rear, the artillery parks were withdrawn, and orders went forth for tbe destruction of the bridges on the Inn.

Informed of the near approach of the enemy, and being much inferior in numbers, Kutuzoff adopted a wise course. He avoided a general action, and decided to make up for his inferiority in numbers by rapidity of movement. He did not await the arrival of the French, but evacuated Braunau on the 26th, retiring by way of Altheim, Ried and Haag on Lambach and Wels. Kienmayer was ordered to abandon Salzburg, and to march on a level with the Russians, covering their left flank with a detachment of cavalry, which would also serve to keep up the communications. Nostitz was directed to march from Passau to Linz. Prince Bagration was to assume command of the Russian rearguard, and was to be supported by Miloradovitch, who, with a large reserve, was to follow the army, always keeping half a day's march from the rear-guard. Merveldt very strongly objected to this course of action, but all his remonstrances had no effect on Kutuzoff.

As the various French columns reached the left bank of the Inn, they found all the points of passage on the left shore occupied by detachments of the enemy, placed there to give warning and to prevent the re-establishment of the bridges, all of which had been either broken or burnt.

Dumas remarks on the fallacy of considering the passage of rivers, even of the broadest, as an operation difficult to accomplish, for the simple reason that the passage is, generally speaking, surprised, being effected where it is least expected, or otherwise forced at any cost. In this instance the French did not allow all the defences which the enemy had run up to stop them for a moment; they jumped into boats and crossed in the face of musketry and grape. The emperor justly surmised that Kutuzoff, dreading being turned from the side of the mountains, would not seriously contest the crossing of the rivers, and he was right.

Bernadotte's march had only been delayed for an instant by the destruction of the bridges of Wasserburg and Rosenheim; these were restored under the fire of his artillery in one day, and without pressing a trigger his troops entered Salzburg.

Marmont, who had followed the same road as Bernadotte, and had crossed the Inn at Wasserburg, was ordered to proceed in the direction of Steyer with the object of threatening the enemy's left, should he appear at all disposed to hold his ground in rear of the Traun or to defend the line of the Enns.

Davout, though he found the enemy strongly entrenched on the right bank, with well-located batteries which rendered the restoration of the bridge at Mühldorf a matter of difficulty, worked steadily during the night under fire, and by midday on the day after his arrival a portion of his corps was able to effect its passage. On the morning of the 28th, Montbrun's light cavalry crossed over and sabred the Austrian rear-guard. The Salza was crossed with less difficulty at Burghausen.

Murat, who came from Ampfing took advantage of the bridge of Mühldorf to send one of his brigades across; this protected the repairs of the bridges of Neu Ötting and Markl.

Lannes was more fortunate, and having marched from Landshut by way of Eggenfeld and Traun, approached Braunau. The bridge of Braunau, which constitutes the principal means of communication between Bavaria and Upper Austria, had been broken. Surprised at seeing no appearance of life on the walls of the city on the river front, Lannes sent over in two boats a large detachment of infantry, to whom the inhabitants opened the gates. As soon as it was known that the French had secured the passage of the Upper Inn, the city had been evacuated by the Russians. In Braunau Lannes found a considerable amount of supplies, 45 guns, a magazine full of every description of ammunition, a considerable quantity of clothing, 40,000 rations of bread, and over a thousand sacks of flour.

On the side of Bavaria, Braunau was covered by the Inn, and on the Austrian, by a bastioned wall with lunettes, a good covered way, wet ditches and drawbridges. The fortifications were in a fine state of repair, protected by fraises, and palisades, all in good order.

Braunau was found to be a capital place for a secondary base of operations.

Napoleon, alive to all the advantages it offered, determined to make of it the principal depot for his army, and ordered that all the stores which had been provisionally collected at Augsburg should be transported there. Lauriston, who had just arrived from Spain after the battle of Trafalgar, was appointed commandant of the stronghold.

By the 29th and 30th of October, the French Army had crossed the Austrian frontier, and what was more fortunate was that it then ceased to press on the friendly country of Bavaria to meet its wants. The Austro-Russian armies had drawn much from the country round Braunau, still there remained abundant resources.

At Lembach Napoleon had proofs, if any were wanting, of how pillaging impaired the moral tone and relaxed the discipline of the army. There, coming across Soult's corps, he demanded in a loud tone of voice if the provisions were distributed with due regularity. Soult, evidently thinking it would please the emperor, replied that the soldiers did not fall short of anything. Hardly had he spoken than twenty voices from the ranks contradicted him flatly.

There were officers who blurted out the whole truth; General Macon was of the number. He was a brave man, to whom Napoleon had taken a liking in the days of Marengo. He had been made commandant at headquarters, but for all that had not lost any of his republican bluntness. As the emperor mounted his horse the following day, he met the general, and asked him gaily what he had to tell him. Macon, excited by a scene of plunder which he had been unable to put a stop to, replied:

> Really, sire, that you are followed by a horde of plunderers, who will bring dishonour on your army and on yourself if you do not soon take steps to re-establish good order.

The reproach, though made a little too openly, was well merited, still it did not please the emperor, who pleaded that this disreputable horde of laggards and plunderers was an inevitable evil, the outcome of forced and sudden marches, which, in reality, had done more for the success of the operations than anything else. That it was the absence of supply arrangements which had conferred mobility to his army, which had been the key-note of its success.

The theory was correct, for living on the resources of a country pushes an army forward, because as the country around gets soon emptied the troops are compelled to move onwards to procure something to eat. Relying on the provision columns, on the other hand, has the effect of checking the pace to give time to the supplies to overtake the troops.

Napoleon's offensive strategy depended on the facilities given by good roads, and on the products found on the lines of march; these enabled his armies to move rapidly, and to find the means of subsistence in the lands they crossed.

When it was made clear to Napoleon at Linz that the evil was increasing, and that it was thinning the ranks, he issued strict orders (7th of November) to have all the laggards and absentees tracked and driven back to their respective companies, where they were deprived of their loot, and received a sound beating from their comrades.

★★★★★★

In 1813 Lord Wellington crossed the Bidassoa and assailed Napoleon in his own country. As soon as they were on Gallic soil, the Spanish troops commenced to plunder, scared the peasants away, and stopped supplies being brought to the provision markets. Sir William Napier describes in the following words Lord Wellington's action: "He put to death all the Spanish marauders whom he could take in the act, and then, with many reproaches, and despite the discontent of their generals, forced the whole to withdraw to their own country. Morillo's division alone remained with the army. These decisive proceedings, marking the lofty character of the man, proved no less politic than resolute. The French people immediately returned, and, finding the strictest discipline preserved and all things paid for, adopted an amicable intercourse with the invader."

The following instance will show how soon the soldier forgets the distinction between *meum et tuum*. Captain Smith, of the 95th Rifle Regiment, afterwards Sir Harry Smith, known to fame in the Punjab and South Africa, had married a Spanish lady of good family whom he had rescued at Badajos. The young wife marched with the army, and in a French village she and her husband were hospitably entertained by a French widow lady, who in their honour produced a choice basin of Sevres porcelain. Much was the surprise of Mrs. Smith in beholding on the breakfast-table at the next halting-place this valuable bowl. The soldier-servant, when questioned about it, simply said that *it was too pretty an article to be left behind them*. Mrs. Smith, greatly annoyed, at once ordered out her horse and groom and rode thirty miles through a dangerous country to restore the piece of china to the rightful owner.

Mrs Smith's story is one of three in *Ladies of Waterloo, The Experiences of Three Women During the Campaign of 1815* by Charlotte A. Eaton, Magdalene de Lancey & Juana Smith, published by Leonaur.

✶✶✶✶✶✶

The allies had shown no disposition to defend the passage of the Inn, and nowhere did they hold their ground stoutly.

On the 30th, Murat overtook the Austrian rear-guard at Mernbach, and attacked it with the 1st regiment of Chasseurs. The Austrians retired on Haag, and their cavalry turned on the French horsemen and, until the latter were joined by Beaumont's dragoons, checked the pursuit. Even then the French cavalry were delayed by a brisk musketry fire coming from wooded eminences which bordered the road. What with this and the darkness, the Austrian column was able to slip away.

On the following day, Murat again overtook this rear-guard not far from Lambach. Schustek was then supported by eight Russian battalions, with which Bagration was covering the demolition of the bridge over the Traun. Murat had with him Bisson's division, belonging to Davout's corps. For many hours the Russian infantry sustained Bisson's attacks, and was ultimately broken by a vigorous charge of dragoons and *chasseurs*. Schustek had some difficulty in withdrawing to the right bank of the river; but he did so, and as soon as his troops were safely over, he destroyed the bridge.

This was done by the Pawlograd hussars, who were commanded by Count Orourk, an officer who greatly distinguished himself with the rear-guard in this retreat.

This was the first occasion on which the French and Russians came face to face in the campaign, and both sides fought with great fury. Kutuzoff, in his dispatch to the Minister of Foreign Affairs, states that the allies kept the French at bay for five hours.

On that same day, Davout's advanced guard reached Lambach. Soult was on the heights of Ried. Lannes, who had moved down the right bank of the Inn as far as Schärding, had his advanced posts about Efferding on the Linz road. The Imperial headquarters and the Guard were at Braunau.

The Emperor of Austria appeared at Weis on the 19th or 20th of October (Russian style) and held a council of war. It was at this council of war that, when questioned by the emperor as to his plans for future operations, Kutuzoff told him that he considered it his duty to propose a painful measure, the abandonment of the city of Vienna to the French, there not being the least prospect of holding it. His plan was to defend vigorously the passages over the Enns, then to take his army over to the left bank of the Danube and prevent the French following. He would compel them to remain on the right bank till all the allied forces had gathered together and a fresh campaign could commence. The emperor put up with this sacrifice, but Kutuzoff was urged to remain on the right bank of the Danube as long as possible; first in rear of the Enns, and afterwards at the bridge-head of Krems, a work only quite lately begun.

On the 1st of November, Napoleon who did not relish proceeding beyond the Traun without having first made his flanks secure, or undertaking any serious engagement without having concentrated his forces, ordered Murat to extend his left up to the banks of the Danube, and to see that the bridges at Weis and at Ebelsberg were repaired. Davout was to assemble his corps at Lambach, with a simple advance-guard to reconnoitre the Steyer road. Soult was to take up a position at Weis, whilst Lannes was to march on Linz and take possession of that city. Marmont was to discontinue his march on Steyer and to close on Lambach. Bernadotte, whose presence was no longer required at Salzburg, was to be ready to rejoin the army on the Traun. Deroy, with a Bavarian division of the 2nd Corps, was directed to proceed to Reichenhall, so as to turn the fortress of Kufstein, and finally to co-operate with Ney's operations.

However stubborn the opposition the rear-guards might offer to the French, their sole object was to gain time, for Kutuzoff's purpose was to retire on the main body, fully aware that there was no other way of evading a crushing defeat. So enterprising, however, were the French, that he was not able to gain a few marches on them and cast off the pressure of pursuit.

The Austro-Russian Army continued its retreat, and on the 3rd of November, on the left bank of the Enns, there only remained Bagration and Nostitz's rear-guards. Kutuzoff was at Stringberg, not far from the Danube; Kienmayer occupied Salaberg with thirty-six squadrons of cavalry; Merveldt was at Steyer. The French were between the Traun and the Enns, their cavalry beating back all the enemy's advanced posts.

On the 4th of November, both at Enns and at Steyer the French had a stiff fight with the enemy's rear-guards. Merveldt had been posted at Steyer and ordered to throw up some entrenchments so as to hold the ground by the river, as Kutuzoff had promised to do. The French, however, attacked and defeated the Austrians and drove them out of Steyer, which compelled Kutuzoff to hasten his retreat. To remain longer at Enns was not possible, so he went to Amstetten, closely followed by the French.

Lannes was marching on Enns by way of Ebelsberg, Soult on Kronsdorf by Neuhofen, and Davout by Steyer on Kremsmünster. Marmont was at Lambach, and Bernadotte's advanced guard was showing beyond Frankenmarkt.

The French left, having no serious obstacle to overcome, marched swiftly and by the shortest way. On the morning of the 5th of November, Murat, with his light cavalry and Oudinot's grenadier division, took up the pursuit of the Austro-Russian forces, and the same day overtook, not far from Amstetten, their rear-guard, which was commanded by Bagration. This consisted of nine battalions of infantry, the Pawlograd's hussars, four battalions of Croats, and a few squadrons of Hesse-Homburg's hussars.

At this point, the main road to Vienna passed through a fir forest. The Russians had taken post in a clearing of the forest which left an open space on both sides of the road. In the centre of this clearing and somewhat forward, Bagration had posted his artillery, supported by cavalry; in the forest in rear he had the best of his infantry. The object of the Russians was to gain time for their main body and the baggage to get across the Ips.

The day was cold, the ground was covered by a thick sheeting of snow. The long branches of oak, pine, and other forest trees bent under the heavy weight of frozen snow and icicles. On issuing from a defile, Murat, though at the head of a small body of horsemen, dashed boldly at the enemy. The French attacked with such spirit that Kutuzoff, who was present, did not anticipate being able to hold the ground for any length of time.

The allies attacked Murat in their turn, and drove him back. A fearful *mêlée* followed, in which Murat's horse was killed under him, and order was only restored by a young artillery officer, fresh from the military school, who fired two guns loaded with canister in the very face of the enemy. The Russian infantry held their ground stoutly, and for several hours both sides fought with the greatest determination. The French admit that the Russians displayed extraordinary bravery.

Miloradovitck came to Bagration's assistance with troops drawn from the reserve at the moment when the latter had commenced to retire. He brought to the prince's aid the grenadier regiment of Little Russia and Apchéron, the Smolensko Fusiliers, the 8th Rifles, and the Marioupol hussar regiment.

Murat tried to overcome the Russian right, but was repulsed by the grenadiers of Little Russia; he next attacked their left, but could score no advantage over Witgenstein. He next had to sustain a fierce charge made by Miloradovitck at the head of two battalions of the regiments of Apchéron and Smolensko, which forced back Oudinot's grenadiers with the bayonet. The contest in the forest did not cease until both sides were thoroughly exhausted. The Russians fought with desperate courage, and defended themselves to the last breath. The wounded and maimed continued fighting with fury until they were disarmed or stunned by their captors. The prisoners attacked their escorts.

The Russians claimed the victory, but, though they state that the French retired in disorder, they themselves retreated, and Murat, pressing them vigorously with the 9th and 10th Hussars, made over a thousand prisoners.

The sounds of fierce strife which had disturbed that peaceful region were over, but in the forest silence lay many a brave heart which would beat no more.

For stubbornness, for obstinate tenacity, for passive obedience, the Russian soldier has always been renowned. He is not only brave to a fault, but he is a splendid marcher, he endures extremes of heat and cold, he supports hunger and thirst. The theory in 1805 was, as it is still now, that the Russian soldier must unhesitatingly obey the orders of his superior, and is not made to take care of himself. In point of fact, he could not compete in equal terms with the French soldier whose mind had expanded in the wars of the Revolution, and who had learnt to follow his own initiative. The Russians did not get the training the new order of things demanded. Gallant and reckless their officers are, but, like our own, they know very little of the art of war.

On the 4th of November, Napoleon transferred his headquarters to Linz, where he remained till the 9th. It was during his sojourn at Linz that General Giulay presented himself before him, deputed by the Emperor of Austria to propose an armistice. The Emperor Francis had taken this step alarmed at the near approach of the French Army, and irritated by the arrogance and excessive demands of the Russians. But Napoleon was not slow in discovering that the proposed armistice was simply a device for gaining time.

Peace was possible, but before opening negotiations he demanded the evacuation of Venice and the Tyrol, and also an immediate separation from the Russian alliance. As far as a suspension of arms was concerned, he could derive no benefit whatsoever from it, inasmuch as he was marching at the head of 200,000 men, and there was no Austrian Army in front of him to stop him. The terms of the *ultimatum*, however, were considered too severe by General Giulay, who returned to Vienna to receive fresh instructions from his emperor.

Before crossing the Enns and plunging his troops deeper into the great defile formed by the Danube on one side and the spurs of the Styrian Alps on the other, Napoleon deemed it desirable to take fresh measures of precaution and to protect his line of operations. It was at Linz that, taking Gazan's division from Lannes' corps, Dupont's from Ney's, and Dumonceau's from Marmont's, he formed of these three divisions and Klein's division of dragoons a fresh corps, the command of which was conferred on Mortier.

This corps was to facilitate the march of the army on Vienna, and to cause the Russians some anxiety anent their communications in Moravia. Possibly the emperor looked forward to capturing the bridge of Krems, by which the second Russian Army could effect a junction with Kutuzoff. That bridge, once in his hands, the battle which he hoped to fight at St. Polten would have been fought with every chance of success on his side.

Mortier was to keep advancing along the left bank of the Danube, conforming with Lannes' movements on the right bank of the river; always, however, taking care to keep somewhat in rear of the 5th Corps. He was enjoined to keep a careful eye on Bohemia, and on the roads of Moravia, a precaution which had become more than ever necessary since there was a possibility of a Prussian Army joining the allies and entering Bohemia.

The communication between the two shores of the Danube, between Mortier on the left and Lannes on the right, had not been overlooked. This was to be maintained by a flotilla, which was placed under the command of Lostenge, a naval captain. That officer had been authorised to enlist all the boatmen he could find in the country and to collect as many boats as he could procure on the Danube and its affluents.

To diminish the danger incurred by this detached corps, Mortier had been directed to push forward parties of cavalry and to explore to a considerable distance.

Napoleon conceived that the Austro-Russians would strive to defend Vienna, and that with such an object in view they would most probably deliver battle in rear of the Drasen, on a favourable position on the important rocky ridge behind St. Polten. This was a defensible position in front of Vienna, which covered the junction of the roads running to Italy through Leoben with the great route down the valley of the Danube to the capital. The foot of this position was covered by the Drasen, the bed of which in the direction of the Danube is enclosed by high rocks. He was strengthened in this opinion by the obstinacy with which the Russians had defended the position of Amstetten. Kutuzoff for all that had decided otherwise, and this notwithstanding the repeated orders he had received from Vienna, enjoining him to contest the crossing of all the rivers.

After Murat's engagement with Bagration's and Miloradovitch's rear-guards on the 5th of November at Amstetten, and Davout's recontre on the 8th of the same month with Merveldt's corps in the mountains at Mariazell, Kutuzoff suddenly vanished. The news of Mortier's appearance on the left bank of the Danube had alarmed him, and persuaded him that Napoleon intended to drive him into a corner, to invest him when he had his back on that river. He decided without hesitation to quit St. Polten. He marched speedily and gained the left bank of the Danube by taking his army across the wooden bridge of eight and twenty arches at Mautern-Krems. This very handsome structure was the only existing bridge between Linz and Vienna, and was burnt by Miloradovitch as soon as his troops had crossed the river. There was little to be gained by defending the hastily constructed and unfinished bridge-head of Krems.

★★★★★★

The Emperor Francis had, on the 4th of November, given the following instructions to Kutuzoff:—

1st. Should circumstances press on you the hard necessity of abandoning the right bank of the Enns, your retreat should be conducted as slowly as possible. You will direct it towards Krems, where I am having a bridge-head constructed, which, though it may not be found completed at the moment you reach Krems, should be defended at any cost, and those works I will have continued until they are in a perfect state of defence.

2nd. If, as I did order you yesterday, stronger forces compel you to withdraw, it must only be done step by step towards Krems, where it is of the greatest moment for you to await the reinforcements which are coming to you, and that you protect at any price the construction of the bridge-head which I am having erected in front of Krems, and which will need several weeks before it can be confided to a simple garrison. I trust too much in your intelligence to enter into details on all the importance which I assign, first, to the defence of the right bank of the Enns, next to that of a very slow retreat towards Krems, lastly to the holding of a bridge-head in front of that place.

★★★★★★

Once across the Danube, Kutuzoff might have adopted one of the following courses. First, he might have halted at Krems, there to await the arrival of the second Russian Army. Secondly, he might have descended the Danube, keeping on the left bank until opposite the city of Vienna, seized the great bridge there, and waited to be joined by the rest of the Russian forces coming down by the main road of Moravia. Thirdly, it was open to him to advance on Mortier, attack him and force him to fall back on Linz. Lastly, to abandon the banks of the Danube altogether, make for the capital of Moravia, and effect as soon as possible his junction with the second Russian Army, and with such of the Austrian troops as he might be able to rally.

Kutuzoff could never hope to have been able to defeat Napoleon's entire army with his 40,000 men. Had he given battle in front of Vienna, in all probability the Russian general would have been beaten and compelled to cross the Danube hastily, either at Vienna or below that city. More than likely, he would have been cut off from Brünn, and from the reinforcements coming down from Moravia. But Kutuzoff had received positive orders from the *Czar* not to risk a battle before the arrival of the rest of the Russian forces; and, as Buxhowden's column had not yet reached the Moravian frontier, there was no hope of being able to effect this junction on the right bank of the Danube.

Though placed under the orders of the Court of Vienna, Kutuzoff would not follow, as Souwaroff had done in 1799, the injunctions of the Aulic Council. Whilst always appearing to approve of the measures proposed by the Austrian generals, he nevertheless abstained from being influenced by their opinions. He acted throughout in accordance with his own ideas. This was the characteristic trait of his conduct during the first part of the campaign.

With singular inconsistency, whilst the Emperor Francis was urging Kutuzoff to undertake a stubborn defence of the rivers, he uncovered the general's left by ordering Merveldt to separate himself from the Russians, with the object of shielding Vienna more directly.

On the 10th of November, not a single Russian battalion was remaining on the right bank of the Danube. The road to Vienna lay open, and Murat pushed boldly along. When, however, he had reached a point some few miles from the capital, peremptory orders called him back to Burkersdorp, for the rest of the army had been ordered to concentrate so as to assist Mortier, who had got into trouble.

On the 10th of November Napoleon arrived at the abbey of Mölk, and it was there that he learnt that the Russians under Kutuzoff had crossed the Danube at Krems, and were taking the very road he intended Mortier should follow.

Captain Colbert, Berthier's *aide-de-camp*, was sent by the emperor's orders to Mortier to warn him that the enemy had crossed the river, and to recommend him to advance with caution. Colbert proceeded on his mission, but could find no boat of any description with which to cross the Danube, which at that point was a quarter of a league broad. The peasants were unanimous in declaring that the Austrians had removed every boat. By using his wits, after some time Colbert, however, found in a house a kind of rough canoe, a large scooped-out tree. The owner of this primitive craft, when addressed by Colbert, replied in Latin, "*Ego sum piscator,*" ("I am a fisherman.")

The French officer settled quickly for the hire of this rickety boat, and was rowed by this strange fisherman to the left bank, though it took a long time to get across, having to contend against a very strong current. After landing, Colbert met Captain Lapointe, Mortier's *aide-de-camp*, who undertook to deliver the emperor's warning to the marshal.

Here was a bitter disappointment for Napoleon, who had been diligently preparing to fight a decisive battle at St. Polten. By crossing to the left bank of the Danube, the first Russian Army escaped him, and would now experience no difficulty in effecting a junction with

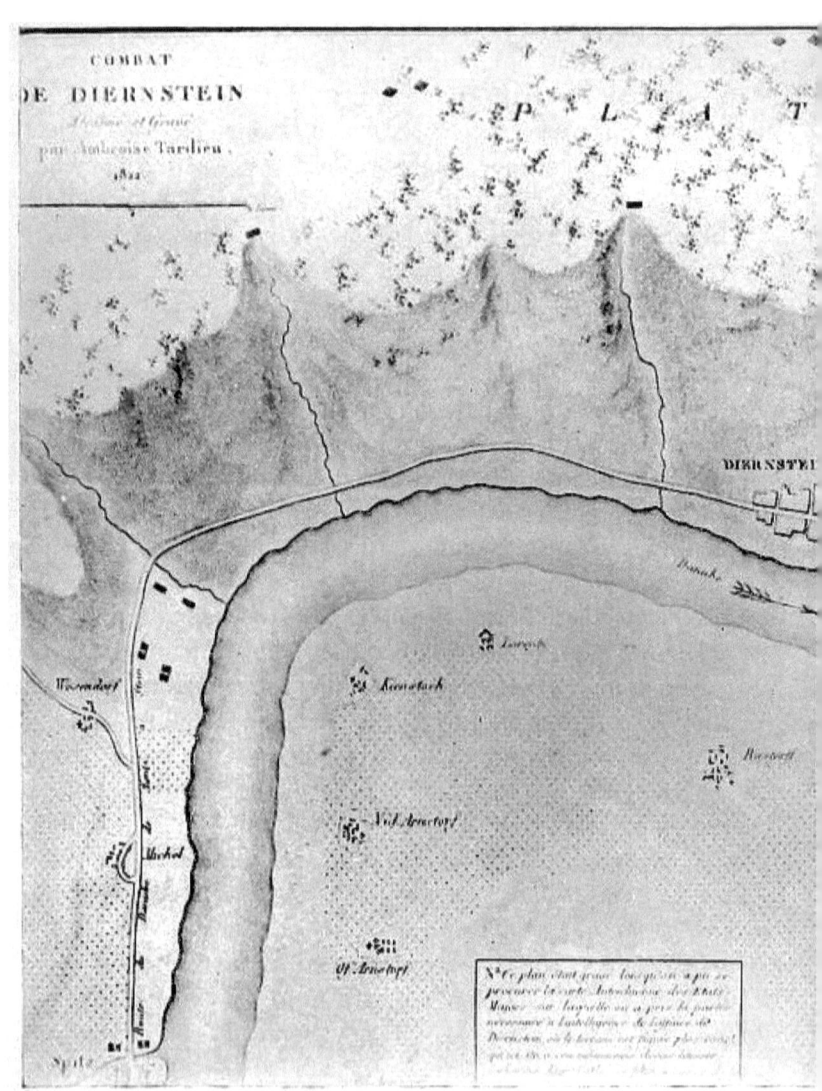

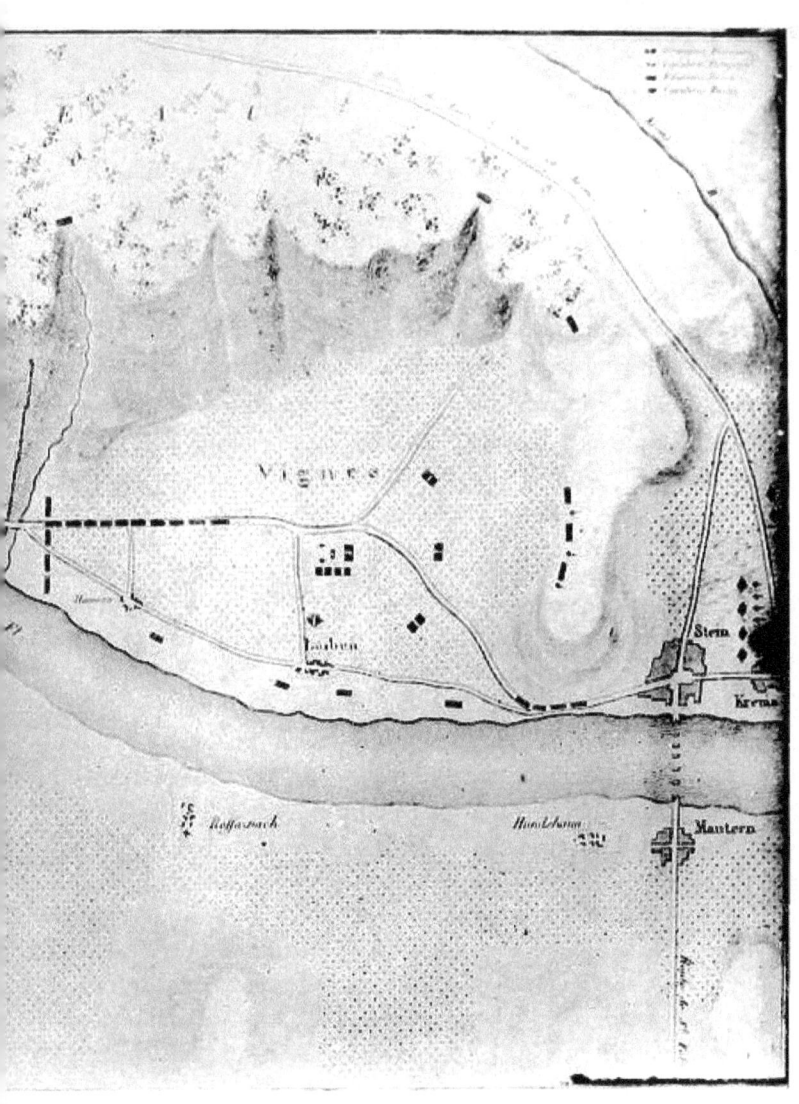

STEIN.

the second. The emperor realised at once the full meaning of that manoeuvre: that it would make the war recede, that it would draw him further away from his frontiers, that it would give time to the Archduke Charles to come up from the south, and to the Archduke Ferdinand to gather fresh forces and increase in audacity.

The crossing of the Danube by Kutuzoff upset all the strategical combinations Napoleon had made since his departure from Munich. He was not slow to detect the danger of Mortier's position on the left bank of the Danube, he therefore at once stopped the advance of his army on Vienna.

Rapp relates what Napoleon told him:

> Murat runs forward like a blind man; he goes as if there was nothing else to do but to enter Vienna; the enemy has no one in front of him, he can employ all his forces to crush Mortier. Go and tell Berthier to stop the march of the columns. *Mémoires du Général Rapp (Rapp: the Last Victor: The Career of Jean Rapp, Aide-de-Camp to Desaix & Napoleon, Premier Consul, General of France* by Jean Rapp is also published by Leonaur.)

Had Mortier been able to seize the bridge at Krems before the Russians, Kutuzoff would have been in a sore plight. But the marshal had been placed in a critical position through the crossing of the Russians, a thing which had not been anticipated. His command was not concentrated, and two of his divisions were marching at a day's distance in rear of him; for communicating with the rest of the army there was nothing but Lostange's flotilla, which was descending the Danube on his rear. Most of Klein's cavalry was far away exploring in the direction of Bohemia.

Gazan had with him the 4th Light Infantry, the 100th and 103rd of the Line, 2 squadrons of the 4th Dragoons, and 2 field-guns.

On the 9th he bivouacked at Spitz, Dupont and Dumonceau bivouacking at Marbach. Mortier, whose orders were to keep abreast of the corps on his right which were advancing on more open ground and more direct roads, was obliged to force his march, and could not wait for his other two divisions, which, however, had been ordered to rejoin him by forced marches.

The marshal reached Weissenkirchen on the 10th, where his reconnoitring parties made him aware of the presence of the Russians at Krems and Stein. These he could have avoided, but believing that all there was in front of him was a rear-guard detached from the main body to cover its retreat, and being eager to inflict loss upon the Russian troops which he fully believed to be hurrying towards Moravia, be decided not to await the arrival of his other divisions.

Kutuzoff, on the other hand, was well acquainted with Mortier's isolated position, and with the scattered state of his forces. Some French marauders belonging to Lostange's flotilla, captured by Miloradovitch, declared that Mortier was at Dürrenstein with Gazan's division, and far in advance of the rest of his command. Emissaries sent by Kutuzoff confirmed these statements, adding that Dupont's division was at Spitz, about twelve kilometres from Dürrenstein, and that Dumonceau followed Dupont. By their accounts, the French cavalry was exploring to the left in the direction of Zwetteh.

Though not able to cope with Napoleon's army, Kutuzoff felt quite equal to attempt the capture of this isolated division, and taking advantage of the local knowledge possessed by the Austrian General Schmidt, he made his dispositions for an attack.

Measures were taken to confirm Mortier in his idea that there was only a Russian rear-guard under Miloradovitch in front of him at Stein, and that Kutuzoff was merely resting his troops previous to resuming the retreat. Emissaries were also sent to the French camp to spread a report to that effect, for Kutuzoff feared lest Mortier, hearing of the presence of the Russians at Krems, might halt at Dürrenstein to await the arrival of the remainder of his forces.

Kutuzoff had with him 38 battalions and 23 squadrons to meet Mortier's weak division. His plan was to attack Mortier's left and cut him off from Dupont's and Dumonceau's divisions. To effect this, he divided his forces. Miloradovitch with 6 battalions and 2 squadrons of hussars was to withstand Mortier's frontal attack, whilst Dochtouroff with 21 battalions and 2 squadrons was to proceed by a mountain road—which Schmidt declared to be very practicable—and attack the left flank and rear of the French column.

Between Weitenek and Krems the road is very narrow, and in most places, it is cut out of the solid rock. After Dürrenstein, towards Stein, the defile opens out and leads through a succession of vineyards. These vineyards are divided by walls from three to four feet high which separate each property. On the right, the Danube runs very swift, and the main road, which is bounded by loose stone walls, is only broad enough to admit of a column with a front of seven men.

Docktouroff had divided his forces into three parts. The first column, led by Gerhardt, destined to take Mortier in flank, marched by Scheiben-Hof towards the ruins of the old castle to the north of Dürrenstein, celebrated in the history of the Middle Ages, as it was there that Richard Coeur de Lion was imprisoned on his return from the Holy Land.

******

At St. Polten in the campaign of 1809, a guide pointed out to the emperor the ruins of the castle prison of Richard Coeur de Lion. Having looked steadily at them for a while, Napoleon said: "He also had been campaigning in Palestine and Syria; he was more fortunate than we were at Saint Jean d'Acre, though not pluckier than you, my brave Lannes. He was sold by a Duke of Austria to an Emperor of Germany, who imprisoned him, and whose name is only kept alive by that cruel deed."

******

The second column under Docktouroff marched also on Scheiben-Hof, turning then by way of Pfaffenthal on Wadstein, to fall on the rear of the French. General Schmidt, who commanded the third column, moved in the direction of Resell; he was to come on the Danube at the top of the bend, and was to prevent Dupont coming to his chief's assistance.

At 8 a.m. of the 11th of November Mortier with Gazan's division and the 4th Dragoons quitted Ober Loiben and Unter Loiben, where he had passed the night, and marched for Stein and Krems. He soon came into contact with Miloradovitch, who had advanced to meet him, and drove him back on Stein; there Kutuzoff reinforced him with a few battalions.

There was an obstinate contest at Unter Loiben, which was captured and recaptured several times. Kutuzoff, expecting at any moment to hear of Dochtouroff's arrival at Dürrenstein, ordered Miloradovitch to fall back; Mortier followed him.

The ground being difficult for wheel carriages, the only battery belonging to Gazan's division was embarked on board of the flotilla, the horses being led by hand. When Mortier ordered the division to attack, the artillery officer who commanded the battery, Fabvier, landed the guns and took up a position. The fire of these guns caused the Russians serious losses, consequently they formed in mass, flung themselves on the guns, and captured them. The guns were taken and retaken; the fight at this point lasted half a day.

Mortier, attacked on the left flank by the regiment of Boutyrsk, which was descending from the hills by Egelse, discovered too late that it was not with a rear-guard only that he was contending. He thereupon tried to withdraw to Dürrenstein in the best possible order; General Stryk's vigorous attack on his left flank impeded his following up his intention of carrying Stein, and a sanguinary contest took place.

The Russian flanking and turning columns had moved slowly. Dochtouroff's guides had lost their way in the mountains, which were thickly wooded. Schmidt had asserted that the turning movement might be completed by 7 a.m., but the morning was dark and cold, the ground covered with snow. In place of being 7 or 8 o'clock, Dochtouroff's advanced guard, commanded by Oulanius, only descended the mountain and approached Dürrenstein at 5 p.m. The place was held by a small detachment of French, which defended the gates with three small guns; this detachment was soon driven out. Oulanius then drew up his detachment, facing Krems. The regiment of Wiatka was posted on the other side of Dürrenstein facing Spitz, for Dochtouroff had already noticed Dupont's progress in that direction.

On hearing of the Russians having appeared in his rear, Mortier sent his dragoons to Dürrenstein, but they fell in with Oulanius' troops, and were repulsed. He then formed a rear-guard to keep Miloradovitch in countenance, and with the rest of his troops marched on Dürrenstein to extricate himself.

At three in the evening, there was a pause in the battle; the Russians began to fall back on Stein. As soon, however, as Miloradovitch noticed the retreat of the French, he resumed the offensive. Mortier was caught between two fires; assailed both in front and in rear, the marshal all the same continued to fall back slowly. He himself being conspicuous in the thick of the combat, fighting hand to hand with the Russian grenadiers.

The French soldiers fought bravely, and so did their officers. Earlier, we have seen the Archduke Ferdinand setting a bad example to the Austrian Army by quitting Ulm, and by so doing weakening General Mack to the extent of some 15,000 men. At a most critical part of the battle of Dürrenstein, whilst Mortier, sword in hand, was fighting at the head of his men, some of his officers, lest a marshal of France should fall into the hands of the Russians, entreated him to avail himself of a boat that was handy for crossing the Danube, and so place himself in safety on the right bank. Mortier, however, was made of finer metal. "No," replied the brave marshal, "one does not abandon such brave men. It behoves to get free, or to perish with them."

★★★★★★

Marshal Mortier was accompanying King Louis Philippe at a review which was to he held on the 29th of July 1835. On arriving at the Boulevard du Temple, the aged marshal complained of the distress which the excessive heat caused him. Someone advised him to withdraw, but he refused. "My place," he said, "is by the side of the king, amongst the marshals, my brothers-in-arms." Hardly had he finished these words, so like the sentiment he expressed thirty years before at Dürrenstein, than Fieschi's infernal machine exploded and wounded him mortally. He was carried to a cafe close by, where his glorious career very shortly ended.

★★★★★★

Mortier determined not to give in, and to hold out until reinforcements should come to extricate him from his perilous situation. The marshal had no reason for despairing, for he knew that he had brave men with the colours. And what soldiers he had! Soldiers whom nothing could daunt; struggling for twelve hours against great odds, with foes on three sides of them, and a swift stream on the other, they fought with a full determination to conquer. It is well known with what devotion the French fought when under the eyes of their beloved emperor, but in this campaign, and in others too, they fought as bravely when he was far distant. Their great virtue was to endure, never to give in. Making toilsome marches over roads destroyed by the inclemency of the weather, enduring privations and discomforts of every sort, often without bread or provisions, never counting the odds, these heroic men fought and fought for nothing more than honour and glory, for rewards in those days were scanty.

Mortier was compromised by the distance which existed between Gazan and Dupont's division, and by the position in the rear of the flotilla. Cooped up between the river and a wall of rock, the French were mown down by continuous discharges of musketry. Destruction appeared inevitable, and they often despaired of overcoming their assailants. Fortunately, however, Dupont, coming from Marbach, had marched past Spitz in the direction of the cannonade, followed, though, at a considerable distance by Dumonceau's division.

Dupont's troops reached Weissenkirchen late in the afternoon. At 4 p.m. the 1st Hussars, who had been ordered to push forward some reconnoitring parties beyond Weissenkirchen, reported to Colonel Rouvillois that the Russians were seen descending from the mountains overhanging Dürrenstein. Not a moment was to be lost, and Colonel Meunier advanced with the 9th Light Infantry against the enemy, detaching some companies to the heights on his left, so as to take the enemy in flank. Dupont followed him with the 32nd.

This corps advanced to the charge and attacked the Russian regiment of Wiatka; both sides fought with the bayonet and with the butt-ends of their muskets. It was a terribly confused contest, what with the limited space, the intense darkness, the heavy rain, and the shouts of the enraged combatants, who could not use their arms freely. At last Dupont collected all he could get out of the 32nd and 9th and opened a heavy fire, to which the Russians could not reply.

Dupont directed another portion of his troops to oppose the third Russian column, which had not yet issued from the gorges. Dochtouroff soon found himself placed between two fires, for Dupont's onslaught helped Mortier, who made a last effort and with his troops entered Dürrenstein by one side, whilst Dupont penetrated by the other.

The Russian commander found himself in a most critical position; he had no artillery, whilst the most intense darkness and tempestuous weather concealed the enemy's movements and prevented his making suitable dispositions. The only open retreat lay through impracticable defiles. Both sides fought desperately for three hours, darkness being lighted only by the discharges from the cannons and the flashes of musketry. In battle the zest grows with the fray; so, it did in this instance. The contest continued till 9 o'clock at night, both sides fighting with fury, hemmed in the narrow streets of the village. Finally, Dochtouroff had to give way and leave Dürrenstein to what was still remaining of Gazan's division.

The Russians could claim the day, for the French had been driven back, and Gazan had lost two thirds of his men. (Danilevski sets down the French losses at five guns, a standard, and 1500 prisoners. On the Russian side he estimated the casualties, which were never made officially known, at 2000 men.) Kutuzoff had given a proof of his skill. He had been retiring before Napoleon, as he did not consider himself strong enough to measure himself with his army. Now that the odds were in his favour, he had shown no hesitation in attacking.

Mortier had evidently calculated on Kutuzoff's steady withdrawal, and imagined that his having taken the shortest road to join the Czar indicated, if anything, that he purposed to continue his retreat. However, Mortier was rash in attacking before he had concentrated his forces. Berthier's injunctions were to explore with cavalry to a *con-*

siderable distance in front, and so prevent his being surprised. This precaution was apparently disregarded, for very shortly after Gazan had quitted Unter Loiben he came in contact with Miloradovitch, who was moving up the Danube in his direction.

Owing to the great weariness of the troops, Mortier deemed it desirable to get back to Spitz, where the flotilla was lying. In compliance with fresh orders issued by the emperor the following day, he ferried his troops to the right bank of the Danube. As soon, however, as Napoleon heard the result of the fight and knew that Mortier was safe on the right bank, he issued orders for the army to resume its march on Vienna. No enemy was there, covering the Austrian capital, and there was a fair prospect of his being able to seize the bridges over the Danube.

De Ségur describes the great state of anxiety Napoleon fell into as soon as he heard that Kutuzoff had crossed with his army to the left bank of the Danube. In the strained conditions which at that period existed between France and Prussia, it was more than ever desirable not to allow the enemy to score a victory, however small it might be. Probably on the 10th Napoleon was not fully aware that Kutuzoff's entire force had crossed at Krems, or, if he was, he may possibly have felt convinced that the Russian commander would think of nothing else but of continuing his retreat on Brünn and Olmütz as his only resource.

The temptation for Kutuzoff was very great, but by his attacking Mortier he endangered his army, as it delayed his retreat, and in that way gave Napoleon time to cut him off on the road to Brünn. Kutuzoff's object was to retire and effect a junction with Buxhowden's corps. He could not have imagined it probable that he could destroy Gazan's division without a serious engagement, which would lead to the loss of a large number of men. As it was, he lost about 2000 men at Dürrenstein, and 3000 more at Hollabrunn, and this was nothing else but the result of his not having continued to retire on the 11th of November. He lost therefore to no purpose several thousand men, who would have proved invaluable on the field of Austerlitz. (Danilevski sets down Kutuzoff's loss in killed and wounded from Braunau to Brünn at 5810 men: other writers make it even greater.)

As in other military operations, what militated against success in Dochtouroff's flank march and saved Gazan's division from utter destruction, was want of unity and the absence of any maps showing the nature of the ground and roads in the neighbourhood of Krems and Dürrenstein. All the information available was gathered from the reports of the inhabitants, who, confident in the possibility of turning the enemy's position, eagerly volunteered to lead the columns.

Dürrenstein proved to the French, if the combat at Amstetten had not already done so, that in the Russians they had enemies who were as brave as they were, as warlike and as circumspect.

The Emperor of Austria was very much elated on hearing of the fight at Dürrenstein, and at once sent to Kutuzoff the insignia of the order of Maria Theresa of the first class. However, the victory was nothing of any great account. Kutuzoff's aim was to capture Gazan's division, and in this he failed. He failed because the French, though in dire circumstances, proved themselves better soldiers than the Russians. Notwithstanding that he attacked with forces fully four times as numerous as those Mortier had, the latter's 5000 men succeeded by dint of hard fighting in making their way through and joining Dupont. The disproportion between the two sides demanded the greatest courage and tenacity on the part of the French.

Napoleon was seriously disturbed by the distant sounds of the conflict. He advanced from Mölk to St. Polten, to get as close as possible to the noise of the battle; still there was nothing to be done but to await patiently for what fate had in store. As his agitation increased, he sent officers and *aides-de-camp*, every one he had near him, to gather news. Full of Mortier's peril, he suspended the march of invasion, in rear of him at Mölk, the advance of Bernadotte and of the flotilla, in front of him. (The Abbey is one of the finest in Europe, in a strong position commanding the Danube. By the Romans it was called the *Iron House*.) Murat, and even Soult, who followed the latter, were ordered to fall back. On the 12th of November, at about two in the afternoon, Thiard and Lemarois returned to calm his anxiety; they were soon followed by one of Mortier's *aides-de-camp*.

Napoleon was singularly annoyed by Kutuzoff's success at Dürrenstein, in which the enemy had shown signs of capacity and courage. This was the first real engagement of the Russians, and they had come out of it victorious. He wrote an indignant letter to Murat, full of reproaches, in which he reminded him that whereas his orders were to follow the Russians, and to bear hard on them, he had got away from them by forced marches. He upbraided him with thinking only of the glory of entering Vienna at the head of his cavalry, when he should have asked for fresh instructions as soon as he found that the Russians had crossed the Danube at Krems.

As by the time of his hearing that Kutuzoff had crossed the Danube at Krems the bridge at Mautern had already been destroyed, it would be difficult to say what assistance Murat could have rendered to Mortier. Besides which, the nature of the country on the left bank of the Danube was not well adapted for cavalry.

Between the valley of the Enns and that of the Trasen there were at that time but two roads practicable for an army. The one on the left, the most northerly of the two, was a fine postal road, which went by Strengberg, Amstetten, Kemmelbach, Mölk, to St. Polten. The other, more to the south, was a tortuous and difficult mountain road, which went by way of Waidhofen, Gaming, and Annaberg; this road for a great portion of the year was impassable for cavalry and artillery. Kutuzoff had withdrawn his army by the first, but Merveldt, rather than face the obstacles of the second, had made a considerable detour. Napoleon chose to avail himself of both.

Imagining that Kutuzoff would cover Vienna, Napoleon, on quitting Linz, had arranged that the corps of Davout, Marmont, and Bernadotte were to constitute his right wing, which was to endeavour to turn the left of the Austro-Russian Army. Soult was to attack the centre, whilst Lannes, with Oudinot's and Suchet's divisions and the entire cavalry under Murat, was to manoeuvre round Kutuzoff's right, and strive to surround it.

Davout, whose corps led the march on the southernmost road, had to face serious difficulties, which were only overcome by the resolution and endurance of his troops. The rains were certainly over, but a good deal of snow had fallen in the first days of November. The 3rd Corps made some marches of ten or twelve leagues over ice and quagmires, marching till late into the night. The cavalry and artillery made unheard-of efforts.

On becoming acquainted with this state of things, the emperor was constrained to alter the orders for Bernadotte's and Marmont's corps. Bernadotte was ordered not to go beyond Waidhofen, and to come down the Ips as far as Amstetten, where he would fall in with the great road. Marmont had to take to his right by the mountains of Styria, and to reach Leoben and Bruck, then to come down on St. Polten by way of Mariazell.

It is surprising how the French were able to get over the ground, and how they proved themselves enduring enough to overcome every obstacle. What was at the bottom of all this? Was it a matter of habit or enthusiasm brought about by their past victories? Was it a strong *esprit de corps?* or was it, as we believe, that Davout was at the head of the

3rd Corps? It was Davout's corps, we should recollect, which showed most discipline a few years later in the advance on Moscow, and in the deplorable retreat from that city.

Napoleon was at St. Polten when he received the details of the fight at Dürrenstein, and was much relieved in finding that, after all, the combat had not been as disastrous as he had first imagined. He was greatly pleased with the conduct of the troops.

The Emperor Francis had determined to spare the inhabitants of his capital the ordeal of a siege, a humane resolve, for as the walls which surrounded the suburbs were not of any great solidity, they could have been easily broken down. Nevertheless, at that moment, it would have proved a great advantage to the allies to retard the advance of the French, were it only for a few days. Count Wurbna, the chief chamberlain, the intimate friend and confidant of the Emperor Francis, was intrusted with the negotiations for the occupation of Vienna.

The inhabitants of Vienna, headed by Prince Linzendorf, waited on Murat at St. Hypolite to declare the emperor's intention to deliver the capital in order to preserve it from the horrors of war. The prince added that in so doing the Emperor Francis depended on Napoleon's justice and generosity to carry his benevolent wishes into execution. In reality there was no other alternative, for Vienna was threatened with famine.

The Viennese evinced more friendship for the French troops than for their allies the Russians, for they were thoroughly disgusted with the rude habits and barbarous manners of the latter. The fate of the Austrian Army at Ulm and the recent defeats had brought about a complete discouragement, which did not promise well for the future. Terror had crept into every corner of the empire and brought about a complete disorganisation of all the sections of the administration. The people were against the prolongation of the war. There was still means of saving the empire, had anyone desired to do so, but no one dreamt of such a thing.

When the Austrian Government renounced to undertake the defence of their capital and withdrew the troops to the left bank of the Danube, Vienna was left completely uncovered. General Count Auersperg with 13,000 men drawn from the garrison of the city had been detailed to defend the great wooden bridge of Tabor. The count had received distinct orders to defend, and in any case to destroy this important work on the Danube.

Napoleon was not satisfied with the glory of having occupied the capital of the German Empire; what was of more consequence to him was to end the war. He was keen to make up for the disaster at Dürrenstein by pushing forward as rapidly as possible and trying to forestall the Russians at the spot where the road from Krems falls into the great road of Olmütz. If he could only secure the bridge of Tabor, there was every possibility of intercepting General Kutuzoff's retreat, and to make him experience the fate which had befallen Mack. However much he desired the occupation of that important point of passage, Napoleon was not slow to foresee what chances there were that it had been already destroyed by the Austrians.

To the west of the city of Vienna numerous suburbs had sprung up, and beyond these flows the Danube, its course leading through a number of well-wooded islands, connected together by a series of wooden bridges. A larger bridge than the rest—the bridge of Tabor—crossed the broadest arm of the river and completed the communication between the two shores.

Napoleon ordered Murat not to enter Vienna, but to skirt the walls of the city and gain possession of the bridge of Tabor. The instructions were, "Succeed! Honestly if you can—but succeed." Having captured the bridge, Murat was at once to hasten after the retiring Russians, so as to intercept their retreat.

Murat and Lannes, two men who yielded to each other in nothing where bravery and daring were concerned, moved at once in the direction of the Danube, followed by a detachment of Oudinot's grenadiers and a small squad of hussars, which they concealed in the bushy copses which border the river. Their military experience had accustomed them to stratagems. They knew that audacity was often crowned with success.

Accompanied by some *aides-de-camp*, by General Bertrand, and Colonel Dode de la Brunerie, an engineer officer, the marshals moved up to the bridge-head. This was closed by a wooden barrier, which they pulled down. A hussar sentry which was stationed a little further away discharged his carbine and galloped back. He was followed by the French officers, who, having crossed the bridges on the minor branches of the river, arrived at the great one over the main stream.

It is customary with the Austrians when defending the passage of a river to keep the bridges intact till the last moment, in order to retain the power of making a counter attack. In this instance they had made everything ready for firing the great bridge; every measure had been taken to destroy the flooring, which had been all laid over with combustibles, ready to be set on fire at any moment. At the further end of the bridge, at Spitz, they had a strong battery of artillery and 6000 men, under the command of Count Auersperg.

French officers were never over-scrupulous in their dealings with the enemy, and often had recourse to artful and discreditable stratagems. In this instance, as there was abroad a rumour of an armistice which might lead to the conclusion of peace, the marshals made use of this report to hoodwink the Austrians in charge of the bridge.

They advanced towards them waving white handkerchiefs. A non-commissioned officer of artillery approached, torch in hand, to set fire to the combustibles placed under the arches, but Colonel Dode, with great presence of mind, seized hold of the man and stopped his doing so. The French officers reached the other extremity of the bridge and spoke to the Austrian gunners of an armistice actually signed, or if not, about to be signed. They told the Austrians that they no longer nursed any hatred towards them, and their only desire was to reach the Russians. They indicated their wish to parley with the Austrian officer in command; they conversed with him with great assurance of negotiations going on for the conclusion of the war, which they declared were well in progress. Rapp states that reports of peace had been studiously circulated, as the preservation of the bridge was the important point. The marshals requested to hold conversation with Count Auersperg, and Bertrand and Dode were taken to him. To the count they repeated the same story, and assured him of Napoleon's pacific intentions. (It is said that Bertrand gave his word of honour that their statements were the strict truth.)

Evidently Auersperg did not apprehend any low trickery from two of the most renowned marshals of France. However, he forgot the principle that a good soldier in presence of the enemy should everywhere and at all times be on his guard.

Whilst the French officers were in this manner to cajole the Austrians, Murat had arranged for a detachment of grenadiers to advance under cover of the large trees which rose by the river-side, and screened by the windings of the road which meandered through the wooded islands. Crossing the smaller bridges, and their advance concealed, this detachment suddenly appeared. The Austrians, detecting that they had been deceived, made ready to fire, but Lannes, Murat, and the rest of the officers approached the gunners, spoke to them plausibly, and made them hesitate, thus giving the grenadiers time to rush at the guns and overpower the gunners.

Napoleon was filled with joy when he heard of the successful result of Murat's stratagem.

The river being crossed by a succession of bridges, it appears that Auersperg erred in having reserved his measures entirely for the last, though the most important. A slight resistance at one of the minor bridges, caused by the marshal's stratagem being suspected, would have given ample time to set fire to the main one. As the last work was of the greatest consequence, it stands to reason that the more advanced ones should have been contested.

It will seem very extraordinary that on such a vague assertion, and nothing more, Auersperg and his officers should have suffered themselves to be taken in and should not have disputed the possession of this bridge to a handful of men. However, Auersperg knew that the war was unpopular, that the population of Vienna and all the leading Austrians were crying loudly for peace; that the idea of an armistice was widespread, and no one would believe that any person existed who wished to prolong the war—a war which held no hope of success, and might lead the monarchy to its ruin. As the Emperor Francis had already on the 3rd of November endeavoured to open negotiations with Napoleon, and Count Giulay had several times been to Napoleon's headquarters, these well-known facts, no doubt, gave some semblance of truth to Murat's statement.

We do not know who is most deserving of censure in this affair, whether the officers who put forward statements which they knew to be absolutely false, or the officer who believed in such fables, and who, in the face of the positive orders he had received, did not arrest or drive away the two daring marshals. The immense importance of securing the possession of the bridge, one might feel inclined to think, would condone the way in which it was tricked out of the enemy. The French, in fact, call it a *ruse audacieuse*, and appear to have acted on the common saying that all is fair in love and war.

Whether fair or not, *à la guerre l'art de réussir n'est souvent que l'art d'oser*, (in war the art of succeeding is often only the art of daring); and the truth of this saying was made evident in this instance, as this act of daring and presence of mind had great influence on the course of events, for had the bridge been destroyed, it would have involved a delay of twelve or fifteen days, which might have changed the fortune of the campaign.(Marbot calls it a not wholly creditable trick, and was of opinion that the stratagem employed by the marshals was not permissible.) Count Auersperg was brought before a court-martial, and was replaced in his command by Prince John of Liechtenstein.

Thus, taken by surprise, the Austrians never thought of an orderly retreat, and withdrew by the Brünn road, undecided which way to go. This occurred on the 13th, and Napoleon, who had hoped to sign peace at Vienna, strove to turn this unexpected windfall to good account. He had wished all along to destroy Kutuzoff before that general could effect a junction with the *Czar*, and had it not been, as we shall see hereafter, for Murat's stupidity in letting the Russians gain some marches on him, he would have been successful.

CHAPTER 10

Action of the Archdukes

We have seen earlier how the Archduke Ferdinand quitted Ulm, was pursued by Murat, and almost destroyed.

After Jellachich's surrender on the 14th of November, Augereau, whose services were no longer necessary to Ney, was sent to Suabia, and later on to Franconia, where, with Baraguey d'Hilliers' dismounted dragoons, he was to keep an eye on the movements of the Archduke Ferdinand.

At Czaslau, where he had been since the 25th of November, the archduke had collected a small force of 14 battalions and 18 squadrons, in all about 9000 men. Bernadotte had been left to watch him, but in the expectation of a battle, the marshal was called up to Brünn with orders to leave Wrède's Bavarian division at Deutsch-Brod to hold the archduke in check. Wrède had 10 battalions and 12 squadrons, or, more or less, 6000 infantry and 1200 horse. (As we are treating on the operations of the three archdukes, we may be excused in anticipating the share taken by the Archduke Ferdinand in Bohemia.)

On becoming acquainted with Bernadotte's withdrawal, the archduke advanced on Deutsch-Brod, which was evacuated by the Bavarians. On the 2nd of December, the day of the battle of Austerlitz, Ferdinand, having formed his force into three columns, marched out of Deutsch-Brod, the main body making for Iglau by the main road, the right column marching on Windisch-Jenikau, and the left on Polna.

With 8 battalions and 8 squadrons Wrède had taken post at Stoecken, the remainder of his force he kept in reserve at Tglau or watching his flanks. Vigorously attacked on the 3rd of December, he was compelled to fall back on Iglau, where two days later he had a very stiff engagement with the Austrians. The Bavarians defended their position stubbornly and incurred serious loss, but when threatened with being surrounded, they found it necessary to evacuate Iglau. This was done during the night. At this moment the news of the suspension of arms arrived and stopped the Austrian pursuit.

Massena's Army of Italy.

After Napoleon's coronation at Milan in the spring of 1805, the kingdom of Italy had been organised on the model of the French empire. A number of French troops remained there at the disposal of Eugène de Beauharnais, who, possessing all Napoleon's confidence, had been left in Italy to represent him as viceroy. Joubert had been sent to Italy to act as his mentor.

Napoleon's intention was to employ an army of 50,000 men in Italy, under the command of Massena. Notwithstanding, however, all the exertions of Prince Eugène, the viceroy, the troops collected at Monte Chiaro on the Chiese, in front of Brescia, when Massena arrived on the 8th of September to assume command of his army corps, did not amount to more than 28,000 men.

Everything tended to indicate that the Austrians would assume the offensive in Italy; the choice of the general and the strength of his army pointed in that direction. The weakness of Massena's force, especially in artillery, did not trouble Napoleon very much, for all he needed at that time was that Massena should hold his own long enough to allow the *Grande Armée* to deliver in Germany the decisive strokes which he had been meditating.

Massena had been advised to concentrate his forces as soon as possible between Peschiera and Verona, occupying the latter city strongly. The Treaty of Lunéville had given Verona to France, but oddly enough the suburb of Veronetta and San Giorgio, with the defences on the left bank of the Adige, had remained with Austria. Massena was instructed to await the enemy's attack, and to be careful not to make an offensive movement, unless he saw evident prospect of deriving some real advantage thereby.

The emperor believed that with his right covered by the Adige, which the cavalry and light artillery would guard as far as Legnago, if not even as far as Rovigo, and the left solidly resting on Monte Baldo, Massena was nearly invincible, and could safely complete the organisation of his army.

Napoleon made a right forecast when he wrote to Massena:

Everything besides leads me to believe that you will not remain more than fifteen days in your position at Verona without the enemy drawing large detachments from its army in Italy to reinforce the one they have in Germany; then you will march against him and push forward to the Isonzo.... I will frequently inform you of the progress which we shall make in Germany, and shall send you orders which will serve to guide your conduct. Everything, after all, will depend on circumstances and on your ability.

The operations in Italy did not play a very important part in this campaign, and may well be considered as an accessory.

The state of affairs at Genoa in 1800 was very similar to this. Massena had to play a very secondary part, and by his firm attitude was to keep the archduke and his army tied down to Italy and away from the Danube. Contrary to his being urged to commence operations as Moreau had been in 1800, Massena was reminded of the necessity for playing a waiting game in Italy until the emperor had commenced the execution of his plan in Germany, a plan in which all the parts were so well connected together that they were to afford each other mutual support.

Napoleon wrote:

It may be possible, that the enemy, reckoning on French impetuosity, would like to await you on the battlefield of Caldiero, but nothing urges you, and you should in that case fortify yourself in front of Verona.... You should tarry in that position until the enemy becomes weakened by hurrying to the help of Vienna. Above all, you should keep your troops together and not scatter your army; from 40,000 to 50,000 French commanded by you are invincible, as long as they are in a good position.

Prince Eugène and Massena were indefatigable, and by great efforts they managed to double the strength of the Army of Italy.

★★★★★★

When Murat made over the command of the French returning from Moscow to Prince Eugène, the prince told him, "You cannot make it over to me; only the emperor can do that. But you can run away in the night, and the supreme command will devolve on me the next morning."

★★★★★★

On the 26th of September, the date when the emperor crossed the Rhine, it numbered already 53,000 men. Of this number, 11,000 men formed the garrisons of Mantua, Legnago, Peschiera, and Roc-ca d'Anfo. There remained over 41,000 men—81 battalions and 68 squadrons. These were divided in five divisions of infantry commanded by Gardanne, Verdier, Molitor, Duhesme, and Séras. General Partouneaux commanded a reserve division (grenadiers). The cavalry was divided into three divisions. One (advanced-guard) of *Chasseurs à Cheval*, commanded by Espagne, one of *cuirassiers* under Pully, and lastly one of dragoons under Mermet.

In conformity with the emperor's instructions, these forces were posted in two lines between the Mincio and the Adige.

Gardanne, with 12 battalions and 4 squadrons (5600 men), occupied the west of Verona and the villages thereabout on the right bank of the Adige. Verdier, with 13 battalions and 4 squadrons (5700 men), was on Gardanne's right at Valese, Isola Porcarizzo, etc. His cavalry posts were pushed forwards as far as the Polesina.

Molitor's 15 battalions (5700 men) were stationed in rear of Verona at Villafranca and neighbourhood. Duhesme had his 13 battalions (6800 men) at Somma Campagna, Sona, and Castel-Nuovo, on Molitor's left. Séras, further still to the left, with 16 battalions and 4 squadrons (7500 men), spread out from Bussolengo to La Corona and Rivoli, occupying also on the opposite side of the lake of Garda Salo and the outlets of the Val-Sabbia.

Partouneaux, with 11 battalions of grenadiers and 4 squadrons (4900 men), was on the Mincio at Valeggio; Espagne, with 16 squadrons of *chasseurs* and 1 battalion of grenadiers (2000 men) was on the Adige below Verona, at Santa Maria and at San Giovanni. Mermet had his 20 squadrons of dragoons (2000 men) in rear of Verdier at Isola della Scala and Salizzolo. Pully's *cuirassiers*, 16 squadrons (1600 men), were still further in rear at Roverbella and at Castiglione.

Lastly, the artillery park was at Provigliano, and detachments from the garrison of Mantua held the passes on the Lower Mincio at Governolo and of the Po at Ostiglia. The headquarters with the reserve of grenadiers were at first at Valeggio; they were afterwards shifted to Villafranca, and later on to Alpo.

It was intended that the English and Russians should land, either at Taranto, Naples, or Ancona, a number of troops which they had concentrated at Malta and Corfu. Together with the Neapolitan army, these troops were to surprise Gouvion Saint Cyr's 20,000 men, who were at that time occupying the fort of Pescara and the northern frontier of the Neapolitan Kingdom, after which they were to march on Genoa by way of Tuscany and through the duchy of Parma and fall suddenly on Massena's rear. This diversion, proposed to the Cabinet of Vienna, was the plan of General Dumourier, who recommended it to Nelson, and demanded to be appointed its leader. Napoleon had foreseen something of the kind, and while the Queen of Naples was dreaming of fresh successes, he wrote to Saint Cyr:

> Occupy Naples, drive out the court, dissolve or destroy the Neapolitan Army before the English and Russians can even have learnt that hostilities have commenced.

Archduke Charles

Towards the middle of October 1805, the Archduke Charles had at his disposal about 65,000 men, forming 107 battalions of infantry and 80 squadrons of horse. General Hillier, with 17,000 more, was in the Southern Tyrol.

Hillier, with Lusignan's and Mitrowski's divisions, had been located between Trent and Botzen, so as to connect the Austrian armies in the Tyrol and in Italy. Soon, however, his corps joined in the operations of the Archduke John.

In Italy, both the Archduke Charles and Massena awaited the turn of events. The archduke was strong enough to assume the initiative, to undertake a vigorous offensive, carry his army into Italy, and drive Massena beyond the Mincio, if not beyond the Po; but he had to wait till the Russians joined Mack on the Lech. The Austrian and French commanders alike had to subordinate their operations to those of the armies in Germany.

The archduke, well acquainted with Napoleon's brilliant talent, and having a poor idea of Mack's capacity, pondered deeply on what there was to be gained by entering Italy and reaping some dubious advantages over the French, which in the end were too likely to prove fruitless, and in which he was certain to lose many good soldiers—soldiers whose blood would be more profitably shed in the defence of the hereditary states. In this he gave evidence of great perspicacity, and having not the least confidence in the officer who had been selected to command the army in Germany, he felt more than sure that before long the army of Italy would be made to retrace its steps.

✶✶✶✶✶✶

Speaking of Mack, "This man is mad," said the archduke to Cobenzel. "What does it matter?" replied the minister. "He is expedient, and that is sufficient." The archduke called him insane, and certainly his actions during the campaign have furnished history with abundant proof to justify such charge.

******

A few victories gained in Italy would not have modified to any appreciable extent the events which occurred round Ulm, whilst they would have increased the distance the archduke's forces would have had to march if called up to the assistance of the threatened capital. The only advantage which might have accrued from such successes would have been that the French beaten in Italy would possibly not have been in a position to pursue their adversaries with the energy they eventually displayed. How often, however, have we seen that the very fact of an army being in pursuit acts as a stimulus and adds miraculous vigour to the pursuers?

The archduke's forecast turned out correct. The Cabinet of Vienna, alarmed by the danger which Mack's army was exposed to by Napoleon's rapid march across Germany, and the long way the Russians were still from the Lech, sent instructions to the archduke to keep on the defensive and to direct on Ulm all the troops he could well spare.

Though the archduke commanded a larger army than Massena, the military reputation his adversary rightly enjoyed compelled him to be cautious. Massena was a redoubtable opponent; by his victory at Zurich in 1799 he had rendered France a very great service, and had delivered her from further molestation by Russian forces, whilst his obstinate defence of Genoa the following year had made his name even more famous.

It was Massena who struck the first blow in Italy. Deeming it very desirable to secure the passage over the Adige at Verona, on the morning of the 18th of October, under cover of darkness, he made a body of troops approach the bridge of Castello Vecchio, whilst Verdier made demonstrations on the Lower Adige and Zevio. At break of day, the bridge to the north of Veronetta was rushed, and a stubborn fight took place. Vukassovich had only a small detachment on his side of the bridge, and this was easily overcome. He soon came up from Avesa with two battalions and a squadron and took the advance party of the French in flank, but Gardanne, who had taken his division across the bridge, carried the Austrian intrenchments and engaged in a murderous combat in the suburbs of San Giorgio.

The Austrians eventually retired to the heights of San Leonardo, the suburbs remaining in the hands of the French. Vukassovich, having reformed his troops and received reinforcements, made another attempt to recapture the lost ground, but in vain. A storm which broke at about 4 p.m. put an end to the combat. General Chasseloup speedily covered the bridge on the left bank with a bridge-head, which gave Massena the power of crossing at any time to the left bank of the Adige.

In this engagement, the French admit a loss of 400 killed and wounded; the Austrians are said to have lost 1200 men, of whom by far the greater part were captured. The French possibly lost more men than they would acknowledge.

Until the 29th of October, Massena undertook nothing further; he was attending the result of Napoleon's advance into Suabia. On his side the archduke had received far from comforting news, and had become more than ever convinced that the time was last approaching when he would find himself compelled to retire. Resolved, nevertheless, to retard the pursuit as much as it lay in his power, he laboured diligently in fortifying the position of Caldiero.

Caldiero was already by nature a strong position and difficult to turn. One side rested on the mountains and the other on the marshes which border the Adige. To render it still more formidable, the archduke had thrown up a series of defensive works, the fire from which crossing each other, left not a single dead angle. With singular skill every vantage of ground had been utilized; batteries were placed in commanding positions and all points of access were covered by fraises, palisades, *cheveaux de frise*, and abatis. The hill of Colognola constituted the centre of the defence.

During the night of the 24th-25th of October the archduke received the news of the capitulation of Ulm; a piece of information which was kept strictly undivulged. Preparations continued to be made in the rear, a bridge was thrown athwart the Bacchiglione above Vicenza, the magazines at Palma-Nuova were cleared, and positions fit for defence were strengthened as a precaution in case of a retreat.

The news of the French successes in Suabia only reached Massena on the evening of the 28th; by that date his arrangements for an advance were, however, well forward, and at break of day on the 29th his army was put in motion and crossed the Adige. The French had some smart fighting with Frimont's brigade, but the Austrian general, who had been driven out of several positions, halted his troops at last at the foot of the Caldiero position. That same evening the Austrians, quitting their camp at San Gregorio, moved to the localities respectively assigned to them at Caldiero.

Around this position the archduke had 71 battalions and 41 squadrons, making a total of 40,000 infantry and 5000 cavalry. Simbschen commanded the right, Bellegarde the centre, and Reuss the left. Massena was inferior to him in numbers, for he had not more than 33,000 men. Molitor was on the French left by Ca dell'Ara with 15 battalions and 8 squadrons, and he was instructed to carry the heights of Colognola. Gardanne, who was at Rotta with 12 battalions, formed the centre; Duhesme and his 13 battalions on the Gambione road constituted the right. In second line, the French had Partouneaux's 12 battalions of grenadiers, 20 squadrons of d'Espagne, and 8 of Mermet. Massena had ordered Verdier to turn the Austrian left by crossing the Adige at Persago with his infantry and Pully's *cuirassiers*. It was the marshal's intention not to assault the position of Caldiero until Verdier's attack was well under way.

On the 30th, in spite of a dense fog, the archduke sent troops from both flanks in the direction of Ca dell'Ara and Sabionora to discover the enemy's intentions. Soon a heavy musketry fire opened. As the archduke's intention was to draw the French under the fire of his redoubts, he ordered Simbschen and Nordmann to recall their troops. Massena, under the impression that he heard the sound of Verdier's artillery, ordered a general attack. Molitor was to advance on Colognola, Gardanne on Caldiero, and Duhesme on Gambione.

Verdier's attack miscarried, and in place of falling on Nordmann's rear he had to deliver a frontal attack. Getting the worst of it, he withdrew his troops and brought them back to the right bank of the Adige.

Duhesme was driven back by Nordmann, ably supported by the Prince of Reuss, and by the end of the day he was not farther advanced than Gambione.

In the centre about Caldiero a fierce battle was raging. There Bellegarde had driven Gardanne out of the village of Caldiero, as far even as Rotta. Massena, however, re-established the fight by calling up the reserves. Both Bellegarde and Reuss were driven back to the foot of the intrenchments. Caldiero taken, lost, and retaken, remained at last to the French; nevertheless all their efforts to advance beyond it were frustrated by the fire of the Austrian position, and by the attacks of the Austrian reserves.

Molitor had scaled the heights and carried the village of Colognola-Olta and one of the principal Austrian redoubts, but Simbschen, reinforced by a battalion of grenadiers, drove him out and forced him to retire from the hill. Urged by Massena, he then tried a second attack, but with no better result. Night put an end to the combat; both sides had lost heavily. Only soldiers who have fought know what kind of a night is passed after a sanguinary and doubtful combat.

Massena had not abandoned the intention of capturing the Austrian position; on the 31st, he returned to the attack, this time directing his efforts on the Austrian left. Duhesme and Verdier at the same time made a combined attack on Nordmann, who occupied a large redoubt at Chiavica del Cristo. A very hot engagement ensued, but the Austrians continued to hold Chiavica del Cristo in the evening.

The Archduke Charles had now made up his mind to retire, and to hide his purpose from the enemy as long as possible by making demonstrations on Massena's flanks, and in that way to keep him tied to Verona. Waiting to discover the archduke's intentions, Massena had concentrated his forces around Vago. A combat ensued between General Hillinger and Colonel de Loverdo; the latter, reinforced by General Carpentier—Massena's chief of the staff—surrounded Hillinger and forced him to lay down his arms. The Austrians had thus about 2000 men taken prisoners.

The archduke, seeing how Reuss and Nordmann had checked the French attack on the 31st, and how Rosenberg's and Davidovich's demonstrations had attracted Massena's attention, issued his orders for a general retreat. At daybreak on the 1st of November, the various columns set out. Bellegarde and Simbschen marching by the main road up to Montecchio-Maggiore, halfway from Montebello to Vicenza; Reuss and Nordmann by Arcole and Orgiano on Albettone; Davidovich by Bevilacqua and Montagnana on Este.

Frimont was left at Caldiero with a rear-guard composed of 4 battalions and 12 squadrons. These few troops were to impose on the French by making a great show; numerous bivouac fires were also lighted to convey a false idea of numbers. But the French, who had noticed the great noise made by the enemy during the previous night, sent out reconnaissances in the early morning; these returned stating that there were no guns in the intrenchments and little infantry. On this information, Massena pushed forward d'Espagne's *chasseurs* and Gardanne's light infantry to examine the ground.

These troops found the redoubts which flanked the main road occupied by the enemy. But Frimont, now believing that the main body had gained a sufficient start, commenced falling back on the 2nd.

There was possibly more skilful manoeuvring on the frontier of Italy than in any other part of the theatre of war. Massena and the Archduke Charles, in all that regarded military knowledge, were well matched. Had not the necessity for hastening to the succour of Vienna pressed heavily, the archduke might have engaged in an obstinate defence of the lines of the Bacchiglione, Brenta, and Piave. The defence of these positions he left to his rear-guard, which was enjoined to retard as long as possible the crossing of each one of these rivers.

At Vicenza he decided that Vogelsang, with 4 battalions of grenadiers and 8 field pieces, should stop the French, were it only for one day, or at any rate till Frimont had taken his troops across the river. Vicenza was enclosed by a fortified wall, which was still in a pretty fair state of repair, whilst the swelling of the Bacchiglione prevented the city being turned.

Frimont was retiring, hotly pursued by the French, for as soon as it became quite evident to Massena that the enemy had disappeared from his front, he had taken all possible measures to start a vigorous pursuit. D'Espagne, with his *chasseurs*, followed on the footsteps of the Austrians, and overtaking them the same day at Villanova, and later at Montebello, captured many prisoners.

Massena appeared before Vicenza and summoned the place. On the commandant refusing to unclose the gates, the French opened fire; their field pieces, however, were not in a condition to produce a sensible effect. The attack, therefore, was suspended till the arrival of the heavy ordnance. When it arrived in the morning the Austrians had disappeared. Vogelsang had quietly quitted the place during the night and joined Frimont.

The Austrian Army, having already crossed the Brenta, was marching for the Piave. Frimont, who had found a favourable position in front of the Brenta at San Pietro Engù, halted and confronted the enemy for some hours. The few hours, however, which he gained for the retreat of the Austrian Army were gained at a great sacrifice of life, and with difficulty the Austrian rear-guard succeeded in getting across the Brenta at Fontanavia.

The archduke with Rosenberg, Bellegarde and Simbschen, crossed the Piave at Nervesa and San Spersiano on the 5th. Two days later he was at Sacile, on the left bank of the Livenza, and on the 8th, having crossed the Tagliamento at Ponte della Delizia, above Valvasone, he halted at Codroipo.

The Prince of Reuss and Davidovich effected their junction at Zero, crossed the Piave at Ponte di Piave on the 6th, the Livenza at La Motta on the 7th, and the Tagliamento at Ponte della Delizia on the 9th. On the evening of that day the entire Austrian Army was concentrated at Codroipo.

Reuss and Davidovich had both small engagements with the advanced guards of Digonnet's and Pully's forces which were marching from Vicenza to Padua.

When the French arrived on the Brenta, they found the bridge at Fontanavia destroyed. This, however, did not detain them long and they soon followed in the wake of the Austrians. The archduke, seriously alarmed at the news of the rapid progress Napoleon's army was making, decided on quitting Codroipo and marching on Vienna by the Frioul and Carinthia road. For all that, he intended that Massena's army should be detained on the Tagliamento for a while. On reaching the banks of that river at the head of his cavalry, Massena was bent on forcing the passage, but he met with a warm reception, fire being opened on him from several batteries well posted on the left bank, to which he could only reply with his light guns. In the evening, his infantry having come up, he designed to deliver a general attack on the following day.

His plans, nevertheless, were frustrated by the archduke, who, not desiring to bring on a general engagement, had decamped early on the morning of the 13th. The Austrians marched in three columns which crossed the Isonzo on the same evening at Podgora, Gradisca, and San Canciano. On the 16th, the Austrian Army took up a position at Prewald. General Vincent, with 9 battalions and 16 squadrons, was left to dispute the passage of the Isonzo.

On learning the enemy's dispositions, Massena had arrived at the conclusion that the archduke had decided to retire altogether from Italy, and that possibly he might not hold the ground in rear of the Isonzo. D'Espagne, who had reached the right bank of that river on the 15th, had been apprised of Vincent's preparations for defence. Massena thereupon conceived an elaborate plan for dislodging him, but for various reasons the attack had to be postponed. Vincent had a serious engagement at Sant' Andrea with Duhesme, after which he suddenly withdrew.

Massena had reached the Venetian frontier, but for some time had not received any news of the *Grande Armée*. He was also ignorant of Ney's operations in the Tyrol, for the inhabitants had risen and intercepted the communications. From various disturbing reports that reached him, he conceived that it was advisable not to push the pursuit any further. The country in his front was mountainous and difficult, whilst his rear had been left insufficiently guarded. He accordingly suspended the march on the 16th and took post on the Isonzo, bent on attending the development of events. Lacour, with 3 battalions and 8 squadrons, was sent towards Villach to endeavour to enter into communication with the *Grande Armée*.

Lacour advanced on the 22nd as far as Villach, which the Austrians had only just passed through, and sent detachments in the direction of Styria to endeavour to find traces of Marmont.

The Archduke Charles, leaving Bellegarde at Prewald with 28 battalions and 12 squadrons, marched by Cilli to effect a junction with his brother. This was effected on the 26th of November at Windisch-Feistritz. The archduke thus gathered together 155 battalions and 96 squadrons, an army, in round numbers, about 80,000 strong.

There remained nothing for the archduke to do but to strive and effect as speedily as he could a junction with the two Russian armies, which, by the latest accounts, had already come together. He imagined, nevertheless, that the two emperors would temporise, and try to march in his direction. He was also anxious to be joined by the rear-guard he had left at Prewald and to give some rest to his troops. He therefore established his army on the Drave, and only resumed the march on the 2nd of December, moving to Körmend, in the valley of the Raab.

THE ARCHDUKE JOHN.

The Archduke John commanded the Army of the Tyrol. In the closing days of October, this army was divided into four principal parts.

The main body of Chasteler's corps, 10 battalions and 8 squadrons, was at Rattenberg, in the Unter-Innthal; one of these battalions held the intrenchment at the Col de Lofer, and another formed the garrison of the fortress of Kufstein.

Saint Julien's corps, 8½ battalions and 9 squadrons strong, was more scattered. Saint Julien himself was at Innsbruck with 1½ battalion and 1 squadron; 2 battalions held the defences in front of Scharnitz; 1 battalion the redoubt of Leutesch; 4 battalions and 8 squadrons, under the Prince of Rohan, were at Reutte, watching the Knie pass and the Füssen road.

Jellachich, with 13¼ battalions and 13 squadrons, troops which for the most part had effected their escape from Ulm, was in the Vorarlberg. He occupied principally the strong position of Hobenems on the right bank of the Rhine, between Feldkirch and Bregenz. Jellachich, who had shown no desire to rejoin Mack after Spangen's surrender of Memmingen, still considered himself as belonging to the Army of the Danube, and trusted to be able to reach Bohemia marching through Suabia.

Festenberg was at Innsbruck with the reserve, 9 battalions and 6 squadrons; 2 more squadrons were attached to headquarters for employment as orderlies, to furnish escorts, etc.

There were besides 2 isolated detachments, one of 6 battalions and 2 squadrons under Szenassy at Werfen, the other, under Colonel Spauer, of 1 battalion and 1 squadron, posted at Nauders, to keep open the communications with Hillier's corps.

The peasants of the Tyrol had the reputation of being very brave and expert marksmen. They organised themselves into bands affiliated with regular troops, and this augmented the Austrian means of defence.

Napoleon enunciated the principle of spreading the troops to diminish the difficulties which always attend their subsistence in war, on condition, however, of being able to concentrate them speedily for fighting. There can be no gainsaying the correctness of such a principle, but the same is based on the fact that the troops are judiciously posted, so that no delay may arise when the concentration has to be effected. The Archduke John had scattered his forces all over the Tyrol and in small detachments, not to obtain better commissariat conditions, but evidently moved by a desire to guard every point in a long line. Consequently, with a force consisting of 48 battalions and 41 squadrons, he was weak alike in every direction.

It has been shown earlier how, under the terms of the capitulation, Ney's corps was bound to occupy the city of Ulm till the 25th of October. When that period was over, in obedience with his orders, he marched to invade the Northern Tyrol. To superintend the evacuation of the prisoners, and the removal of arms and ammunition still in Ulm, half of Loison's division and most of Ney's cavalry had to remain in the city.

Dupont's division had already been taken away from the 6th Corps, so that Marshal Ney's force was greatly reduced in numbers. When he marched for Landsberg, he had only 14 battalions and a few platoons of *chasseurs* and hussars, in all not more than 8000 men. With this small force he was ordered to operate in a very difficult country where the Austrians had more than 25,000 combatants. But Ney's force well concentrated, directed by a daring and capable general, looking at the scattered condition of its adversaries, was likely to give a good account of itself.

Ney, who had been informed of the scattered state of the archduke's forces, determined to pierce their line, to cross over from Bavaria into the Tyrol. He was at Landsberg, and not far from him was the Scharnitz pass, which led directly on Innsbruck, the heart of the country. In advance of Scharnitz, the Isar valley was closed by a bastioned front, and to the west a redoubt guarded the lateral valley of the Leutesch. Not only were these works open at the gorge, but they were feebly garrisoned. The first was held by two battalions and some 500 Tyrolese militia, the other by two companies of militia.

Quitting Landsberg on the 31st of October, Ney marched by Weilheim, Murnau, and Partenkirch, reaching Mittenwalde on the 3rd of November. He then divided his corps in two columns; Malher, with the first, composed of his division, was to carry the works at Scharnitz by a frontal attack; the other column, 5 battalions, under Loison, guided by some Bavarian foresters, went by hunters' tracks to turn the Leutesch redoubt. Malher's attack, though prepared by the fire of eight field pieces, failed; but Loison soon issued in rear of the Leutesch work, enveloped it, and obliged its defenders to lay down their arms. Informed of this event, which exposed his works to be attacked in rear, the commandant of the Scharnitz fort determined to beat a retreat, which he carried into effect at night, after having spiked his guns. Ney had foreseen the likelihood of such an event occurring, and had dispatched a column to Seefeld. The retreating Austrians were cut off, attacked, and after a bold resistance compelled to surrender.

The French column now continued its advance, and by noon on the 5th entered Innsbruck without meeting the slightest resistance. Only the previous day the Archduke John had received orders from his brother, the Archduke Charles, to quit all the positions he held in the Tyrol, and to retire by the Pusterthal with the object of joining the Army of Italy, which was retiring either on Carinthia or Styria. On receipt of these orders, he sent instructions to all his lieutenants to fall back on the Brenner, where the concentration was to be effected, he himself moving thereto with Festenberg's corps and what troops Saint Julien still had at Innsbruck.

How much better would the archduke have done had he from the very first kept his troops concentrated on the Col of Brenner, a point from which he could have darted easily in any direction when threatened, which besides lies on the lines of retreat by the Italian Tyrol on Carinthia. When he did so it was too late, for he had already received

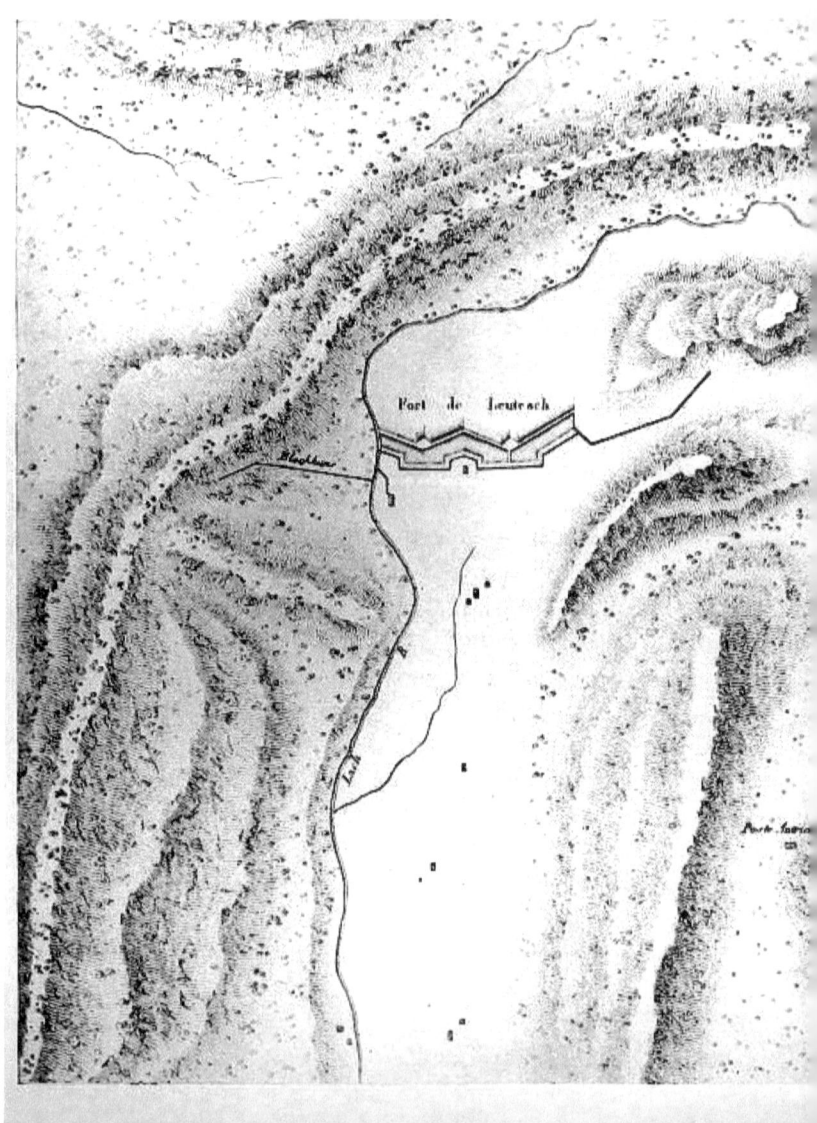

INTRENCHMENTS

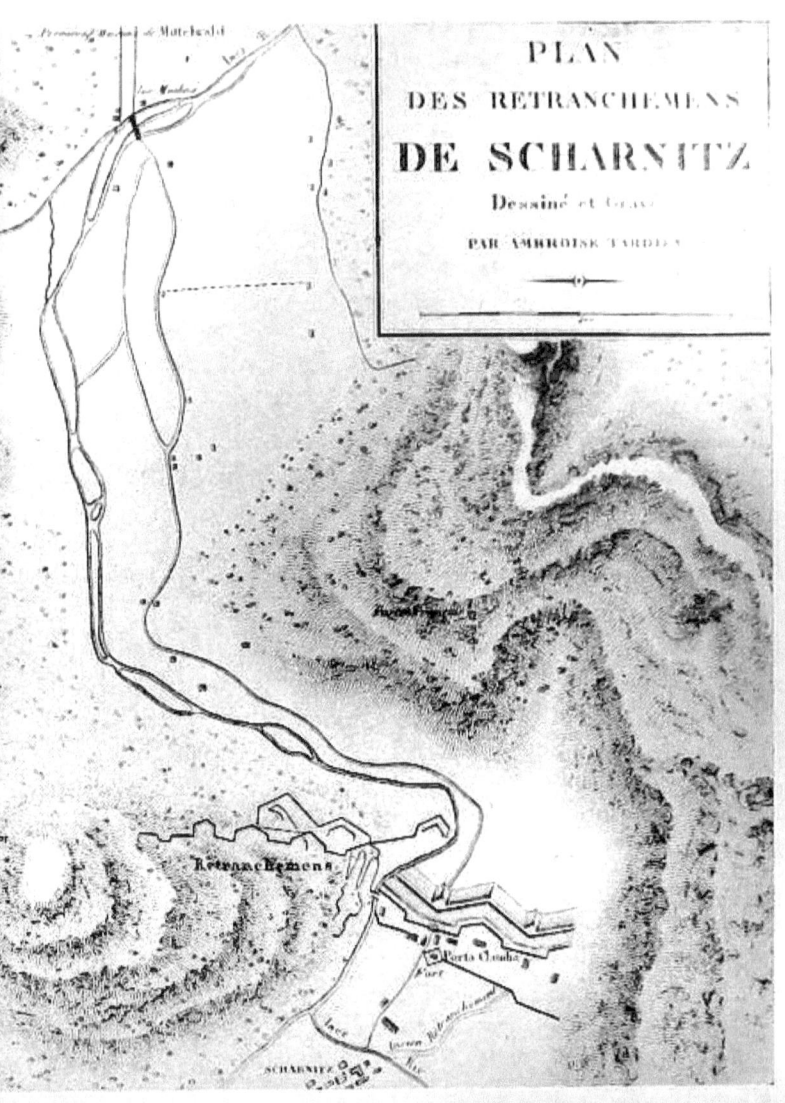

AT SCHARNITZ.

peremptory orders to evacuate the country.

The fortress of Kufstein had been invested by a portion of Deroy's Bavarian division, sent by Bernadotte when he recognised the difficulty of forcing the passage of Lofer. The garrison of Kufstein, as we have already said, consisted of one battalion, but the place, being difficult of access, was capable of being defended for a long time. The citadel was built on a scarped rock, and could only be reached by a spiral and vaulted staircase. After a few feeble demonstrations the civil authorities insisted on a suspension of hostilities, and a convention was arranged, in virtue of which the Bavarians were to occupy the town, the garrison retiring to the fortress. The Austrian commander, getting soon tired of his inaction, obtained leave to march out with his 750 men and 2 guns. He quitted the place on the 10th of November, and proceeded to rejoin Chasteler.

With the other commanders, Jellachich had received orders on the 4th to fall back on the Brenner, but he made no move till the 10th, when, alarmed by the approach of Augereau's corps, he tried to retire on the Upper Adige by way of Bludenz and Landeck. Jellachich, in fact, had not renounced the idea of opening himself a way to the north. On the morning of the 13th, he started 12 squadrons in that direction, and these, marching by way of Wangen, Biberach, Ehingen, Ellwangen, and Ansbach, finally reached Bohemia.

Possibly the rest of his troops would have followed had he not been vigorously attacked near Bregenz by Maurice Mathieu's division. Jellachich's boldness did not equal his obstinacy, and this attack made him believe he was lost. Accordingly, he concluded a capitulation with the French commander at Dornbirn; 9¼ battalions laid down their arms and were led up to the Bohemian frontier, bound for the rest of the war not to fight against the French in Germany nor in Italy.

There remained the Prince of Rohan and his 6000 men near Nauders and Finstermünz. He had received the order to retire from Reutte in time and had regained the valley of the Inn, fully persuaded that he could get to the Brenner by the Innsbruck road. On reaching Landeck, however, on the 9th of November, he became acquainted with the progress made by the French, and how Malher was in the neighbourhood at Imst.

The prince then tried to make a detour by way of Nauders, Glurns, Meran, Botzen, and Brixen. In this also he was foiled, for he was about being anticipated by Ney. To avoid the marshal, he crossed the Venetian frontier, but this did not avail him much, for after having cleared the mountains and passed Bassano, he was attacked by Saint Cyr and completely defeated at Castel-Franco. Seeing no possibility of escape, the prince and his five thousand men laid down their arms.

CHAPTER 11

The "Grande Armée" Enters Moravia

Napoleon made his entry into Vienna on the 14th of November, and took up his quarters at the imperial castle of Schönbrunn. No time was lost in prosecuting military operations. Margaron's light cavalry division was started, after Auersperg's troops, in the direction of Wolkersdorf, whilst Walther's division of dragoons went in the direction of Stockerau, to try and discover Kutuzoff's whereabouts. (The Austrians had formed a fine magazine of clothing, camp equipment, harness, etc., at Stockerau. The French troops pillaged everything.) Mortier's divisions, which had suffered so severely at Dürrenstein, were directed on Vienna to constitute the reserve.

Of the other corps, Bernadotte was sent to the left bank of the Danube; Soult's, minus Saint Hilaire's division left at Mautern, was brought to Vienna, there to join Murat and Lannes; Davout was recalled from Modling to Vienna.

In a campaign so full of admirable measures no disposition was more remarkable than the distribution of the French forces round Vienna. Deeming that Marmont was too far off at Leoben, Napoleon bid him close up, and assigned him a position on the Styrian Alps, where he was to watch the main road leading from Italy to Vienna. He enjoined him to abstain from fighting, but should the archdukes endeavour to retake possession of that road, he was to break down the bridges, tear up the roads, and do all which is enjoined in mountain warfare for staying the progress of a superior enemy. Massena was brought closer to Marmont, and the two were placed in direct communication.

Davout was stationed close to Vienna, with one division, Gudin's, in the direction of Neustadt, so as to be in a position to give a hand to Marmont if necessary; the second division, Friant's, remained in the direction of Pressburg, to watch the roads leading from Hungary;

the third, Caffarelli's, was in front of Vienna, on the Moravia road. Dupont's and Gazan's divisions, which had suffered greatly at Dürrenstein, formed the garrison of Vienna. The other corps, Soult's, Lannes', and Murat's, advanced into Moravia. Bernadotte, who had crossed the Danube at Krems, followed Kutuzoff step by step, ready to join the other French corps, which were soon likely to come to blows with the Russians.

Napoleon had disposed his troops round Vienna so that he could combine his forces and proceed in any direction at the first notice he received of the presence of the enemy.

The emperor was determined to allow no breathing time to the Russian Army, nevertheless he found his own so exhausted by fatigue that he considered it prudent to halt the troops and rest them for a day.

He remained at Schönbrunn until the news came that his troops had regained touch of the enemy. These two days he devoted in giving some definite organisation to the occupied territory. Amongst other appointments, General Clarke was nominated commander of the city of Vienna, Daru, Commissary-General of the occupied provinces, with instructions to turn to good profit the abundant resources of the country. Mathieu Dumas says:

> The conqueror exacted much, but with all the consideration which could lighten this burden of a great calamity.

When Kutuzoff by his sudden flank march took his army across the Danube on the 10th of November, he looked forward to his being able to gain by that manoeuvre a little time over his adversary, and, covered by the Danube, to be able to effect his junction with Buxhowden's column unmolested.

Once the Danube made him secure from a frontal attack, he had no reason for quitting Krems, and his intention was to remain some time in that neighbourhood. He found it necessary to give a rest to his troops, who were much fatigued, and this was the first time, after two weeks of marching and fighting, that they were not menaced by the enemy. Knowing what orders had been issued to Auersperg, enjoining him to make a stubborn defence at the Tabor bridge, Kutuzoff entertained no doubt that the French would be stopped there. Napoleon had foreseen this, and not being able to attack the Russian general on the right bank of the Danube, he resolved to deal him a decisive blow on the left bank of that river by occupying Vienna and the bridge beyond.

Bernadotte and Mortier were ordered to take post opposite to Krems. They were to gather speedily the materials necessary for a bridge, and to cross the river by means of the flotilla at the first news of Kutuzoff's retreat. They were directed to place him between their two corps and Murat's troops.

Being in the habit of paying his emissaries and spies generously, on the evening of the 13th of November the Russian general was informed that the French had crossed the Danube at Vienna that very day, and were marching on Korneuburg and Wolkersdorf. The spies assured him that the French were making for Brünn, though they were unable to tell him exactly in what numbers.

In a letter to Miloradovitch, dated the 26th of January 1806, Kutuzoff avows that his intention had been to defend the crossing of the Danube at Krems, and there to await quietly for reinforcements, but that it was the capture of the bridge at Vienna that had forced him to retire on Hollabrunn. He then perceived the impossibility of remaining any longer at Krems, and the urgency there was for a speedy retirement on the road which led to Brünn, where he intended to effect a junction with Buxhowden. Since his fight at Dürrenstein one reinforcement had joined him, but this was a small one, under De Rosen, which swelled his force by 9 battalions and 5 squadrons; he was not strong enough yet to measure himself with the French Army.

On the night of the 13th-14th of November, he accordingly set out from Krems, having left his wounded there to the merciful care of his adversary, so that they might not hamper his movements. His retreat had to be conducted with the utmost speed, on unmetalled roads, at a very advanced period of the autumn. In the afternoon of the 14th he was at Meissau; there he received the unwelcome news that Murat's cavalry was already showing itself on the side of Stockerau, evidently bent on cutting him off on the Brünn road.

Kutuzoff lost no time, and, on reaching Ebersbrünn, detached Bagration with some 6000 or 7000 men on his right, with orders to take up a good position by Ober Hollabrünn, where the roads followed by the French and Russians crossed. There with his troops and Nostitz' small Austrian corps he was to detain the French until the rest of the Russian Army should have passed in his rear on the road leading from Znaim to Prosmeritz.

While Kutuzoff was marching on Brünn by Znaim, Prince John Liechtenstein, who had been appointed to assume the command of Auersperg's troops, was making for the same city, following the

Nikolsburg road.

Bagration's troops, coming from Krems, had only reached Ebersbrünn when they were ordered to continue their march to Hollabrünn. The distance from Ebersbrünn to Hollabrünn is not more than 12½ miles, still the march was a hard one, for the night was pitch dark and the roads bad, knee-deep in mud. Bagration, who personally led the troops, had learnt in Souvarow's school the difficult art—an art which his general understood to perfection—of effecting forced marches without utterly exhausting the strength of the soldiers.

Both commanders were determined not to lose a moment of time. Napoleon evidently was eager that Kutuzoff's army should not escape him. Of the several eventualities open to the Russian commander he guessed the right one, that he would make for Moravia by extraordinary rapid marches.

He had consequently directed Lannes to join Murat and to advance with him on the Znaim road. (Znaim was the point where the roads from Vienna and Krems join; it was there that Murat was to hold Kutuzoff in check till the French coming from Krems attacked him in rear.)

Soult was to follow the two marshals at a distance of half a day's march and support them. Bernadotte, who had replaced Mortier on the left bank of the Danube, was to follow the retiring Russians, being supported by Mortier, if deemed necessary. The inclement weather, however, had kept Bernadotte from crossing the river, a fact which Miloradovitch hastened to communicate to his chief.

On the morning of the 15th of November, Murat set out from Stockerau with d'Hautpoul's and Nansouty's *cuirassiers*, Walther's dragoons, Lannes' light cavalry, and Oudinot's grenadiers. His advanced guard had not proceeded far from Stockerau when it came into contact with 8 squadrons of Austrian hussars and some *sotnias* of Cossacks under Nostitz, posted in front of Ober Hollabrünn. Bagration, having failed to hit upon a favourable position at Ober Hollabrünn, had fallen with his main body further back, intending to dispute the village of Schoengraben.

He had with him the grenadier regiment of Kiew, the fusilier ones of Azoff and Podolia, the 6th Foot Chasseurs, a battalion of fusiliers of Narwa and of Nowgorod, Pawlograd's and Hesse-Homburg's hussars, Tchernigoff's dragoons, two regiments of Cossacks, and a company of artillery.

Just as the action was about to commence, Murat, remembering

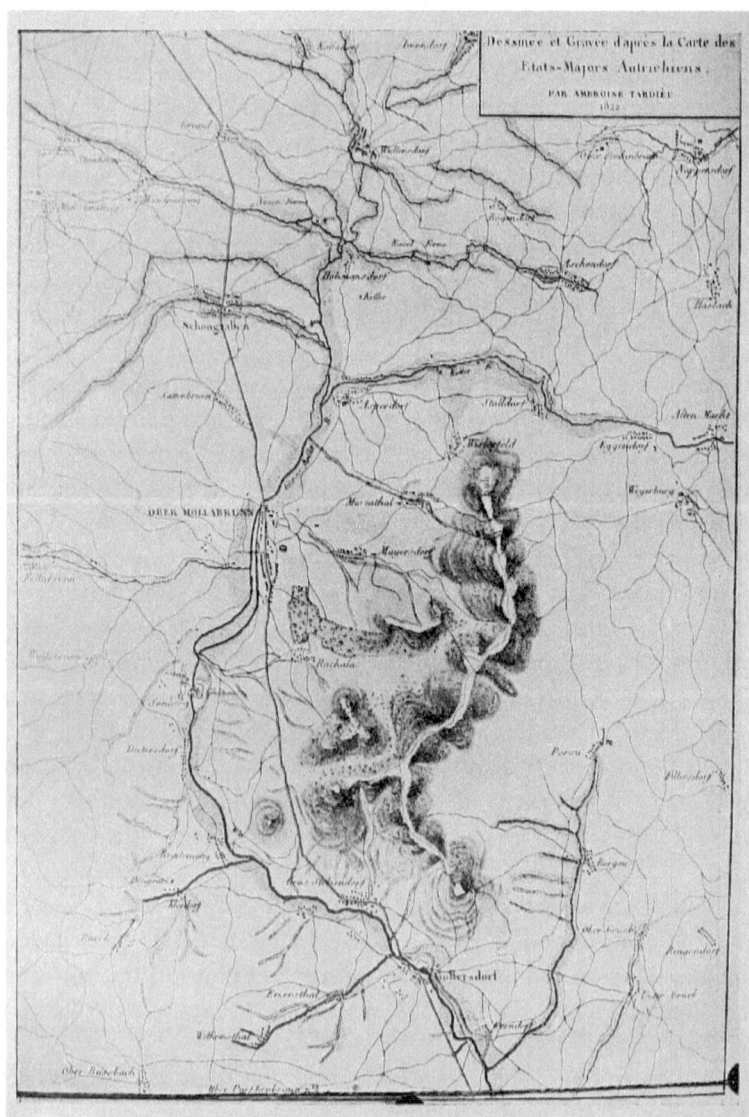

HOLLABRÜNN.

how successful he had been with his stratagem in seizing the bridge at Vienna, and what poor effort he could make with the little infantry he had with him, thought of gaining time by imposing on the Russian commander, the more so as he was desirous to be the first to reach Znaim.

Napoleon was eager to crush Kutuzoff, who had escaped him at Krems. This could only be done by displaying the greatest energy, and it is unaccountable how he should have, against his usual habit, relegated to Murat the management of a manoeuvre which promised such great results.

Count Nostitz, who had command of the advanced guard at Hollabrünn, had with him two regiments of Cossacks and the Hesse-Homburg hussars. When Murat came up with the vedettes of the latter corps he sent word to Nostitz that a separate peace had been concluded between Napoleon and the Austrians, as could be seen by the uncontested passage of the Danube by the French troops. Nostitz put faith in Murat's statement and refused to fight any longer side by side with Bagration.

Bagration tried his very best to undeceive him and to convince him that Murat's statement was simply a *ruse de guerre*, that he was playing on his credulity; but all in vain, and Nostitz withdrew his hussars. Bagration was suddenly attacked; he had to retire and abandon 100 carriages.

Murat, finding the ground cleared by the retreat of the hussars and Cossacks, approached Schoengraben, which, by Bagration's orders, was evacuated by the 6th Foot Chasseurs.

He next tried by cunning to stay Kutuzoff's retreat till his own infantry had time to join him and Bernadotte and Mortier had time to fall on the Russians' rear.

With this object he sent a flag of truce to Bagration to propose an armistice. This proposal was referred to Kutuzoff, who was at Jetzeldorf. Here was an unexpected piece of unheard-of good luck for the Russian commander, and he avidly seized an opportunity which would allow him to get out of his embarrassment. It was no longer with a straightforward unsuspecting Austrian that Murat had now to deal, but with a semi-Asiatic general, renowned in his country for diplomacy and finesse, well skilled in the art of dissimulation. Kutuzoff showed himself most amicable in his reception of the news, and appeared to enter cordially into the negotiations. He dispatched Winzingerode—one of the emperor's *A.D.C.*—to the French camp to propose terms of peace.

Received the same day at the outposts by General Belliard, Winzingerode framed with him a convention by the terms of which the Russian Army was to regain at once its frontier by the road it had come and clear out of Germany. On this condition Murat undertook to suspend his advance into Moravia. It was in any case stipulated that the convention was not to come into operation unless with the approval of the Emperor Napoleon.

In the meantime, the two armies were to remain in the positions they were respectively occupying. Murat, who imagined that by this clever stroke he would end the war by having broken the alliance between the *Czar* and the Emperor of Austria, was tricked. Whilst Bagration remained stationary before the French outposts with his seven thousand men, Kutuzoff was turning to good account the fifteen or sixteen hours required by Murat's staff-officer to reach Schönbrunn and return; besides which, Kutuzoff had caused a further delay by holding the articles of convention back for a day with the object of getting a start on the enemy and saving the army. In his report to the *Czar* he wrote:

> I have delayed my reply for twenty-four hours with the object of continuing my retreat, and I have succeeded in putting the distance of two marches between myself and the French.

Lannes was not so easily taken in as Murat. When Prince Bagration, on visiting Murat, made some flattering speeches to Lannes, the marshal bluntly replied that, had he had his own way, they would be fighting at that moment, and not exchanging empty compliments.

It has been pleaded for Murat that he did not consider that his cavalry and Oudinot's grenadiers were of sufficient strength to close the road to the Russians. However, he was at the head of 50,000 men, and all he had to do was to attack and drive the enemy vigorously before him up to Znaim, where he would have forestalled and probably captured the Russian field-marshal.

On receiving on the afternoon of the 16th Murat's letter, Napoleon, far more foreseeing that his lieutenant, became greatly irritated, and dispatched General Lemarrois at once with a severe reprimand to the prince. He could not find, the emperor wrote, terms sufficiently strong to express all his discontent. Murat was at once to break the armistice and march against the enemy, attack the Russian rear-guard, and press so hard on it that Kutuzoff should find himself compelled to halt and support it. Napoleon wrote:

> Should the *Czar* ratify the convention in question, I shall ratify it, but it is simply a stratagem; march, destroy the Russian Army; you are in a position to capture its baggage and its artillery. The Austrians have allowed themselves to be taken in with regard to the passage of the bridge at Vienna, you allow yourself to be deceived by an *aide-de-camp* of the emperor.

So distrustful was he of Murat that he himself set out for Hollabrünn, bidding the Imperial Guard and Caffarelli's division to follow. So anxious was he to make up for lost time, that, after having gone a short way with the troops, he got into his carriage and started at a gallop for Hollabrünn.

The emperor was likewise dissatisfied with Bernadotte's slack pursuit of the Russians. The marshal had experienced considerable difficulty in throwing a bridge over the Danube at Spitz, and had shifted his corps over to Mautern, hence another lamentable delay.

Kutuzoff on his side repudiated the conditions contained in the armistice. It was an intense grief to him having to sacrifice Bagration and his brave soldiers, but their mission was to lay down their lives for the good of the main body. Their gallantry and death were to save the Russian Army. On quitting the prince, Kutuzoff blessed him before the troops.

It was late in the evening, close upon five o'clock, when Murat began his attack. Prepared for a sudden and impetuous onslaught, Bagration had made a careful distribution of his troops. The small village of Grund was occupied by three regiments. It had been covered with intrenchments and flanked on the right by a regiment of dragoons and on the left by a regiment of hussars. The artillery was posted on the main road in front of the centre.

Murat had at his disposal Lannes' two divisions, Suchet's and Oudinot's, likewise two of Soult's, Legrand's and Vandamme's. (The 4th Corps crossed Vienna on the 23rd Brumaire (14th November) without halting, and pursued its march to Moravia.) He had besides most of the cavalry, but that arm was not of much avail there on account of the ground, which was marshy. He entrusted the attack to Oudinot's grenadiers; these tried soldiers advanced in two columns against the Russian centre, whilst Legrand threatened their right flank and Suchet the left; Vandamme was ordered to remain on the road as a reserve.

Deeming the position at Schoengraben too exposed, Bagration

had withdrawn his troops. Oudinot's grenadiers were much troubled by the smoke and sparks which the Russian artillery had raised by setting fire with shells to the village of Schoengraben. Nevertheless, the French reached Bagration's centre and threw it back on the principal street of Grand, whilst Legrand and Suchet worked gradually round the flanks and rear.

The Russian right was attacked first by the horse grenadiers. Oulanius, who commanded on that flank, had under him the grenadiers of Kiew, the 6th Foot Chasseurs, and Tchernigoff's dragoons. The infantry received the French cavalry with a well-nourished fire, which emptied many saddles, and repulsed two charges. Tchernigoff's dragoons and the Cossacks pursued the French, whilst Oulanius, covered by artillery and skirmishers, continued the retreat. The French horsemen returned to the charge, but such was the order in which Oulanius drew back that they abstained from attacking.

On the Russian left, the attack was more powerful, and the French were in greater numbers. After several attacks, the French separated Pawlograd's hussars from the infantry, and compelled the latter to take another road to rejoin the army. After this success, Lannes surrounded the regiments of Azoff and Podolia, which had already twice cleared their way with the bayonet.

The French centre, which had been held back for some time by the conflagration of Schoengraben, moved forward and rushed at Bagration who was in the act of retiring by the main road, and opened a severe artillery fire on his troops. The French surrounded the Russians on every side, their cavalry not losing a single chance of attacking either centre or flanks. In the narrow streets, alleys, courts, and gardens of Grand the Russians lost many men. The carnage was frightful. They fought in good order, and with great steadiness; Bagration all the while setting an excellent example of courage. On this and other occasions, he handled the rear-guard with great skill.

The Russians approached Guntersdorf where Bagration had already sent two battalions of infantry and some Cossacks, with orders to let the rest of the Russian forces pass, and then to form a rear-guard. At the village the French pressed hard, but before arriving at the other side darkness had set in. Desperate fighting went on till midnight; the two sides had got into indescribable confusion, and Napoleon, on coming up to Murat, seeing the fruitlessness of continuing the contest, ordered the "cease fire" to sound.

Bagration was eventually able to reach Neu Schallersdorf on the morning of the 17th, and Frainspitz, where he overtook the main body of Kutuzoff's army, on the 18th. He had lost one-half of his men, either fallen in the fight or captured. The fight spoke loudly for his fine generalship, for, at the head of 6000 or 7000 men, he had kept at bay an army of 25,000. Tranchard de Laverne states:

> The Russian rear-guard lost that day 12 guns, 100 baggage wagons, 2000 prisoners, and 2000 men who remained on the field of battle.

Both sides behaved with singular intrepidity. Some of the senior officers of the French—Generals Oudinot, Dupas, Legrand, and others—set a fine example and fought like ordinary grenadiers. In Saint-Chaman's opinion, at Hollabrünn the Russians displayed greater spirit than the French. This he partly attributes to the French being under Murat, the poorest (*plus triste*) general he ever came across; also, to the fact that the French, as fighters, were of less account at night than in the day. He adduces as the cause for this that the French soldier likes to be remarked by his officers and comrades, and is not roused by a simple consideration of duty.

From Pohrlitz, where he was joined by Liechtenstein with 13,000 Austrians, Kutuzoff marched speedily to Brünn, and there on arrival received the welcome intelligence that Buxhowden with his column, 27,000 strong, was only one march and a half beyond him on the Olmütz road. Kutuzoff did not allow any delay, and on the 18th the two armies effected a junction at Wischau.

By rapid marching and alertness, the Russian general had escaped a defeat; for it would certainly have gone hard with him had the French overtaken him. In this manner he had upset the second part of Napoleon's plan, which, as we have seen, was to destroy the first Russian Army before it could effect a junction with the rest of the Russian forces.

Though a masterly retreat brings to the front the soldierly qualities of a commander, it is always a very distasteful operation. In this instance it was not of Kutuzoff's choosing, but it had been forced on him by Mack's imprudence and want of skill. He had brought his soldiers through Austria with the full intention of undertaking a brisk offensive; but once he heard of Mack's disaster, he saw himself compelled to retire on or behind Vienna.

However irritating Murat's action at Hollabrünn may have been, and how much Napoleon may have been nettled by the Russians having escaped from him, nothing in the end could have been more fortunate. The Battle of Austerlitz was the crowning event of his brilliant campaign, and that decisive battle would never have been fought had not the Russian and Austrian forces concentrated around Olmütz.

A few days after quitting Brünn, the Austro-Russian forces were mostly bivouacking in the camp of Olschan to the south of Olmütz; there they remained for eight days, to enjoy some little rest of which they were much in need, and to wait the arrival of reinforcements. Both the *Czar* and the Emperor of Austria had their headquarters at Olschan.

The army mustered about 90,000 combatants. Kutuzoff had brought back from the Danube some 35,000 men, Buxhowden's corps and the Imperial Guard mustered 40,000, which made the Russians 75,000 strong. To this should be added 15,000 Austrians, bringing up the total to 90,000 fighting men. The 6000 or 7000 men the Russians lost in the fights on the 11th and 16th of November would have proved very serviceable at Austerlitz.

As for the French Army, Murat entered Brünn on the 19th of November, capturing many Russians as he went along, and on the following day Napoleon established his headquarters in that city. Thus, the capital of Moravia, with considerable magazines, fell into the hands of the French without their having fired a single shot.

On the 21st, Murat had an engagement with Buxhowden's cavalry at Santon. Klein delivered several charges without success, but, reinforced by d'Hautpoul's *cuirassiers* and four squadrons of the Guard, drove the Russians back to Olmütz. After this skirmish the French advanced posts were established at Wischau.

It was to the advantage of both armies to gain time. Napoleon wished to give his troops a short period of rest after the long marches from the shores of the Channel, after all their fatigues and discomfort. His soldiers were worn by exposure, had suffered from cold and often from hunger. The ranks were thinned, and the waste since taking the field amounted to about one-fifth of the total. A certain leisure was also required for issuing articles of clothing and boots of which the troops were very much in want. The allies on their side hoped to gain time for their last reinforcements to arrive and for the archdukes to join them.

General Stutterheim states that some generals of the combined army were in favour of an immediate resumption of the offensive now that Kutuzoff and Buxhowden had joined forces, as the allies were then superior in number to the French. (The Austrian Major-General Stutterheim wrote an account of what he saw of the battle in French, a language, as he says, more generally known than that of Germany.) But the reinforcements which the Grand Duke Constantine was bringing had not yet joined the army, and so fatigued were the Russian soldiers by continual marches—Kutuzoff's falling back from the Inn on the supports, and the supports in hurrying forward to join him—that it was decided to take up a position about Olmütz, and to give some days' repose to the troops.

The allied army at Olschan was posted with the left resting on the river March, the right extending in the direction of the heights in rear of the Tobolan. The forces, under the command of the General-in-Chief, Kutuzoff, numbered 101 battalions, 20 of which were Austrians, and 159 squadrons, 54 of which were Austrians, and 40 Cossacks.

Prince John of Liechtenstein commanded the Austrian forces; his infantry was composed of a number of sixth battalions, which had been recruited, armed, and organised not longer than a month. Kienmayer formed a part of the prince's corps.

On the 25th of November, the Grand Duke Constantine arrived at Olmütz with the Russian Imperial Guard. After a long and forced march from St. Petersburg, this magnificent body of soldiers, composed of men of enormous size, joined in perfect order. The corps consisted of 10 battalions and 18 squadrons, a total of 8,500 men under arms. This reinforcement swelled the number of the Russian Army to more than 75,000 men.

Napoleon, when he arrived at Brünn, did not dare to attack the allies, estimating their position far too strong. The allies got him out of the difficulty by coming to meet him.

Stutterheim again deplores that an advance was not made on the day when the Grand Duke arrived with reinforcements. By the general's own statement, however, the allies had no sort of information as to the position and strength of the enemy. Prince Bagration ignored the situation occupied by the French advanced guard, and the Austrians, who, being in their own country, might have been expected to possess means for procuring intelligence, had only very vague details to go upon. With such meagre information regarding the position and strength of the enemy, it would have certainly been the height of folly to resume the offensive.

General Giulay and Herr Stadion waited on Napoleon at Brünn to discuss the conditions of peace, but the stipulations on which the emperor based his acquiescence appeared to them singularly hard. Napoleon, who looked upon these delegates purely in the light of military spies purposely sent to his headquarters with a view of penetrating his designs, made them clearly understand that he did not at all relish having political agents in his camp, and, as they were not authorised to treat on behalf of Russia, he dismissed them, and ordered them to proceed to Vienna to discuss matters with Talleyrand, his foreign minister. Napoleon by this prevented the Austrian emissaries meeting Haugwitz and making their demands in conjunction with him. Haugwitz had been detained purposely at Iglau.

However able and artful these negotiators may have been considered in their own country, they were no match for Napoleon in sagacity and acuteness; their conversation was not sufficiently guarded that one of them did not let out the fact that Prussia had entered into a treaty with Austria and Russia. Some hint of this had already reached the emperor from Monsieur Laforest, his minister at Berlin, and the danger of following the Russians beyond Moravia was now fully revealed to him. Since the occupation of Vienna and the combat at Hollabrünn, many of his principal officers had been urging Napoleon to conclude peace, and he was equally willing to end the war by concluding peace—as long as the conditions proposed appeared fair—or to fight a battle, should the enemy offer him a favourable opportunity.

That his army was much exhausted there could be no question. Count de Ségur relates a long conversation Napoleon had with a dozen of his officers on the eve of Austerlitz, when Mouton, in answer to Junot, who was rejoiced to behold the ardour of the troops, spoke out:

> The army was wearied; it had had enough of it; and if it were intended to drag it on still further, it would obey, though reluctantly; lastly, that if it displayed such spirit on the eve of battle it was simply because it hoped to have done with the war on the morrow and to return home.

Circumstanced as Napoleon was, his advance into Moravia had been a bold step, if not a risky one. Here, at Brünn, he had ventured to the furthermost frontier of Moravia, and had no more than 65,000 men within reach. The *Czar* confronted him with 90,000 Russians and Austrians at Olmütz, the Archduke Ferdinand, at the head of some 20,000 Austrians, was advancing through Bohemia in his rear; and the Archduke Charles, already in Hungary, was hurrying up on his right with 40,000 men. Prussia, with 150,000 men, was ready to seize his line of retreat. The danger was great, and greater it became the longer the *Czar* remained inactive. Nevertheless, the emperor knew too well that once the offensive has been assumed it is most paying to abide by it to the last extremity. He decided to end the war by beating the allies thoroughly before the armies in Bohemia and Hungary would have had the necessary time to reinforce the allied sovereigns.

The further the *Grande Armée* advanced, naturally the more its combinations became multiplied, and the more the emperor was compelled to disperse his forces. The same did not apply to the allies, who, on the other hand, could concentrate their forces as they retired. This consideration, and the length and weakness of his lines of communication, gave the emperor matter for deep reflection.

A little less than a day's march divided the two armies. Since the cavalry engagement on the 21st, they had remained inactive, contenting themselves by simply watching each other. Lannes and the Guard occupied Brünn and the country in its neighbourhood; Soult was at Austerlitz and at Pratzen; Murat, with his cavalry, on the main road from Brünn to Olmütz. Caffarelli had remained in rear between Znaim and Brünn.

A battle was not improbable; indeed, both sides were expecting it. However, in the camp of the allies opinions were divided. Kutuzoff desired to temporise, to withdraw further with the object of procuring provisions, for scarcity was already prevailing in the eastern provinces of Austria; besides, it had never been contemplated to concentrate 90,000 men round Olmütz. The Russians, who had not the skill of the French in requisitioning, laid their hands on everything and appropriated the little there was with the brutal rapacity of a savage horde. They went beyond living on the resources of the country, for they devastated any locality they occupied.

The younger and more fiery followers of the *Czar* rejected Kutuzoff's arguments, and, looking at Napoleon's perilous position at Brünn, so far advanced from his base and from France, were eager to fight and overwhelm the *Grande Armée*. They disdained to await either the cooperation of the Prussians or the arrival of the Archduke Charles.

On seeing Napoleon stop in the midst of the advantages he had already gained, the Russian staff interpreted that fact as a clear indication of timidity, when, on the contrary, this delay was well calculated, and arose from crafty motives. They could not bring themselves to believe that he could possibly have any other reason than fear for staying his pursuit of the allies.

Before trying the issue of a battle, Napoleon endeavoured to negotiate. Accordingly, on the 25th of November, he directed Savary to repair to the Russian headquarters, bearing a letter for the *Czar*. Savary, who was an officer at the same time discreet and cunning, had evidently been selected with a view to observing the exact condition of the allies, learning their feelings and discovering their projects. (The Russians held Savary in horror, and looked upon him as d'Enghien's executioner.) Napoleon's letter was complimentary; he felicitated the *Czar* on his arrival in Moravia, assured him of his esteem in the most pleasing language, and expressed a wish to merit his friendship. Savary had a long interview with the *Czar*, which he gives in detail in his memoirs. He returned, bringing back a letter, not addressed to the emperor, but to the *Chef du Gouvernement Français*. In handing this letter to Savary the *Czar* seemed somewhat embarrassed, and kept the address from sight till the last, when he explained that the address meant nothing more than a *régle d'etiquette*.

******

When in 1806 Fox wrote to Talleyrand to report the proposal made to him by the so-called Guillet da la Gevrilliére to assassinate the emperor, he used the words *chef du Gouvernement Français*. In a private letter he explains to the, foreign minister how, in the actual situation of the two courts, it would not have been fitting for a minister to use any other expression.

******

Savary spoke highly of the civility he had received from the Czar Alexander and the Grand Duke Constantine; besides the conversation he had with the *Czar*, he reported how the Russian headquarters were full of youths of the best families who dreamt of nothing else but battle, so much so that he looked upon a contest as inevitable. He added that, from conversations he had held with a number of officers, who under different titles were about the *Czar*, he had detected that presumption, inconsiderateness and imprudence governed the decisions of the Russian military cabinet.

******

Czartorinski wished Novosiltzoff to return to the French camp with Savary, to have an interview with Haugwitz. Savary distinctly refused; he would not entertain such an idea for an instant.

******

Savary met the emperor near the outposts not far from Wischau. After he had explained the result of his mission and his conversation with the *Czar*, he was directed to return at once to the Russian camp and propose to the *Czar* a personal interview on the following day, at any convenient time, with the proviso of a suspension of arms for twenty-four hours.

The *Czar* refused the proposed interview on the plea that he wished to consult the Emperor Francis who was at the time some distance off, but he sent Prince Dolgorouki, his first *aide-de-camp*, back with Savary. He explained that it was in the prince that he had the greatest confidence, and that to him alone could he intrust such a mission. Whilst Savary was with the *Czar*, information was brought in that the French were retiring; in fact, no sooner had Savary quitted Napoleon than the latter commenced the movement to the rear, which he had prepared beforehand, and which was to lead his army to the position which he had attentively surveyed some days previously and adopted as the best on which to give battle. All the young people at headquarters, who could not appreciate the object of this movement, really believed that the French were scared, and that they were trying to escape from the Russian Army.

Napoleon, who generally received the bearers of flag, of truce at his headquarters, received Prince Dolgorouki at the outposts, and only let him see as much of the army as would tend to deceive him. He walked about with the prince on the main road. This officer allowed himself to be imposed upon by the artfully feigned attitude of the French. Everything seemed to indicate that a strong feeling of fear oppressed their army, strong guards were visible in every direction, fortifications and field works were being thrown up in great haste.

Dolgorouki appears to have displayed little tact in what he was ordered to say by the *Czar*. In the report made to him on his return, he states that during the conference with Napoleon he never once gave him the title of Imperial Majesty. He spoke, it is said, in the haughty and overbearing tone in which he was wont to speak to the Russian officers. This young man (the emperor in his bulletin calls him a *freluquet*, puppy), who had never yet done anything worth recording, had the impudence to advise the emperor to abandon Northern Italy and Piedmont, to withdraw from Belgium, to confer the iron crown on one of his most determined enemies.

★★★★★★

When sending Prince Repnin to the *Czar* after the Battle of Austerlitz, Napoleon complained that instead of agreeing to an interview before the battle, the *Czar* had sent him a young man who had nothing but impertinences for him. "*Au lieu de cela, c'eat un jeune homme qu'il m'envoie pour me faire entendre des impertinences, et où? au milieu des mes colonnes!*"

("Instead, it's a young man he sends me to make me hear impertinences, and where? in the middle of my columns!"

★★★★★★

The emperor calmly listened to these extraordinary proposals, then drily replied:

If it is that only that you have been directed to say, go and report to the Emperor Alexander that when I asked to see him, I did not anticipate such dispositions. I would have only shown him my army, and would have appealed to his justice for the conditions. He desires it; we shall fight. I wash my hands of the consequences.

In any case, was it not expecting too much to hope that the conqueror should give up all his conquests, the fruit of all the blood France had shed since the commencement of the Revolution? Who would believe that the most able sword in Europe would tamely submit to demands of such a nature?

Lanfry makes out that Dolgorouki's deportment was not at all disrespectful; that his proposals were nothing more nor less than the programme drawn up by the Emperor of Austria, the *Czar*, and the King of Prussia. He thinks that Napoleon's account of the interview with the prince should be received with caution. De Ségur, who was in attendance on the emperor, and who states that he and other staff officers could hear part of the conversation, condemns Dolgorouki's deportment. The habit and determination to conquer always suggests to an experienced general the means.

Napoleon desired to be attached, consequently he felt bound by his words, by his attitude, and by his movements, to inspire in the minds of his adversaries a false idea of their superiority over him. Always bold, he suddenly showed himself irresolute. His cavalry, ordinarily so enterprising, seemed to have lost its daring. His advanced posts allowed themselves to be surprised.

His attitude and his patience were taken as clear indications that he was afraid. It was an accepted thing that the French Army should be attacked, and that the allies were so to manoeuvre as to cut him off from Vienna.

In vain did Czartorinski strive to prove that if Napoleon did not advance from Brünn it was not because he was afraid. Only soldiers without experience would ever believe that such a man could be afraid. If he did not advance, it was because he estimated that he had already advanced quite far enough. He was not likely to follow the Russians beyond Moravia.

★★★★★★

Czartorinski may possibly have heard of Bonaparte's reply to one of his councillors after the explosion of the infernal machine on the 3rd *Nivôse*, when recommended to have no fear. "I fear! Were I afraid, France would be indeed unfortunate."

★★★★★★

In the allied camp, there were several far-seeing and prudent men who were decidedly against risking the chances of a battle. Prince Adam Czartorinski, a Polish nobleman, who seconded the more enlightened views of the *Czar* for the ulterior good of Poland and for a return of its national institutions, an early friend of the *Czar*, and who had a certain influence over him, wished to get Alexander away from the army. (The Czar Paul was not pleased to see the intimacy which his son Alexander, had contracted with Prince Adam Czartorinski. At one time he removed him from St. Petersburg by making him Minister of Russia at the Sardinian Court).

He judged that his presence at army headquarters, surrounded as he was by giddy, ignorant, and presumptuous youths, must necessarily destroy the authority of the generals and absolve them from all responsibility. He urged his return to St. Petersburg. As to hostilities, he drew an unfavourable comparison between the French soldiers, accustomed to fight and to conquer, and the Russian, who had been steadily retiring from the Inn to Olmütz. He called attention to the French commander-in-chief, a general who, besides being young and daring, had commanded in many battles, who was the most experienced of all living captains, if not the greatest, who had overcome all the generals of Europe, whilst of his present opponents not one had yet risen to fame.

Czartorinski often presumed on the *Czar's* friendship and on his own abilities and good sense in blaming his sovereign for his inconsistency. Nothing was more disagreeable to the Czar than the sound advice the prince gave him at this time. (The Dolgorouki party were opposed to Czartorinski's views, and even accused him of betraying his sovereign.) Alexander craved to shine on the battlefield, his youthful entourage had made him undervalue the knowledge of his generals, and encouraged him to imagine that he would be better inspired and show more skill than his aged and pedantic lieutenants. Flattery had ended in persuading him to place himself in the midst of his army, and had convinced him that he possessed all the high qualities to be looked for in a commander; also, that his presence amongst his troops would surely kindle their enthusiasm.

Others of his most devoted subjects, besides Czartorinski, were displeased to see the *Czar* in camp with the army. What we ask of our *Czar*, they said, is not the passive courage of the recruit whose only virtue lies in braving death, but the high courage of deliberating, of deciding, of acting for 50,000,000 of souls. According to them, what was needed was a heart in the centre of the body to transmit strength to the hands that fight.

Kutuzoff, Bagration, Dochtouroff, Miloradovitch, face to face with the possessors of Imperial favour, could only hint that the arguments of the latter were not sound, but all alike seemed to dread pressing their views on their Imperial master, lest by so doing they should forfeit his esteem. Kutuzoff, being a courtier, did not oppose the wishes of his master as strongly as his experience and his position entitled him to do.

Discord reigned in the allied camp. The Russians having come, as they considered, to assist the Austrians, had grown in a certain measure to despise them. They held them cheap, and even accused them of weakness. The combats of Dürrenstein and of Hollabrünn had raised their self-esteem to such a pitch that the only fear they entertained was lest Napoleon should succeed in escaping from them.

The Austrian Army, truly enough, lacked enthusiasm, and their officers were weighted down by recent disasters: nevertheless, the haughtiness of the Russians, the *Nasha Russki Mallatchi* —our Russian bravery, a catch phrase of the Russian Army—had so seriously irritated the Emperor Francis and all ranks, that they were not loath that their allies should receive a lesson. (The Russians say that it is the hardships they have to endure that has made their soldiers the best troops in the world. As a rule, they are very ignorant.)

In their foolish pride, the young Russian courtiers despised the Austrian Army, which they held, and with much reason, to have compromised the fate of the war at Ulm. But strange enough, with all the insults heaped on the Austrians, the military youths who surrounded the *Czar* permitted an Austrian general, Weyrother, to have veritable authority at headquarters. This general had guided Buxhowden's army in its march through Galicia, and had inspired the Russians with confidence. He had also succeeded in persuading Alexander's courtiers that he had elaborated a splendid plan which of a certainty would destroy Napoleon. This consisted in turning the French right, cut it off from Vienna and throw Napoleon back on Bohemia, thus separating him from the forces he had in Austria and Italy. It is noteworthy that the Emperor Francis was quite ignored in the arrangements for the coming battle.

The hot-headed young officers who virtually directed the affairs of the Russian Army were eager for action, they revelled in their natural presumption. They had persuaded themselves that if the French had hitherto done so much in the course of the campaign, it was owing to the cowardice of the Austrians.

There were not wanting, nevertheless, generals and superior officers of the Austrian Army, men who had fought several campaigns against the French, to disabuse them and to warn their allies that it was not with that unbounded confidence that one ought to march against tried soldiers and officers of the highest merit. These Austrian officers, having too often felt the weight of Napoleon's hand, had become cautious.

They stated how they had on several occasions seen the French emperor, when reduced to a handful of men, repossess himself of victory under the most difficult circumstances, and by rapid and unforeseen operations, destroy the most numerous armies. That, as far as matters had yet gone, the Russians had not obtained any real advantage; that what they had yet accomplished in the campaign were rear-guard engagements, which had, if anything, ended in favour of the French.

Such had been the brilliancy of his victories that not only his soldiers, but even his adversaries, had begun to believe that there was no difficulty from which Napoleon could not triumphantly extricate himself.

The *Czar* and his advisers were oblivious of the fact that they were about to contend against the most able and successful general of the age, and unmindful of how his power would augment should he in the coming contest be able to score a further victory.

The young officers kept extolling the bravery of the 80,000 Russians; they pointed to the enthusiasm inspired by the presence of their *Czar*, to the picked corps of the Imperial Guard; and what more than anything else seemed to astonish them was that the Austrians should be so blind as not to acknowledge their superior talents. In their judgment, not to deliver battle was a most glaring fault, simply an act of arrant cowardice. These men were eager to fight and have done with it, to set their faces again towards their frontier.

Alexander hearkened to the counsels of such as clamoured for battle. He was influenced by young men full of ardour, courage, and illusions, who were impatient to distinguish themselves in the eyes of their sovereign. These men, who had no experience, held Kutuzoff's dilatory attitude in contempt.

The prudent advice of Kutuzoff, Dochtouroff, Langeron, Bagration, and Miloradovitch—the most tried soldiers in the army—had less weight at the *Czar's* headquarters than the rash eagerness of young staff-officers like Prince Dolgorouki and Baron Winzengerode. There were, nevertheless, weighty reasons which made a delay desirable, if not even a necessity. First of all, Essen's corps was fast approaching, and would soon have brought a reinforcement to the army of from 10,000 to 12,000 men. Secondly, the time agreed by Prussia for casting her lot with the coalition had nearly arrived. She only waited for Napoleon's reply to her ultimatum which Count Haugwitz had been directed to present.

Then a fine army of 120,000 men would commence its march from Bayreuth and Bamberg with the object of seizing the French communications. Who could foretell what effect a lost battle would have on the mind of the wavering Prussian monarch; if he would be only too glad to find in the event an opportunity for releasing himself from his obligations? Thirdly, by delaying for two or three weeks, it was hoped that the archdukes would have effected a junction with the main Austro-Russian Army, raising the total of the two to 170,000 men.

Czartorinski, who was the Russian minister of foreign affairs, who had accompanied the *Czar* to Berlin and had sounded the agitation in the Prussian capital, used all these arguments to dissuade the *Czar*. He had not become prudent through age, for he was in the prime of life, but he was rightly jealous of his sovereign's reputation. The young Emperor Alexander, having as yet no experience of war, shared the impatience of his entourage. Both he and his staff were eager for a speedy trial of strength with the enemy.

Certainly, it was imperative soon to decide one way or the other, for supplies were getting scarce. Not anticipating a check, the allies had not established magazines in their rear. The army had not been at Olmütz one day before it was obliged to have recourse to forced requisitions. These, executed with violence and in a disorderly manner, were injurious to the discipline of the army. Irregularities and disorders went unpunished under the pretext that the army was starving. It was, nevertheless, possible to draw back a few marches as Kutuzoff proposed, thus quitting a district which the passage and occupation by a large number of troops had utterly exhausted. Better still, there was the alternative of marching towards Hungary to meet the archdukes. This difficulty of provisioning was not to be solved simply by an inconsiderate march in the direction of the enemy.

Notwithstanding these and other considerations set forth at a council of war held on the 24th of November, it was resolved to undertake a grand offensive movement. The allied army, having taken two or three days to collect provisions for a few days, quitted the neighbourhood of Olmütz on the 27th of November and marched in the direction of Brünn. By that date, the allies had received the reinforcements brought by the Grand Duke Constantine, and heedlessly thought that nothing was to be gained by a further delay. They believed their forces to be sufficiently numerous to contend with the French, and superior to them in quality.

The Austro-Russian Army consisted of 113 battalions, 153 squadrons, and 5 regiments of Cossacks, making a total of 80,000 combatants—70,000 infantry and artillery and 16,000 cavalry. The Russians had 93 battalions and 99 squadrons, a total of 72,000 men. The Austrians had at the most 14,000 men, divided into 54 very weak squadrons of cavalry and 20 battalions. Three-fourths of the combatants were Russians.

The allies could not look forward to being joined by the archdukes for some time, considering that on the 15th of November the latter were only at Layback. To gain Hungary they had first to make a considerable detour, they had then to cross the length of that country before entering Moravia and proceeding to Olmütz. This entailed a march of fully 150 leagues, which would at the very least demand 20 days. Napoleon, who was at Vienna on the 15th, had only 40 leagues to march to arrive under the walls of Brünn.

The fire-eaters had before them a deeply calculating adversary; a master of the art of war, who could thoroughly penetrate all their motives and intentions. Their eagerness accorded excellently with Napoleon's plans; he consequently did all in his power to encourage their aspirations. He did even more, for he ordered his lieutenants to abandon ground wherever they found themselves attacked.

As at Marengo, fortune favoured Napoleon, for the allies lacked the ability to comprehend that their best policy was to play a waiting game.

The army was set in motion on the 27th, though orders had been issued on the 24th for an advance to take place on the following day. What led to this delay was that it had been considered expedient to take two days' provisions, and that there was no way of collecting them till the 26th. Then, as some of the generals were uncertain regarding the proper meaning of their orders, one more day was lost.

The accounts derived from the people of the country were very contradictory, and the outposts could give no information whatever.

On the 27th, Bagration who commanded the advanced guard made no movement, the better to conceal from the enemy the march of the allied armies. This was carried out over five roads, parallel to each other. The two right columns moved along the foot of the mountains, to the right of the causeway, and were composed entirely of infantry; the centre one was on the great Prosnitz road; the fourth advanced parallel to it on its left, and at no great distance; the fifth, composed entirely of cavalry, was in sight of the fourth, and had the country in its front thoroughly open.

The Austro-Russian Army moved forward with the greatest precaution; and naturally enough, for it was uncertain of the exact position occupied by the French Army. The orders were to refuse the left and to allow the right, which was moving along the mountains, to gain ground, in order to turn the enemy's left. In the afternoon of the 27th, the allies halted between Prosnitz and Proedlitz. It was ascertained during the evening that the French advanced posts were still holding Wischau, and that apparently, they had not been reinforced. On this information, Bagration received orders to attack them early on the following day.

On the 28th, in the morning, the prince formed his corps into three columns; the centre one was to attack Wischau in front, the other two were directed to go to the right and left, so as to turn the position. Lannes had there a brigade of hussars, eight squadrons, under General Treilhard. Two other regiments of cavalry were in rear of the town in reserve, and General Sebastiani was at Huluboschau with a regiment of dragoons. Treilhard had received orders to retire on the approach of the enemy. His retreat was effected, but not as promptly as it should have been.

A cloud of Cossacks, supported by regular cavalry, Szechler's and Hesse-Homburg's hussars, surrounded the small town of Wischau and captured a squadron of the French. Murat advanced to protect Treilhard's retreat, but Prince Bagration sent forward all his cavalry and that of the 4th column to support the attack of his advanced guard. He occupied the heights of Rausnitz, where he took up his position.

Napoleon, hearing what was occurring, repaired speedily to the advanced guard, and having examined from the top of a hill the ground Murat was disputing, ordered him to abandon the defence of Rausnitz and to retire. Murat fell back on Posoritz, and the allies took post in front of Wischau. Their army was not more than twenty miles from the city of Brünn.

Insignificant as this skirmish was, it had, nevertheless, decisive results in the campaign. It emboldened the allies, who definitely decided to advance in search of the French Army and bring it to battle, a thing which to all appearance they thought that Napoleon seemed to dread. Believing that his army was bent on retiring, their great anxiety was lest the French should be able to baffle the attack. Napoleon, who had guessed the intentions of the allies and the plan they would most probably adopt, endeavoured to encourage them by ordering his advanced guard on the Olmütz road to fall back, by withdrawing the advanced posts from the Littawa and bringing Soult from Austerlitz and Pratzen to the right bank of the Goldbach. Rausnitz and Austerlitz were evacuated to animate the enemy with a show of success. All the emperor's measures more or less indicated a wish to obtain peace without fighting.

Not only had Savary, in his interviews with the allies, gained very valuable information, but Napoleon, in his conversations with Stadion and Giulay, sent to his headquarters with the object of gaining time, had come to know the condition in which the allied army around Olmütz was. Dolgorouki, with his presumptuous assurance, had unwittingly enlightened him on many doubtful points.

Mikhailovski-Danilevski writes:

> Ocular witnesses affirm that the information furnished by Prince Dolgorouki on the demeanour of the French troops and the apparent hesitation on the part of Napoleon were the reasons which determined the allies to resort to an immediate attack. The prince was fully convinced that the French Army was on the brink of ruin.

After the encounter at Wischau he wrote:

> *Les chances sent pour nous, il ne s'agit que d'avancer, l'ennemi rétrogradera ainsi quil l'a fait à Wischau.* (The chances are all in our favour, it is only a matter of advancing, the enemy will retire as

he did at Wischau.)

The Emperor Francis himself had exhausted every argument to dissuade the *Czar* from offering battle, but it was all in vain.

In view of a battle which he foresaw to be imminent, Napoleon had taken the wise precaution of calling to his side all the troops he could well dispose of. He had brought within reach of him at Nikolsburg a portion of the 3rd Corps. Davout, with Friant's division and Bourcier's cavalry brigade, who were intended to form the right of the line of battle, were hastened up to Raigern, where they arrived on the night of the 1st of December, only five miles from the Goldbach. Caffarelli was likewise brought up and placed under Lannes to form part of the French left.

Bernadotte, on the evening of the 28th, had been directed to leave Wrède's Bavarians at Iglau in front of the Archduke Ferdinand, and to bring his two other divisions to Brünn as speedily as possible. By these arrangements, on the evening of the 1st of December the emperor had under him, not counting Davout's troops which had not yet reached Raigern, some 70,000 combatants.

Chapter 12

Dispositions for the Battle

The mountains of Bohemia and those of Hungary are connected together by those of Moravia. The latter slope gradually down in the direction of the Danube, and in the vicinity of that river Moravia opens out in a vast plain. Round Brünn—the capital of the Province—at the foot of the Spielberg, the mountains have ceased to be anything more than lofty hills, covered with dark firs. The level nature of the plain impedes the flow of the streams; these run sluggishly, and in their course open out into a succession of ponds. By different outlets the water makes its way to the Morava, and hence to the Danube.

On the west of the plain lies the main road of Moravia, leading from Vienna to Brünn. At Brünn the road turns sharply to the right, and, passing by Bellowitz, goes on to Olmütz. On the east, the road coming from Hungary crosses the village of Austerlitz, then inclines to the north-west, and falls into the Brünn-Olmütz road at the Posoritzer post-house.

The Schwarzawa River, after passing the city of Brünn, flows into the Morava, joining the Danube near Presburg. In the middle of the plain runs the Goldbach brook, which rises on the north of the Brünn-Olmütz road, and falls into the small pond of Mönitz. This stream, flowing along the bottom of a little valley, separated the two armies; and on its banks are situated the villages of Telnitz, Sokolnitz—with its park and *château*—Kobelnitz, Puntowitz, and Girzikowitz.

Up to a certain point, parallel with the Goldbach, flows the Littawa, which, dividing into several branches about Birbaum, bends to the south-west, and flows into the ponds of Satschan and Mönitz. The Austro-Russian left was near the pool of Satschan and the swampy ground around it.

One of the principal features of the battlefield has disappeared. The ponds which played such a conspicuous part in the termination of the battle were artificial ponds, constructed for the purpose of fishing. Napoleon had them drained many years ago.

Napoleon confirmed the maxim that the best reconnaissance of country over which a commander has to manoeuvre his troops is that made by himself. Riding back from Wischau on the 21st of November, he ascended the Bosenitzerberg, a hillock which lies close to the Olmütz road; then riding in a southerly direction, he proceeded slowly across an elevated plain about three leagues in length and about two in breadth, taking in all its most prominent features. Several times he enjoined his marshals to "study this ground attentively, for this will be a battlefield, and ere long you shall have an important role to play on it."

He had with his far-reaching eye appreciated all the advantages of this position, and had selected the ground between the Goldbach and the Littawa for his battlefield, where he would await the enemy's attack. From the day he rode beyond Brünn, the coming battle with all its details occupied his mind. The little town of Wischau was to be occupied only by four regiments of light cavalry. Rausnitz and Austerlitz were to be evacuated on the first appearance of the enemy.

★★★★★★

Thiebault states that in riding across the Pratzen plateau on the 21st of November the emperor told the officers who accompanied him, "Take a good look at those heights; you will be fighting there in less than two months." Lejeune, at that time on Berthier's staff, and a captain of Engineers, relates in his memoirs: "The emperor then sent me, with other officers of Engineers, to reconnoitre and study the ground in the neighbourhood of Brünn, where he desired to draw the Russians and offer them battle, with the ground in his favour. He himself chose the position, and caused the advanced guards to fall back for several leagues, in the direction of the heights, which nature appeared to have set to be the theatre of such a mighty event."

★★★★★★

On the left were the wooded hills of Moravia, and the rounded knoll of Bosenitzerberg, a pretty steep hillock, to which the French soldiers from Egypt gave the name of Santon, because it had on the summit a little chapel with a spire suggesting a minaret. In the centre, between the Goldbach and the Littawa, stood a group of heights which, though of no considerable elevation, commanded all the ground around. These formed the plateau of Pratzen, so named after the village which stood about their centre. On the left of this plateau was the village of Stari Winobradi.

To the west, between the Goldbach and the Schwarzawa, some insignificant heights and the Turas wood, to the south of the Latein chapel, could afford a second defensive position in front of Brünn.

The heights, generally speaking, are bare, with nothing which might impede the movements of cavalry and artillery. The soil is clay, muddy and slippery during a thaw, as it was at the period of the Battle of Austerlitz. The thaw, however, had been moderate, and the ice on the ponds was still bearing. There was no snow, but the weather was very cold.

On the 30th of November, Napoleon fixed his bivouac on a knoll to the right of the Olmütz road, a little in advance of the village of Bellowitz. From this point, which was subsequently called Kaiserbühl (the emperor's hill), could be seen all the country around for a very great distance, and from this point the enemy's movements were plainly visible. Those of the French, on the contrary, were concealed by the undulations of the ground. It was from this knoll that the emperor settled his general line of battle.

In the Marengo campaign, after the capture of Ivrea, the First Consul might have destroyed the Austrians in detail; he wished, however, to crush them in one decisive battle, in a battle worthy of the name. It was the same at Austerlitz. Mathieu Dumas relates how Napoleon, on making a careful reconnaissance of the ground from Bosenitzerberg to Pratzen Hoehe, and going through the villages of Girzikowitz, Puntowitz, Kobelnitz, Sokolnitz, and Telnitz, addressed his generals as follows:

> Had I the intention of simply preventing the enemy from passing, it is here where I would post myself, but this would only lead to an ordinary battle, whereas were I to refuse my right, withdrawing it in the direction of Brünn, and the Russians abandon these heights, if there were 300,000 of them they would be lost without hope.

In an ordinary battle the allies would have retired, soon to gather strength for a fresh contest; but Napoleon was keen to end the war.

The Austro-Russian Army had been moving westwards, marching in five parallel columns of uneven strength. On the 29th of November it crossed the Wischau stream and advanced in the direction of Austerlitz, with its right on the Olmütz road and its left on both banks of the Littawa.

The allied army was divided thus:—

RIGHT WING.

The Infantry General: Buxhowden.

First Column.
Lieutenant-General: Wimpfen.
Major-Generals: Müller, Slichow, and Stride.
18 battalions of Russians. 1 company of pioneers.
2½ squadrons of Cossacks.
8,320 men. 250 horses.

Second Column.
Lieutenant-General: Langeron.
Major-Generals: Kaminsky, Alsufieu.
18 battalions of Russians. 1 company of pioneers.
2½ squadrons of Cossacks.
11,420 men. 250 horses.

CENTRE.

General-in-Chief: Kutuzoff.

Third Column.
Lieutenant-General: Przybyszewsky.
Major-Generals: Orosoff, Lieders, Lewis.
24 battalions of Russians.
2 companies of reserve artillery.
13,800 men.

LEFT WING.

The Austrian Lieutenant-General: Prince John of Liechtenstein.

Fourth Column.
The Austrian Lieutenant-General: Kolowrat.
The Russian Lieutenant-Generals: Essen and Miloradovitch.
The Russian Major-Generals: Szepelow and Repninsky.
The Austrian Major-Generals: Carneville, Rottermunde, and Jurecek.
32 battalions, of which 20 were Austrians.
1 company of reserve artillery.
5 companies of pioneers.
30 squadrons of Russians, of which 8 were Cossacks.
22,400 men. 3,000 horses.

Fifth Column.
The Austrian Lieutenant-General: Prince Hohenlohe.
The Russian Lieutenant-General: Ouvaroff.
The Austrian Major-Generals: Stutterheim, Weber, and Caramelli.
The Russian Major-General: Piritzky.
70 squadrons, of which 40 were Austrians, but very weak.
2 companies of light artillery.
4,600 horses.
The Reserve.
The Grand Duke: Constantine.
Lieutenant-Generals: Kollagrivoff and Malutin.
Major-Generals: Jankewitz and Depleradovich.
10 battalions of guards, 4 companies.
18 squadrons.
8,500 men.

Recapitulation.

	Bat.	Comp.	Squad.	
1st and 2nd columns ...	36	2	5	19,740
3rd column	24	2	—	13,800
4th and 5th columns ...	32	8	100	27,000
Reserve	10	4	18	8,500
Advanced corps under Prince Bagration	12	—	40*	12,000
General Kienmayer ...	—	—	14	1,000
	114	16	177	82,040

* 15 of these were Cossacks.

The above is the detail of the allied armies as furnished by General Stutterheim, who was present. Lieutenant-General Mikhailovski-Danilevski computes the total at 80,000 men.

In the cavalry the squadrons were weak, and the total number of horsemen did not amount to more than 16,560 men.

According to Jomini, the allies had 330 guns; however, they made no use of their superiority in that arm. A large number of guns was with the left wing, evidently intended for the anticipated battle on the right bank of the Goldbach.

The advance of the Allied Army on Brünn by their right, to turn the left of the French, was suddenly abandoned, as the impression was steadily gaining ground that Napoleon desired to avoid a battle and escape from the allies by the Vienna road. The order of battle was accordingly changed, the intention being to manoeuvre by their left, to outstrip the French Army on that road, and drive it into Bohemia.

The allies laboured under the false impression that Napoleon's line of retreat must be the Brünn-Vienna road; they fully believed that once his army was cut from that road its ruin would be certain. But the emperor had the line Brünn-Pilsen through the Bohemian mountains at his command. He had also changed his line of communications, and shifted it more to the north by way of Krems, so that he was no longer dependent on Vienna.

The Austro-Russian staff wished to cut the French Army from Vienna because it was by the bridges of that city that they expected to effect their junction with the Archduke Charles. Napoleon, however, had provided for this by leaving Marmont's corps near Vienna, with instructions for the marshal to contest the crossing of the Danube. Iglau was held by a division, and the French could march speedily to the Danube, cross the river at Linz, and appear under the walls of Vienna in no time.

On the 28th of November, the allied army moved to Lultsch, Nosalowitz, heights of Noska, and Topolan. On the 29th it marched from Lultsch and the heights of Noska to Huluboschan and Kutscherau. Prince Bagration pushed forward his advance guard to Posorsitz, and General Kienmayer moved to Austerlitz. (The *château* and park of Austerlitz belonged to the family of Prince Kaunitz.)

The movements of the Austro-Russian Army for the last two days had been singularly slow, the natural consequence of want of information and provisions. Through the incapacity of their staff for efficient reconnaissance work, the allies were in complete ignorance of the strength and distribution of the French Army.

All the cavalry of Kienmayer, Liechtenstein, and Ouvaroff, making a total of 177 squadrons, did nothing in that direction. (It is strange how soon the employment of cavalry beyond the battlefield is forgotten; how in peace time it is seldom exercised in the most important cavalry duties of scouting, patrolling, and reconnoitring.) The staff had neglected to employ still more efficacious means—emissaries and spies—for obtaining reports of the enemy's doings, and the army moved slowly over bad cross-country roads, feeling its way as it went, for, though campaigning in a friendly country, it received from the local authorities no enlightenment whatsoever.

How contrary was this neglect in acquiring information to the principal maxim of their able opponent, who considered the general who does not know how to acquire information to he ignorant of his trade.

For all that, their own manoeuvre was perfectly safe, inasmuch as the route followed by their army brought it closer to the Hungarian border, in the direction where it was hoped to effect a junction with the forces the archdukes were bringing up. Their plan, however, was executed in a bungling and wavering manner, and no provision was made for unexpected events.

If the Russians feared that the French would evade a battle and retire without fighting, Napoleon, on the other hand, had good reason to dread that the enemy, abstaining from fighting, might manoeuvre in the direction of Hungary, seeking to form a junction with the army of the Archduke Charles. This, the soundest plan the allies could have adopted, would have placed all the resources of Hungary at their disposal, and would have induced Prussia to declare itself against Napoleon, in which case he would have been compelled to evacuate Moravia and part of the Austrian territory.

On the 1st of December the combined armies occupied the plateau of Pratzen, which rises to the south of the Brünn-Olmütz road, between the waters of the two marshy brooks of the Littawa and Goldbach, and which, as we have seen, after running between several ponds, converge towards Mönitz. The Austro-Russian columns did not reach their destination that night before half-past ten.

Finding themselves in presence of the enemy, they decided to leave on their centre, at Pratzen, a thin screen of troops, so as to deceive the French, and then to bring forward and engage the wings, one of which was to make a secondary attack on the right, on the Santon (Bosenitzerberg), a height which commanded the Brünn road, and thus to rivet the enemy's attention in that direction, whilst the other wing, the left, was to deliver the principal attack on Telnitz and Sokolnitz. The object of all this was to drive the enemy's right back towards Turas and Brünn, occupy the favourable ground which extends in the direction of Maxdorf and Turas, and cut the French off entirely from the Vienna road. A reserve was to remain in front of the Austerlitz village, to help their right or left according to circumstances.

The movements of the allied armies were made with so little disguise that already on the eve of the battle their general object was too evident. Before dawn on the 2nd, Napoleon felt perfectly sure that he had not been deceived as to what the enemy's plan was. The fires of the bivouacs and the frequent reports coming in from the outposts all tended to show in the clearest possible manner that the allies, having left the plateau of Pratzen weakly occupied, were steadily closing on their left.

The allies, as we have said, possessed scanty information regarding the French Army. On the 1st of December, they had noticed Bernadotte's arrival by the Olmütz road, and the position taken up by the reserve. On the side of Kobelnitz and Sokolnitz they had discovered few troops, from which fact they hastily concluded that Napoleon was weakening his right to reinforce his left. The energy displayed by Lannes in intrenching and fortifying the Santon, and the very position of the emperor's bivouac, led them into error, and they worked steadily in carrying forward their entire left wing, which, in reality, constituted the bulk of their forces.

On beholding the Austro-Russians tending to the south-west of the Olmütz road, Napoleon at once grasped the purpose of their manoeuvre. With the object of encouraging the enemy, he had ordered his cavalry to withdraw to the right bank of the Goldbach. Soult had been directed to do likewise, abandoning Austerlitz and Pratzen.

The line of battle Napoleon had chosen ran, generally speaking, along the Goldbach brook. The valley of this stream is low and possibly marshy at the end of the year, therefore passable for all arms at certain well-known points only; the infantry alone might have found other points of passage. *Though a great deal of importance has been attached to the Goldbach by most writers, it is at least now nothing more than a narrow brook which any second or third rate jumper can easily get over. It was principally a feature of the ground.* The French left rested on the Bosenitzerberg, or Santon, a hillock which the emperor caused to be entrenched and well-armed with artillery; the right was posted by the Mönitz marshes.

On the left, Lannes' divisions, Suchet's and Caffarelli's, backed by Murat's cavalry, were athwart the Olmütz road, to hold in check at any cost the Russian right under Bagration. On the right was Legrand's very weak division, and Margaron's cavalry, both forming part of Soult's corps. These latter were to hold the ground between Pontowitz and Telnitz, nearly one-half of the total front, and were to detain the enemy on the Goldbach, and, if possible, to prevent him getting as far. They were to be supported in the morning by Davout. Friant's division and Bourcier's dragoons belonging to his corps were to come from Raigern at a critical moment and close the *débouché* from Telnitz.

In the centre was Soult with Bernadotte in second line, and it was to these troops that the decisive role was assigned. When the Russians had incautiously extended their left too far, and massed in the low ground with the object of acting against Legrand and Davout, and by doing so had weakened their centre, Soult, at the head of Vandamme's and Saint Hilaire's divisions, was to scale the denuded plateau of Pratzen; wheeling then to their right, the divisions were to advance on Hostieradek-Aujezd, and close Buxhowden's retreat.

Bernadotte, with Rivaud's and Drouet's infantry divisions, was to hold the plateau in front of Austerlitz, backing according to circumstances either Lannes with his centre or Soult with his right.

Napoleon held in hand a powerful reserve on the high ground overlooking Schlapanitz. This reserve was composed of ten battalions of the Imperial Guard, and ten battalions of Oudinot's grenadiers. (Oudinot had been wounded at Hollabrünn. In his career this gallant soldier received no less than thirty-two wounds.) These troops were drawn up in two lines of battalion columns at deploying distance, with 40 guns in the intervals. In rear of the infantry, came the cavalry of the Imperial Guard: 4 squadrons of Horse Grenadiers, 4 squadrons of *Chasseurs à Cheval*, and 1 squadron of Mamelukes, all under the command of General Bessières.

Murat's cavalry bivouacked in second line in rear of Lannes' right and Bernadotte's left.

In the first line was Kellermann with his hussars and mounted rifles. In second line came Walther's and Beaumont's dragoons. In the third, as a reserve, stood Nansouty's and d'Hautpoul's *cuirassiers*.

The imperial headquarters were on the right of the main road to Olmütz, in front of Bellowitz.

Not only had Napoleon deemed the ground well adapted as a battlefield in a general way, but with his penetrating sight he had been able to form a just idea of how it could be best occupied. He had recognised all the importance of the plateau around the village of Pratzen, the faces of which slope down to the Goldbach from Blasowitz to Sokolnitz; he saw what capital ground for cavalry there was between Pratzen and Blasowitz, also what little effect in the result of the battle the allied troops sent on the low ground would have. In studying his order of battle, one is astonished to find such a thorough reconnaissance, such an able appreciation of ground, and such a masterly distribution of the forces with so close relationship between the different arms.

It was Soult who was to do most of the work. He had with the 4th Corps to occupy some ten kilometres of ground, and one of his

Mameluke and Russian Dragoon in combat

Mameluck.
GARDE IMPERIALE.

brigades, Merle's, was spread over fully four of these. His third division had to withstand the efforts of the three leading columns of the enemy until Friant's division could arrive on the field. Soult had 21,000 men, and Merle's brigade numbered about 3,500, consequently Soult had about two men per each running yard on his left and centre, and less than one per yard in the part held by Merle's brigade.

The troops on the right wing were divided into small detachments and posted between Pontonitz and the Mönitz marshes. The distance from the Olmütz road along the Goldbach as far as Telnitz is about 7½ miles, and as the emperor had not sufficient troops to occupy the position thoroughly, he only held one part of it in force, and from Koblenitz to Telnitz satisfied himself with guarding the passages across the Goldbach. It resulted that, when the battle commenced, nearly one-half of his line of battle was defended by one division of infantry, Legrand's, and Margaron's brigade of light cavalry.

Legrand had posted three battalions in Telnitz, and two in the village and castle of Sokolnitz. One of his brigades lay in front of the Kobelnitz defile, ranged in two lines, the first deployed, the second in column; a single battalion was posted beyond the defile.

Davout's corps was far away in the rear; its first division, Friant's, ten battalions strong, was still on the main road between Vienna and Brünn. (Gudin's division of Marshal Davout's corps, coming from Presburg, had advanced as far as Nickolsbourg, on the right of the French Army; it was to keep in check tome 4,000 men of De Merveld, then at Lundenbourg.) On the night of the 1st of December, it reached the cloister of Gross-Raigern, situated seven miles from the city of Brünn and about twelve miles from the village of Austerlitz.

Marching before daybreak from Raigern, Davout had to confront the enemy at the village of Telnitz. Should he find on arrival that the Russians had advanced beyond that village, he was to contain and harass them as much as he could. He had been enjoined not to attack them vigorously until he should see that they had been cut off, and that the Pratzen heights were in the hands of the French.

To hasten the movements of his division, Davout had ordered it to march in three small columns; the one on the right was to consist of two battalions, the other two consisted of four battalions each. The divisional artillery was partitioned amongst the three columns, and Bourcier's division of dragoons, which had been provisionally attached to Davout, was directed to take post on the right flank and to cover the advance of the infantry. These columns, marching in echelon from the right, advanced at a brisk pace and took post in succession from right to left in the very order they were intended to deploy.

General Friant made a creditable march, for in forty-eight hours his division covered a distance of nearly ninety miles, from Vienna to Gross-Raigern. On the night of the 1st of December, 1805, which was extremely cold, the division bivouacked at the latter place, and was therefore within easy marching distance of the battlefield.

Friant's soldiers were weary to excess; one-twentieth part of them arrived at their destination with the columns, the rest rejoined from hour to hour. Officers had been left purposely along the road to pick up the stragglers, and after a brief rest were to conduct them forward to their respective regiments. Though there were many voids in the ranks of the French, still, for troops that had marched steadily for three months, there were fewer laggards than are generally seen in other armies under similar conditions. The spirit of the troops can be judged by the eagerness with which the soldiers, left from different causes in rear, hastened to rejoin their respective corps.

Friant brought 4,000 men from Raigern. All he could do in conjunction with Legrand was to compel the enemy to deploy the greatest number of troops possible, to deceive him completely with regard to the aim the emperor had in view. It was not difficult to foresee that Friant and Legrand together would be unable to withstand the mass of their assailants; in their action, however, they could further the emperor's plan by retiring in such a direction as would draw the Austro-Russian forces as far as possible away from the point where the fortune of the day was to be decided.

Davout with his small force was to keep in check 35,000 of the enemy. It was calculated that the villages on the Goldbach would enable his troops to oppose a determined resistance. Napoleon knew his men, and could depend on his general. When Davout could withstand the enemy no longer, he was to show a bold front, withdrawing as slowly as possible, so that the centre of the allies, in prolonging their turning movement, should become more and more ungarnished, losing little by little its consistency.

What seems open to adverse criticism is that Napoleon should have detailed only part of one corps to occupy one-half of the battlefield, and that this important position—being the right flank of the French line of battle, where he knew that the principal effort of the enemy would be made—should have been assigned to troops which, owing to recent severe marches, were not in a vigorous state to contend against a comparatively fresh enemy. The state of lassitude Davout's troops were in can be gathered from the fact that, as we have said, the soldiers of the 3rd Corps came into line by driblets.

The nature of the position, nevertheless, was much in favour of the French, for the Russians could not well deploy their forces before reaching the right bank of the Goldbach. In fact, the marshes caused by the sluggishness of the current turned the villages on that stream into really difficult defiles. Nor could the extreme right of the French be attacked without the allies making a long circuit, in doing which the attacking force would have had to extend several leagues southwards, getting further and further away from the Olmütz road, which was their proper line of retreat. Having penetrated the intention of the allies, Napoleon invited an attack on his right and withdrew from their path, but only to aim his blow at the centre of their line, which the allies had laid bare and which was held by less than one-third of their force.

On the left flank, Colonel Sénarmont had fortified the Santon, and armed it with eighteen pieces of heavy artillery. The defence of the hill was entrusted to the 17th Light Infantry. In front of the Santon lay the village of Bosenitz, and the Russians could not attack the hill unless they first carried that village, as in doing so they would have been taken in flank. Sénarmont had taken this circumstance into consideration, and he had posted most of the artillery on the Santon, so as to batter the Russians when making their efforts against the village, and pound them thoroughly should they ever succeed in occupying it.

Baron Crossard, who thought that the allies should have attacked the left of the French, and not the right, inspected the ground the day before the battle. In his *Mémoires Militaires* he states that the Santon was commanded by the hills on the north, where batteries should have been placed; that the mamelon was well within range of mortars and howitzers. He wrote:

> A chain of mountains, practicable on their summit even for vehicles, runs parallel to the road (Brünn-Olmütz)., and commands the Santon.

We much doubt if the ordnance of those days could have carried so far with any real effect.

On the evening of the 1st of December, the dangerous manoeuvre performed by the Austro-Russians was too plainly revealed. Bagration alone remained on the Olmütz road, his front extending from Kowalowitz to Kruh. On the opposite wing, Kienmayer's advanced guard was already beyond Aujezd. On his right rear on the eastern slope of the heights, and reaching as far as Krenowitz, where the chief headquarters had been established, stood echeloned the four columns of Dochtouroff, Langeron, Przybyszewsky, and Kolowrat.

The allies were so slow and clumsy in all they did that nothing was concealed. With his extraordinary quickness of penetration, Napoleon saw their purpose as if reading a book. He followed their movements hour by hour, and the little he did not see he could well guess. Dolgorouki's assertion that the emperor received information of the dispositions made by the allies has remained a current belief, but nothing more, for it has never been proved. By that vague statement, Dolgorouki apparently wished to soften to the *Czar* the mortification of the defeat, but Danilevsky, himself a Russian, writes that Napoleon, that born leader of men, had genius enough to do without an informer.

From the heights, where he reconnoitred steadily the whole day, he detected with undisguised satisfaction the Austro-Russian Army commencing at 3 o'clock in the afternoon a flank movement to turn the French right, carried out within three gun-shot lengths of the French position. (That morning the 11th French Hussars were sent to reconnoitre the Pratzen heights, about a league in front of Sokolnitz. At about 10 they were attacked by some 4,000 or 5,000 irregular Cossacks, and were compelled to withdraw.)

The enemy appeared in front of the French posts; they defiled by a flank march on a depth of four leagues, all the details being visible with the naked eye. The allies sped bravely along the whole front of the French Army, which apparently did not dare quit its position, as if paralyzed by what it saw of its opponent's irresistible power. The only fear which oppressed the allies was that the French might possibly escape them.

The allies forgot that nothing is so rash and so contrary to principle as to make a flank march before an army in position. It might be argued that in consequence of the greater range of firearms a flank march like that of the Austro-Russian Army on the 1st and 2nd of December would in our days have been carried out at a considerable distance from their adversaries, and therefore entirely out of the adversary's sight. The detection of the plan of the allies would, nevertheless, have been possible at any time, given that there was a competent and alert chief to watch what was passing. At Austerlitz, Napoleon had plenty of cavalry and enterprising cavalry leaders to push far to the front to reconnoitre and unveil the enemy's plans, and he would no doubt have sent forward the eyes of the army to gain information as to what was passing in his front.

The emperor desired to be attacked; consequently, by his words, by his attitude, and by his dispositions, he endeavoured to inspire his enemies with unbounded confidence. He himself, always so audacious, had to feign irresolution; his cavalry, generally so alert, allowed itself to be surprised. Everything was done to confirm the enemy in his idea of the bad plight the French were in. Murat, the daring cavalry leader who had pressed so steadily after Kutuzoff in his retreat, sent out on the plain a small column. All at once this column abruptly halted, as if struck with dismay by the sight of the immense forces of the enemy, wheeled about, and withdrew in rapid haste.

Wishing to raise the over-confidence of the enemy, the emperor had forbidden all enterprise against the enemy's outposts.

By his craftiness, he had provoked a false movement, and the favourable moment for taking advantage of it was fast approaching. The occasion he had been so anxiously looking forward to had arrived. His aim and hope was to induce the allied army to attack his; he wanted them to extend their line unduly, so that he might break it with the greater ease. What he had foreseen was about to occur: the enemy, by denuding its centre of troops, was leaving a dangerous gap between its centre and the right wing.

Instead of imitating the enemy's deployment, he determined to hold his troops concentrated until the allies had well engaged on the low ground of the Goldbach. To be able, however, to act in mass at the most opportune moment, all the troops of the first line were ordered to cross the Goldbach on the evening of the 1st of December; the remainder had their special bridges assigned to them.

On the eve of this momentous battle, when Napoleon was eagerly expecting to be attacked by the Austro-Russian Army, Haugwitz presented himself at the French headquarters. He had tarried on his voyage as much as he could, to gain time for the Russian Army to concentrate. The count, in this first interview, did not disclose all the conditions imposed by King Frederick William, but confined himself to proposing the intervention of Prussia. Napoleon received him with great courtesy, but, knowing his real mission too well, told him that, being on the point of fighting a battle on the morrow, he would attend to his business after that event, unless a chance shot were to do away with him. He added that after the battle, it struck him, would be the proper time to come to an agreement with the Berlin Cabinet.

Haugwitz was directed to start that same night for Vienna, where De Talleyrand would confer with him. Evidently with the sole intention of impressing the ambassador with the dire results of war, he was, by the emperor's orders, conducted through the battlefield of Hollabrünn, which presented a horrible sight. With regard to this order, Napoleon wrote to Talleyrand:

> It is desirable that this Prussian should learn with his own eyes the manner in which we make war.

******

The story is often told how Napoleon addressed Haugwitz when he complimented him on his victory: "Here is a compliment of which the fortune of war has changed the address."

******

The emperor quitted Brünn early on the morning of the 1st of December, and spent the whole day on horseback making a personal inspection of his army, regiment by regiment. He spoke to the soldiers, he examined each separate arm, all the field batteries. He then visited the field hospitals, and ascertained what means for transporting the wounded had been collected. All this done, he returned to his bivouac, a hut in rear of the French sentries, at a point where the view took in the bivouacs of both sides. There he assembled all his marshals; he conversed with them regarding all that they should do on the morrow, and of all that it was possible for the enemy to attempt. The Duke of Rovigo tells us in his *Memoirs* that one could have written a volume on all that fell from the emperor's lips during those twenty-four hours.

On the evening of the 1st of December, at the moment when Napoleon was gathering his marshals around him to give them his final instructions, he caused the following proclamation to be distributed amongst his troops:—

> Soldiers,
> The Russian Army appears before you to avenge the Austrian Army of Ulm. They are the identical battalions which you have beaten at Hollabrünn, and which you have constantly pursued ever since.
> The positions which we occupy are formidable, and whilst they march to turn my right, they present me their flank.
> Soldiers, I will myself direct my battalions. I shall keep out of the zone of fire if, with your customary bravery, you will carry disorder and confusion amongst the enemy's ranks. Should,

however, victory be but for an instant uncertain, you will behold your emperor exposing himself to the first blows, because victory should not hesitate this day, when it is a question of the honour of the French infantry, which is so dear to the entire nation.

Let no one under the pretext of removing the wounded attenuate (*degarnisser*) the ranks; let everyone be filled with this thought, that it is absolutely necessary to crush these auxiliaries in the pay of England, who are filled with such intense hatred against our nation.

This victory will end the campaign, and we shall be able to go into winter quarters, where we shall be joined by fresh armies now in the act of being formed in France. Then I will conclude a peace which will be worthy of my people, of you, and of me.

In this proclamation, which savours of the antique, the emperor, by recalling recent victories, works up the confidence of his troops. He then appeals to the devotion, self-esteem, and military pride of his soldiers, not omitting to revile the hatred nourished by the adversary. Lastly, he holds out prospects of rest and of an early peace. In this proclamation he flatters his men by identifying the glory of his people, of the army, and of the emperor in one sentence.

The emperor was disturbed by some brisk skirmishing which took place on his extreme right, fearing it might conceal some unexpected movement of the Russians. It turned out that they had been trying to seize a village at the foot of their position, so as to have the way clear in the morning.

The night was fine, with a shining moon. An immense quantity of bivouac fires burnt bright. When it was well advanced, Napoleon, accompanied by Marshal Soult, visited the bivouacs. Quietly as this was done, the emperor was soon recognised. Then an outburst of sudden enthusiasm broke forth and stirred the hearts of his chilled troops; in an instant a most grandiose and inspiriting scene was spontaneously enacted. The soldiers gathered the straw of their bivouacs, and having twisted it into bundles, which they bound on to poles, they set it alight. The emperor marched in the midst of this impromptu illumination, the air resounding with the cheers of his troops, who, in their devotion for their illustrious chief, deprived themselves of the little straw they had to lie on. This extraordinary spectacle, being so strange in an army which was declared to be disheartened and in retreat, can-

BIVOUAC ON THE EVE OF THE BATTLE OF AUSTERLITZ

THE NIGHT BEFORE THE BATTLE OF AUSTERLITZ

not have escaped the attention of the allies, and did no doubt raise in many prudent minds sinister forebodings; Lejeune states that the allies passed the rest of the night under arms.

This spontaneous illumination should have shown to the allies the positions occupied by the French Army, had they not been preoccupied with a plan based on erroneous suppositions. They credited Napoleon with being so blind as not to perceive their endeavour to work round him; many even interpreted the glare from the torches as a further proof that the French were about to retire.

Marbot seems to infer that it was the picket of *chasseurs* forming the emperor's escort moving with lighted torches that inspired this impromptu illumination. Some 60,000 torches alight, with loud shouts of "Long live the Emperor!" and the sound of many bands of the French regiments, all demonstrated the high pitch of enthusiasm which animated the French.

A grenadier, Jean Archer, of the 46th of the Line, became spokesman for his comrades. Stepping in front of the emperor, he assured him that he would not have to expose himself on the morrow. In the name of the grenadiers of the army, he promised that he would only have to fight with his eyes, that the soldiers would take it upon themselves to hand him over the standards and the artillery of the Russian Army to celebrate the anniversary of his coronation.

How thorough was the fascination which Napoleon exercised over his soldiers! A personal magnetism which few could resist, and the very least incident was sufficient to make it burst forth. On the eve of this most eventful battle how flattering must have been to the emperor this sudden acknowledgment of his dominion over the heart of his troops!

What a day for any mortal to have lived through!—first to see his calculations with regard to the enemy gradually taking a greater development and portending a brilliant victory on the morrow; then the enthusiasm and love of his soldiers, their confidence in their commander, and their eagerness to display their prowess before his eyes!

Returning to his bivouac, a miserable roofless hut, which the grenadiers had improvised, Napoleon gave vent to his feelings:

> Behold the most glorious night of my life! but I feel sorry that I shall lose many of those brave fellows. I feel, from the regret which oppresses me, that they are really my sons; in fact, I often reproach myself for this feeling, for I fear that in the end it will

prevent me from waging war.

★★★★★★

The story is told in different ways. Lejeune states that Napoleon and Berthier went unaccompanied and on foot to hear, without being seen, the conversations the soldiers held round their bivouac fires; that he was recognised. The Duchesse d'Abrantes writes that at 11 p.m. the emperor ordered Junot, Duroc, and. Berthier to put on their cloaks and follow him. That in passing by a bivouac fire he was recognised. "The Emperor!" exclaimed the men. "*Vive l'Empereur!*" they cried—an acclamation which was instantly taken up by the whole line of bivouacs.

★★★★★★

Saint-Chamans accompanied Soult as he went round the outposts with Napoleon. He relates how the emperor himself questioned the commanders of the advanced posts; how they unanimously declared that the enemy was making a considerable movement to its left, evidently to come in contact with the French right. Saint-Chamans states:

> We decidedly heard the rumbling of artillery carriages and the sound of horses on the march leading in that direction.
> "*A vous la balle, maréchal Soult, dit l'Empereur en se tournant vers lui.*" "*Sire, je m'en félicite, repondit le maréchal, en saluant Sa Majesté.*" ("To you the ball, Marshal Soult," said the emperor, turning to him. "Sire, I am glad of it," replied the marshal, bowing to His Majesty.) *Mémoires de Saint-Chamans*:

Stutterheim states that there was a good deal of firing during the whole morning of the 1st along the entire chain of outposts. That the French were seen from the break of day continually reconnoitring along the heights in front of Pratzen and Kruh. Several cavalry movements took place, but they were of no importance, mostly tending to encourage the allies to attack.

Napoleon, as we have said, spent most of the day examining personally the adversary's dispositions; but on the side of the allies we hear of no eager spirit unceasingly directing the small reconnaisances so necessary to maintain a constant knowledge of what is doing in the enemy's camp.

The allies had only very vague reports regarding the situation of the French Army, though scarcely out of range of its musketry. During the day, they had noticed the movements on the Brünn-Olmütz road, caused by the arrival of Bernadotte's corps and the location of the reserves—possibly nothing else than the posting of Suchet's and Caffarelli's divisions to support the Santon. In the direction of Sokolnitz and Kobelnitz they could discover few troops, as Davout was at that moment still miles away from the position he was to occupy during the battle. They took the movements they saw as clear indications that Napoleon was reinforcing his left at the expense of his right. What possibly helped to deceive them in this sense was the activity Lannes displayed in strengthening the Santon with field works.

Firm in their supposition, they persisted in their plan of overlapping the French Army in the direction of the ponds by pushing forward their left, the bulk of their forces. They imagined that they would have little difficulty in mastering the defiles by the villages, situated at the base of the Pratzen plateau. Once their forces had got across at Telnitz and at Sokolnitz, the attack was to be continued on all the ground which stretches towards Maxdorf and Turas. The movements of their left wing in that direction would have thrown the French right on to its centre, at the same time that Bagration, supported by Liechtenstein, would on his side have borne on the French left. It was expected that the two wings of the allied armies would come together in the neighbourhood of Latein; they would both then bear on the French Army, throw it over the Schwarzawa, and cut its communications with Vienna.

The Russians had not the least doubt as to the good result of their manoeuvre. Colonel Orouck writes that Prince Dolgorouki went to his advanced posts and gave him instructions to watch carefully the road the French Army would take in retiring, as no one could for one moment doubt that such was their intention.

We have remarked on the scarcity of information the allies were able to gather. Much of it is often obtained from the outposts, and one is struck with astonishment in learning from General Stutterheim that during the whole night which preceded the battle there was no chain of outposts established in front of the position occupied by the combined armies.

Baron Lejeune, on the other hand, writes:

> The shouts and the illuminations alarmed the enemy, who, fearing a surprise, came from every side to reconnoitre our outposts, and remained under arms all night.

At about midnight on the 1st of December, the leaders of the several columns were summoned to the presence of Prince Wolkonsky, the general of the day. He then led them to Krenowitz, where Kutuzoff had established his headquarters. There they were told that at 7 o'clock in the morning the enemy would be attacked in the positions he occupied. In a pedantic style Weyrother read out his plan of operations. After he had explained the task assigned to each column, the intended movements, and other details, he added that the combined armies were to give battle on the ground between Brünn and Austerlitz, ground which he knew perfectly, the Austrians having manoeuvred there the previous year. Thereupon his A.D.C., Colonel Count Bubna, told him in a blunt manner, "Take care not to repeat the faults you made in the manoeuvres of last year." This caution, though given in full hearing of Kutuzoff, does not appear to have given rise to any misgiving. The commander-in-chief never uttered a word.

The following were the orders issued to the different columns after the midnight meeting on the 1st of December. As they had to be translated, copied, and despatched, they were not in the hands of the respective generals before 8 o'clock, that is, after the columns had set out on their march:—

1st Column: Lieutenant-General Dochtouroff, with 21 battalions of Russians, from the heights of Hostieradek, by Aujezd, upon Telnitz. After having got through the village and defile, the column was to move forward to the right towards the ponds, till its head should arrive parallel with that of the 2nd column.

2nd Column: Lieutenant-General Langeron, with 18 battalions of Russians, marching like the first column by its left from the heights of Pratzen, was to force the Goldbach between Telnitz and Sokolnitz, and then dress on the 1st column.

3rd Column: Lieutenant-General Przybyszewsky, with 18 battalions of Russians, was also to move by his left, from the heights to the right of Pratzen, crossing the stream close by the castle of Sokolnitz; from whence the heads of the three columns were to move forward, between Sokolnitz and the ponds situated behind it, as far as the village of Kobelnitz.

4th Column: Lieutenant-General Kolowrat, with 27 battalions, 15 of which were Austrian, moving forward by his left, from the heights in rear of the 3rd column, was to pass the same valley, and the ponds of Kobelnitz, and bring the head of his column parallel with that of the three former.

The advanced corps under Kienmayer, was to protect, with its infantry, the movements of the 1st column. In point of fact, by this arrangement that column was reinforced by five Austrian battalions, and consisted altogether of 29 battalions.

The heads of these four columns of infantry were to present an imposing front, and four battalions of the 1st column were to occupy the wood of Turas. The remainder of this column and all the others were then to move forward between this wood and Schlapanitz, and attack the right of the enemy with strong bodies of infantry, while three battalions of the 4th column should be busy in carrying the village of Schlapanitz.

5th Column: Lieutenant-General Prince John of Liechtenstein, with 82 squadrons, was, first of all, to move from the foot of the hill, in rear of the 3rd column, towards Blasowitz and Kruh, to protect the formation and march of the columns on the right, afterwards to advance upon the plain on the right and left of the causeway, between Kruh and the Inn of Lesch, as was before mentioned.

The advanced corps, under Lieutenant-General Prince Bagration, consisting of 12 battalions and 40 squadrons, was to maintain its position, and gain the heights between Dwaroschna and the Inn of Lesch, in order to place on these heights strong batteries of cannon. The prince was to manoeuvre against the French left; advancing at an early hour, he was to carry the Santon height, and then push directly on for Brünn.

The corps of reserve, under the Grand-Duke Constantine, consisting of 10 battalions and 18 squadrons, was to move from the heights in front of Austerlitz to the rear of Blasowitz and Kruh; it was to serve as a support to the cavalry of Prince John of Liechtenstein, and to the corps under Prince Bagration.

Weyrother was the author of this plan. It does not require much wisdom to see the faults it contained. To start with, there was not the slightest foundation for presuming that Napoleon's right was weak and isolated; secondly, the movements of the wings had deplenished the allied centre out of all proportion, had left ungarnished of troops a position of easy access, and which commanded the entire battlefield; thirdly, there was no connection between the principal sections of the line of battle; and, lastly, it rested on Weyrother's imagination alone that all that Napoleon could do was to remain stationary behind the Goldbach, and defend his line step by step. The Austrian general gave to Napoleon 40,000 men at the most, and felt fully convinced that by awaiting the attack he courted a defeat. When he was told that the French had extinguished their fires, and that one could hear a considerable noise in the direction of their camp, he declared it to be a sign that Napoleon was either retiring or shifting his position.

The general took no account of those circumstances which often militate against the success of a well-devised plan. Weyrother had omitted to indicate to Buxhowden how he was to fall back on Waschau or Niskowitz, should the contest in the centre take an unfavourable turn. The commanders of the three left columns had nothing to guide them in case the turning of the French flank should be found impracticable.

Evidently Weyrother did not inspire much confidence. Stutterheim, *A Detailed Account of the Battle of Austerlitz,* depicts his character in the following words:

> But the quartermaster-general, as it has been mentioned before, though an officer of great personal courage, had not that confidence in himself which could enable him to give advice at headquarters where the greatest wisdom was requisite. Without regarding the difficulties thrown in his way, this officer too easily abandoned his own opinions to adopt those of other people.

Baron Crossard does justice to his courage, but describes him as a man of grand ideas, but of little stored knowledge. He possessed, he goes on to say, creating genius, but lacked the talent which understands how to direct it to advantage by basing it on accepted standards.

The object of the allies' right wing was to menace and contain Napoleon on the side of the Olmütz road during the time his own right wing was being turned. It was after the success of Buxhowden's forces that Bagration was to deliver his main attack, moving in a westerly direction while the other wing would advance towards the north.

CHAPTER 13

Battle of Austerlitz

DIE KAISER-SCHLACHT—THE BATTLE OF THE EMPERORS
(Also called by the French Army *bataille de l'Anniversaire, bataille du Couronnement.*)

At four o'clock on the morning of the 2nd of December, Napoleon, who desired to judge if his suppositions had turned out to be correct, mounted on horseback and proceeded to the outposts. He rode as far as the village of Pontowitz, on the banks of the brook which separated the two armies. The moon was setting and the morning was dark and cold, with a thick fog shrouding the low ground. He waited for daylight to show if the enemy were persisting in their plan. The dragoons on vedette duty reported that up to 2 a.m. a confused rumble had reached their ears, the sound of troops in motion; also that the lights had gradually increased in the direction of Aujezd and the south-eastern quarter of the horizon. On the Pratzen, the bivouac fires were nearly out, and the rumbling of wheels, the striking of hoofs, and the jingling of steel, indicated too clearly a march of the allies in the direction of the ponds.

The heights of Pratzen, which on the evening of the 1st of December had been covered with artillery and troops of all arms, were now nearly deserted. The enemy's columns had evidently descended to the low ground to carry out the plan of outflanking the French.

Savary, sent to the extreme right to see if the allies had any infantry in front of Telnitz and Sokolnitz, and in what number, sent in his report, which reached the emperor at midnight of the 1st. It stated that a strong force, not only of cavalry but also of infantry, was in position in front of General Merle.

What a contrast with Napoleon's personal activity was what Thiers

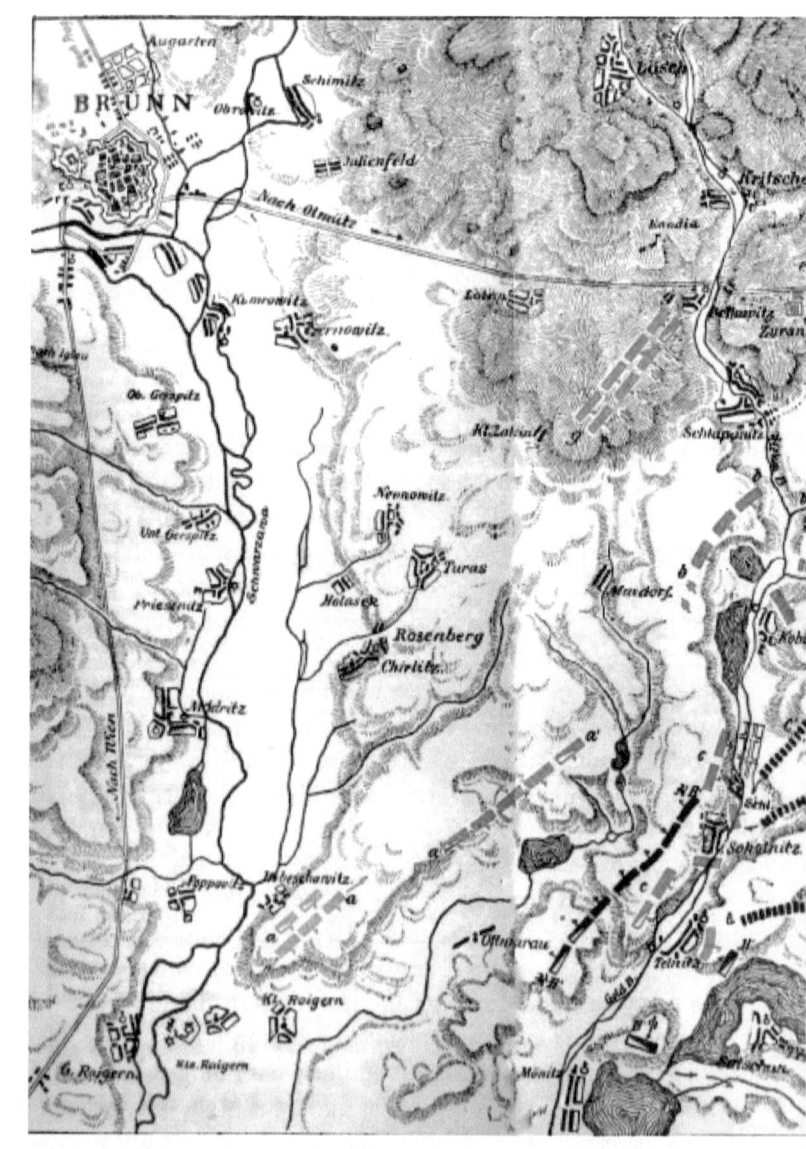

cites from the manuscript memoires of General Langeron. The general states that towards 11 p.m. of the 1st of December, all the leaders of columns, barring Prince Bagration who was out of reach, were summoned to Kutuzoff's headquarters at Krenowitz, to hear the reading of the dispositions for the morrow's battle.

> At one o'clock in the morning, when we were all congregated. General Weyrother came in, deployed on a large table an immense and very exact map of the country about Brünn and Austerlitz, and read us his dispositions in a very lofty tone, with an overbearing air, which plainly proclaimed a full persuasion of his own worth and pity for our inferior capacity. We might really have been taken for a pack of schoolboys, but he was far from being a good professor. Kutuzoff, who was sitting dozing when we arrived at his abode, ended, before our departure, by falling into a profound sleep. Buxhowden listened standing, and for a certainty did not take in a single word; Miloradovitch kept silent; Przybyszewsky remained in the background, and only Dochtouroff stood alert, attentively examining the map. When Weyrother had finished his harangue, I was the only one who spoke.

Of the *commandants* of the Russian corps, one alone, Dochtouroff, had listened with attention; another, Langeron, was inclined to raise objections, but Kutuzoff put an end to all discussion and sent the officers back to their respective quarters.

At daybreak, the French Army fell in. A thick fog prevented anything from being seen beyond ten yards, but as the morning advanced the fog gradually lifted. Deep unbroken silence reigned along the ground occupied by the French troops; one would have hardly believed it possible that so many thousands of eager combatants could have been concentrated in that limited space.

Napoleon had summoned his marshals to receive their final orders on the hillock which now bears the name of *Butte de l'Empereur* (the emperor's hillock). (As he buckled on his sword that morning before mounting, he said to his staff, "Gentlemen, let us commence a memorable day.") He could not see the movements of the Russian left in the direction of Aujezd, because they were carried out down in the valley of the Littawa. It was only when the fog cleared that he could see how small was their force holding the heights of Pratzen. As soon as, from the intensity of the firing on his right, he judged that the enemy's attack had developed in earnest, he ordered his lieutenants to repair to their respective commands, and take their share in the battle. It was then about 8.30 a.m.

Napoleon had taken advantage, in a masterly manner, of the faults committed by the allies. His troops, concentrated in massive columns, were ready to act as circumstances would demand.

Action against the French Right.

On the evening of the 1st of December, Lieutenant-General Kienmayer, at the head of his column composed of 22 squadrons of Austrians, 10 of Cossacks, and 5 battalions of Croats, marched from Pratzen and made for Aujezd, where he arrived at nine and bivouacked.

The first shots in the battle were fired on the allies' left that evening, when a preliminary attack was made on the French right by O'Reilly's light cavalry belonging to Kienmayer's advanced guard. The general wished to clear the way for the morrow, as he had to lead the troops moving on Telnitz.

At seven the following morning (2nd December), the three first Russian columns commenced descending from their bivouacs on the Pratzen plateau, marching in the direction of Telnitz and Sokolnitz, as specified in their orders. On a hill in front of the former village, the French had posted several companies of infantry, with the object of defending the approaches to the village; some detachments of cavalry were on their right, resting on the lake of Mönitz.

Kienmayer, who attacked at daybreak, ordered a detachment of cavalry to advance towards the right of the French and a battalion of Szecklers' infantry to attack the hill on which the several French companies were posted. The French were reinforced, and defended themselves with obstinacy. The Austrians, supported by a second battalion, persisted bravely in their efforts. The cavalry which had taken post on the flanks of this infantry, particularly the hussars of Hesse-Homburg, suffered severely from the fire of the enemy's sharp-shooters. Several attacks were made on the hill, which it was necessary to carry in order to drive the enemy from the village beyond. After repeated failures, General Stutterheim finally succeeded in getting possession of it.

The French held Telnitz and the vineyards all round the village with the 3rd Regiment of the Line and two battalions of Corsican sharp-shooters. Two more battalions were kept in reserve on the right bank of the Goldbach brook. The troops in the village fought stubbornly. Telnitz was situated in a sort of natural intrenchment, the ground about it being cut up by ravines, the vineyards being surrounded by deep ditches, of which the French held possession.

The Austrians at one time succeeded in penetrating as far as the village, but Legrand, having sent the 26th Light to the assistance of the 3rd Regiment, speedily drove them out in the direction of Aujezd. It was then 8.30. The allies maintained themselves on the hill in front of the village with some difficulty. In these attacks Szecklers' regiment, which fought with great valour, lost in killed and wounded about two-thirds of its number.

Not till after the contest had been kept up for an hour did Buxhowden appear, coming from the direction of Aujezd at the head of the first column. The starting of the several columns had been delayed partly by the clumsiness of the organisation, partly from the fact that the staff-officers were unaccustomed to handle large masses of troops, and partly also by the copies of the orders not having reached the hands of the column commanders till about 8 a.m.

Buxhowden sent a battalion of the 7th Rifles to support the Austrians, and one of General Loewis' brigades (the regiments of Yaroslaw and of New-Ingrie) to form a reserve for Stutterheim. The Austro-Russians thereupon delivered a fresh attack on the village and gained possession of it. On the approach of such superior forces, the French evacuated the defile and drew up on the further side of the Goldbach, in the direction of Ottmarau. Kienmayer crossed the brook and skirmished with Margaron, but without any special success.

The French did wonders against the first three Russian columns. All that Legrand had to do was to compel the enemy to employ against him as many troops as possible, and to deceive him completely with regard to the aims the emperor had in view. Though vigorously attacked, he sustained the shock bravely, and, as on all other occasions, behaved like an able general and a valiant soldier. After 2000 Frenchmen in the neighbourhood of Telnitz had kept Kienmayer and the first Russian column in countenance for fully two hours, they received a reinforcement. It was Friant's division of Davout's corps—4000 men—which had hurried up from Raigern.

Davout, who quitted Raigern at about 5 a.m., had been marching on Turas and Sokolnitz when he received news of the fight going on round Telnitz; he at once changed his direction, sending the 1st regiment of Dragoons forward to support Legrand. Taking advantage of a thick fog which suddenly enveloped the entire valley, Heudelet's brigade advanced to the attack. The French recaptured the village and pushed on beyond it, as far as the hill where the combat had commenced.

Battle of Austerlitz

At this time a mishap favoured the allies. Merle's brigade, which, after rallying, had followed Heudelet's, mistaking in the fog their comrades for Russians, opened fire on them. This caused some confusion of which Nostitz took ready advantage, and at the head of two squadrons of hussars he charged the French, and made some hundreds of them prisoners. Some accounts say that the Russians were on the point of surrendering when Merle's men fired into Heudelet's brigade. The fog having cleared, the allies again advanced on Telnitz and drove the French out of the village. The first Russian column deployed in several lines and opened a brisk cannonade. Prince Maurice of Liechtenstein and General Stutterheim's cavalry passed the defile without opposition and drew up in battle array on the other side. Davout, who was attacked at this time, could make no further effort at this point, and, leaving Bourcier in front of Telnitz, marched with Friant's five regiments in the direction of Sokolnitz. (According to Stutterheim, tire French "entirely abandoned the plain between Telnitz and Turas.")

Buxhowden, oblivious that his manoeuvre required to be executed with celerity and vigour, that the valley between Telnitz and Sokolnitz was to be passed with all speed, hesitated, and missed a good chance. Had he pushed his column forward before the arrival of the whole of Friant's division, he might have turned the French right. He did not do so, it is said, because the communication with the 2nd column had not yet been established, and his orders enjoined him to keep on the same level with that column.

While Buxhowden maintained a fruitless skirmish with the French infantry, waiting to hear of the progress made by Langeron and Przybyszewsky, Bourchier, with several charges delivered at opportune moments, prevented the Russians gaining more ground.

In the meantime, the second and third columns (except two regiments of the former left in reserve on the Pratzen plateau) had quitted the heights. At 8.30 a.m. they were approaching Sokolnitz. Their advance had been delayed by Prince of Liechtenstein's cavalry, which had crossed their line of march to gain its assigned place on the battlefield. (For no given reason this cavalry had bivouacked on the night of the 1st between Aujezd and Pratzen, though intended in the early morning to move northwards and form up at Blasowitz on Bagration's left.) The march of the third column in the direction of Sokolnitz had also been considerably retarded by its having to cross the village of Pratzen, as also vineyards, canals, and ravines.

Sokolnitz was occupied by two battalions belonging to Legrand's

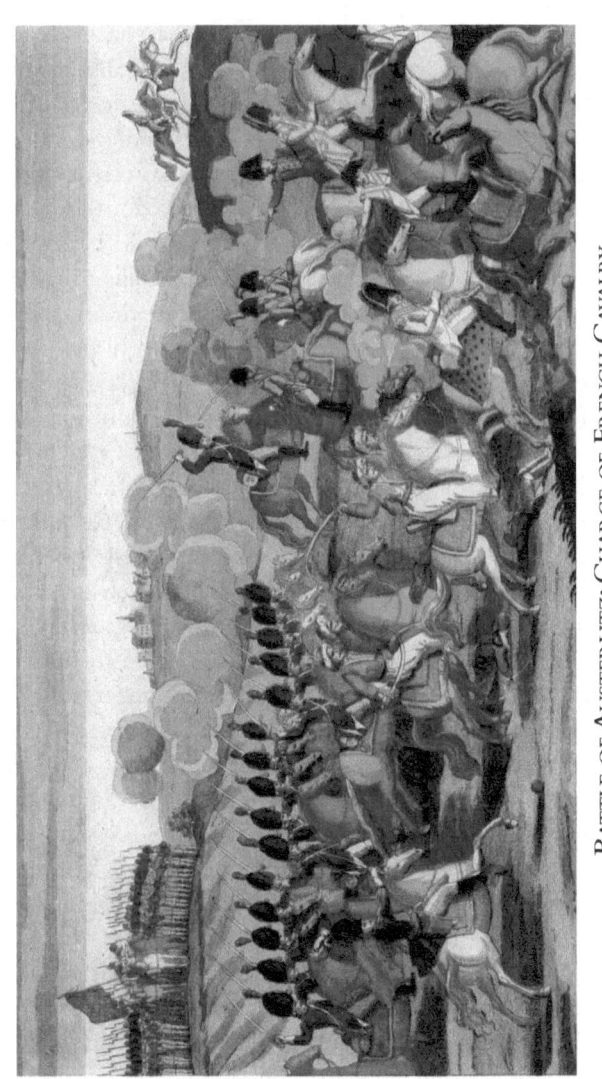

Battle of Austerlitz: Charge of French Cavalry

division, a reserve holding Kobelnitz. These troops opposed some resistance to the Russian light infantry which led the attack. The French had also posted some artillery on a hill between Sokolnitz and Kobelnitz, and the Russians opened a heavy cannonade against Sokolnitz, which nearly destroyed the village.

Both columns, without concerning themselves with the progress made by the first column, having neglected to establish any direct communication with it, and taking no particular notice of the offensive movement the French were on the point of undertaking on their right rear, continued their operations against Sokolnitz, its castle and park, in strict accordance with the original dispositions.

After a long and fruitless cannonade, Langeron's three regiments captured Sokolnitz at 9.30 a.m., and General Müller, belonging to the third column—who was severely wounded— chased the French out of the castle and beyond Sokolnitz. The two columns, in passing through the village, at that time enveloped in a thick fog, crossed each other, from which cause, they were thrown into confusion. At about this period a serious battle was commencing on the Pratzen plateau.

Legrand, attacked by the 2nd and 3rd Russian columns, was compelled to evacuate Sokolnitz and to retire to the heights in rear of it. The Russians were already gaining ground on the right bank of the Goldbach brook, and Davout, fearing lest the French line might be severed, directed Friant to concentrate his three brigades and fall on the enemy as he emerged from Sokolnitz and tried to form on the heights. Friant sent the 48th regiment against Sokolnitz, supporting it with the 111th and Kister's brigade. The Russians were overthrown and driven back through the village, which, with six guns and two flags, remained in possession of the French. These latter, however, could not so easily shake off their adversaries; the Russians returned to the attack with fresh troops, and all the efforts of Friant's soldiers could not prevail.

The 111th, who held the left of the village, were driven back, and Lochet, with the 48th on the right side, had to sustain a terrible contest in the streets, in the houses, in the barns, for three-quarters of an hour. Friant came to his assistance with Kister's brigade, drove the Russians back for a moment, and occupied the village with the 15th Light Infantry. Still he was not able to effect much; after a most vigorous resistance this regiment, as well as the 33rd, had to give way. After capturing and losing the village several times, Lochet was driven back by the Russians step by step beyond the Goldbach.

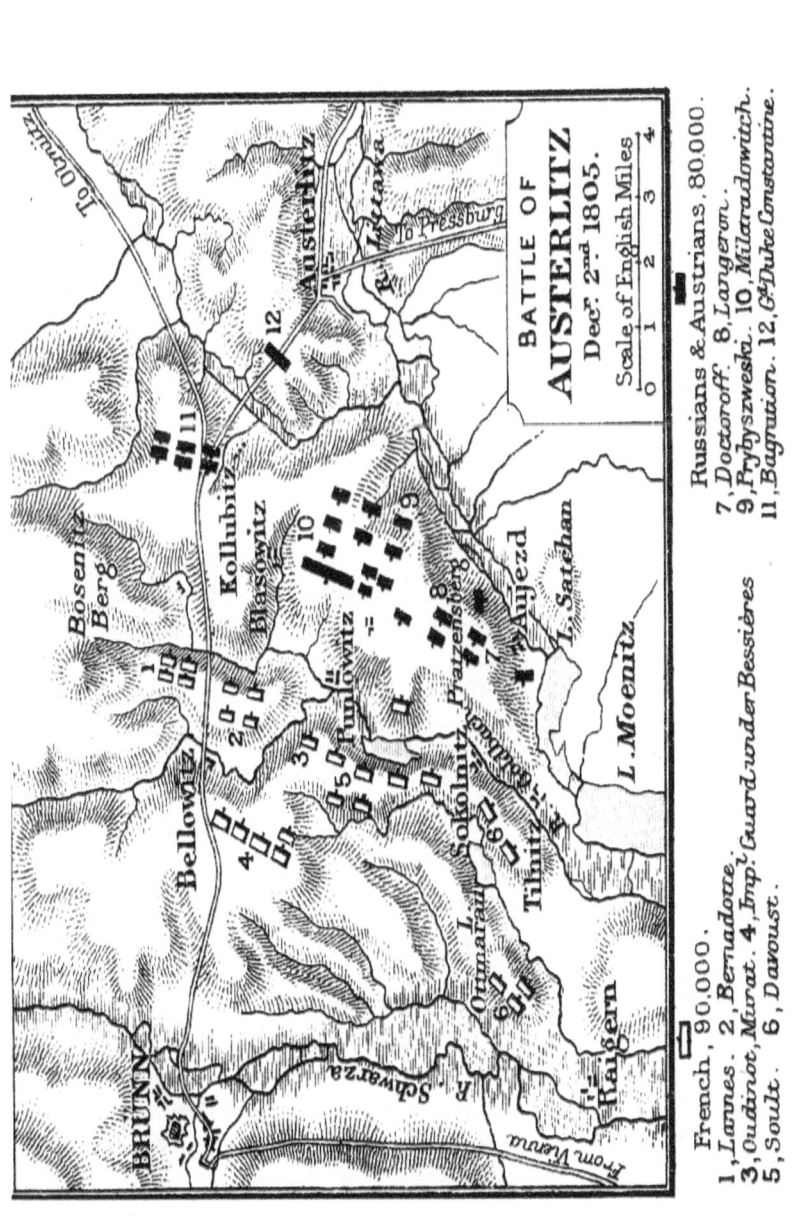

By ten o'clock Davout held a position with his right in rear of the pond of Ottmarau and the left extending in the direction of Sokolnitz castle. Przybyszewsky had taken ten battalions of his column across to the right bank of the Goldbach in front of Davout's left; the other seven battalions remained on the left bank of the brook and constituted a reserve. Another of his battalions, which had been routed in an engagement with La Vasseur, rejoined him about this time. At ten, Langeron attacked Davout's left wing. Had the Russians advanced with energy and united the three columns of their left wing in one body, this manoeuvre would have menaced Napoleon's rear, and more than probably it would have stayed Soult's advance up the Pratzen heights. Davout, who fully recognised all the importance of the task assigned to him, was resolved to do everything in his power to avert the danger, and as a first step he concentrated the whole of his forces on his left.

The 2nd and 3rd Russian columns extended along a row of ponds, and when about to attack were thrown into disorder by the fire of Davout's batteries, which had been skilfully posted. They managed to recover their array, but the artillery soon opened a deadly fire on them and cast them into confusion. Davout succeeded in retaking Sokolnitz castle, but could not hold it on account of the numerical majority of the enemy. At eleven o'clock he abandoned Sokolnitz, but managed to make his position good on the line of ponds and hills of the Goldbach.

The three Russian columns of the left wing numbered 38,000 men and 4,000 horses; these troops were for three hours held at bay by 10,000 men and 2,500 horses under Davout. The marshal was enjoined to keep on the defensive, as the emperor did not imagine that with his scanty forces, he would ever remain victorious. His struggle had been continuous and terrific. Buxhowden's utter want of enterprise was inexplicable, for had he pressed vigorously on Davout when that marshal withdrew from Telnitz and took all his troops from the right to reinforce his left, notwithstanding all his determination, Davout would not have been able to make head against the allies. Buxhowden lay inert waiting until Langeron and Przybyszewsky had fought out their fight with the French, whereas he should have complied with his orders and pushed forward determinately towards Turas.

Round Telnitz and Sokolnitz the combat continued the greatest part of the day. At these points the opposing forces were very unequal in numbers. Still, nothing would equal the tenacity with which the French disputed their ground. The allies who had clumsily crowded considerable forces in the bottom of Telnitz and in the swampy valley bordering on the pools of Satschan and Mönitz, did not know how to employ them.

Having seen how the allies fared in the forenoon of the 2nd in the low ground on their left, we must turn to their centre, where a fierce battle was raging. The action on the French right and that on the centre were intimately connected, for what the emperor earnestly desired was to see the enemy fully occupied in forcing the defiles of the Goldbach before he attempted to pierce their centre and wreak their ruin.

Defeat of the Allies' Centre.

On the evening before a battle, it was customary with Napoleon, instead of giving orders to extend his lines, to converge all his forces on the point he had decided to attack, and as he aimed generally at some weak point he had discovered in the adversary's dispositions, he soon carried all before him.

At daybreak, Kutuzoff was with the 4th column, destined, as we have seen, to march on Kobelnitz. Kolowrat's column, which was in reality Kutuzoff's reserve, was the weakest of all, and was composed of troops of both nationalities. It was made up of fifteen Austrian battalions and the grenadier regiments of Little Russia, Smolensko, and Nowgorod, with the Apchéron fusiliers; the latter were all weak regiments which had suffered considerably in the encounters with the enemy during the retreat from Braunau. Nevertheless, the Russian battalions constituted the backbone of the 4th column, for the Austrian battalions consisted, for the most part, of recruits who had never been, under fire.

Kolowrat's march was delayed, his way being barred by Liechtenstein's cavalry, which was filing off to the right across his front to occupy the ground which had been assigned to it. When at last the way was clear, Kutuzoff made no move, as if he were troubled by a presentiment that Napoleon meditated some startling manoeuvre.

On the far east a ruddy glow heralded the near approach of the coming day. The summits of the hills gradually lighted up, and as the French were dashing forward towards the village of Pratzen a crimson rim appeared above the horizon, and slowly the entire orb, the sun, the legendary sun of Austerlitz, rose in unclouded brilliancy as in the glorious days of spring. But ere that sun whose early rays gilded the bright arms of the two contending sides had run his daily course, grim death had made sad havoc among the brave warriors of the three nations.

Taking of an Eagle at the Battle of Austerlitz:

At about 9 a.m., the *Czar* and the Emperor Francis arrived on the ground.

※※※※※※

Mathieu Dumas states that the fourth column commenced moving at about 8 a.m., but as it had to give time to the other columns to force the defiles of Telnitz and Sokolnitz, it possibly set out somewhat later. The Russian account makes it nearer to 9 a.m.

※※※※※※

Wolkonsky, who was by Kutuzoff's side, relates how Alexander, finding the columns with piled arms, inquired of Kutuzoff the reason why he did not move forward.

"I am waiting, sire," replied the general, "till all the troops of the column are together."

The *Czar* retorted, "We are not on the parade ground, when one waits till all the troops have arrived before commencing the exercises."

"It is just on that account, sire, that we are not on the parade ground, that I do not commence," spoke Kutuzoff. "However, you can please, sire, give your orders." (Lieut.-Général Mikhailovski-Danilevski, *Rélation de la Campagne de 1805, Austerlitz*.)"

Napoleon held his troops well in hand for the decisive stroke. Of Soult's corps, St. Hilaire's division, with a company of light artillery, was formed for attack on three lines in front of the village of Puntowitz; he was to be supported by Le Vasseur's brigade of Legrand's division, which was to prevent any attack being made on his rear. Vandamme's division, formed in the same order, lay in front of Girzikowitz. The attack which had been planned by the emperor depended on the rapidity with which the centre could master the heights of Pratzen.

As word was brought to him that the enemy's troops who had passed the night in the vicinity of Pratzen were leaving it and moving in the direction of Telnitz and Sokolnitz, he turned to Soult and asked, "How long will your troops take to ascend the Pratzen plateau?" to which the marshal replied, "Twenty minutes at the most."

"In that case let us wait for another quarter of an hour," rejoined Napoleon.

Frequent reports of the continued advance of the enemy's left were reaching him. As the sun was just rising, an *aide-de-camp* brought him word—prematurely as it turned out—that the last of the Russian troops which had bivouacked on the plateau were leaving it and moving to their left.

THE VICTORY OF THE BATTLE OF AUSTERLITZ:

Seeing, then, how the left of the allies was getting away from the centre, and that the heights were being abandoned, the emperor issued the order to advance. At that moment the third column of the allies had but quitted the heights of Pratzen to march on Sokolnitz.

It was near nine o'clock as the 4th column, preceded by an advanced guard of two battalions of Miloradovitch's corps, of the regiments of Nowgorod and Apscheronsky, with some dragoons of the Archduke John's regiment, arrived on the ground which Przybyszewsky had occupied during the night.

★★★★★★

Two battalions of the regiment of Nowgorod having run away at Austerlitz, it was ordered by the *Czar* that the officers should wear their swords without sword-knots; that the soldiers should be deprived of their swords and compelled to serve for five years beyond their proper term.

★★★★★★

It was then that Kutuzoff detected the massive columns of French infantry in a bottom in front of Pratzen, advancing on Kolowrat's right. The French, in order of battle, were on the point of assailing the allied army while in column of march. It was Soult's corps. Saint Hilaire had orders to seize the plateau in rear and to the right of the village of Pratzen. His orders distinctly specified that he was not to send any troops against Pratzen, even if that village should be found occupied by the enemy. Vandamme was to ascend the plateau and approach Pratzen, but always keeping at a certain distance from the village, the intention being to isolate what troops the Russians might have in the village and to place them between two fires. The plateau was to be seized in the first moment of surprise. Soult feared lest an attack on the village might lead to unfortunate delays.

The French had the advantage that, being in the low ground, where the smoke of the bivouac fires and the fog did not clear for some time, their long array of columns ready to march to the attack was concealed from the enemy. At last they advanced, Vandamme's division on the left, Saint Hilaire's on the right. At this unexpected sight the advanced guard of the 4th column was pushed forward up to the village of Pratzen, which it occupied, and it also took possession of a small bridge beyond it before the enemy's sharpshooters had time to come up. A battalion was then posted upon a hill to the left in front of the village (which had not yet been quite vacated by the rear-guard of the 3rd column); the other battalion of the advanced guard remained in occupation of the village itself.

The allies had never dreamt of the possibility of being attacked on the heights of Pratzen. Kutuzoff, taken entirely by surprise, felt all the importance of maintaining these heights, commanding as they did all the ground around, whilst at the same time they were necessary to protect the rear of his third column. It was the possession of these heights which was to decide the fate of the day. This was the key of the position, which the allied commanders had carelessly abandoned.

When the allies were marching to the assault, by a masterly counterstroke they found themselves being attacked. It was only then that Kutuzoff realised that his plan was based on wrong suppositions; that Napoleon, far from retreating, was bearing heavily on the allied army in the hope of cutting it asunder. What Kutuzoff lacked in prevision he made up in energy at that moment. When he saw the French columns so near, he promptly issued his orders to hold the heights, to show a bold front to the enemy. He was still in time to retrieve the fortunes of the day; it needed only a spark of genius to run to the left, withdraw the troops of Buxhowden from the hollows they were jammed in, and lead them to the plateau of Pratzen to recapture the key of the battlefield.

Saint Hilaire was rudely attacked as it was; had Buxhowden received timely notice of Soult's manoeuvre, and acted with energy, he might have made the marshal's ultimate success very problematical. De Ségur relates that things at one time looked very black, and that Napoleon was alarmed at the advance of the Imperial Guard, which he mistook for a Russian column.

Let us admit that Napoleon was not the commander to give Kutuzoff or Buxhowden a chance; nevertheless, it would have been something gained for the Russian commanders to have got an open retreat for the allied left on Austerlitz, and to have got it clear of the abyss in their rear. Nevertheless, the left wing of the allies imprudently continued to advance for the purpose of turning the French Army in a position which it did not occupy.

The centre of the allies barely amounted to more than 17,000 men, and was attacked by double that number. By a more able arrangement of his forces, by being more concentrated, Napoleon's numbers at the principal point of attack doubled that of his opponents. The offensive movement made by the French, declares Stutterheim, upset the whole plan of the allies, and from that moment all concert ceased.

The French had climbed the heights, and were moving forward

in well-dressed lines at steady pace. To the troops, as they went by, the emperor said:

> We must end this campaign with a clap of thunder which will turn the pride of our enemy into confusion.

A part of Bernadotte's corps now also made its appearance to the north of Pratzen: for Napoleon, having remarked that the space which Liechtenstein's cavalry was intended to occupy had been left bare, ordered Rivaud's division of Bernadotte's corps, Caffarelli's division, and Kellermann's cavalry to march on Blasowitz. These troops, by occupying the vacant space, were intended to separate the Russian right from the centre.

Kutuzoff sent orders to occupy the heights, and the battalions which were already there to be supported. He directed the Austrian brigades of Rottermunde and Jurecek, twenty battalions, which belonged to Kolowrat's second line, with a powerful artillery, to advance on the heights to the left of Pratzen and defend them in conjunction with the reserve which Langeron had left there. The Russians under Miloradovitch were ordered to deploy and defend Pratzen and the side of the plateau which extends from that village to Stari-Winebradi. Intimation was sent to the Russian Imperial Guard to incline towards the centre, and an urgent demand was made to obtain from Liechtenstein some regiments of cavalry. In response to this the prince sent to Kutuzoff four Russian cavalry regiments.

The crisis of the battle had arrived, and the action became very warm when the allies strove to regain the ground lost by their advanced guard. There was no other chance of retrieving the fate of the day but by making a general and desperate attack at the point of the bayonet.

On the French side, Morand had been detailed to lead Saint Hilaire's advanced guard with the 10th regiment of light infantry. Thiebault was ordered to drive the enemy out of Pratzen, which having done, he was to rejoin the advanced guard on the plateau. Mazas attacked the village with the first battalion of the 14th, but he omitted to ascertain the nature of the ground in front of him and the strength of the enemy. Coming suddenly on a broad ravine and under a most murderous fire, which the Russians opened on him, his attack failed. (Saint Hilaire believed, and told Thiebault, that only the enemy's pickets were likely to be occupying Pratzen, consequently the brigadier attacked weakly.) The assault was resumed by Thiebault with the second battalion of the same regiment, supported by the 36th. The 14th flung itself into the ravine, attacked the Russians with the bayonet and routed them.

Morand, advancing with one single regiment, was nearly surrounded by some Austrian battalions, and had to fall back. Saint Hilaire, with the first battalion of the 14th, came to his aid, and posting this battalion on the right of the 10th, restored the fight. The enemy's centre was renewing its efforts to recover the Pratzen plateau. The fourth column, marching from Kobelnitz in column of companies, wheeled to the right into line, and aided by a powerful artillery, confronted Thiebault's brigade. As Thiebault came up he saw four regiments of the allies coming from the direction of Krenowitz and bearing on his left flank.

Thiebault ordered the 36th to deploy with its right resting on Morand's regiment, and placed the second battalion of the 14th in column on the left of the line. He had three guns with him, and six more were brought up by Major Fontenay, sent by the emperor, who deemed the position of the brigade rather critical. These guns, loaded with canister and grape, were posted between the two battalions of the 36th, and masked by infantry; the brigadier then went forward with Morand to reconnoitre, one of the enemy having called out not to fire on the troops, as they were Bavarians. This artifice was, however, soon detected. Thiebault allowed this formidable mass, which was commanded by Kolowrat, to approach till it was some thirty or forty yards from the French, then the guns were suddenly unmasked, and opened a deadly fire on the allies. This fire, well directed and briskly kept up, threw the Austrians into disorder; after a long resistance, unable to hold their ground, they retired, and in great confusion went down the eastern slope of the plateau.

During the time this fierce contest was being carried out on Soult's right, Vandamme was hotly engaged with the enemy. In the early morning, his division lay in front of the village of Girzikowitz, when he received orders to scale the heights of Pratzen, march on the enemy, and attack its centre.

The instructions for Saint Hilaire and Vandamme were to maintain always their divisions in two lines. According to this order, Vandamme formed his troops in two lines by brigades; one of the brigades deployed into line, the other in column by battalions covering the intervals of the battalions of the first line. We see this formation everywhere on the French side at Austerlitz. The light cavalry or light infantry were to take post in front, and also the guns ready to open fire. This formation was adopted as best calculated for making head against the numerous cavalry of the allies.

Whilst Kolowrat was striving to recapture the heights on the left, Miloradovitch was making every possible effort to resist Vandamme's attack and to hold the ground on the right.

Saint Hilaire had destined his left brigade, commanded by General Varé, to form his reserve and to come into action only as Vandamme's division should come level with it. Nevertheless, no sooner had these regiments—the 43rd and 55th of the Line—beheld Saint Hilaire's first success, than they dashed forward, turned the village of Pratzen (which the brigade was originally ordered to observe) on the left, and seized the heights, taking in flank two Russian regiments which were intended to support the troops in the village. These two Russian regiments had not quite completed their formation when they were overthrown. Pratzen was evacuated and the Russians pursued. Nothing was able to restrain the ardour of Varé's brigade.

Kutuzoff had formed up the 4th column in several lines, the right being drawn back towards the heights of Krenowitz, which were bristling with artillery.

At this moment Vandamme came level with Varé's brigade and within range of the enemy. Miloradovitch led his troops against the advancing French, but, deprived of their generals, Berg and Repninsky, both of whom had been wounded, the troops lost confidence. The imposing sight of the enemy's infantry, their number and steadiness, advancing without ever firing a shot, damped their ardour; the attack lacked the dash necessary for success; the pace became slow, accompanied by an ill-directed fire of musketry. When well within range, Vandamme fired several deadly volleys, followed by a bayonet attack; he was soon on them. Nothing could resist his vigorous onset.

Miloradovitch, who behaved with great spirit throughout, strove to hold firm and to get the Austrians to rally in his rear, but his efforts, though aided by some of his bravest officers and men, were of no avail. Neither his brilliant courage nor the affection his soldiers had for him could persuade them to hold their ground. He was beaten back and rallied his troops in rear of the Austrians. These latter, decimated by the enemy's fire and weakened in no time by a loss of 2,388 men, did not hold out much longer, and went down the heights, carrying with them Miloradovitch's troops.

The Emperor Alexander, who personally witnessed this disaster, ordered Miloradovitch to gather his men and retire on Austerlitz.

A mamelon concealed six Austro-Russian battalions which were intended to turn Vandamme's left. These battalions were supported by a strong body of artillery. In spite of a severe plunging fire, the 4th regiment of the French attacked them in front, while Schiner with the 26th Light Infantry fell on their flank and, without firing a shot, overthrew them, cut them to pieces, and captured their guns. A Russian regiment of the Grand Duke Constantine and an Austrian regiment of Salzbourg were almost annihilated.

The Russians lost a great portion of their artillery, which stuck in the deep clay that prevails in that part of the country. Great labour was experienced throughout in moving the artillery, partly on account of the broken nature of the ground, and also from the fact that the draught cattle had been weakened by being insufficiently fed. (The Russians had failed to recognise the great fact that the proper feeding, of the horses in a campaign is a vital precaution. No pains should ever be spared, to keep up their strength by sufficient nourishment.)

Danilevski states that, at the moment when the defeat of the 4th column took place, the confusion was so great that the *Czar's* entourage lost sight of him completely, quitted the road, and only rejoined him during the night, some even one or two days after the battle. During a portion of the contest on the plateau, Alexander had at his side only Wyllie his surgeon, Jaehne his equerry, a groom, and two Cossacks. Another version relates that General Toll found the *Czar* weeping by the wayside, accompanied only by one adjutant.

The contest on the Pratzen plateau lasted a long time, for the combined armies made considerable efforts.

Delivered from Kolowrat's column, Morand and Thiebault had to change front to their right to meet a fresh enemy, Kaminsky's brigade, with whom they had a fierce contest. These two regiments—the grenadiers of Phanagoria and the fusiliers of Riajsk—had remained in reserve on the heights, where the 2nd column had bivouacked the previous night.

Langeron had marched for Sokolnitz, with the 8th Chasseurs leading. These were followed by the regiments of Wibourg, Prim, and Koursk. In rear came the other brigade, with the grenadier regiments of Riajsk and Phanagoria. This brigade, commanded by Count Kaminsky, was moving in the direction of Sokolnitz, following the rest of the 2nd column, when Kaminsky perceived the French advancing up the heights of Pratzen. He sent at once to warn Langeron, halted his brigade, and placed it at right angles to the French right. By taking the enemy in flank he hoped to cause a favourable diversion.

Saint Hilaire's extreme right had formed in an angular direction to make head against the rear of the 2nd column. The Russians, shouting, according to their usual custom, rushed at the French, who received them with steadiness and a well supported fire, which did great execution. In this first onset Kaminsky's brigade was overpowered.

At that moment Kutuzoff, accompanied by Prince Wolkonsky, arrived on the ground. The prince, seizing a flag of the Phanagorian regiment, reformed the brigade and led it again to the charge. The Russians attacked the French vigorously and captured two guns. Again overpowered, they lost the two guns, but Wolkonsky rallied the men and led them anew against the French. The attacks of this brigade, which lasted some time, occupied the attention of Soult's right, but in no way arrested the progress of the centre. The Russian brigade reformed, and was reinforced by two squadrons of St. Petersburg dragoons and a hundred Cossacks of the Issaief regiment.

Thiebault, who commanded a brigade, writes that the Kaminsky brigade, reinforced by two regiments, restored the fight and made the French position highly critical. It was a principle with the French not to leave the enemy time to count their numbers; here they struggled desperately for the ground they held against an enemy who seemed maddened by the resistance it met. The position of Morand and Thiebault, with only six battalions and no reserve, appeared hopeless. A terrible tussle went on for twenty minutes, then followed a short breathing-space, then a brisk fire almost at point-blank range.

The situation had become unbearable, but the men behaved with a magnificent determination, and offered a strenuous resistance. The Russians delivered several furious charges, but for half an hour the French held their ground stoutly like brave men, till in their turn they executed a decisive charge, broke the enemy's line, captured their batteries, and remained undisputed masters of that part of the plateau.

Le Vasseur's brigade had been posted in reserve at Hobelnitz. His brigade marched on the flank and rear of the allies when they attempted to retake the heights of Pratzen, and greatly contributed to their defeat.

Thiebault says of this fight:

> In those terrible shocks, whole battalions of them (Russians) were killed without one man leaving his position in the ranks,

and their corpses lay in the lines in which the battalions had stood. Up to the last moment of that battle, we captured no prisoners, except such as contrived to constitute themselves so.

Under the recent conditions of fire, troops nowadays must be prepared to suffer heavy losses if a serious attack is to be pushed home. Even a hundred years ago, with the slow-loading firearms then in use, a stubborn enemy could not be dislodged from a position without incurring heavy losses. In their repeated attacks on the French the Kaminsky brigade left a large number of its gallant men on the ground.

General Kaminsky and his brigade fought very bravely during the whole of the battle, as the French learnt to their cost. The Russians, even when too severely wounded to be able to march, would take up their arms again after the enemy had gone forward, reload them, and put their conquerors between two fires. The 14th and 36th of the French had two-thirds of their officers killed or wounded; of 236 grenadiers of the 36th, only 17 answered their names at roll-call that night. This Russian attack alone seemed at one time capable of re-establishing the balance of power in the action on the crest of the hill. It might have found some work for the French reserves to do, but the stubbornness displayed by Thiebault's brigade rendered it unnecessary.

Kutuzoff made the greatest possible efforts to retake the Pratzen heights. Four combats were maintained for more than three hours, but all his efforts could not repair the mistake of having paid so little attention to the key of the position.

Seeing the impossibility of resisting with this brigade and a few details which had joined it, and finding his retreat on Austerlitz cut off, Kutuzoff retired on Hostieradek, and descended the valley of the Littawa. He had sent orders to Buxhowden to retire with the three first columns.

No sooner had Kaminsky's brigade retired than Langeron, with the regiment of Koursk, arrived at the very spot where the brigade had fought so stoutly. On nearing the Goldbach, Langeron, as we have seen, had received a report from Kaminsky to the effect that the French were seizing the heights of Pratzen, and that this unexpected move having stayed the march of the regiments of Phanagoria and Riajsk, he was unable to follow him in the direction of Sokolnitz. Langeron at first refused to accord credit to this report, but a heavy cannonade in his right rear soon convinced him of its truth; so, taking the regiment of Koursk, he marched to his comrade's assistance.

Kaminsky's brigade had quitted the battle-ground, and, left alone, the regiment of Koursk found itself exposed to the attacks of an immensely superior force, and was nearly destroyed. No less than 1,600 men of that regiment were killed and wounded in the battle.

The Kaminsky brigade and the regiment of Koursk disposed of, Saint Hilaire's division and Le Vasseur's brigade were ordered by Soult to attack Sokolnitz, chase and destroy all that there was of the enemy in that direction, and join the other two of Legrand's brigades. At that moment, Vandamme, reinforced by Varé's brigade, was about forcing the village of Aujezd; the allies' left was isolated and hemmed in between Aujezd, Telnitz, and Sokolnitz. Morand and Le Vasseur advanced to carry the Sokolnitz chateau on either side, whilst Thiebault attacked it in front. Here a great massacre took place, for the Russians fought desperately. Houses, stables, barns, everything served them for shelter, and everywhere they fought to the last extremity.

To strengthen this attack, Napoleon sent Duroc with a brigade of Oudinot's grenadiers by way of Koblenitz to attack Langeron's and Przybyszevvsky's columns.

Kister's brigade had been turned on its left, but by ordering the 33rd regiment to effect a change of front, Friant rallied his three brigades and pounced on the enemy at the very moment that Saint Hilaire had the castle of Sokolnitz attacked by the 36th. The 14th was turning the village from the left, and Morand, taking the 10th Light and the 43rd, followed the ponds on the right so as to cut off the enemy's retreat. The Russians held a strong position, and defended the castle with obstinate bravery. The 36th suffered severely, but by the aid of the 33rd and 111th it overcame all resistance, drove the enemy out, and cut it to pieces. The Russians suffered a loss in killed, wounded, or captured of 5,000 men; a number of wagons and guns fell into the hands of the French.

Stutterheim writes:

> When the Russians who were in Sokolnitz and those who had pushed beyond it saw themselves surrounded, they immediately surrendered.

A column of the allies, 3,000 strong, having three generals at its head, had issued from Sokolnitz and got beyond Legrand's left. At that moment some light cavalry belonging to Soult's corps was arriving on the battlefield. Franceschi, at the head of the 8th Hussars, his horses wearied by a forced march, charged the Russians, seized the general in command, and ordered the troops to surrender. All promptly laid down their arms. The 11th and 12th Chasseurs, who had gone round to attack the column in front, found their manoeuvre forestalled.

* Loss of the Third Column.

7th *Chasseurs* of 1925 men	...	...	...	...	700
Regiment of Galisch of 1478 men		...	...	...	1100
„ Boutyrsk of 1709 men	...	...	...	...	1600
„ Narwa of 1552 men		...	...	...	1300
„ Podolia of 709 men		...	...	...	180
„ Azoff of 909 men	...	...	...	...	400
Total of the column before the battle			...	8282	
Casualties	...	...	...	...	5280

Alarmed at the progress the French were making in the centre, Kutuzoff, leaving Ouvaroff with his squadrons to maintain the communications between the centre and the right wing of the allies, ordered up a large portion of Liechtenstein's cavalry, with the evident intention of making a fresh effort against the enemy on the heights of Pratzen. Napoleon, however, had a superiority of forces at this point, for besides Soult, already victorious, he had at his disposal the whole of Bernadotte's corps, the Guards, and Oudinot's grenadiers, the entire force estimated at 25,000 men.

Kolowrat's troops were in imminent danger, and on the French left Lannes and Murat were making steady progress. Disturbed by what he saw, the Grand Duke Constantine brought forward the Russian Imperial Guard; descending from the heights, it advanced about midway between Blasowitz and Pratzen to meet the French, but the Guard was met by Vandamme's division, and a furious combat ensued.

Defeat of the Russian Right.

Before proceeding to show the further development of the French central attack, it will be as well to turn our eyes in the direction of the left of the French line of battle, and to see how the Russians fared there.

At the same time as heavy fighting was progressing on the French right and centre, Prince Bagration found himself attacked by the French left wing. The action in that part of the field may be regarded more or less as a distinct battle.

The Emperor Napoleon had sent repeated orders to Lannes and Murat to attack the enemy early and vigorously, so as to prevent Bagration rendering any assistance to the centre of the allies, on which the principal blows were to be struck. Bernadotte, who had occupied Girzikowitz the moment Vandamme's division had advanced, was directed to quit that village and to occupy with his divisions the heights of Blasowitz. Drouet was to form on the right, Rivaud on the left. The cavalry reserve, Walther's, d'Hautpoul's, and Nansouty's divisions were to follow and form in several lines on Bernadotte's left between his corps and that of Lannes.

The marshals had surprised the Russians on their line of march, and the Russian right wing, while advancing without any conception that the enemy was close at hand, was astonished to find itself all at once attacked by Suchet's division.

When Prince Bagration read the dispositions for the battle as they were handed to him in the early morning of the 2nd of December, he remarked to the officers who were about him, "We shall lose the battle"—a show of want of confidence in the commander-in-chief which did not portend well.

His command lay athwart the main road leading from Olmütz to Brünn. The infantry was formed in two lines, being under the command of Prince Dolgorouki. On the evening of the 1st he had been reinforced by some regiments of hussars and dragoons. His cavalry he had disposed as follows: On his left flank was Ouvaroff with the Elisabethgrad hussars, Kharkoff and Tchernigoff dragoons, which were posted in front of a ravine. On the right were the Mariopol and Pawlograd's hussars, and in reserve the *cuirassiers* of the empress, the dragoons of Iwer and of Saint Petersburg. Wittgenstein and Tchaptily commanded the cavalry on the right and the reserve.

It had been intended that at the commencement of the battle the prince should remain in front of Pohorlitz and hold that position. Then, as he learnt the success of the four columns on his left, he was to assume the offensive, moving on Bosenitz and manoeuvring against the French left. He was to advance on both sides of the Olmütz road, carry the Santon hill, and afterwards march straight for Brünn. He had been enjoined to take special care not to be turned on his left.

Bagration commenced moving forward to oppose Lannes' left, which was known to be in the direction of Kowalowitz. He occupied the village of Kruh, situated in a hollow some few hundred yards from the Olmütz road. Here General Ulanius was posted with three battalions of light troops. Ouvaroff, at the head of thirty-five squadrons of cavalry and a few battalions of infantry, was on the road itself.

Bagration endeavoured to capture the small eminence of Santon. His troops descended into a valley which extends at the foot of that eminence and carried the village of Bosenitz; they then engaged in an artillery duel with the French artillery posted on the hill, but did not make any strong effort to carry it with their infantry.

✶✶✶✶✶✶

The Russians were directed to deposit their packs before charging, their generals evidently thinking that packs would be in the way of the men when fighting. They assured the soldiers that they would capture those of the French, which were well filled with gold. Apparently they did not lose much, for all the French found in them were sacred images, reliquaries, and rations of black bread, consisting more of straw and bran than of flour.—Lejeune, vol. i. (Volumes 1 & 2 also republished by Leonaur.)

✶✶✶✶✶✶

Lannes repulsed all the attempts of the enemy to seize the Santon hill, and drove him steadily back to the other side of the Olmütz road in the direction of Blasowitz. The ground there, being more level, was better suited for cavalry, and Murat executed some brilliant charges.

Lannes caused his troops to advance as Napoleon gained ground on the Pratzen plateau, and, as news reached him of the successes gained by the emperor in that direction, he assumed a vigorous offensive.

At 7 a.m., Kellermann with his light cavalry had been sent out along the Olmütz road to screen Suchet's division, which rested on Bosenitz, having Caffarelli's on his right. Liechtenstein, in consequence of having experienced considerable delay by the third column marching across his front, was not able to deploy on Bagration's left as it had been originally intended, and the Russian Imperial Guard which had been told off to form the reserve of the right wing found itself in the end in first line. It lay close to Blasowitz, and soon became engaged with Bernadotte's skirmishers and Kellermann's hussars.

A cloud of Cossacks masked the dispositions of the Russian cavalry, and as the Cossacks cleared away a numerous artillery opened a destructive fire on Kellermann's light horse. Kellermann still advanced covering Caffarelli's division which had been ordered to move on Blazowitz. Ouvaroff, coming from the left of his artillery, prepared to attack Kellermann, who thereupon retired.

Liechtenstein in the meanwhile appeared at the head of thirty-two Austrian squadrons and the lancers of the Grand Duke Constantine. He determined to form his cavalry in order of battle, and to charge the enemy. The Grand Duke's lancers, one of the finest regiments of the Russian Army, was the first to deploy; this done, it rushed at the enemy without waiting for the formation of the rest, and without supports. The lancers attacked prematurely with far too much impetuosity, and so became victims of their own misplaced courage.

To avoid being driven back in disorder by the Russian lancers on to the first line, Kellermann retired through the intervals of Caffarelli's division and reformed in two lines between Caffarelli's first and second line, but not scatheless, for his rear was overtaken and attacked. The lancers in their pursuit came under the terrible cross-fire of the French infantry squares, and suffered severely.

Kellermann had retired only to await a favourable opportunity for charging, and, as the Grand Duke's lancers turned about like a wave recovering from the recoil, his light horsemen fell on their decimated ranks and sabred many. The Russian regiment was completely routed; it had 16 officers and 400 non-commissioned officers and men put *hors de combat*. What was left of it retired and reformed in rear of Prince Bagration's corps. The Russian general, Essen, was mortally wounded in this charge.

★★★★★★

A body of 12,000 Russians coming from Brest-Litowski was not far from the battlefield. This reinforcement, which might have been of great assistance to the allies in the battle, though marching with all possible speed, could not, on the 2nd of December, get beyond Presau, three marches from the field of Austerlitz. Its commander, General Essen, seeing no chance of leading his troops in the battle, rode forward and offered his services to Liechtenstein, and fell gloriously at the head of the Grand Duke's lancers.

★★★★★★

The 1st Russian Hussars and 2nd Dragoons advanced to the help of the hard-pressed lancers. Kellerman formed his division in echelon to meet the attack. (Kellermann had the 2nd, 4th, and 5th Hussars, and the 5th *Chasseurs à Cheval*.) His 4th Hussars were surrounded by 800 of the enemy and cut to pieces, but the three following echelons fell on the enemy's flanks and, aided by Sebastiani's dragoons, soon overthrew their opponents.

At the same time as Kellermann's charge occurred, Lannes attacked Blasowitz with the loth Light Infantry, supported by the 17th of the Line. Suchet's division attacked Bagration's infantry, which on the extreme right had made constant demonstrations against the Santon hill, all of which had been readily met by Claparède and the 17th Light Infantry.

The charge of the 4th Hussars

Prince John of Liechtenstein had, after a time, completed the deployment of his numerous squadrons, and intended to take part in the battle, but he was met by Nansouty's division. Whilst the prince was aligning his forces, Nansouty had ranged his division into two lines, but, careful not to be outflanked, he bid the *carabineers* take ground to their right. When they had got sufficiently far in that direction, he wheeled them into line and moved forward. The Russian guns opened and inflicted heavy losses on the French, but did not stop them for a moment. The Russians withdrew their guns, and Nansouty, deeming his men sufficiently close, made a most brilliant charge. Liechtenstein's first line was hurled back on the second, which advanced in its turn. The 2nd and 3rd Cuirassiers came to the assistance of the carabineers, and defeated the second line of the Austrian cavalry. The enemy's squadrons were disordered and destroyed, and only rallied on the other side of a brook under the protection of a powerful artillery fire.

This charge of Nansouty separated Liechtenstein from Prince Bagration's corps. After this combat, the French horsemen were reformed in rear of Caffarelli, and were soon rejoined by the 3rd Cuirassiers who, having ventured too far, had been vigorously repulsed.

For all that, Liechtenstein did not consider himself quite beaten; if he could do no more, he at least strove to check or retard the success of the French. Having reformed his cavalry into two lines, he attempted an attack on Caffarelli's right, but Caffarelli stopped him by a deadly fire. Nansouty then trotted out his heavy horsemen, and, passing through the intervals of the infantry, deployed in two lines and attacked the enemy. The Austrians were overturned, their first line being driven on to their second.

It was now the turn of Nansouty's second line; the squadrons advanced and delivered three charges, the enemy losing heavily; being overthrown and broken, the Austrians retired. This movement, besides dividing the allied army into two, gave the French possession of the heights of Kruh and Holubitz which led to the fall of the two villages of that name. In this charge the French captured eight guns and routed completely all the troops on the left of the main road. Nansouty's loss was relatively not very considerable.

Whilst Kellermann was engaged with the enemy's cavalry, Lannes was gaining ground. Suchet was pushing forward in the direction of Kowalowitz, bent on overlapping Bagration's right. Caffarelli followed along the high-road.

After a desperate resistance, Blasowitz had been carried by Lannes' right and Bernadotte's left. As the 17th regiment was in the act of escorting to the rear 1,200 prisoners captured in Blasowitz, and disarming an Austrian battalion, a body of Russian dragoons suddenly appeared beyond the right of that regiment. General Debilly promptly threw the 17th and 61st into square, and as the Russians charged, they came under the cross-fire of the two squares. They were taken aback, disorganised, and decimated by this warm reception.

Two mishaps occurred at this time: the Russian dragoons, striving to find an escape, fell on the Austrians, whom they had failed to recognise. Murat, taking them for Bavarians, had, ordered the fire to cease. The Russian horsemen came up quite close to where he was before the error was detected, and, but for a timely charge at the head of his escort, the great cavalry leader would have been captured.

Dumas writes:

> The combat of Lannes and Bernadotte on the left, was remarkable for the complete success with which the troops, arranged in the order prescribed by Napoleon, baffled all the efforts of the allies whose numerous and magnificent cavalry had there a full opportunity of acting. The first line was uniformly drawn up in battle array, the second in battalion squares, the artillery and light horse in front, with the heavy cavalry deployed in several lines in rear of the whole. Thus, if a charge of horse, which was frequently the case, broke the first array, it passed, while disordered by success, through the intervals between the squares in the rear, from whose front and flanks it sustained a heavy fire. If they escaped that, the horsemen were suddenly assailed, when blown and dispersed, by a solid mass of heavy cavalry in the rear, which never failed to bring them back in confusion through the squares, who by this time had reloaded their pieces, and whose flanking fire completed the destruction of their gallant assailants.

At about noon, three regiments of Caffarelli's division, (the 17th, 30th, and 61st), were ordered to attack the infantry on Bagration's left. The latter had endeavoured to cover its front by taking post in rear of the ravine formed by the small stream Owaruschna, which lies at right angles to the grand route. After a stout resistance, the French advanced with the bayonet and dislodged the enemy with a loss of 1,500 prisoners. Six guns that they had captured on the heights of Kruh were at once turned on the enemy. It was at that time that Kruh and Holubitz were abandoned, their defenders retiring beyond the Welspitz stream.

The prince sent in that direction Kaminsky, with the regiment of Archangel. The regiment fought with great determination, and offered a stubborn resistance. It was, nevertheless, surrounded more than once by the French cavalry and attacked on every side; when the cavalry sheered off, it was pounded by the artillery. At last it retired in disorder, but not before it had left 1,600 men on the ground. Kaminsky had his horse shot under him, and was only able to get back to his men by an officer having given him his own charger.

The centre of the Russian right, posted on the main road, had been pierced, and it was with considerable difficulty covered by Ouvaroff's cavalry. Bagration, nevertheless, was able to reform his troops in rear, the left resting on the Posorzitzer post-house, the right being near Kowalowitz.

The cavalry of the allies, which at the first moment had moved forward in support of the 4th column, was suddenly stayed in its progress by Murat, who was advancing with all his cavalry in the direction of Blasowitz. As Ouvaroff came forward on the Posorzitz plateau, Murat called up Walther's and d'Hautpoul's divisions, and sent Sebastiani's and Rogers's brigades against Ouvaroff's horsemen, and drove them back in rear of Bagration's infantry. The Russian infantry held its ground, but d'Hautpoul rushed at it with his division of *cuirassiers*, and by an admirable charge overthrew it, capturing a flag, 11 guns, 1 and from 1,200 to 1,800 prisoners.

There was soon no unanimity in the enemy's opposition, and the infantry which had occupied Bosenitz was well shaken. Lannes then directed Suchet and a portion of Caffarelli's divisions to advance, bringing the right forward. The battalions of the first line broke the enemy's array, driving them towards their right, and penetrating between Prince Bagration's left and Ouvaroff's cavalry. Suchet then recaptured Bosenitz, and Lannes had a battery of eighteen guns put in position between Bosenitz and Kowalowitz, to the left of the causeway leading to Brünn.

The infantry of the allied right wing had concentrated in one compact mass. In vain did Murat, with Sebastiani's brigade, Walther's dragoons and d'Hautpoul's *cuirassiers*, try and force it to lay down its arms. Suchet's battalions, supported by a battery of eighteen pieces placed to the north of the Olmütz road and protected by Kellermann, were more successful. The Russians could not withstand the shock of his charge; they were broken and dispersed in the Kowalowitz valley, leaving their artillery and 1,200 prisoners in Suchet's hands.

Bagration's fight with the French left had no connection with the rest of the battle. His troops had fought bravely, and he was allowed to carry out his retreat. As night came on, protected by Ouvaroff's cavalry, he made for Austerlitz by a flank march executed within striking distance of Suchet's division, halted then beyond Rausnitzerbach in the direction of Wellesowitz. The intense darkness of the night, however, rendered this movement less dangerous.

Bagration's march towards Austerlitz uncovered the high-road to Wischau, primitive line of operations of the allied armies, and on which all their baggage and other *impedimenta* had been left. However, the allies could not think of using it any longer as a line of retreat, for it was impossible for their centre and left to regain it. There was consequently no other alternative remaining for Bagration than to continue his retreat in the direction followed by the rest of the army.

The Action of the Russian Imperial Guard.

The Russian Imperial Guard was intended to form the reserve of the right wing of the allied armies. This corps, commanded by the Grand Duke Constantine, had bivouacked during the night of the 1st in front of Austerlitz, and in the morning, guided by Colonel Bülow, set out at the appointed hour, crossed the Walkmühl stream, and took up a position in the direction of Blasowitz.

Not only was the extent of front occupied by the allies too great for their numbers, but their reserve not in due proportion to their forces. An unforeseen accident, moreover, prevented the reserve being used as intended. The position in which Prince Liechtenstein bivouacked on the eve of the battle interfered with the march of his squadrons on the morning of the 2nd. This delay led to a considerable gap being formed in the line of battle; this had to be made good by the reserve, so that when the pinch came there was none. Under these circumstances, there was no other course open for the Grand Duke Constantine but to occupy the vacant space and deploy the Guard.

No sooner had the Grand Duke completed his deployment than the French artillery opened fire on his troops. Thereupon Count Saint Priest, with a battalion of *chasseurs* of the Guard, was ordered to occupy Blasowitz, being soon reinforced by a battalion of the Séménowski Guards.

It was not long after this that an order from the *Czar* directed the

Grand Duke to attack in the centre and to send a reinforcement towards Pratzen. In compliance with the last part of this order he sent a battalion of the Izmailowski Guard, under Colonel Khrapowitski, in the direction of Pratzen; but this battalion only appeared at the moment when the 4th column was retiring routed.

Rivaud and Caffarelli, with their two divisions, as we have already seen, supported by Walther's dragoons and Nansouty's *cuirassiers*, attacked the Russians under Saint Priest, and compelled them to evacuate Blasowitz. The village captured, the French turned their guns on the main body of the Russian Guard. At this moment Liechtenstein appeared and posted his cavalry on the left flank of the Guard.

The Grand Duke, receiving no news of the progress of the battle, was in a strange situation. He found the forces at his command very weak. He had in hand no more than six battalions and ten squadrons, with inexperienced generals and no reserve. Disdaining to retire without orders, he took ground to his left, hoping by so doing to rejoin the centre. Unaware of the defeat of the 4th column, he soon beheld heavy masses of the French bearing in his direction. What followed was the last effort that the allies made on that day.

The Grand Duke formed up for attack and deployed the Guard into two lines. In the first were the Préobragenski and. Séménowski regiments, between the two was a company of the. Grand Duke Michael's artillery. In the second line he had the Ismaïlowski regiment and the Foot Rifles of the Guard. On the right of the battalions were two field-guns. In rear of the infantry were the Hussars and the *Cuirassiers* of the Guard. The rear-guard of the corps, placed under the orders of General Malioutine, was composed of the *regiments chevaliers-gardes-cuirassiers*, the grenadiers bodyguard, and the Cossacks of the Guard.

In this formation the Guard moved a short way to its left, when it came into full view of the French columns, at that moment advancing on their right. The Guards attacked with the bayonet and drove back the cloud of skirmishers, who were covering the march of the French. Soon the latter's guns opened a heavy fire which did considerable execution.

Vandamme, who had held his own valiantly against Miloradovitch on the Pratzen plateau, received an order to execute a change of front to his right, advance on the heights and village of Aujezd, and attack the rear of the allies' left. Drouet's division had been rushed forward to replace him on the plateau. Vandamme's first care was to recall Schiner's brigade, above all the 1st battalion of the 4th regiment and the 2nd battalion of the 24th Light, two Infantry battalions which, after the capture of Stari-Winobradi, had allowed themselves to be carried away too far in their pursuit of the enemy, and had lost their formation.

At this moment the Grand Duke's regiment of Horse Guards made a vigorous charge on the enemy's flank; having first checked and driven back the French cavalry, they pushed forward and rushed at their infantry. All of a sudden Schiner's battalions found themselves about to be attacked by the reserve of the Russian Imperial Guard, a body of 2,000 heavy horsemen, and a mass of infantry led by the Grand Duke Constantine in person. Barely had they time to break into column preparatory to forming square, when the cavalry were on them, attacked them impetuously, and trampled over them, inflicting great loss. The battalion of the 4th, (nicknamed *the impetuous*) suffered most; it was literally cut to pieces, and, what was worst of all, lost its eagle.

The nature of the ground had partly concealed from the emperor, who was then near Blasowitz, the advance of the Russian Guard corps.

Saint Chamans at this time, by Soult's orders, had conducted to Napoleon General Berg, commander of the grenadiers of Little Russia, who had been made prisoner on the Pratzen heights. The emperor was closely questioning the general from the eminence where he was, when, writes Saint Chamans, a crowd of infantry could be distinctly seen coming back in disorder.

Berthier observed to his Majesty, "Behold, sire, what a crowd of prisoners they are bringing you!"

Napoleon, having very carefully examined with his field-glasses what was occurring, ordered Rapp, one of his *aides-de-camp*, to go forward with the *Chasseurs à Cheval* of the Guard and act as circumstances demanded.

★★★★★★

Rapp was an Alsatian, a man of middle height, with a bullet head, round, chubby face, small nose, and round eyes. He was a very useful officer, as he spoke and wrote German as well as French. Desaix took him to Egypt as one of his *aides-de-camp*, and after the death of that fine soldier at Marengo, out of respect for Desaix's friendship, the First Consul took Rapp on his personal staff.

He was a simple-minded man, with a good heart, but as he gave vent to his thoughts without fear, his blunt way of telling the truth often displeased Napoleon. His defence of Dantzig after the return of the army from Moscow, aided by two engineer officers, General Campredon and Colonel Richmond, was a fine action.

Rapp restored discipline, established hospitals, and protected the inhabitants from depredation. He turned the churches into stores, the schools into hospitals, the monasteries into barracks. He broke into the Dantzigers' cellars and took their wine for the sick; their storehouses he placed under the strictest guard. The Alsatian general said with his grim humour: "We are one united family in a narrow house, and it is I who keep the store-room key."

The city had to be placed in a state of defence during an unusually rigorous winter, the soil being frozen to the depth of three feet; the river which protected it was frozen hard, and presented no obstacle to the besiegers.

******

The cavalry of the Russian Guard, by a vigorous charge, had put Marshal Soult's left in disorder and caused the confusion which had been observed. As for the prisoners announced by Berthier, it was the 4th regiment of the Line which had been routed by a well-timed charge, and nothing more. There was but one moment of uncertainty: this attack brought the two Imperial Guards face to face.

Rapp set out at a gallop, formed as follows: first line, two squadrons of *chasseurs*, one squadron of mamelucks; second line, to the left, two squadrons of horse grenadiers. A light battery belonging to the 1st Corps moved forward with him. In his right rear came Bessières with four squadrons of horse grenadiers and *chasseurs* and two batteries of the Imperial Guard.

In their impetuous outset the Russian cavalry had crossed Drouet's division, which was advancing in line of columns in rear of Vandamme, and approached close to where Napoleon with his staff officers were stationed. Rapp arrived on the ground at the moment when Schiner's brigade was being cut up. Charged vigorously by the *chasseurs* and mamelucks, the troopers of the Russian Guard turned about and retired through the intervals of Drouet's division and over the dead bodies of the square they had only just broken, receiving the fire of such of the 4th Regiment of the Line as had laid down to let them go by. The Russian cavalry reformed under the protection of four guns. The French horsemen pursued onwards, captured the guns, and drove the ten squadrons of the Russian Guard on to their infantry. The mamelucks of the French Imperial cavalry cast themselves on the Préobragenski regiment, at that time dispersed in the vineyards and acting as flankers. In the combat which ensued the mamelucks lost heavily.

To attack the Russian infantry, Rapp had to dispose of eight squadrons of the second line of the Russian cavalry of the Guard (*Chevaliers Gardes* and Cossacks) which had moved forward to the rescue. The *Chevaliers Gardes* was a superb regiment, in which all the privates were well born; they were well mounted and good riders. The formation of the two guards was different. Rapp's squadrons were drawn up in echelon; the two squadrons of *chasseurs* and the mamelucks, forming the centre, were in front, his two squadrons of horse grenadiers in rear on the left flank. Bessières' four squadrons were in echelon on the right. The Russians, whose evident intention was to surround their enemy, advanced in echelon of squadrons from both flanks.

The orderly array of the two cavalries was soon succeeded by a tangle of men and horses as the two forces became engaged, and the combatants of both sides commingling, a sanguinary contest ensued, the men all fighting hand-to-hand. A clanging combat in which sword clashed upon steel breast-plates and artillery belched fire and iron. Horse and man went down in the *mêlée* and were trampled underfoot amidst shrieks and stern oaths. In this terrible shock, the French leading squadrons were driven back with the loss of their colonel. But the triumph of the *Chevaliers Gardes* was of short duration, for a battery of the French Imperial Guard came into action, and opened fire on them; this favoured the action of their opponents.

Bessières came up to the rescue at the head of the horse grenadiers of the French Imperial Guard, all picked men and well mounted. Both French and Russians fell on each other with desperate determination, but the valour and better swordsmanship of the French could not be denied, and Bessières' men triumphed over their adversaries.

Rapp states that the Russian infantry did not venture to fire, that all was confusion, that the troops fought man to man. The *Czar* and the Emperor of Austria, stationed on an eminence at a little distance from the field of battle, witnessed the Guard, which was expected to decide the victory, cut to pieces by a handful of brave men. A decided advantage was gained with a very small force over the enemy's chosen troops.

Bernadotte's infantry, which had come up at the double on the trail of the cavalry, rushed at the infantry of the Russian Guard. Then the Russian infantry and cavalry all retired pell-mell, and in the greatest disorder recrossed the Krenowitz stream. Of the many charges delivered on that eventful day none was so well fought and effective as this. The combatants on both sides were the flower of their army, and were worthy of each other. From that moment the battle was lost and won.

This sanguinary engagement of the two Imperial Guards, the most desperate that had taken place in the whole campaign, did not last more than five minutes. It decided the fate of the day, for the Russians, pierced through the centre, fought no longer for victory, but for existence. It cost the *Chevaliers Gardes* a loss of 16 officers and 200 *cuirassiers*; nevertheless, it gained time for the infantry to get out of the broken ground. The 3rd and 4th squadrons, which charged the French cavalry when it was engaged fighting with the Séménowski regiment, fared worst. Attacked in front and in flank by the French horse grenadiers and *chasseurs*, they experienced a terrible carnage. Of the 4th squadron only eighteen men survived. Prince Repnine, the commandant of the squadron, and several severely wounded officers, were captured.

This regiment was recruited from the young Russian nobility; it lost heavily because the troopers had swaggered and boasted of what they would do to the French. Rumour of this had reached the ears of the French soldiers, and had greatly irritated them. As they closed with their antagonists they cried out, "Now we shall give the ladies of St. Petersburg something to cry for!"

What remained of the *Chevaliers Gardes* crossed the stream and reformed. While this bloody encounter was taking place, three regiments of Drouet's division, led by Gérard, had advanced in the space left vacant by General Vandamme, and covered the rallying of the two battalions so severely punished by the Russian cavalry. Drouet soon advanced and drove the Russian Guard on to the village of Kreznowitz, captured it, and made many prisoners. Both the cavalry and infantry of the Guard had to give way, and their standards and their artillery were lost. At this moment General Lobanoff arrived with the regiment of Bodyguard Grenadiers, and deployed its three battalions in front of the village of Austerlitz. A manoeuvre which deceived Napoleon, who, believing it to be the head of General Essen's corps, issued orders not to press the action any further in that quarter. (Lieutenant-General Mikkailovski-Danilovaki, *Relation de la Campagne de 1805 (Austerlitz)*.

This brilliant feat of the French Imperial Guard decided the day. Following it, the reserve of the allied army had been borne back above a mile from the battlefield. It was 1 p.m., and there could exist no doubt about victory siding with the French. There was no longer any connection between the centre and the flanks of the allies; the second act of the drama was about to open with a vigorous attack on their left.

The following instance will show with what determination the French horsemen engaged. On the evening which preceded the battle, a cavalry non-commissioned officer wagered his watch against fifty golden dollars with one of his comrades that in the morrow's battle he would gain the cross. In a brilliant charge against superior forces, this non-commissioned officer plunged into the midst of the enemy's squadrons, killed five men, and captured a flag. He was all covered with blood; above all, on the face, so that his eyes were no longer visible. As he was returning to his corps, which had formed up in rear of the emperor, Napoleon met him, and told him, "You have done enough, my friend, for your share in the battle; go and get your wounds looked to."

Wiping his face with the captured flag, the non-commissioned officer gaily replied, "I am not at all wounded; this, sire, is not my blood, but the blood of others."

Pleased with this spirited reply, the emperor promoted him on the spot, and gave him the cross.

Strangely enough his comrade, the man with whom he had waged the bet the previous evening, came up about the same time badly wounded by a pistol-shot fired at him by a general officer whom he was bringing in prisoner. When he presented his antagonist to the emperor, Napoleon laughingly said, "What another cross of honour? Why, if this continues much longer, we shall have either to suppress the order or decorate the entire army."

After the defeat of the Guard cavalry, the allies had no more hope left, and did not attempt any important attack. The combat lingered still for some hours on their extreme left; but then the battle went on, not for victory, but for dear life, and to gain a retreat. All honour to the brave who would not abandon the contest without a further effort, though for some time they had begun to look on victory as gone.

Having chased the allies from the plateau, and being master of the villages of Pratzen and Blasowitz, Napoleon not only suspended all action against the Austro-Russian centre, but did not molest its retreat.

Vandamme's change of front to the right was not completed until after the overthrow of the Russian cavalry. Leaving Bernadotte in position on the heights of Krenowitz, the emperor now brought forward his Guard and Oudinot's grenadiers, bent on finishing the contest on his right. It was 2 p.m. when he arrived on the heights of Aujezd with his Guard, which was ordered to occupy the *Chapelle de Saint Antoine*. Oudinot's grenadiers at first were left on the heights of Pratzen, subsequently a brigade was sent under Duroc in the direction of Kobelnitz, with the object of taking Przybyszewsky's and Langeron's columns in flank. Davout was to resume the offensive.

Buxhowden sent a portion of the 1st column (about 6,000 men) by way of Aujezd to the help of the centre. This force tried to charge Saint Hilaire's division. Vandamme, however, was already arriving on the plateau of the Chapelle Saint Antoine, and he sent General Ferrey, at the head of his brigade, composed of the 46th and 57th, forward to attack the advancing Russians. Ferrey charged and destroyed them, Aujezd fell into his hands, with over 3,000 prisoners and all the enemy's artillery.

After the defeat of the allies' right and centre, the French descended from the Pratzen plateau and marched with all speed to take the enemy's left wing in rear at the moment when Davout was about to attack them in front. Lejeune carried the emperor's orders to Davout to advance briskly and support the centre. That marshal, however, had already commenced that movement, and was striving hard to carry Mönitz. A desperate fight ensued round that village; its main street, four or five hundred yards long, and fairly wide, was chocked up with the dead and wounded of both armies, piled one on the top of the other. Davout had driven the Russians out of it three times. By a further effort, he cleared the village once more and drove the Russians under the fire of Saint Hilaire's and Legrand's divisions, which attacked them in their turn and routed them.

The Austro-Russians found themselves placed between two fires, and fell into an indescribable confusion. All ranks got mixed together, each man seeking nothing else but to save himself by flight.

All who had crossed the Goldbach were hustled by Legrand and Friant, and either captured or driven on to the Kobelnitz pond. Others, who were endeavouring to escape to the north, were surrounded by Oudinot's grenadiers and compelled to lay down their arms.

Danilevski declares that the determined resistance of the 3rd column favoured the retirement of Dochtouroff and Langeron, for, as long as Soult had to contend with Przybyszewsky, he was prevented from sending any of his troops to act on their rear. As the French captured Sokolnitz, they made the reserves of the 3rd column under Wimpfen prisoners; Przybyszewsky, ignorant of what was occurring elsewhere, his soldiers having expended the whole of their ammunition, and receiving no orders, then marched in the direction of Kobelnitz, hoping to join the 4th column which had been detailed to march in that direction, but the French were on him, the whole of his force was killed or captured, including Przybyszewsky, Stryck, and Selkhoff.

Legrand came up with a Russian column which had reached Kobelnitz, and drove it into the marsh, where the greater part were drowned. The rest endeavoured to reach Schlapanitz, but were captured.

We have stated that after the defeat of Kamenski's brigade Kutuzoff despatched orders to Buxhowden to retire. Notwithstanding these orders, Buxhowden did not retire, for, not knowing that the battle in the centre had been hopelessly lost, he thought that by hurling back the French right he would be able to restore the chances of victory. Kienmayer and Stutterheim were of the same opinion. It was only when they beheld the French coming down on their rear that they became convinced of the uselessness of a longer resistance beyond Telnitz. Buxhowden then began his retreat with Dochtouroff's column through that village, Langeron being ordered to conform. He himself was fortunate in withdrawing and reaching Austerlitz with a few battalions.

Deprived of the regiments of Phanagoria and of Riajsk, which had followed Kutuzoff, and after the defeat of the regiment of Koursk—sent, as we have seen, to the assistance of Kaminsky—Langeron wended his way back to Sokolnitz, where Olsoufieff, with the 8th Foot Chasseurs and the regiments of Wibourg and Perm, was very hotly engaged with the French. When he eventually retired on Telnitz, he could only bring away two of his regiments; the regiment of Perm had been almost entirely destroyed by the enemy. This regiment alone lost in killed, wounded, and prisoners, 5 superior officers, 39 company officers, and 1,684 non-commissioned officers and men; also 6 guns.

Dochtouroff, who was an able and stubborn general, was in no way deterred by the fate which had overtaken the 2nd and 3rd columns, and offered a very determined resistance. He recalled Kienmayer's cavalry, which was at the time contending in a desultory manner against Bourcier's dragoons, and directed General Loewis to form a rearguard at Telnitz, which should hinder the French as long as possible, so that they might be kept from molesting his rear. Having then rallied what remained of Langeron's troops, he took post in front of the lakes of Mönitz and Satschan. There, aided by the fire of thirty-eight field-pieces, he tried to stay the progress of Saint Hilaire's division.

The village of Telnitz, which was surrounded by ditches, offered a certain protection, which was fully taken advantage of to stay the enemy. A Russian regiment which General Loewis had posted behind these ditches defended itself with resolution.

In rear of Telnitz, between that village and Mönitz, was some high ground, the right of which rested on the pond. To this point the Russian infantry retired, under the protection of the Austrian cavalry, whose ranks were thinned by continuous discharges of grape.

The cavalry occupied the above-mentioned hill in order to protect a portion of the column, which had fallen into great confusion. The French had by this time succeeded in getting possession of Telnitz, in which village they captured many Russian stragglers. After which they opened a heavy fire on the flanks of O'Reilly's cavalry, putting a large number of horsemen *hors de combat*. Nothing, however, could prevent these brave men from continuing to protect the retreat of the Russians; they held their ground with the greatest intrepidity. General Degenfeld's artillery played on the French, and interfered with the accuracy of their fire.

Soon the end of the battle came. As the French were advancing on all sides, Dochtouroff commenced his retreat. The first column had to march exposed to the fire of the artillery of Napoleon's Guard in action on the heights of Chapelle Saint Antoine. On nearing Aujezd, it encountered Vandamme's division which barred the way. The head of the column was then directed to the right towards the marshes of the Littawa. The bridge over that stream broke down under the weight of the guns, and the troops were thrown into disorder by the enemy's cannonade; unable to move forward on the crowded dyke, they attempted to find a way across the frozen lake of Satschan. The ice was thin, and under the weight of the men, and pounded by the French guns which had been brought to bear on the lake, it broke, and some hundreds of men were drowned. Dochtouroff, who brought up the rear, gave up retiring in this direction. Protected up to the last by Kienmayer's cavalry, he wended his way back in the direction of Telnitz; then, following a poor and narrow dam running between the ponds of Satschan and Mönitz, he led the remains of his force to Ottinitz.

★★★★★★

There having been some controversy regarding this catastrophe on the ice, the statements of various writers have been gathered in the Appendix. The account in the official bulletin was evidently a great exaggeration; still, most writers agree that the ice did break under the weight of the troops, and that a number of men were drowned.

Chapter 14

After the Battle

As the short December day closed and night came on, the noise of the contest gradually died away. The thunder of the artillery slackened, and soon ceased altogether; only the groans of the thousands of unfortunate wounded covering the field in every direction, and the voice of the search parties, disturbed the solemn silence of the night. And this long winter night was intensely dark.

Availing themselves of the darkness, the allies retired from the gore-deluged field. As the two monarchs were withdrawing from the scene of their defeat, the loud shouts of the French greeting their emperor reached their ears. The *Czar* was distracted.

The defeat had been complete: and in reality, of the allied forces only Bagration's corps, though severely punished, retained its formation; the rest were in a frightful confusion.

Kutuzoff and Prince Wolkonsky were marching with the regiments of Phanagoria and Riajsk on the road to Hungary; Buxhowden and Langeron, having got round Aujezd and crossed the Littawa, with two battalions, were marching up that stream, making for Austerlitz; the Russian Guard was formed up in rear of that village. Prince Bagration, unable to withstand Suchet's attack, had directed his forces on Rausnitz; his left was between Austerlitz and Krenowitz. Ouvaroff and Liechtenstein were with the remnants of the 4th column. The Rausnitz and Littawa brooks separated the contending armies.

After the battle, Napoleon occupied about the same position which the allies held on the 1st. Lannes and Murat were in sight of Rausnitz; Bernadotte on the heights of Prasnitz; Soult was beyond the Pratzen heights by Aujezd; he had in second line the Imperial Guard and Oudinot's grenadiers; Davout was close to Telnitz and Sokolnitz.

The termination of the contest on their right had compelled the allies to abandon their natural line of retreat, the road to Olmütz, and they followed the road leading towards Hungary by Göding. They were saved from a greater disaster by retreating in that direction, for the Olmütz line of retreat lay too much in rear of their right flank, and could only with difficulty be reached by their centre and left.

On the right, it was about midnight when Bagration, who at first commenced to withdraw in the direction of Olmütz, in doing which he misled the French, reached the village of Austerlitz. There he found Miloradovitch with some troops, purposely posted to retard the pursuit. Liechtenstein, and what there remained of Kolowrat's column, had some time before taken the road to Hungary.

The *Czar*, with his Imperial Guard which had rested for some time at Hodiezetz, resumed the march for Göding as soon as he received the news of Bagration's arrival at Austerlitz. Early on the 3rd of December, the Austro-Russian right and centre were united at Cejtsch. There they were soon joined by the broken remnants of their left wing.

Having passed the dyke, the Austrian generals who protected Doctonroff's retreat halted on the heights of Neuhoff, or Neudorf, and tried to restore order in the Russian battalions, which still formed a corps of at least 8,000 men. It was then over four o'clock in the afternoon, and it was already beginning to get dark. The retreat was then continued to Beschowitz; the troops, drenched by a heavy fall of rain which completed the destruction of the roads, marched the whole night. Much of the Russian artillery stood still harnessed on the edge of the water or overturned in the ponds. The few guns still available sank in the sloughs and were abandoned. The regiments of O'Reilly alone brought off their artillery. The cavalry furnished the rear-guard, which the French, who had halted at the dyke, did not think of pursuing.

The Austrian cavalry retired by Reichsmanandorf, and as soon as all the remaining squadrons and artillery had got to a safe distance, Kienmayer took post at Nischkowitz to watch the enemy's movements.

Essen's corps received orders on the 3rd to go by way of Kremsier to Ungarisch Hradisch, moving south, following the course of the march.

From Cejtsch the allies, formed in a single column, proceeded to Coding, and on the 4th arrived at Holies on the Hungarian side of the March. Bagration's rear-guard, subsequently reinforced by Kienmayer's squadrons, covered the movement on the side of Uhrzilz.

Merveldt, who was bringing a small detachment from Hungary, had reached Lundenburg on the day of the battle. He was kept on the left bank of the river, and ordered to advance as far as Eisgrub. The object of this movement was to retard the French as much as possible.

On the 3rd, the weather was simply dreadful; the French found, a quarter of a mile from the great pond, abandoned in the marshes, a park of over one hundred guns with their wagons. At every instant, isolated or wounded Russians were captured, unfortunates who really did not know which way to turn. The entire desertion of the artillery and of their baggage showed too clearly the condition the allies were in.

War, that most detestable scourge which periodically afflicts poor humanity, had left its gruesome mark all over the battleground. The angel of death had visited the land and laid his ruthless hand over the strong and brave sons of three mighty empires. The battlefield was a real *Glen Fruin* (a glen of sorrow). In places where the fight had been most stubborn, and the two opposing sides had poured volleys into each other, or had closed with the bayonet, bodies in all attitudes lay stretched in long lines. In others the dead lay in little groups, as if they had crawled to breathe their last together, comrades in life and in death. Single bodies showed where skirmishers had fallen.

Where the steel-clad *cuirassier* and the bold Austrian or Muscovite dragoon had crossed their weapons, some of the finest specimens of humanity had been done to death. Their beauty, their strength, and their daring, now all a thing of the past.

The cruel artillery, vomiting case and canister, had spared no one in the attacking columns. Large wedge-shaped masses of men covered the ground, soon to be thrown into deep long trenches, and wept alone in some humble home or cottage far, far away. Glorious war! Can it be so with the anguish and sufferings of women and children?

The ground all round reddened with gore, the fetid smell of the battlefield prevailing all. Wounded men restlessly tossing about in their last agony, uttering piercing cries of pain, demanding a draught of water to cool a piercing thirst. Others patiently waiting for some sick bearer, if not a loving comrade, to take him to a place of safety, where his injuries might be attended to.

Of the dead, some are mutilated beyond recognition, others lying with a look of peace, with parted lips which seem to be smiling. A vile horde of scavengers, men who follow in the wake of every army, are busy rifling the dead.

Muskets, sabres, lances, knapsacks, helmets, and a multitude of other head-gear, dismounted cannon, useless limbers, abandoned wagons, lie in all parts of the field with the dead around them. The ground is cut up and rent as by an earthquake, and the soil is furrowed by shot. Horse, the companion of man, has not fared better than his rider. Hundreds lie dead all over the battlefield, in most cases by the side of the men they carried so gallantly in their last charge. Hundreds lie maimed and wounded in patient agony, bearing their pain till some pitying soldier kindly ends their sufferings. The horses lie in all directions, such as are not yet dead, wagging their pain-racked heads to the right and to the left, emitting that very peculiar plaint of the dying horse so dolorous and heart-rending.

There are still other horrors for the poor wounded, owing to the many riderless and scared horses which rush all over the battle-ground in search of their companions. In their mad gallop, the poor beasts crush the dead and finish the wounded.

It took three days after Austerlitz to clear the field of battle completely of the wounded.

The Emperor Francis had not followed the *Czar* in his retreat to Holitsch. He had decided to stand by his bad fortune, cost him what it would. Between seven and eight on the evening of the battle, he sent from Cejtsch one of Lis officers to Napoleon to propose an armistice and arrange for an interview. Before taking this step, Francis II. had asked the *Czar* if he approved of his holding a conference with the conqueror.

"Act according to your own interests," replied Alexander; "as for myself, Napoleon will see me again in a year."

Prince John of Liechtenstein, the officer sent by the Emperor of Austria, did not reach Napoleon's headquarters which, late after the conclusion of the battle, had been established at the post-house of Posoritz, much before 4 a.m. of the 3rd.

Crossard, on the authority of Colonel Wimpfen, of the Austrian headquarters, states that the prince told the Emperor Francis after the battle:

> Your Majesty has led us into difficult circumstances, and must face them like the rest of us.

The prince, who, as proprietor of almost the whole of Moravia, must have been particularly hit by the course of events, evidently alluded to his strong opposition to the war, which had been disregarded by the emperor. Napoleon did not refuse either the armistice nor the interview, but, being keen to gather all possible fruits from his victory, delayed his interview with the Emperor of Austria till the following day. In the meantime, he issued his orders for the pursuit, which he intended should be conducted with all possible vigour.

Murat's obstinacy, however, retarded the operation, for he put the army on a false scent. Having passed the night near Rausnitz, the prince had become persuaded that the Austro-Russians were tailing off in the direction of Olmütz. Napoleon came to the same conclusion, for it was not impossible that a portion of the allies might have regained during the night their proper line of retreat. On the 3rd of December, Murat, at the head of seventy-two squadrons of cavalry, started at a gallop towards Wischau; Lannes and Bernadotte, who had been directed to support his movement, followed him, and so did most of the army. It was only later during the morning, when the army headquarters were transferred to Austerlitz, that Napoleon became aware that, in retiring, the allied army had followed the road to Hungary. He then immediately countermanded the orders, and recalled Murat.

Had Bernadotte properly executed a manoeuvre which had been assigned to him, the entire army of the enemy might have been captured. He had been ordered to attack the infantry of the Russian Guard; but having done so, broken and chased the flying corps for a league, instead of pursuing his advantage, he fell back to his first position, where Napoleon, to his great surprise, found him remaining inactive in the evening. By continuing to advance, he would have obtained possession of the road from Austerlitz to Holitsch, and thus have intercepted the retreat of the Austrians and Russians. (De Ségur, *Un Aide-de-Camp de Napoleon.*)

The meeting of the Emperor Francis and the victor of Austerlitz took place at the Spalenymuhl mill, where Napoleon awaited him. Saint-Chamans narrates that, whilst the two emperors were talking, the French staff officers entered into conversation with the Austrians. The latter openly avowed their detestation of the Russians, disgusted as they were by their haughtiness and insolence. One of them kept telling us, whilst rubbing his hands with delight, "What a battle, gentlemen! You have killed 30,000 Russians, 30,000 Russians!"

In his interview with the Emperor Francis, Napoleon appeared willing not to demand any cession of territory if the Russians were included in the peace, and would agree to close their ports to British trade. Otherwise, the territory of Venice was to be incorporated with

Napoleon and Francis II

the kingdom of Italy and the Tyrol bestowed on Bavaria. The *Czar* firmly rejected the clause relating to the exclusion of British exports, and Austria was left to bear the consequences.

At Holitsch, the *Czar* took the resolution of breaking off entirely with Austria. Depressed by the scenes of horror which he had witnessed in the battle, and disgusted with the part of generalissimo, Alexander was too willing to ratify the terms by which alone Napoleon conceded an armistice to the Emperor of Austria.

There were not a few Russians, and officers also, in high position, who reviled the Austrians with having betrayed them. These men urged the necessity of seeking vengeance on them, and demanded to be led back to Russia as quickly as possible, averring that their army was incapable of fighting any longer.

The Russian account relates how, on the 5th day of the retreat, Kutuzoff received, through the Austrian general, Strauch, a despatch from the Emperor Francis to ask, should the armistice be broken, if he were authorised to resume hostilities. The necessity for ascertaining this point had arisen from the demands Napoleon had made in the preliminary discussions. The Russian general replied that his sovereign had pledged his honour to Napoleon, and as for himself, having received an order to take his troops back to Russia by the shortest route, he was no longer at liberty to retrace his steps.

After the surrender of Ulm, most of the Austrian generals confessed how disagreeable the war was for them, and with what intense displeasure they saw a Russian Army in their country. In the latter portion of the campaign, everything tended to show that the understanding between the allies was anything but cordial. Czartorinski confesses that they soon came to detest each other, and that they hated the French less.

The Russian generals had supplicated the *Czar* before Austerlitz to leave the army, as his presence rendered the operations very delicate and difficult. They were very desirous that he should not expose himself to useless dangers. Czartorinski wished him to keep away from the army, leaving it entirely to its generals, and keeping just near enough to give that impulse which the operations required.

Napoleon was generous towards the vanquished, and let the Russians return to their country unmolested, though, by continuing his operations after the battle, he might have surrounded and captured them. Austerlitz, with their great losses, should have incapacitated them from playing any military part in Europe for a number of years to come; yet in little more than two years Prussia beheld Russia by her side in the plains of Poland.

Austerlitz is the most celebrated of Napoleon's battles, and may be justly regarded as the most splendid of his many victories. What made Austerlitz a masterpiece was the simplicity of the conception and the precision of the execution. It decided not only the day, but the campaign, and not only the campaign, but the war.

It showed all the truth of Souvoroff's remark:

> A moment decides a battle, an hour the result of a campaign, a single day the fate of empires.

Never before had the emperor gained such an overwhelming- victory, such a thorough success; though it must be admitted that never either had he been so much aided by the faults of his opponents. That he allowed them to fall into errors, and even encouraged them to commit them, only tended to enhance his great genius, to show his grasp of the art of war.

A French author wrote, "*Et s'élançant du sol des Pyramides pour voir briller le soleil d'Austerlitz.*" ("And darting from the floor of the Pyramids to see the Austerlitz sun shine.") The Austerlitz sun brightened the battlefield principally in the forenoon. In the latter part of the day, the sky became overcast. As the Russians were lost to sight in the neighbourhood of the ponds, the sun disappeared behind a bank of dense clouds. Snow soon fell, as the curtain drops at the conclusion of the last act of a drama. The sounds of strife were hushed into silence with the advent of an early winter night.

Napoleon could well say, "Soldiers, I am satisfied with you" ("*Soldats, je suis content de vous*"), for he had not won the battle with the whole strength of his army. Many corps, part of Bernadotte's, the infantry of the Guard, Oudinot's grenadiers, had not done more than fire a few shots. The Russian accounts made the French Army stronger than theirs by 20,000 men, but it was not so. Thiers declares that 45,000 French had fought against 90,000 allies, and his estimate, after all, was not very far from the truth.

At Austerlitz, the confidence of the French troops in their superiority was sufficient to make up for their inferiority in numbers. In an interview Savary had with the *Czar*, he challenged the accuracy of the Russian account. On the contrary, he declared that the French forces numbered 25,000 men less than the army of the allies. He avowed that Napoleon "had manoeuvred much, and that some divisions combated at many points in different directions. It was that which apparently multiplied our numbers." What influence being well commanded has on the operations of war! The emperor proved that sagacity and clear-headedness are more potent than any other force.

The French soldiers were drunk with joy and incessant in their acclamations, but the battlefield was dreadful to behold; it presented a most horrible spectacle. Napoleon remained on the ground till nearly midnight to supervise personally the removal of the wounded. Here and there some brave old warrior mortally attained would by a superhuman effort raise himself to utter for a last time a feeble *Vive l'Empereur* as Napoleon went by, not unlike the cry of the Roman gladiators in the arena, *Ave Imperator, morituri te salutant*.

A century ago infantry manoeuvred on the battlefield in masses, and large bodies of infantry in that compact formation were easily handled. Now the destructive power of firearms, even at long ranges, has necessitated a greater development of the fighting line; to reduce casualties, the infantry must occupy a more extended space, with less depth.

In the campaign of 1805, the French troops were more elastic than those of the allies; the intellect of the soldiers had been expanded by the scenes of the Revolution, and by many campaigns in foreign lands. While in those days the much cherished ideas of equality had conferred on the French soldier a great measure of initiative, their Russian adversaries were still nothing better than mere machines. The keen intelligence of the French gave their officers great superiority in point of manoeuvring.

In the opening stage of the battle of Austerlitz, when the left of the allies strove to cross the Goldbach, the rifle of the present day and the better quality of the powder would have been of great assistance to the French. The power which long-range arms give to the defence would have enabled Soult's and Davout's men to hold the enemy at bay with far greater ease. For the same reason, the charges of cavalry against infantry would in most cases have been regarded as impracticable.

The advantages of accuracy and range of modern small arms have brought about a system of fighting utterly different from what obtained at Austerlitz. Then, fighting was done in close order, shoulder to shoulder, the opposing forces, as a rule, being well in sight of each other. Now fighting is done in extended order, the men being enjoined to take all possible advantage of cover. In those times, a general could personally control the progress of the battle; in our days the soldiers are very much less under the control of their battalion and company officers. In the early part of last century, and for many years after, canister and case-shot were very effective, and each discharge swept away a number of men from the enemy's ranks; now we do not possess anything equal to them for the successful checking of an advance, we have no thorough substitute for them; shrapnel is the nearest to them, but it has very much less effect, as the troops manoeuvre in extended order.

Contented as we are with our present army rifle, with its lightness, its handiness, its facility of loading, and the certainty of its fire, even at long ranges, we can barely conceive the difficulties the conquerors of Europe had to contend against a hundred years ago. Here are some in the words of Jean Morvan, (*Le Soldat Impérial*):

> When he intends firing, the soldier must tear his cartridge between his teeth, drop the powder it contains down the barrel of his gun, wad it, by using the iron ram-rod—which gives more animation to the fire—by pushing down a portion of the casing of the cartridge, then spit the ball into the barrel, pushing it down till it rests on the wad, which is often a difficult matter, inasmuch as the arm soon becomes foul; then cock the piece, pour some powder into the pan and the touch-hole. These operations accomplished, he may hope that the shot will go off, if the flint will only give a spark, which seldom happens more than once in fifteen times, and if the touch-hole has not been choked by the preceding shots.
>
> Under such conditions he may count on discharging four bullets in three minutes; given, however, that he has been adequately instructed and is not deployed three deep. When, however, firing is continuous, and it may become necessary to cleanse his weapon, in any way he best can—often by making water down the barrel—and to free the touch-hole with the pin, the rapidity of fire is considerably reduced....
>
> Firing will be effective up to 100 metres, and accurate up to 200. To reach an opponent beyond that, it was necessary to aim above the enemy's head, for a distance difficult to lay down with exactness, or to use the thumb in the way of a sight, a practice which militated greatly against precision. Given that the powder was of good quality, the bullet could kill to a distance of 450 or 500 metres. Rifled muskets were more deadly, but the ball having to be forced home with a mallet, although

it gave a more satisfactory weapon, did so slacken the fire that they were reserved for the Tyrolese chamois hunters.

Each infantry soldier and dragoon was provided with fifty cartridges and three flints, and kept the lock covered with a piece of linen. Old campaigners added to the regulation bullet another cut into four parts.

Returning to our subject, General Foy writes, (*History of the War in the Peninsula*):

The Battle of Austerlitz, may be accounted as the most scientific in modern history, and was not the least decisive one.

It made Napoleon the master of Europe, the giver of crowns.

Austerlitz was greater than Marengo. At Marengo the battle for the French commenced with defeat and ended in victory; at Austerlitz the French were victorious all through. In this campaign everything appeared to partake of the marvellous; still Napoleon had left nothing to chance, had penetrated the enemy's intentions, had struck promptly, and held his reserve, and a large one too, in hand, in case it should have been needed.

The glory of the campaign, and of its crowning event, the battle of the 2nd of December, were all his. Unlike in the Marengo campaign, there was no brave Desaix, nor dashing Kellermann, whom the envious and the ignorant could make partakers of his glory. The brilliancy of his genius shone forth in all its lustre, proclaimed to the world by this campaign. In several instances he had been risky, but he was young, and could well pin his faith on fortune which had befriended him hitherto in a most providential manner. A man like him who had found himself in many difficulties, and had emerged triumphantly from them all, soon learns to hope and trust in his star.

Not only did Napoleon show his accustomed vigour but also consummate ability in drawing the allies to the battlefield of his own selection. Subtlety more than force was to come to his aid. Savary says of the emperor that such infallible insight had he in scenting the approach of an event, that it rendered him able to make it turn in the way which most suited his purpose.

After having gone back for two days, Napoleon left the initiative in the attack to his adversaries. He had guessed what was their object, how they would take measures for overlapping his right with the intent of cutting his army off from Vienna. He encouraged them so to do; but in carrying out this manoeuvre the Russian general unwittingly denuded his centre, which was exactly what Napoleon was anxiously waiting for. He was tarrying only for the opportune moment to seize the Pratzen plateau, to cut the allied army in two, and to take in reverse the columns that were intended to overcome and destroy his right.

The Prince of Liechtenstein, in his interview with Napoleon after the battle, when the Emperor Francis sent him to sue for peace, told him:

> Your Majesty has nothing more to conquer; your victory is so complete that nothing can be added to it.

Langeron, speaking of this battle, said:

> I had already seen several lost battles, but could never have conceived such a defeat.

Decision never excludes circumspection; with all his well-known repugnance to a retreat from the battlefield, in referring to his dispositions for the battle of Austerlitz, we find Napoleon writing:

> All was ready for the retreat as for the battle; the marshals, grouped round the emperor, awaited his last orders. Everyone knew his role in either operation.

Everything had been foreseen, even the loss of the battle. In such a case, a double line of retreat had been indicated, either on the Danube by the Krems bridge, which was carefully guarded, or across Bohemia by way of Iglau.

De Ségur (*Un Aide-de-camp de Napoléon*) writes:

> Never was a battlefield better reconnoitred and better prepared. What seemed to draw his (Napoleon's) attention most on the 29th was the defence of the Santon. He hastened to have it fortified, armed, and provisioned like a fort. Several times he sent me there to repeat his orders, and to see that they were executed: not satisfied with this, he went there himself and mounted the acclivity on foot.

Napoleon mistrusted Bernadotte, and Ségur relates how he was ordered to go to the marshal to repeat his orders and see to their execution. Bernadotte, who resented Napoleon's having become his master, had shown a want of good-will; but, for all his obduracy, he was one of the most able and most cunning generals the emperor had.

In this campaign, Napoleon's genius overcame many dangers, for he really had no assured communications, nor did he stay his advance after Ulm to form a reliable base in Bavaria. He would listen to no remonstrances, to no timid counsels; he went forward, and fortune, which always befriends the brave, gave him Vienna, the passage of the Danube, and a retreating enemy nearly up to Olmütz.

At Austerlitz, the army had manoeuvred as if on parade. The French generals acted their part and handled their troops with that ability which is the natural result of a military eye and experience combined. They advanced boldly when necessary; otherwise, taking advantage of the inequalities of the ground, concealed their movements and sheltered their troops from the enemy's fire. Drilled for two years in extended movements at the camp of Boulogne, the French ascended the heights of Pratzen with remarkable precision and quickness, and fell like a terrible avalanche on the flank of the enemy's fourth column. The French cavalry maintained the high reputation it had acquired under Moreau at Hochstett; it dashed at the enemy with its ordinary spirit, and in many brilliant charges inflicted serious losses on their opponents.

So gallantly did the French troops conduct themselves in the battle that Napoleon was not obliged to bring forward his reserves. A fact which caused the deepest sorrow to a number of brave soldiers who were deprived of an opportunity of distinguishing themselves.

Bravery is not all that is required to gain battles; that quality must go hand-in-hand with a sound knowledge of the art of war. Perhaps few of the French officers of that period were well read in books referring to the military art, but they had served a good apprenticeship in the many wars of the Republic. Most of them had gained much useful experience and had seen a good deal. Probably in the allied armies there were generals every whit as brave as the French; none, however, were quite so daring and enterprising, none had in so full a measure quaffed the cup of victory or were so eager for glory. The French had now come to look upon victory as their right, and they bravely held out under the most trying circumstances until it was theirs.

******

On the eve of Austerlitz, Napoleon, while inspecting a corps of grenadiers, threatened a soldier with arrest on account of his uniform. The soldier replied, "An arrest is too small a matter; you may dismiss me, provided always that the dismissal takes place after tomorrow, for I do not relish being dishonoured."

✶✶✶✶✶✶

Napoleon's rewards for the lower ranks were very simple—more honour than honours—and could give no offence.

It will be quite sufficient for you to say, 'I was at the Battle of Austerlitz,' to which people will reply, 'Behold, a hero!'

Had he rewarded his generals with the same Spartan measure, they might have proved more faithful to him in 1814; but they were full of honours and riches, and this very naturally made them anxious to enjoy these good things in peace.

The reader may perhaps think that we have over-estimated the bravery displayed by the French Army in this campaign. He may think so; nevertheless, he will look through the annals of war in vain to find any troops that fought with the same spirit and confidence in themselves and their leaders for such a long period of years as did the French soldiers of the first Republic and the first Empire. In the first period they were exalted by love of country and national glory; in the second, inspirited by love of glory and infatuation for their warrior emperor. To such a pitch did events raise their courage that they were able to conquer most of the nations of continental Europe.

The enemies they met on the field of Austerlitz were in every way worthy of them. General Mikhailovski-Danilevski relates how, on the 2nd of December 1820, the Czar Alexander, having at his court come across Miloradovitch, addressed him thus: "General, this is a sad anniversary of an unfortunate day for our army. I remember it well after fifteen years." (When the Russians occupied Paris in 1814, the *Czar* refused to destroy the bridge of Austerlitz, or even to change its name. "It is sufficient for me," he said, "that it has been crossed by my armies.")

"Your Imperial Majesty will allow me not to be of the same opinion," replied Miloradovitch; "I cannot call a day in which our officers as well as our soldiers fought like lions disastrous."

✶✶✶✶✶✶

Savary relates a curious fact to show the endurance of the Russian soldiers. He states that when he went to the Russian headquarters at Olmütz, he observed that the soldiers slept without their clothes, some without even a shirt, round the bivouac fires, and this at the end of November—*Mémoires du Duc de Rovigo*, vol. ii.

✶✶✶✶✶✶

Doctouroff conducted the retreat of the Russian left in a most masterly way, and was only overwhelmed after a most spirited resistance. Loewis held to the village of Telnitz, and kept the French at bay for a considerable time. Kienmayer and O'Reilly covered the retreat, quite regardless of their cruel losses. The regiments of Hesse-Homburg, Szeckler, and O'Reilly were the last to quit the battlefield.

The bitter recollection of Austerlitz was never effaced from the *Czar's* memory: the angel of death had visited too many of the families of his mighty empire. No one more than he could seriously bewail his great inferiority to Napoleon as a general. Though the Russian soldiers behaved with heroic bravery, their commanders failed to make the best use of the splendid material at their disposal.

The Russians admitted a loss in killed, wounded, and prisoners of 21,000 men, with 133 guns. The Austrians lost 5,922 men; their loss in guns has never been stated. French writers set down Napoleon's loss at less than 8,000 men, of which number 760 were not accounted for. Bernadotte, as he returned from Austerlitz, computed the French loss at 12,000 men.

Mathieu Dumas makes the number of the allies placed *hors de combat* from all sources to amount to more than 40,000 men (out of 82,000 combatants). He reckons 10,000 killed in the battle, 19,000 Russians and 600 Austrians captured, and about 10,000 men wounded, dispersed, or missing. The artillery fire, playing on dense columns huddled in the low ground, cannot but have been very deadly. Amongst the prisoners were 3 lieutenant-generals, 20 superior officers, and more than 8,000 other officers.

Eighteen thousand Russian prisoners left Brünn for France, divided into several columns, escorted at the rate of one French foot soldier for every ten Russians, one horseman for every hundred. (Saint-Chamans relates that he saw 20,000 Russian prisoners march out of Brünn, that the convoys moved in great order, that the soldiers were fed with, regularity and were comfortably clad.) These prisoners might have been sent by the most direct route over the bridge of Krems, but Napoleon never lost an opportunity of impressing the imagination of the populations with the magnitude of his power; these prisoners, therefore, were marched with much show through the streets of Vienna.

The French garrison of Vienna was to make their passage a sort of feast day. The prisoners were not to stop an instant in Vienna or in the suburbs. It was ordered that they were never to march by night.

In the final disposition of his forces made by the emperor on the 7th of December, Gouvion Saint-Cyr was directed to march his troops back to Naples to oppose the Anglo-Russian corps commanded by Lascy. Augereau received orders to make by forced marches for Mayence, to protect Holland, seriously threatened by a combined army which had landed in Hanover under Tolstoy.

Whilst for the victorious troops Napoleon had nothing but praise, he could be severe on those he considered to have disgraced themselves. Some days after his return to Vienna from the field of Austerlitz he reviewed Soult's army corps. Having come abreast with the 4th regiment of infantry which had lost its eagle in the charge delivered by the Russian cavalry of the Guard, he halted and called the officers to the front. Then in a loud and fiery tone he spoke to them these words—

> Where is your eagle? (*a pause of intense silence*). Yours is the only regiment of the French Army to which such a question can be put! I would much sooner have lost my left arm than lost an eagle! It is about to be carried in triumph to St. Petersburg, and still in another hundred years the Russians will show it with pride; the forty banners that we have from them are not worth as much as your eagle! Have you forgotten to defend yourselves against cavalry? Who commanded the regiment? What measures did he take when he saw himself charged by cavalry? Where were your officers, your grenadiers? Had you not all to die before losing your eagle? I have seen many regiments who have hardly any officers or soldiers left in the ranks; but they have kept their flags, their honour; and you, I look at your numerous and strong companies, and I cannot trace my eagle in your ranks! ...
>
> What will you do to repair that disgrace, to silence your old comrades in the army, who in seeing you will exclaim, 'Look at the regiment which has lost its eagle?' (*a pause of intense silence*) On the first occasion your regiment must bring me four of the enemy's flags, then I shall consider if I can restore it an eagle.

Napoleon's reproach was not entirely deserved. The three non-commissioned officers who had in succession carried the eagle had been killed in defending it, and almost the entire detachment which had rallied around it was placed *hors de combat*. To make up for their irreparable loss, the 4th brought back two of the enemy's flags, which they had captured. (An eagle was given to the regiment at a review held in Berlin in 1806.)

Napoleon had to put up with a good deal from his marshals. After Austerlitz, Lannes was grievously offended because the emperor had made no personal mention of the part the marshal had played in the battle. Irritated by this, he had quitted the army and posted to Paris. It seems a strange state of discipline when an officer commanding a corps can throw up his command at his pleasure. In this instance, Lannes was not ordered back to his post, and Napoleon simply expressed a hope to see him back with the army should the arrangements for peace fall through.

Lannes had a quarrel with Soult at the post-house in rear of Welspetz on the 28th of November, and called him a dirty sneak for having given an evasive answer on the situation to the emperor. He wanted to press his demand for satisfaction on the battlefield. Soult silenced him by saying, "We have got more important matters to attend to today." Berthier also was jealous of Soult, in whom he had recognised superior ability, and the greater estimation in which he was held by the emperor.

Various officers were loud in their complaints of what appeared in the bulletins. Their inexactitude had become a proverb in the camp. It was said, "*Menteur comme un bulletin*" ("As great a liar as a bulletin").

In Thiebault's memoirs that general is very wroth with Soult, the commander of the corps he belonged to. He positively asserts that Soult did not exert any command during the action, and that he was nowhere to be seen on the battlefield. (Could Thiebault have contracted some ill-feeling against Soult at the siege of Genoa? It is not unlikely.) On the other hand, the Duchesse d'Abrantes writes (*The Home and Court Life of the Emperor Napoleon and his Family*) that, according to her husband (Junot), the success of the day was mainly due to Soult. Junot had declared to her that Soult's conduct had considerable influence on the result of the battle.

With regard to Thiebault's insinuations, Saint-Chamans, who as Soult's *aide-de-camp* should have had opportunities for knowing the truth, says, (*Mémoires*), that out of 22,000 men which Soult had on the morning of the 2nd of December only 16,000 remained to him in the evening. The 4th Corps and the marshal himself had contributed more than any others to the victory, and had fought from 8 a.m. to 5 p.m., all the time against superior forces. On the point of the marshal's personal courage, he states that Soult admired energetic enterprises, provided, however, that he was not called to run great personal risks, as he did not possess the brilliant courage of Marshal Hey and Marshal Lannes. He might even be reproached for an excess in a contrary direction and for sheltering himself carefully from danger. This fault had come to him with the great fortune he had acquired, and it was not at all rare to come across officers who had not feared death when they were nothing but colonels or simple generals, but who later on placed themselves well in safety under the shelter of their marshal's baton.

The first rumours of the Battle of Austerlitz did not reach London till the 23rd of December. The *Times*, in its issue of the 16th of that month, alludes to Lady Elgin who had been refused permission to return to England. It added that, after all, she obtained it, but on condition of her starting at once, so that she might confirm the contents of the despatches announcing the triumph of the French over the Austrians by an account of the rejoicings which had taken place in Paris for the victory.

In England the first news of a battle favourable to the French was not believed. The *Times* was incredulous. It wrote on the 24th of December:

> The bulletins from the *Grande Armée* have lost much of their credit on the Continent, and even begin to be suspected in Paris. That they are fabricated nine times out of ten to suit the purpose of the moment, we have had, since the commencement of the present campaign, ample reasons to be convinced.

★★★★★★

> Cobenzl, in his correspondence with Metternich, Austrian ambassador at Berlin, spoke of the battle of Austerlitz as an engagement of little importance, and of the armistice concluded as a suitable delay for burying the dead.

★★★★★★

The first accounts of the Battle of Austerlitz gave the victory to the allies. On the 30th of December, the *Times*, in printing an unofficial account, reported their defeat, but received that statement as false and extravagant.

From the last words in its issue of the following day, we realise the state of feeling which the news of Napoleon's victory produced in England.

> From the Baltic to the farthest extremity of Italy, there is not a sovereign or prince who at this moment may not be said to

hold his power by sufferance from Bonaparte. What this frightful state is to lead to is in the womb of time. The victor may be merciful on the Continent; but we, who despise his power, are not to expect peace from his moderation. He pledged himself to his troops that he would make peace at Vienna before Christmas, and in London before Easter. He has redeemed that pledge in the first instance; we are persuaded he will endeavour to do so in the latter.

Napoleon was disgusted at having been so often deceived by his navy, at having had his dearest hopes crushed. Where was he who only a few months before had demanded from his admiral the command of the Channel for a few days, to find after Trafalgar a fleet with which to cover his daring enterprise? There was no reason for the alarmist tone of our leading newspaper. The nation could safely rely on its splendid fleet, sure that the bravery of her sailors would keep the stranger from treading on British soil. The dreaded invasion was a thing of the past, and there was very clear evidence that Napoleon had come to realise all its dangers.

After Trafalgar, Napoleon decided to attack Great Britain elsewhere than at sea. He took measures to reconstitute his navy, though reserving for it no part in the contest. There was great activity in the building yards, and every year saw some battleships added to the French fleet. Large squadrons were moored in the harbours of Brest and Toulon, all that they needed was the habit of keeping the sea. The emperor, notwithstanding the ardour of both officers and sailors, refused to give them an opportunity of trying their strength with the enemy.

On the fall of the empire, France had an immense quantity of naval material and a fleet superior to the one she inherited from the unfortunate Louis XVI. In 1792 the French naval power was represented by 76 line-of-battle ships and 78 frigates; in 1815 by 103 battleships and 55 frigates.

There remains something to be said of the note furnished by the Emperor Francis through his ambassador in London, in justification of his conduct.

In this note he attributes the unfortunate results of the campaign of 1805 to the following causes:—

1st. To the absence of those diversions in the North which would have forced Bonaparte to divide his troops; from which cause, it resulted that he could not merely dispose of all the forces which came from the coast, but also of the armies of Holland and Hanover.

2nd. To the violation of Prussia's neutrality, which placed the Austrian Army in the alternative of retiring to the Inn or of finding itself enclosed and destroyed.

3rd. To General Mack's fault, who, instead of choosing the alternative, which offered some chance of success, of retiring to the Inn and effecting a junction there with General Kutuzoff, remained on the Iller, and so allowed himself to be surrounded.

4th. To the delay experienced by the second Russian column which was stayed for more than a month by the armaments Prussia was making, and which appeared to be directed against Russia.

5th. To General Count Auersperg's neglect in not burning the bridge of Tabor, which opened to the enemy the country on the left bank of the Danube, and exposed the first Russian Army to the danger of being cut off or destroyed before it could effect its junction with Buxhowden's army which was approaching.

These assertions fail greatly in point of accuracy. That the diversions were not undertaken it is true enough, but much of this was due to the fickleness of the King of Sweden, who was always changing his mind, and to the vacillating conduct of the cabinet of Berlin. Not before the *Grande Armée* having marched from Boulogne *quite suddenly*, the French troops in Holland and Hanover began moving, could the British Government take in hand the despatch of troops to Germany. These only reached the Elbe when Napoleon was chasing the allies from Moravia.

Combined operations are, as a general rule, subject to delays. On the 8th of January the English forces had arrived at Naples as auxiliaries, but in a few days, they re-embarked for Sicily; and the Russians, who had presented themselves on the same errand, set sail for Corfu on the 13th of January 1806.

It was not the violation of the territory of Anspach that made Mack quit his position on the Iller, for the French troops which first appeared on the Danube at Donauwörth belonged to corps which had marched by other routes. None of the corps which had crossed the neutral territory of Anspach took any part in the operations round Ulm. It was Marshal Soult who first cut the Austrian retreat into Bavaria, when he occupied Donauwörth and marched along the Lech up to Füssen; the corps of Ney and Lannes, with Murat's cavalry, the corps principally engaged round Ulm, did not cross Franconia. Why, besides, complain of the violation of the territory of Anspach, when the Austrians had not respected the neutrality of Bavaria?

After their defeat, the allies laid the cause of it on each other. The Russians lay much of the blame for the loss of the battle on the Austrians for their faint-heartedness; but the Austrians, though many of them only raw recruits, fought well, and conspicuous amongst them were the regiment of Saltzbourg and a battalion of Auersperg. Napoleon himself, in the *Moniteur*, contradicted the Russians. His words were:

> All who have beheld the battlefield will attest that it was covered with Austrian corpses where the shock occurred.

The Austrians accused the Russians of ignorance in manoeuvring, of the slowness of their infantry, of the weight of their muskets. The causes must be looked for elsewhere, the main being the absence of a competent directing head. In any case, after Austerlitz, the Russians could no longer attribute all Napoleon's glory to the want of courage and energy of their allies.

Whilst the French Army was commanded by only one man, the most able, experienced, and enterprising general in Europe, there was no supreme commander in the opposite camp.

Kutuzoff, the virtual head of the allied armies, as we have already shown, deprecated on very good grounds the course pressed on him. He really had ceased to command; the young staff officers of the Russian Army had no confidence in him, and would have none of him. He had not planned the arrangements for the battle. The day after Austerlitz, holding converse with the officers of the Guard regiment of Izmaïlovski, he said, "Gentlemen, I wash my hands of it." The general opinion in the Russian Army, however, was that he was responsible and to blame, inasmuch as he had not refuted strongly enough the counsels of the men who enjoyed the *Czar's* confidence.

Buxhowden, who was detailed to command the most important attack, was known to be an indolent officer, possessing very limited ability, and to owe his position principally to a court marriage. He did not exert his authority or supervise the movements of the three columns under his orders as he should have done, with the result that there was no concert between them in their action.

A battle, besides, cannot be won without confidence. At Austerlitz, before engaging, Prince Bagration, as it has already been said, looked on the battle as lost; on the other flank, Langeron, who commanded the second column, was always looking over his right shoulder at the plateau of Pratzen, where he had foreseen the great struggle would come off.

As to General Mack, he had other alternatives open to him than the one mentioned by the Emperor Francis. He might have gone to Switzerland by way of Schaffhausen, and there could have been joined by the Archduke John, or he could have retired on the Main, and then on to Hesse, where the ruler would have readily made common cause with him. There in communication with the Hanoverian troops, the Russians, and the Swedes, he might have decided Prussia to join the coalition. Lastly, he could have attempted as he did, but too late, to retire into Bohemia, marching by the left bank of the Danube.

All the reasons to account for the defeat which the Emperor Francis adduced were feeble. The campaign was undoubtedly lost through bad generalship, and by Napoleon, always alert, having anticipated the allies. In any case, prudence would have made the latter avoid fighting on a battlefield which Napoleon had had ample time to study, and prudence again would have suggested abstaining from bringing on a pitched battle until their army had been largely reinforced by the arrival of the archdukes.

Many of the senior officers on the side of the allies were pedants, bound to their fine formations and rigid uniformity; men who in recent campaigns had not been able to grasp all the advantages of the more elastic formations which the Revolution had introduced into the French Army. The French were far superior in skill and manoeuvring; their three arms, worked together better than those of the allies; and they were more agile and ready in the field.

Czartorinski, in a letter he wrote to the *Czar* in 1806, when asking to be permitted to resign the post of Minister for Foreign Affairs, reminds his master that, had he abstained from joining the army, and consented to quit it, the Battle of Austerlitz most probably would never have been fought. For had Kutuzoff been left uninfluenced, he would have been very careful not to give much latitude to Weyrother, his chief of the staff; and he would have insisted in directing personally the army which had been confided to him. His naturally foreseeing character would have kept him temporising so as to avoid coming to an issue up to the moment when the co-operation of Prussia would have commenced; that was the plan of campaign that should have been adopted; this was what Kutuzoff had recommended. (Czartorinski had pressed this delay, the necessity for gaining time till Prussia's co-operation was secured, and had spoken of it to such as were minded to listen.)

Referring to the Battle of Austerlitz, the *Czar* said:

> At the Battle of Austerlitz, I was young and inexperienced. Kutuzoff recommended to me that we should act otherwise, but he should have held more stoutly to his counsel.

It was, after all, Czartorinski continues, of minor importance that the *Czar* should show personal valour in the field, than that he should be the means of saving Europe and keeping the glory of Russia and the honour of its sovereign unsullied. He reminds him that his presence at Austerlitz was not of the slightest advantage, that just where he was the rout was sharp, immediate. and complete.

In one part of his letter, the prince shows what it was that made Napoleon successful.

> We have not had to contend against 500,000 men as we feared at one time; at the most it was 140,000 men with whom Bonaparte subdued Austria, Russia, and Prussia, because without troubling himself with what might follow, he knows too well how to turn the present moment to account. His talent doubles and trebles his forces; the same army multiplies itself, and, victorious in one point, it moves rapidly to another. It is thus that Caesar and Frederick have acted.

The French emperor sent back to the *Czar* with Prince Repnine all the men belonging to the Russian Imperial Guard captured at Austerlitz. This political act of generosity exasperated many of his officers, amongst others Vandamme, who, on hearing of it, was heard to exclaim, "To restore them to freedom today is to permit them to enter Paris in six years." They did so, though it was a little over eight years after Austerlitz.

Given overmuch to believe in the factor of good fortune, Napoleon did not overlook any necessary precaution. During the armistice he was constantly reminding his marshals of the necessity for keeping on the alert, ready to resume hostilities at any moment. His warning was that the war was not at an end, that peace was not concluded, that too much faith was not to be placed in the armistice.

Earlier, we have seen the steps the emperor considered necessary to take at the very outset of the campaign to acquire information on certain essential points. Success had not made him less cautious.

Nothing possibly demonstrates Napoleon's thoroughness more than the mission he intrusted to General Rapp shortly after the brilliant victory of Austerlitz.

Rapp, who had just recovered from the wound he had received on the head when charging the Russian cavalry of the Guard, was directed to set out and gain personal information of the state such corps as had not fought at Austerlitz were in. Under date 25th *Frimaire* an XIV, the emperor wrote:—

> Monsieur Le Général Rapp, you will proceed to Gratz, where you will remain as long as may be necessary to communicate to General Marmont all the details of the battle of Austerlitz. Inform him that negotiations are open, but that nothing is yet concluded; that he must consequently hold himself in readiness for any event which may possibly occur. You must likewise make yourself fully acquainted with General Marmont's situation, and ascertain the number of the enemy's force now before him. Tell him that I desire him to send spies into Hungary; and that he will communicate to me all the information he will be able to collect.
>
> You will next repair to Laybach, where you will find Marshal Massena, who has the command of the 8th Corps; and transmit to me a correct report of his situation. You will inform Massena that if the negotiations are broken off, as it is possible, they may, he will be sent to Vienna. Let me know what amount of the enemy's forces Marshal Massena has in front of him; and report to me the situation of his corps in every point of view. You will next proceed to Palmanova, after strongly urging Marshal Massena to arm and provision that fortress in an effectual manner; and you will inform me of the state which it is in.
>
> Next proceed and examine the posts we occupy before Venice, and make yourself acquainted with the state of our troops. Thence you will journey to the army of General St. Cyr, who is about to march for Naples; you will ascertain the nature and amount of his forces. You must return by the way of Klagenfurth, where you will see Marshal Ney, and then rejoin me. Do not fail to write from every place at which you stop. Despatch couriers from Gratz, Laybach, Palmanova, Venice, and the locality where the army of Naples may be stationed. I pray God to preserve you in His holy keeping.

Napoleon.

On the 29th of December, Napoleon announced to his soldiers the conclusion of peace. On the 1st of January 1806, the standards captured at Austerlitz were taken to the Luxembourg in solemn procession, witnessed by an immense concourse of the population of the capital. At the sight of the enemy's standards, it was unanimously decreed that a lasting monument should be erected in honour of the victor who in a hundred days had achieved such remarkable and vast deeds. *Fêtes* and rejoicings were universal throughout the country.

The emperor returned to Paris on the 26th of January, and was received, as he had been in all the towns through which his journey lay, with unexampled enthusiasm. The Senate and the Tribunate waited on him, and, in the name of the people, invested him with the title of *Napoleon the Great*—a worthy distinction for the man who had undertaken the arduous task of regenerating his country.

Appendix

Nearly a hundred years after the eventful Battle of Austerlitz, when the evidence of the officers who took part in it was past questioning, the generally accepted version of the catastrophe on Lake Satschan, at the termination of the battle, is contradicted.

Professor J. H. Rose, in his *Napoleonic Studies*, refers to the ice incident in that battle, and, on Professor Fournier's researches, decides that it was enormously exaggerated.

The strange part is, that the catastrophe should have been supported by the evidence of so many persons. Ségur, Thiebault, and Marbot relate it. Lejeune writes:

> A few men, indeed, might have got over (the ice) safely; but when a number had reached the middle of the water, the ice began to crack beneath their weight. They stopped, and, the troops behind pushing them on, there were soon some 6000 men collected in a dense crowd on the swaying, slippery ice. There was a pause, and then, in a brief space of a couple of minutes, the whole mass, with arms and baggage, disappeared beneath the broken ice, not one man escaping or even appearing again at the top of the water.

Mikhailovski-Danilevski goes more into particulars.

> Then, moving in the direction of the village of Sartchan, he (Dochtouroff) made his troops march over the bridge of the Littau, between Aujesd and the lake of Sartchan, and by the dike between the two lakes. The bridge broke under the weight of the guns. The troops threw themselves on to the lake, which was frozen. Besides, the dike was so narrow that only two men abreast could pass. Some officers, seeing how it was crowded, led their troops and their guns on the lake. Then the ice, which

was not thick enough to bear them, broke; the men, the horses, the cannon sunk in the frozen water and under the murderous fire of Napoleon's batteries, which showered round shot and shell on so many unfortunates.

Thiers relates the episode in the following words:

> Napoleon, arriving on the slopes of the Pratzen plateau, on the side of the ponds, beheld the catastrophe which he had so well prepared. He made a battery of the Guard cannonade that part of the ice which still bore, and accomplished the ruin of the unfortunates who had taken refuge thereon. Nearly 2000 men met their death under the broken ice.

Mathieu Dumas states:

> Pursued on every side, having no longer a point of support, these unfortunate soldiers would also cross the pond of Menitz (*sic*) on the ice; they crowded on it, the ice broke, and the greater part perished.

F. Schoell, *Histoire Abrégée des Traités de Paix, tome septième*, refers to it in these words:

> A portion of the left wing was driven on to a lake, in which some thousands of men were drowned.

Hamley's account is nearly the same.

> Finally, the victorious centre (Soult and the reserve) falls upon columns one, two, and three in flank, while Davout attacks their front, and they are forced into and beyond the lakes.

Basing their narrative on the exaggerations contained in the official bulletin, some writers have made the drowned Russians to have amounted to many thousands. Count Labedoyère, referring to the catastrophe on the lakes, says:

> That corps was driven from position to position; and the French witnessed the horrid spectacle of 20,000 men precipitating themselves into the lake.

George Moir Bussey relates:

> They were driven into a hollow, where some small frozen lakes offered the only means of escape from the closing cannonade. Many attempted to escape, but the numbers which rushed to-

gether upon the ice, and a storm of shot which followed them, broke the frail support, and nearly 20,000 men perished, by drowning and the effect of the artillery.

Alison is more moderate in his estimate:

> After a brave resistance, they were at length overwhelmed; seven thousand were taken or destroyed on the spot, and great numbers sought to save themselves by crossing with their artillery and cavalry the frozen lake of Satschan, which adjoined the line of march. The ice was already beginning to yield under the enormous weight, when the shot from the French batteries on the heights above broke it in all directions. A frightful yell arose from the perishing multitude, and above two thousand brave men were swallowed up in the waves.

Commandant Romagny, in his *Compagnes d'un Siècle* (1805), speaks of only some hundreds of Russians as having perished under the broken ice.

General Stutterheim, who commanded a brigade of the allies' left wing, is entirely silent regarding the catastrophe at the Satschan pond. He writes:

> At length, however, the famous dike—the only remaining retreat for the wreck of the first column of the allies, and which had justly been the subject of so much uneasiness—was passed.

He says nothing about Napoleon having forced the left of the allies on to the ponds.

On the evidence of a veteran of 1805, Lanfry is said to have refuted the story of the breaking of the ice under the weight of the retiring Russians. Is it possible that we should be called to accept the verbal statement of a veteran against the evidence of so many careful writers? Besides those whose words we have quoted, we find Walter Scott, Rustow, Clemens Janisschek, Karl Schonhals, Lacroix, Moreno and others supporting the story of the Russians lost by the breaking of the ice.

Professor Fournier of Vienna, from careful researches he has mane, contradicts the accepted version. His statement is founded on official documents and the written testimony of the local bailiff and the clergyman of Telnitz.

By Napoleon's own order to the overseer, states the professor, the lakes were drained a very few days after the battle. In doing this were found 28 to 30 cannon, 150 corpses of horses, and only two or three human corpses. These were found in the marshy corners of the Satschan pond, which the Russians had evidently rushed. Nothing was found in the Mönitz pond. It is asserted that no bones or weapons are said to have ever been found where the two ponds once stood, though some often turn up on other parts of the battlefield.

The fact of no weapons having come to light in the many ploughings of the former pond-beds appears in itself very convincing evidence.

What seems evidently strange is that none of the Russian generals who were present at Austerlitz should have attempted to correct the general belief in the occurrence of such a dreadful finale, or should have disputed the accuracy of Napoleon's bulletin.

Though Napoleon is known to have delighted in captivating the French people by concluding his bulletins with a sensational paragraph, we hardly conceive it possible that he would have drawn so much on the imagination unless he had sufficient grounds for supporting his statement. Here was a statement which many eyewitnesses were in a position to refute.

The incident occurred in the uncertain light of a short December evening, and, what with the smoke and the uproar of the battle, may have appeared far more appalling than it was in reality. From this possibly rose the exaggeration.

What adds to the mystery is that, only nine years after the event, the *Czar* himself should have corroborated the statement made by Napoleon in the thirtieth bulletin. If anyone, the *Czar* should have known something positive from the reports furnished by his generals.

What could the *Czar* have had to gain by corroborating the story? We cannot quite agree with Professor Rose's supposition, that the *Czar* may have designedly accepted the story of the catastrophe on the ice, to explain the precipitate flight of his army. It seems impossible, for he had been a personal witness of Miloradovitch's defeat, when he ordered him to collect his forces and retire on Austerlitz, and more so when with his own eyes he had seen the flower of his Imperial Guard, which was to decide the victory, cut to pieces by Rapp and Bessières.

Some marked catastrophe, certainly not on the proportion given in the bulletin, must have occurred. We cannot bring ourselves to believe that learned historians of different nationalities would have followed blindly the lead given by Napoleon.

As for the number of men which the bulletin declared to have been lost in the ponds, if we take into account the heavy casualties sustained by the three Russian columns on the left, the thousands of men captured by the French, and the 8,000 men which are said to have reached Neudorf on the night of the battle with Dochtouroff, we soon see that there were not many thousands to drown.

ALSO FROM LEONAUR
AVAILABLE IN SOFTCOVER OR HARDCOVER WITH DUST JACKET

OFFICERS & GENTLEMEN *by Peter Hawker & William Graham*—Two Accounts of British Officers During the Peninsula War: Officer of Light Dragoons by Peter Hawker & Campaign in Portugal and Spain by William Graham.

THE WALCHEREN EXPEDITION *by Anonymous*—The Experiences of a British Officer of the 81st Regt. During the Campaign in the Low Countries of 1809.

LADIES OF WATERLOO *by Charlotte A. Eaton, Magdalene de Lancey & Juana Smith*—The Experiences of Three Women During the Campaign of 1815: Waterloo Days by Charlotte A. Eaton, A Week at Waterloo by Magdalene de Lancey & Juana's Story by Juana Smith.

JOURNAL OF AN OFFICER IN THE KING'S GERMAN LEGION *by John Frederick Hering*—Recollections of Campaigning During the Napoleonic Wars.

JOURNAL OF AN ARMY SURGEON IN THE PENINSULAR WAR *by Charles Boutflower*—The Recollections of a British Army Medical Man on Campaign During the Napoleonic Wars.

ON CAMPAIGN WITH MOORE AND WELLINGTON *by Anthony Hamilton*—The Experiences of a Soldier of the 43rd Regiment During the Peninsular War.

THE ROAD TO AUSTERLITZ *by R. G. Burton*—Napoleon's Campaign of 1805.

SOLDIERS OF NAPOLEON *by A. J. Doisy De Villargennes & Arthur Chuquet*—The Experiences of the Men of the French First Empire: Under the Eagles by A. J. Doisy De Villargennes & Voices of 1812 by Arthur Chuquet.

INVASION OF FRANCE, 1814 *by F. W. O. Maycock*—The Final Battles of the Napoleonic First Empire.

LEIPZIG—A CONFLICT OF TITANS *by Frederic Shoberl*—A Personal Experience of the 'Battle of the Nations' During the Napoleonic Wars, October 14th-19th, 1813.

SLASHERS *by Charles Cadell*—The Campaigns of the 28th Regiment of Foot During the Napoleonic Wars by a Serving Officer.

BATTLE IMPERIAL *by Charles William Vane*—The Campaigns in Germany & France for the Defeat of Napoleon 1813-1814.

SWIFT & BOLD *by Gibbes Rigaud*—The 60th Rifles During the Peninsula War.

AVAILABLE ONLINE AT **www.leonaur.com**
AND FROM ALL GOOD BOOK STORES

ALSO FROM LEONAUR
AVAILABLE IN SOFTCOVER OR HARDCOVER WITH DUST JACKET

THE 9TH—THE KING'S (LIVERPOOL REGIMENT) IN THE GREAT WAR 1914 - 1918 *by Enos H. G. Roberts*—Mersey to mud—war and Liverpool men.

THE GAMBARDIER *by Mark Severn*—The experiences of a battery of Heavy artillery on the Western Front during the First World War.

FROM MESSINES TO THIRD YPRES *by Thomas Floyd*—A personal account of the First World War on the Western front by a 2/5th Lancashire Fusilier.

THE IRISH GUARDS IN THE GREAT WAR - VOLUME 1 *by Rudyard Kipling*—Edited and Compiled from Their Diaries and Papers—The First Battalion.

THE IRISH GUARDS IN THE GREAT WAR - VOLUME 1 *by Rudyard Kipling*—Edited and Compiled from Their Diaries and Papers—The Second Battalion.

ARMOURED CARS IN EDEN *by K. Roosevelt*—An American President's son serving in Rolls Royce armoured cars with the British in Mesopatamia & with the American Artillery in France during the First World War.

CHASSEUR OF 1914 *by Marcel Dupont*—Experiences of the twilight of the French Light Cavalry by a young officer during the early battles of the great war in Europe.

TROOP HORSE & TRENCH *by R.A. Lloyd*—The experiences of a British Lifeguardsman of the household cavalry fighting on the western front during the First World War 1914-18.

THE EAST AFRICAN MOUNTED RIFLES *by C.J. Wilson*—Experiences of the campaign in the East African bush during the First World War.

THE LONG PATROL *by George Berrie*—A Novel of Light Horsemen from Gallipoli to the Palestine campaign of the First World War.

THE FIGHTING CAMELIERS *by Frank Reid*—The exploits of the Imperial Camel Corps in the desert and Palestine campaigns of the First World War.

STEEL CHARIOTS IN THE DESERT *by S. C. Rolls*—The first world war experiences of a Rolls Royce armoured car driver with the Duke of Westminster in Libya and in Arabia with T.E. Lawrence.

WITH THE IMPERIAL CAMEL CORPS IN THE GREAT WAR *by Geoffrey Inchbald*—The story of a serving officer with the British 2nd battalion against the Senussi and during the Palestine campaign.

AVAILABLE ONLINE AT www.leonaur.com
AND FROM ALL GOOD BOOK STORES

ALSO FROM LEONAUR
AVAILABLE IN SOFTCOVER OR HARDCOVER WITH DUST JACKET

AN APACHE CAMPAIGN IN THE SIERRA MADRE by John G. Bourke—An Account of the Expedition in Pursuit of the Chiricahua Apaches in Arizona, 1883.

BILLY DIXON & ADOBE WALLS by Billy Dixon and Edward Campbell Little—Scout, Plainsman & Buffalo Hunter, *Life and Adventures of "Billy" Dixon* by Billy Dixon and *The Battle of Adobe Walls* by Edward Campbell Little (*Pearson's Magazine*).

WITH THE CALIFORNIA COLUMN by George H. Petis—Against Confederates and Hostile Indians During the American Civil War on the South Western Frontier, *The California Column, Frontier Service During the Rebellion* and *Kit Carson's Fight With the Comanche and Kiowa Indians*.

THRILLING DAYS IN ARMY LIFE by George Alexander Forsyth—Experiences of the Beecher's Island Battle 1868, the Apache Campaign of 1882, and the American Civil War.

INDIAN FIGHTS AND FIGHTERS by Cyrus Townsend Brady—Indian Fights and Fighters of the American Western Frontier of the 19th Century.

THE NEZ PERCÉ CAMPAIGN, 1877 by G. O. Shields & Edmond Stephen Meany—Two Accounts of Chief Joseph and the Defeat of the Nez Percé, *The Battle of Big Hole* by G. O. Shields and *Chief Joseph, the Nez Percé* by Edmond Stephen Meany.

CAPTAIN JEFF OF THE TEXAS RANGERS by W. J. Maltby—Fighting Comanche & Kiowa Indians on the South Western Frontier 1863-1874.

SHERIDAN'S TROOPERS ON THE BORDERS by De Benneville Randolph Keim—The Winter Campaign of the U. S. Army Against the Indian Tribes of the Southern Plains, 1868-9.

GERONIMO by Geronimo—The Life of the Famous Apache Warrior in His Own Words.

WILD LIFE IN THE FAR WEST by James Hobbs—The Adventures of a Hunter, Trapper, Guide, Prospector and Soldier.

THE OLD SANTA FE TRAIL by Henry Inman—The Story of a Great Highway.

LIFE IN THE FAR WEST by George F. Ruxton—The Experiences of a British Officer in America and Mexico During the 1840's.

ADVENTURES IN MEXICO AND THE ROCKY MOUNTAINS by George F. Ruxton—Experiences of Mexico and the South West During the 1840's.

AVAILABLE ONLINE AT **www.leonaur.com**
AND FROM ALL GOOD BOOK STORES

www.ingramcontent.com/pod-product-compliance
Lightning Source LLC
Chambersburg PA
CBHW030216170426
43201CB00006B/102